Beware of Vegetarian Sharks!

Radical Rants
and
Internationalist Essays

(Illustrated)

by Richard Greeman

Published by Praxis Research and Education Center (Moscow and New York)

DEDICATION: To my daughter, Jenny Greeman, and to young people
everywhere. You deserve a brighter world
than the tragic one you inherited.

Credits: *Thanks to Wikipedia, the IWW.org and other anarchist and open-source sites for the free clip-art of which I have made such free use. Thanks to all my radical friends and particularly to Ian MacMahon and Ilene Gex for your attention, help and comment over the years that these essays were distilling. Thanks to the cooperative spirit of* Lulu.com *and the Internet for making it possible for Praxis to publish these Sharks in N.Y., Moscow and around the world* .

Produced by Jenny Greeman
Copyright June 2007 by Richard Greeman
ISBN 978-1-4303-2307-5

Individual orders and free downloads:
www.lulu.com/923573

Bookstore, Distributor and Group discount orders:
rgreeman@gmail.com

Websites and Contact:
www.invisible-international.org
www.praxiscenter.ru

CONTENTS

3

About the Cover: Trying to convince capitalism to reform makes about as much sense as trying to convert a shark to vegetarianism. It is also dangerous, as the two protesters in the shark's maw are about to discover. By its nature, capitalism is no more capable of giving up the ruthless exploitation of humans and nature than a shark can give up blood and flesh. Capitalist sharks have even been known to *pretend* to be vegetarians, the better to eat us up. So beware of 'clean' coal, 'green' Exxon ads, 'humanitarian'

wars, 'job creation' plans devised by Wall St. bankers, actually existing 'socialisms' and the other vegetarian sharks anatomized in these pages.

Author's Preface: Why I Write

Why do I write? Early on in my political education, I came to the conclusion that activism alone was not enough,. Capitalism could not be reformed, and only in a new society could my dream of peace, justice and equality be realized. In addition, by the age of eighteen I had read enough about the nightmarish condition of workers in Communist Russia and China to reject the dogmas of the fellow-traveling 'progressive' milieu in which I grew up - especially after the brutal suppression of the 1956 Hungarian Revolution of Workers' Councils by 'fraternal' Russian tanks, an act that disillusioned my Dad.

Fortunately, I came under the influence of small revolutionary groups in New Haven, New York, Detroit and Paris which were based on the more democratic principles of libertarian socialism and critical, humanist Marxism. As a result, I had the great luck to hang out with older political activists, including veterans of the Russian anti-Stalinist oppositions, the Spanish Revolution and the European anti-fascist resistance. Among these mentors were first rate theoreticians (who were themselves questioning every ideological dogma) including Marxists like Cornelius Castoriadis, Raya Dunayevskaya, Marc Chirik, Max Schactman, Jean Malaquais, Ngo Van, survivor of the Vietnamese Trotskyist movement, Alberto Maso (Vega) and Wilbaldo Solano of the POUM and of course Victor Serge's son Vlady Kibalchich. I also was influenced by veteran Anarchists like Russell Blackwell, Sam and Esther Dolgoff as well as by radical journalists like I.F. Stone and Daniel Singer and. These extraordinary men and women were living links to the revolutionary past. They incarnated its *ethos,* breathed its energy, spoke of people like Trotsky and Emma Goldman as if they had just left the room. I had the impression, in our conversations, of being initiated into an oral tradition which paralleled and completed the reading of history and the 'sacred texts.' Along with my day-to-day activism, such discussions were the 'universities' in which I completed my political education while earning degrees in French from Yale, Columbia and the Sorbonne in my spare time.[1] (For the full story of my political adventures, please see **Part VII** 'My Political Itinerary' at the end of this volume.)

---

[1] In those wonderful bygone days, there were scholarships that included a stipend for living expenses. With a stipend of $1,500.00 a semester, I was able to rent an apartment in Manhattan, buy a used motorcycle and a beat-up piano. After the Sixties, the U.S. government got smart and forced loans on scholarship students, so that they had to work for corporations instead of going out to save the world like we did. Today students, denied normal bankruptcy protection, are reduced to debt peonage for life under profitably ballooning college loans and massive penalties. Some have committed suicide or fled the country. See Alan Collinge, *The Student Debt Scam,* 2008.

With such a political education, I have never been tempted to turn away from Marxist-humanist and Anarchist ideas, which alone are capable of explaining the errors of past revolutionary movements (hopefully to avoid repeating them). It also taught me to cherish and study our collective positive experience, the rare historical moments when the tremendous creative force of revolutionary humanity emerged and briefly lighted the way to the future - from the 1871 Paris Commune to the Russian Soviets of 1917 to the self-managed farms and factories collectivised and defended by the Spanish Anarchists in 1936, to the world-wide risings of the Sixties, culminating in the French General Strike of May 1968 rebellions, to this Century's rising Latin American popular movements. I here attempt to transmit and elaborate for our times these working class, Socialist and internationalist traditions in the hope that coming generations will rediscover and reinvent them.

Two main concepts, borrowed from Victor Serge and Rosa Luxemburg, dominate my outlook: Internationalism and Tolerance. For me, Internationalism is basic: in our age of multinational corporations, the only way to defend ourselves against global capitalism is globally, through the planetary unity of the working, thinking creative people in all countries. This was the dream that united Marx and Bakunin in the First International, and to me 'internationalism' still says it all. Despite the temptations of nationalism, identity politics and despair, we must continue to 'Act locally, think globally.' So with each concrete struggle we ask the key questions: 'Does this tactic increase solidarity with people of other nationalities, or divide us?' and 'Does this tactic move us closer to our ultimate goal – a new society?'

To me Tolerance, respect for the 'other,' is the only means to reach the revolutionary end, if by revolution we mean a new human society in which "the freedom of the individual is the basis of the freedom of all" (Marx). Without respect for the individual, without freedom of opinion, without the right to dissent and the availability of unbiased information, We-the-people will never be able to find our independent path. Instead we billions will forever be mislead by corrupt or fanatical leaders and manipulated by controlled mass media. Instead of an infallible single Party, I propose critical thinking, horizontal organization, and the development of an 'invisible international' woven of thousands of links where people can discuss and decide everything for themselves.

For this reason, I'm uncomfortable with political labels other than 'internationalist.' My Marxist friends consider me an Anarchist because I reject the State and the self-designated Vanguard Parties that aim to conquer it. On the other hand, sectarian Anarchists throw up their hands whenever I quote Karl Marx – forgetting that Anarchism has no political economy of its own and that Bakunin himself translated *Das Kapital* into Russian, and wrote to Marx: "I am your disciple and proud to be one." Victor Serge appeals to me because

8

he was an internationalist with roots in both Anarchism and Marxism, was critical of them both, and rejected sectarians who claimed to hold the monopoly of the truth - and who therefore felt free to manipulate, raid, and split activist groups, to expel dissenters (and to shoot them when in power). In any case, pluralistic and essentially non-violent mass movements represent the only way for the party of Humanity to emerge victorious the coming planetary social struggles.

The Radical Rants and Internationalist Essays in this collection have been selected and organised to present a coherent argument about capitalism's apparent collapse and the possibility of a more egalitarian and ecological future. Our discussion begins in the present with the Crash of '08 and asks the question 'Is there Life After Capitalism?' I propose my alternative in Part I (Is Another World *Really* Possible?) and let my imagination take power by proposing a realistic scenario for a successful 'Mutiny on Starship Earth,' and by demonstrating scientifically and humoristically that my plan might actually work. My Modern Archimedes' Hypothesis is based on historical experience and contemporary theories of cybernetics, chaos, emergence, dialectics, quantum mechanics and Castoriadis' *Content of Socialism*. It connects a historically proven lever of worker solidarity with a 21st Century philosophical fulcrum (planetary consciousness) and a global electronic place to stand (the Internet) where the billions can unite in solidarity in order to 'lift the earth' before it succumbs to capitalist ecocide. The challenge to our age is this: *can* we realistically imagine (without Divine or Extraterrestrial intervention) a technically feasible, ecologically sustainable post-capitalist future and visualize historically possible roads leading to it? For if we can even *imagine* the sleeping powers of humanity awakening, if we can *visualise* billions of people throwing off the fetters of the profit system and establishing a plant-wide cooperative commonwealth, then we have *already* awakened those powers. So watch out for idea-viruses. This book may be catching.

My search for a way out of today's crisis next turns backward into the history of the successes and failures of past social movements. In Part II ('Dissecting our Decadent Decade') I analyse capitalism's economic and ecological crisis, trace its origins and warn of Dangerous Shortcuts that promise to shorten it but won't. In Part III ('Where Are The Riots of Yesteryear?') I look back my experiences in the turbulent Sixties, when many in my generation thought Another World was possible, and try to draw some lessons. In Part IV ('Back in the USSR') I return even further back into history, to the birth of the world's first Republic of Workers' and Peasants' Councils in Russia in 1917. If Russia proved that Other Worlds *are* possible, it also showed that they can turn into nightmares. By returning to the revolution's origins, I attempt to lay to rest the ghost of the Soviet tragedy, which continues to haunt the today's movement for Another World. In Part V ('Killing the Jews') I deal with another 20th Century tragedy: the WWII United Nations' casual abandonment of European Jewry. Along with the casual destruction of Dresden, Hiroshima and Nagasaki, this denial of the *Holocaust* signalled the degeneration of capitalist democracy into a new global barbarism. I then take a break for a few laughs in Part VI (Killing Sacred Cows) because Comedy must follow Tragedy. Finally, somewhere between Comedy and Tragedy, I present the story of my own 'Political Itinerary,' as well as the story of the social movements and revolutionary organizations in which I have been active for fifty years, in the hope of passing on to today's activists something of what I learned in these 'universities.'

NOTE ON THIS APRIL 2009 EDITION; Six of the Sharks in this collection were first released in 2007 the under the title *Dangerous Shortcuts and Vegetarian Sharks*. I prepared this 'Sampler Edition for the first U.S. Social Forum in Atlanta, where I was presenting a panel on "Ecosocialism vs. Capitalist Ecocide." In November 2008, I tour Great Britain with a massive (409 pages) but flawed prototype of the present, definitive edition (until the next).

Introduction

The Crash of 2008, or Is There Life After Capitalism?

As this modest attack on the capitalist system goes to press (March 2009), capitalism's entire globalized financial edifice is visibly collapsing into a bottomless pit of self-destruction. The bursting of the housing bubble in 2007 exposed the financial markets as a vast Ponzi pyramid of leveraged debt and fictitious capital. Credit evaporated, and by the Fall of 2008 trillions of dollars in securities began melting down to nothing - like the Wicked Witch of the West when the Scarecrow threw water on her. Prominent financiers, economists and statesmen were describing the crash as 'an economic Pearl Harbor' (Warren Buffet), 'the edge of the abyss' (Paul Krugman), 'an approaching tsunami' (Jacques Attali), and a 'financial September 11' (Laurence Parisot, head of the French business association).[2] By October 2008, Alan Greenspan, the revered neo-liberal guru who ran the Federal Reserve Bank for 18 years, was being hauled before Congress and forced to confess that had been "mistaken" in his belief in the power of the free market and "wrong" to have encouraged the housing and financial bubbles by lowering the interest rates and lending billions of freshly-printed U.S. dollars to the big banks.[3] According to *The New Yorker* Wall Street traders were talking about "nuclear winter" in the credit markets: "nothing moves or grows."[4]

---

[2] Quoted in *Revue internationale* No. 136, Paris, premier trimestre 2009.
[3] New York *Times,* Oct. 23, 2008.
[4] *The New Yorker,* Oct. 20, 2008.

11

Desperate, the Bush Administration, supported by both Presidential candidates, pushed through a seven hundred billion dollar bailout of the high-rolling Wall Street bankers, financiers, traders and hedge-fund operators: the very speculators who in their greed and recklessness piled up unsecured debt and gambled with other peoples' money – provoking what will be known through history as the 'Great Crash of 2008.' Moreover, there were no regulatory strings attached, inviting the profiteers to go back to doing what they were doing before: speculating, buying up banks, and paying themselves huge bonuses. Less noted at the time was Treasury Secretary Paulson's announcement of what amounted to an open-ended drawing account to *continue* refloating troubled banks with fresh-printed Treasury notes running, the former Goldman-Sachs CEO admitted, into the 'trillions.' And that was only the beginning, as one bailout followed another. Nonetheless, the stocks represented on the DOW industrial average have declined to half their October 2007 value at this writing, with no end in sight.[5]

Naturally these billionaires' bailouts are supposed to be repaid by the victims of their financial scams – salaried taxpayers and their descendants over decades! (Didn't Marx say that the only part of the nation the working people actually owned was the national debt?) Millions of these working middle class families had been seduced by bank ads and tricked by unscrupulous loan officers into refinancing their homes at ballooning variable-rate mortgages. These slick salesmen at the local banks used low initial monthly payments to lure unsuspecting homeowners and naïve prospective first-home buyers into signing complicated mortgage papers most of them didn't understand. The local bankers – usually so prickly about lending people their money without a major down payment and a well-paid secure job – knew perfectly well that many of these poor folks couldn't possibly meet their monthly payments once the variable interest-rates started to balloon but the bankers didn't care. They simply pocketed their lucrative commissions and sold these "subprime" loans in bundles to brokers who mixed them with bundles of more secure mortgages and sold the adulterated products as 5% or 6% bonds. These supposedly safe mortgage-backed securities, deceptively rated AAA by Moodys and allegedly guaranteed by the government through Fanny Mae, were then sold to employee pension plans and retirees like me, who were trying to hedge their savings against inflation. Over the past decade, Wall Street spent 5.1 billion lobbying for deregulation to make these legal scams possible.[6] Now the victims, workers and small investors, were expected to pay the bill while suffering the loss of their homes, their jobs, and their retirement savings as well as the prospect of mass unemployment, foreclosures, bankruptcies and Depression-era poverty. Meanwhile the billionaires prepared to live off their fat in exclusive gated communities and off-shore tax-havens. Some actually went pheasant hunting

[5] *DemocracyNow.Org,* March 3, 2009.
[6] According to a new report by Robert Weissman of *Multinational Monitor,* reported on *DemocracyNow.Org* March 3, 2009.

the day after they got their first bailout payments. As for the rest of us: 'Openings now for security guards: low hourly wages and no benefits.'

Is there any chance these billionaire CEOs, bankers, investors lobbyists and political gofers in Congress will now reform? Can a man-eating shark become a vegetarian? Global capitalism can no more give up its lust for profit than a shark his lust for blood. Of course, these gentlemen in suits will pretend to reform and try to pass themselves off as vegetarians, but now we know to watch out for them. We've been here before. Despite all the neo-liberal hogwash about "free markets," "small government" and "individual responsibility" with which we have been bombarded since the Reagan-Thatcher '80s, we working taxpayers were still paying off the Chrysler and Savings-and-Loan bailouts of the '80s and '90s when the shit hit the fan. According to economist John Kenneth Galbraith, the true name of the 'free enterprise' system we have been living under is 'socialism for the rich:' privatized profit and socialized debt. By the Fall of 2008, even the TV pundits were using these phrases. Indeed, this time around, the American people weren't being fooled by the Fed's flim-flam and the obfuscations of politicians. During the final weeks of the 2008 Election campaign, reports from Congressional offices indicated constituents' calls running 'roughly one hundred to one' *against* this improvised free market give-away of public money to the capitalists.[7]

You might have thought that such an overwhelming demonstration of voter opinion less than three weeks before a crucial Presidential election would have galvanized the two campaigns – normally ultra- sensitive to the slightest ripple in the polls. But McCain remained clueless, and Obama, the Great White Hope of the liberals and progressives, not only went along with this billionaires' bipartisan boondoggle, he openly opposed throwing in a few goodies for the working people, "kneecap[ing] the efforts of progressives [in the Democratic Party] to force much-needed provisions like reform of bankruptcy law, publicly stating that this (minor) concession shouldn't be in the law."[8] Well, you can't say that Mr. Obama – whose campaign received more Wall Street money than Hilary Clinton's and ten times more than McCain's – wasn't loyal to his contributors. Apparently he who pays the piper calls the tune. Even after his stunning popular victory at the polls, President-elect Obama continued reassuring his financial backers by a 'seamless' transition during which he acquiesced in more giveaways to billionaires and nominated staunch friends of Wall Street like Larry Summers and Tim Geithner to run the economy. Now that Obama has actually taken office and established his authority, he must next pay his dues to the voters who elected him in an historic moment of unity among the working people of all so-called races in our race-besotted nation. Liberal hopes are high that he will now 'do a Roosevelt,' that is to say save

---

[7] As reported in *The Nation*, Oct. 20, 2008
[8] See Christopher Hays, "Democracy Inaction", the *Nation*, Oct. 20, 2008.

13

capitalism for the capitalists by regulating their excesses while staving off mass revolt through populist reforms. Having thrown huge chunks of red meat to the financial sharks in the hope of appeasing them, President Obama must now appear to turn on his backers and 'bite the hand that feeds him' just as FDR attacked the 'economic royalists' and 'malefactors of great wealth.' In other words, Obama must square the circle by transforming the capitalist shark into a vegetarian.

If only this were possible!

Alas, the sorry history of five hundred years of capitalist 'progress' points to the conclusion that capitalism can't grow without devouring the environment and chewing up workers' lives – no more than a shark can grow without devouring fresh blood and flesh. The first capitalist sharks were observed as early as 1492, pillaging the Americas, nearly exterminating their native peoples and replacing them with African slaves. These baby capitalist sharks went on to devour the European commons, driving formerly free yeomen farmers off the land and into factories. For two centuries healthy young sharks grew larger by preying on generations of working men women and children, slowly chewing their substance through 14 daily hours of dreary labor in soot-darkened 'Satanic mills' or under the lash on estates and plantations. And since as sharks grow, their appetites increase, by the end of the 19th Century, our now full-grown capitalist sharks fell into a feeding frenzy in their desperate urge to devour the populations and natural wealth of the entire planet. By the 20th Century, they were attacking each other (as sharks in a feeding frenzy will), the larger sharks devouring the smaller and the surviving giants slashing and biting each other all over the planet. By the 21st Century, the big old sharks were being pushed out of their former feeding grounds by younger breeds of fast-growing Chinese, Indian, Iranian, Russian and Brazilian sharks, better adapted for preying on the locals and increasingly more aggressive. Thus predatory capitalism, which from its birth remained profitable by expanding into the non-capitalist areas of the planet, has finally reached its global limits. Markets are saturated. Capital itself has become a glut, and there are no new continents to exploit or new forms of natural wealth to be profitably extracted from the half-ruined global environment.

To return to our analogy, the difference between billionaires and sharks is that the billionaires must present themselves as harmless, indeed beneficial, to their prey. We are all aware of some of the myriad ploys these wily predators employ to pass themselves off as 'vegetarians.' Ads for 'Green' cars. 'Green' oil companies. 'Clean' coal. 'Trickle-down' economics. 'Humanitarian' wars. They finance business and industry lobbies which bribe politicians with legal and illegal campaign contributions. They exert financial (and ultimately editorial control) of the mass media. They organize propaganda campaigns (like the current one blaming the financial collapse on the poor) and finally they finance 'Democratic' (and in Europe 'Socialist' and 'Labour') politicians

14

who 'feel our pain' while privatizing our public services and kicking away the crutches that help us walk through this vicious competitive society.

All these creatures present themselves as 'vegetarians,' and some of them are very good at it. But watch out! Never forget they really are man-eating sharks, and it makes no sense trying to get them to give up human flesh or even go on a diet, as liberal reformers would have it. I've spent a half century collecting specimens from every part of the globe and from both the left and the right. The anatomical descriptions presented in this book are designed to help you recognize the different species as they swim across the aquarium of your TV screens. This humorous taxonomy is my modest scientific contribution to the workers' cause in the class struggle – a struggle the rich have been waging for the past forty years against the poor.

The cream of the jest is that the rich keep bleating "Class War!" whenever some moderate dares to suggest 'taxing and spending', by which they mean *taxing* corporate profits and *spending* on public goods like education, housing, hospitals, infrastructure, the environment, healthcare, retirement, childcare, mass transit, drug and alcohol treatment, etc. So successfully have the billionaires waged this one-sided class war, both locally and globally, that these public goods have been well-nigh eliminated in the so called 'advanced' countries as well as the 'developing' ex-colonial world (through the intervention of the IMF and World Bank). With capitalism on the ropes, it is high time for the billions to turn the tables by uniting globally to prosecute class war against the billionaires.

Why Capitalism Is Collapsing

As for predicting capitalism's apparent collapse – universally considered impossible only yesterday - how come we diehard classical Marxists were right when almost everyone else was wrong? [9] Were little comrade Richard and a handful of other diehards simply smarter than all those professional economists working in brokerage houses, in the Fed, in the business media, in the universities and the think tanks with their supply-side theories and mathematical models designed to prove that the bubble would always get bigger (thus encouraging new investment)? Funnier, perhaps, but not really

---

[9] Notably, Richard Wolf, editor of *Rethinking Marxism*, Paul Mattick Jr. (aka 'the Last Marxist'), Bob Fitch (author of *Solidarity for Sale*) and sociologist Immanuel Wallerstein, Director the Ferdinand Braudel Institute, who has been plotting the historical curve of capitalism's 500-year rise and decline since the Seventies. On the other hand, most of the fashionable post-Marxists and deconstructionists succumbed to the myth of capitalism's immortality and replaced economic analysis with discourse about discourse in books I find impenetrable (as well as sadly lacking in illustrations and jokes).

smarter. However, we did have the advantage of not blinding ourselves with the self-interested optimism of the professionals who needed to convince themselves and everyone else to keep believing in that vast Ponzi pyramid scheme known as the securities market. Marx wasn't just being funny when he called the official economists of Victorian Britain 'paid prize-fighters for the bourgeoisie' after they 'proved,' for the benefit of the factory owners, that shortening the working day from 11 to 10 hours would destroy the economy. But then again, maybe the Crash of '08 was my fault. For example, no-liberal Hannes Gissurarson, the author of *How Can Iceland Become the Richest Country in the World?* writes 'I take some blame for [the fall of Iceland's banks, currency, and government], but, if you think about it, it's not my fault. It's the fault of the left-wing intellectuals, who should have been giving a counter-view!" He added, 'you can't blame people for their successes - you have to blame those who fail. We were too successful with the free-market philosophy.'[10]

But concerning the inevitability of capitalism's collapse, you don't have to be a rocket scientist to doubt the immortality of an economic system based on a fundamental self-contradiction. Corporations survive by paying us salaried and waged workers as little as possible, extracting from us the maximum in effort, and then selling us back the resultant products at a profit. It's a great deal (for the capitalists) in the short run, but obviously such closed cycle can't go on indefinitely. On the one hand, the rich can't make a profit if they pay us wage-slaves enough to buy back what we produce. On the contrary, they are always speeding up production, automating, off-shoring, downsizing and laying off to keep down their labor costs. On the other hand, with fewer and fewer workers making more and more products for less and less pay, the inevitable long-term results are overproduction (glutted markets) on the one hand and under-consumption (hungry, unemployed workers) on the other.

In this respect, capitalism differs fundamentally from previous economic systems under which unemployment was unknown. Indeed, masters normally provided at least minimum subsistence for the slaves, serfs or other domestic animals they exploited. A rational master would no sooner let his slave or serf starve or fall ill than he would his horse. For a corporation however, employees are like drops of water from a tap, to be turned on only when needed and only when it's profitable to do so. Otherwise they are free to live on air. Of course too many unemployed workers would represent a threat to the system, but U.S. capitalism solves this problem profitably by locking up 7.3 million citizens, or about 3% of the population to work for a pittance in privatized prisons at an annual cost to the taxpayers greater than the budgets for education, transportation and public assistance combined.[11] The capitalist free market treats 'labor' abstractly as one element of production, the other being

---

[10] Quoted in *The New Yorker*, March 9, 2009.
[11] According to the latest Pew study, *N.Y. Times*, March 2, 2009.

'materials' (the Earth) and is utterly indifferent to the fate of either (considered as 'externals' to be thrown away). The actual labor*ers* (you and me) being 'free' (unlike serfs and slaves) are effectively free to starve if they are unable to find a capitalist who can make a profit by employing them. Indeed, unemployment - the availability of a supply of idle, needy men, women and children obliged to sell their labor-power to survive from day to day – is a *necessary* pre-condition for capital to perform its profitable miracles. And the more the labor supply (unemployed workers) exceeds demand (jobs), the cheaper becomes the price of labor-power in this Devil's bargain with capital: the 'free' contract under which, to survive, an Indonesian seamstress must sell ten hours of sweated labor for two dollars a day, during which she stitches dozens garments that sell in stores for a hundred dollars each.[12]

The problem for capitalism is that as wages fall and joblessness rises and credit-cards max out, fewer and fewer people are able to pay for $100 anoraks. So why hire anyone to stitch them? Capital itself becomes a glut on the market.[13] From this obvious contradiction, Marx derived his famous theory of the tendency for the *rate* of profit to decline, which academic economists laughed at when the economy was growing and the *mass* of profits was rising (at least on paper). Of course the professional economists were 'right' and we Marxists were 'wrong' during the extraordinary post-WWII period of economic growth. The tendency for the *rate* of profit to decline remained just that, a tendency, invisible in the market place where the *mass* of profits was accumulating at an accelerated rate. But since the '70s, increasing capitalist global competition has been leading to lower and lower prices of manufactured goods, and the *rate* of profit, based on the amount of labor value added to each product, has been getting lower and lower. The manufacturers made up for it in the volume of sales. But the profit margins kept getting smaller. Take for example the falling prices of today's more and more powerful new computers which become obsolete and are discounted after only a year or so on the market. Today, with less and less money in consumers' pockets, computer sales are declining even more rapidly, the value of obsolete inventory is shrinking, outlets and manufacturers are shutting down or laying off in a diminishing cycle that keeps repeating itself as the economy slides deeper and deeper into depression.[14] So much for theory. But if the system is fundamentally contradictory, how come it worked so well all these years? In other words, Mr. Smartypants Marxist, why didn't capitalism collapse before?

---

[12] Cf. Naomi Klein, *No Logo* (HarperCollins, 2000).
[13] Cf. Paul Krugman, 'Revenge of the Glut,' *N.Y. Times* March 2, 2009.
[14] These vicious cycles may be compared to those of the amazing Foo Bird of Junior High School mythology which flies round and round in ever-tightening circles until it flies up its own ass and vanishes.

How Capitalism, Decadent Since 1914, Outlived Itself

To begin with, the world economy did collapse following the crash of 1929, and most economists today are agreed that it was not Roosevelt's New Deal but WWII arms production that got the U.S. out of its last Depression. Capitalism thrives on war, and WWII destroyed vast amounts of previously existing wealth. Thus the endemic plague of over-production was not a problem during capital's 'glorious' thirty-year post-War recovery. But by the Seventies, the defeated Axis powers, Japan and Germany, having rebuilt their industries using the latest technology, were once again serious capitalist competitors for U.S., and the race to the bottom began again, leading to major recessions in 1973, and 1981. Capital's response was to squeeze more value out of its employees in order to keep up the rate of profit. Thatcher and Reagan tore up the post-war social contract, declared class war on labor unions, shredded the social safety net and privatized everything in sight. As a result, wages stagnated for the next 25 years, while corporate salaries and profits soared. Yet recession struck again in 1990 and 2001. Meanwhile, capitalist competition had become truly global with the arrival in the market of the Asian Tigers and a 800 pound gorilla named China spewing out ever cheaper manufactured goods in mass quantities.

For this newly globalized capitalism to thrive, the aggregate *mass* of profits had to keep growing, whatever the human or ecological cost. One solution was to appropriate new values from *outside* the system. Through outright government intervention (under IMF and World Bank pressure) profit-hungry banks and multinational corporations were able to expropriate and/or privatize much of the world's wealth still held in common by indigenous communities in the third world, Socialist Collectives in the second and citizens in the first. Through these new 'enclosures' everything common from forests and oceans to ideas, cultural practices, health and life itself was transformed into merchandise to be bought and sold for profit. Bourgeois civilization, once the bearer of enlightenment, regressed to barbarism. Africa was stripped of its gold, diamonds, oil and precious ores leaving its peoples in a chaos of famine and civil war. Huge fortunes were made, yet markets still remained unstable with currency crashes, regional crises and major countries like Argentina going bankrupt.

Meanwhile, growthmanship, the competition-driven race for faster and faster economic growth, was becoming a frenzy - leading inevitably to global overproduction. The problem for the corporations then became creating what bourgeois economists call 'effective demand.' In other words, how to get people to buy, and more important, *pay* for all this shit? The problem, in Marxist terms, is how to 'realize' (*ie.* cash in) 'surplus value' (unpaid labor embodied in the surplus products). Modern capitalism has come up with three mains ways to get us consumers and taxpayers to pay for stuff we don't need and can't afford: war production, advertising and credit.

18

Let's start with war production, also known as 'military Keynesianism' an ironic reference to the 1930s economist who advocated major government spending on public works as a solution to recession. First of all, war business is a great business for the owners of the means of production (mines, factories, labs, etc). Think 'cost-plus contracts' and 'cost over-runs.' Economically, the means of destruction (tanks, guns planes, etc) are the ideal commodities for realizing surplus value. No matter how many bombs they manufacture, there is never 'overproduction' because the market is virtually limitless. Arms can also be exported and sold to U.S. -friendly kings and dictators who need them to repress their subjects or invade their neighbors. Once sold, weapons either go 'bang' or become obsolete; in either case, they have to be replaced. And foreign competition (the arms race) is a boon, rather than a threat, because it justifies constant increases in peacetime military spending. In any case, the military contractors have a revolving-door relationship with the brass in the Pentagon, who allow them to overcharge shamelessly and further boost their rate of profit. Of course the end of the forty-year Cold War arms race with the Soviet superpower posed a small problem for the military lobby. (Remember the 'peace dividend'?) But new 'threats' (drugs and terror) were soon invented to justify endless profitable wars.[15]

For example, Bush II's Iraqi War alone cost us an estimated three trillion dollars. How much of that mind-boggling sum ended up as profits for Haliburton, Blackwater, Brown & Root, MacDonald-Douglas and the rest of the war-profiteering cost-overrun contractors? A trillion? No wonder there was no money left for body armor or veterans' benefits. Thank the Lord we elected Mr. Obama, who promised withdraw our troops – many of them reservists serving their second, third or even fourth tour of duty - from the Iraqi quagmire. He forgot to say he was sending them into an even deeper quagmire in Afghanistan, while leaving as many as 50,000 troops and 100,000 mercenries behind to get shot at by angry Iraqis who want them out.[16] Nor did our peace candidate mention he would continue, indeed escalate, Bush's mindless 'war on terror.' Or put Bush's Defense Secretary Robert Gates back in charge of it. Forget that Afghanistan is famous for swallowing up foreign armies – including the British and the Russians - since the time of the Ancient Greeks. Forget that massacring Pakistani civilians from the safety of predator drones is probably not the best way to win the hearts and minds of that nuclear-armed nation teetering on the brink of chaos. Let's stick with the cost, that is with the profits. The top brass expect us to remain in Afghanistan until 2025.

---

[15] See Michael Klare, *Blood and Oil: The Dangers and Consequences of America's Growing Dependency on Imported Petroleum*, 2008.
[16] Indeed, it was Bush, not Obama, who in December 2009 signed the Status of Forces Agreement promising total U.S. withdrawal, after the Malaki government, backed by 70% of Iraqis polled, showed us the door.

Figure at least another mind-boggling three trillion, including another trillion for the military contractors.

I suspect one reason they get away with this boondoggle is that our minds fog over when we see all those zeros. But the devil is in the zeros, boys and girls, and the difference between millions, billions and trillions can kill you. According to the math for dummies book *Innumeracy* a million seconds of time adds up to about 12 days. A billion, on the other hand, equals nearly 32 years or half a lifetime. Keep in mind this stupendous difference as the budget figures flicker over your TV screen. As for a *trillion* seconds, they add up to 32 thousand years, which would take us back to the Stone Age (or to 27 thousand years *before* the Creation according to the Evangelicals). If each of the three trillion dollars spent on the Iraqi war were a second, they would stretch back before the emergence of the first modern humans (according to the Darwinists). And who pays the bill? The average taxpayer, that is to say to the 'working middle class' of salaried people subject to involuntary payroll taxes.

A word about taxes. As most of us have long suspected, the once 'graduated' income tax has been stood on its head, taking from the poor to give to the rich. Thanks to loopholes, massive tax cuts for the super-rich, off-shore tax-havens, and 'corporate welfare' in the form of government incentives and bailouts, many corporations and wealthy individuals pay zero net taxes. Moreover, IRS investigative and enforcement personnel have been drastically cut back, and the remaining inspectors are too busy to mount elaborate cases against the complicated tax-dodges of billion-dollar corporations. Trillions of corporate taxes go uncollected, while inspectors concentrate on closing individual taxpayers 'do-able' cases like waitress' unreported tips and teachers' home office exemptions. As a result, the working middle class (which Marxists used to call 'the proletariat'), with its small and shrinking share of the national wealth, pays an astounding 85% of the nation's taxes.[17] Thus, in macro-economic terms, military spending is an indirect transfer of wealth from poor (employees) to the rich (owners) via government intervention. Another miracle of our free enterprise system! Moreover, the portion of national capital invested in military production is sheltered against the generalized capitalist plague of overproduction and its rate of profit is correspondingly high. Moreover, military products are not only profitable, they are useful in defending corporate interests abroad and for putting down the rabble at home when they finally get wise to the corporate scam and start fighting back, as I imagine they will in the not-so-distant future.

Let's now look at advertising. Conceived by the most subtle psychologists and sociologists, designed and produced by the most talented and highest paid

---

[17] See *Free Lunch: How the Wealthiest Americans Enrich Themselves at Government Expense and Stick You With The Bill* by 2001 Pulitzer-prizing-wining former *N.Y. Times* senior reporter, David Cay Johnson.

writers and artists, incessantly beamed at us through media that celebrate consumerism, advertising creates a culture in which people's sense of status depends less on what they really are than on what they wear, eat, drink, or drive. More than competition between brands, advertising is basically 'capitalist propaganda.'[18] Don't laugh. Communist propaganda was easy to recognize (from the outside). It glorified the state, presented an heroic picture of happy workers, and blared its message out of tinny loudspeakers on nearly every corner. Capitalist propaganda is harder to recognize (from the inside). Yet every day the pervasive capitalist message – buy! – flashing from screens and billboards, blaring out of high-tech speakers, TVs and car radios. The product being sold is consumerist capitalism itself, and as French philosopher Jean-Claude Michéa points out that our society spends almost as much on capitalist propaganda (advertising) as on arms.[19] As McLuhan put it: the 'medium *is* the message. Standardized commercial entertainments are everywhere replacing participatory activities like dancing, music-making, sport, story-telling, reading and conversation, leaving a cultural void to be filled through consumption. Basically, advertising aims at making us feel insecure unless we buy more garbage than we can afford or even use. Literally. More than 50% of U.S. consumer production ends up as garbage within one year of its purchase. Indeed, in our throwaway economy waste products are the leading U.S. export – second only to armaments.[20] It turns out there is more surplus value embodied in the throwaway plastic container than there is in the sandwich inside, and that's where the corporate profit comes from. Garbage glut is another of capitalism's ruses for avoiding the consequences of overproduction.

Twentieth Century advertising worked, up through the '70s. It got lots of people *wanting* to buy things they never knew they couldn't do without. But with downsizing, union-busting, automating, inflating prices and stagnating wages, people no longer had the cash. No problem: capitalism had an answer: credit. 'Can't afford that new car? Don't worry. You don't have to pay for it … now. Step right over to our credit department. That smiley gentleman in the sharkskin suit is waiting to take care of you: our Mr. Loanshark. What our brilliant advertising department has cleverly seduced you into buying, our friendly credit department will cheerfully help you pay over time for a small monthly fee. No need to read all that *teentsie little* fine print at the bottom where it says 'interest annualizes at an average of 21.6%. . . .' All through the roaring '80s and beyond, financialized U.S. capital gorged on double-dip profits, making people work for less and loaning them money at interest to

---

[18] Cf. *Propaganda,* the seminal 1928 book by the genius of modern advertising Edward Bernays, who wrote that propaganda was 'necessary in a democratic society' and invented a new name, 'public relations,' behind which to hide it.
[19] Jean-Claude Michéa, *La pensée double,* Paris 2008.
[20] See Heather Roger's splendid and readable book: *Gone Tomorrow: The Hidden Life of Garbage,* The New Press, N.Y. and London, 2005.

keep consuming. Thanks to 'our Mr. Loanshark,' it was a win/win situation for the capitalists, who convinced themselves that this debt-fueled economy could go on forever and that 'overproduction' was a Marxist myth.

So let's take another look at credit, or rather at its dark twin, debt. It's a subject that makes everybody cringe, so let's start with a simple definition: debt means bankers' profits. The more they lend, the richer they get. And thanks to the Miracle of Compound Interest, bank profits pile up quickly and soon overtake the original principal the lender borrowed. If you have trouble paying, Mr. Loanshark will happily offer you new loans to 'consolidate' your previous obligations and spread them over time, thus multiplying your debt (keep thinking 'bankers' profits'). As long as the payments keep coming in, and ballooning, the loansharks don't care if they ever get their principle back. Since personal bankruptcy 'reform,' the finance companies can attach your salary indefinitely so that you are actually working for *them.* This practice used to be known as 'debt peonage,' and was illegal in many states. On the global scale, many 'developing' nations have ended up in debt peonage, paying out more than half their annual GNP year after year in debt service to international banks. As for the national debt in the U.S. (remember, you own it) the first five and a half of your monthly tax deductions go directly into paying it off . In other words, bankers' profits account for all your taxes from January to mid-June, after which you start paying for such 'extras' as the Army, the government and a few social services.

This kind of usury ought to be a crime, and was in fact been outlawed as such until the deregulation of the Seventies when according to Thomas Goeghegan 'we dismanteled the most ancient of human laws, the law against usury which had existed in some form from the time of the Babylonian Empire (Hammurabi's Code c. 1750 B.C.) to the end of Jimmy Carter's term.' As a result, interest (bank profits) on credit cards rose to 30%-50%, and the banks sent out literally *billions* of pre-proved cards to encourage reckless consumer borrowing. With worker productivity rising and workers' wages stagnating, capitalism 'substituted the credit card for the union card.' [21] More recently, short-term high interest (up to 400%) 'Payday Loans' are being offered to low-wage workers through 22,000 stores situated in lower-middle-class predominantly black and brown neighborhoods. Suppose you are living from paycheck to paycheck like so many Americans and your car breaks down so you can't get to work. You need $200 for repairs right away, and payday is at the end of the month. So you walk into a convenient local branch of a Payday Loan chain and sign a post-dated check for $230 and they give you $200 cash on the spot. If you can't reimburse your loan on payday (the case for more than 75% of working poor borrowers), the interest starts multiplying and you

---

[21] Thomas Goeghegan, 'Infinite Debt: How Unlimited Interest Rates Destroyed the Economy,' *Harpur's* cover story, April 2009.

can end up a peon caught in the Debt Trap.[22] Meanwhile, the U.S. has become de-industrialized. What capitalist would invest in wages, plant and equipment to earn 7% when he could earn 50% as a usurer? By the 1990's, GM Finance Corporation was earning more for GM than manufacturing cars.

As we have seen, the Gilded Age which we (or rather the wealthy among us) have just lived through was based on credit, that is to say on debt (keep thinking 'bankers' profits'). The little people down below were all working harder and harder (those of use who hadn't been downsized) to support the banking, insurance and finance industry (billionaire speculators and institutional loan sharks). These financial wizards kept the *mass* of profits artificially high by lending out the same money several times over, piling up risk upon risk through derivatives. Their gamut of slick financial products ran from common credit card debt to homeowner debt, bank debt, leveraged buyout debt, corporate debt and Government debt. By 2007, the U.S. financial sector had grown to 1.8 times the size of the manufacturing sector. The economy was like an inverted pyramid of debt (keep thinking 'bankers' profits') precariously balanced on a tip of actual productive economic activity in the real economy. Every leveraged buyout meant that a company's employees had to produce not just a regular annual profit of 5% or 10% for management and the stockholders, but another 10% on top of that to pay off the financial corporations who had bought the company on borrowed money. Think of all us tiny worker ants struggling to drag food back to the nest each with a big fat drone of a banker-ant riding on our back, and you get the picture.

On what was all this credit based? Where was the collateral? How many actual concrete values were being created at the base of the inverted pyramid? The world economy based on credit was like the Earth resting on a turtle in the ancient myth. And what was that turtle resting on?' Another turtle! It was 'turtles all the way down' in the financial markets, and we ain't hit bottom yet. So now that this credit bubble has collapsed leaving us all in a horrible mess,

---

[22] See Daniel Brook, 'Usury Country,' in *Harpur's* for April 2009.

the free-market speculators are bleating for the government to bail them out and send them back to the gambling tables.

What is the sense of the government pouring good money after bad into an ocean of bad debt? Especially with a maelstrom sweeping up all securities and driving their prices down to the bottom. Why incur new debt to rescue old? Why buy shares in failing banks when their value keeps shrinking? It certainly won't bring about a recovery. The principal effect of Economic Rescue is to transform accumulated capitalist debt into taxpayer debt. To be repaid – I don't know how – by you and me and all those other little people who used to have useful jobs working down at the point of that great inverted financial pyramid of an economy which just tipped over. So far, the ongoing bailout has been bipartisan, the Creator having blessed our glorious capitalist democracy with two pro-business parties (or if you prefer, a single party with two right wings). The bankers get to keep the profits, and now we get to clean up after the high-rollers' party. And since the 'reform' of personal bankruptcy laws, debtors will have to keep paying installments indefinitely on their educations, cars and houses, even after they have been forced to sell at a loss. Apparently the crash was all their feckless fault. According to the *Times*: "A growing chorus in conservative circles is trying to shift the blame for the current crisis to the poor and advocates for the poor?"[23] But in my opinion, if one tenth of one percent of the world population was accumulating billions while an estimated three billion people were living in poverty, the *ultimate cause* of the collapse of global capitalist economy was its built-in *inequality*.

What Next?

Remember that we have only begun to feel the effects of the global financial crash so far. The shit really hits the fan when it ripples out into the real economy of jobs and food and the actual depression settles in. Those who talk about 'recovery' today are simply whistling past a graveyard. Even if the U.S. could save its banks, this is a world depression and our economy is much more globalized than in 1929. Of course, it is theoretically possible that the world capitalist economy will eventually recover. Full-scale production might resume with time, after sufficient existing values have been destroyed, for example over decades of obsolescence. Or more rapidly through war, as in 1939-45. But I doubt many of us will be around to enjoy that hypothetical recovery, given the capitalism's second major crisis: the environment.

If one thing is safe to predict concerning both the financial and environmental crises, it is this: they are worse than anyone thought. In both cases, the latest studies demonstrate that the most pessimistic of earlier estimations of the rate of accumulating damage was overly optimistic.[24] Global warming keeps

---

[23] See N.Y. *Times* Oct. 17, 2008: "Poor Homeowners, Good Loans."
[24] Cf. Peter S. Goodman, 'Sharper Downturn Clouds Obama Spending Plans,' *N.Y.*

accelerating, and we are probably very close to the tipping point, when it will be impossible to slow or stop it - even if humans stopped burning carbon altogether. Just last month, scientists reported that the arctic glaciers and frozen tundra are rapidly melting, releasing mega-tons of methane - a greenhouse gas twenty times more dangerous than CO_2. Worse still, all that brilliant white ice and snow that used to reflect the sun's heat back into space is melting, exposing brown and green earth that absorbs solar heat - thus raising the earth's temperature and causing more melting in a vicious cycle. One of the many vicious cycles that have been observed in both the environmental and economic spheres. Yet capitalism's solution to the crisis is to bail out the auto industry (rather than build mass transit), burn 'clean coal' (rather than going solar) and to institute pro-business 'cap and trade' fiscal flummery rather than effective controls. One might hope that as factories close, there will be fewer carbon emissions. On the other hand, economic 'recovery' gives the polluters a perfect reason to keep putting off expensive conversions. So let's not hold our breath waiting for a 'green recovery.'

Since the problem is systemic, neither bailouts nor re-regulation nor even nationalization of banks and industries will bring recovery. Nationalization is not the same as socialization. State capitalism was tried in the U.S.S.R. under the name of 'Communism' and failed. Despite totalitarian controls, it was destabilized by class conflicts and eventually collapsed. Is there a solution? According to economist Richard Wolf, we could try eliminating 'capitalist class conflict by reorganizing enterprises to position productive workers as their own collective board of directors, thereby removing one key cause of capitalist instability. Such post-capitalist boards' decisions (about technical change, capital accumulation, wages, and so forth) would differ markedly from capitalist boards' decisions.' This kind of 'industrial democracy' deserves a try, but first we have to get rid of the existing boards of directors and history seems to presenting such an opportunity. The capitalist edifice is crumbling, and it's payback time. Take back the earth time. Put people above profits time. And, according to climate scientists, with not much time left,.

I get no *schadenfreude*[25] out of having foreseen this awesome crisis, which will bring untold suffering to the poorest, the most exposed members of the human family. Obviously, there is no way for me to 'prove' that the Crash of 2008 has provoked capitalism's fabled Final Crisis. That can only be known through hindsight, and it took 25 years before the U.S. economy recovered to 1929 levels in 1954. But twenty-five years from now the question may be moot. Existentially speaking, it's now or never in terms of the survival of many species, including humans. In any case, humanity is entering a phase of titanic

---

Times Feb. 27, 2009.

[25] Untranslatable German expression meaning "sick pleasure derived from others' discomfiture"

social struggles - perhaps the 'final conflict' evoked in the chorus of the *Internationale*. [26] As we have seen, neo-liberal capitalist sharks have been waging one-sided class war on the rest of us for the past generation. 'The unacknowledged Marxism of the enemies of Marxism,' Victor Serge called it. Now they're scared of the popular backlash. Bush 'legalized' use of the Armed Forces against 'domestic disturbances' (violating the Posse Comitatus Act), and the CIA recently advised President Obama that social unrest represents a greater threat to the U.S. than terrorism. Food riots in Asia, Left governments and popular movements in Latin America, youth uprisings in Greece, a general strike in Guadaloupe and Martinique, organized resistance to plant closings and home evictions in the U.S., we can already hear the first rumblings. By demanding equality, these class struggles carry within them the only true solution to capitalism's endemic crisis of boom and bust, overproduction and unemployment, obscene wealth and desperate poverty.

Whatever the outcome, one thing is certain : these struggles will have to be international. With globalized banks and multi-national corporations as adversaries, there is no way of winning lasting gains by purely local or even national struggles. These globalized capitalist sharks are masters at pitting one group of workers against another and delocalising to avoid paying a decent wage. For working people in every land, the choice is simple : global unity or the continuing race to the bottom. As I hope to show in these Internationalist Essays, the workers' movement has a long tradition of international solidarity. The international socialist movement began in 1848 under the slogan 'working people of all countries unite.' Today, with modern communications technology (Internet), workers can can actually unite to organize global strikes and boycotts in real time. The 160 year-old dream has become practical reality. Take that, Mr. Capitalist Shark !

Don't let them eat you · organise to resist

---

[26] Written in 1871 by Eugène Pottier, a member of the revolutionary Paris Commune, the *International* has been sung (off key in 27 languages) by workers and socialists around the world.

Part I:

Is Another World *Really* Possible?

Ecotopia: A Bet You Can't Refuse

One Chance in a hundred?

L et's be optimistic! Let's bet there's one chance in a hundred that the Earth will still be habitable at the end of the 21st Century! Think I'm exaggerating? Try answering the following questions honestly:
Do you personally think that weapons of mass destruction are likely to stop proliferating? Do you truly believe that pollution is going to stop getting worse? Can you actually imagine that forests will stop disappearing? That the climate will stop heating up? Do you actually see an end to:

glaciers melting?
icebergs shrinking?
arctic permafrost disappearing?
oceans rising?
coastlands sinking?

famines raging?
epidemics spreading?
cities deteriorating?
global unemployment rising?
poverty increasing?
armed conflicts erupting?
refugees multiplying?
petty crime flourishing?
corporate crime expanding?

real wages declining?
useless wealth piling up?
rich people withdrawing into gated communities?
youth despairing?
drugs spreading?
AIDS spreading?
prisons boiling over?

religions fanaticizing?
nationalists killing?
womens' rights shrinking?
government security hardening?
civil rights disappearing?
danger of atomic war increasing?
danger of nuclear accident growing?

women being degraded?
wars dragging on forever?
small farms dying?
forests shrinking?
droughts spreading?

biofuels starving peasants?
storms increasing?
deserts extending?
world hunger increasing?
the struggle for water intensifying?
animals and fish disappearing?

Need I go on? You know as well as I do that each of these trends will lead to foreseeable disasters if left unchecked. Now imagine all these trends interacting in horrid synergy. Atmospheric warming leading to glacier melting leading to ocean rising leading to coastal flooding leading to fleeing refugees leading to worldwide epidemics leading to social chaos leading to martial law leading to … you name it. Not a pretty picture. Small wonder we rarely allow ourselves to actually visualize such a future and to imagine ourselves living in it. I dare you to close your eyes and try it, right now, just for thirty seconds…

Denial and Distraction

Hard to stay focused on that picture? Our situation reminds me of people in the Robert Louis Stevenson story who were living in a city built on the edge of a volcano. We get (more or less blithely) through the days without cracking up thanks to a single powerful psychological factor: *denial*. (Didn't they name the longest river in the world after it?) Feeling the need to turn your eyes away from immanent global catastrophe? Today's marketplace provides a full spectrum of diversions for whiling away your time on the way to extinction!

Shopping is a sure-fire way to take your mind off the horror; so are TV and losing yourself in work. Grass is great if it helps you laugh at the absurdity of it all, but if it makes you paranoid, stick to booze. (I find alcohol excellent for momentary forgetting.) If you have access to anti-depressants, tranquilizers and Perkidan; they're the drugs of choice for the quietly desperate. Of course, extreme sports are more of a thrill, and a lot of people get their rocks off competing for more and more money, more and more power. Gambling gives you the same rush.

Cocaine and speed can be cool too if you like the fast lane, but don't knock old standbys like opium and heroin if you just want to forget. Alas, the downside of the opiates is they inhibit sex, which satisfied customers consider the best bet for an inexpensive, healthful, peaceful diversion. On the other hand, beating up on your family or on people from other groups can be diverting up to and including murder and mutilation. For the more introspective, there's suicide (martyrdom optional). And speaking of martyrdom, let's finish off this list with the least expensive diversion on the market: obliterating yourself behind a group identity. Identities are packaged in a variety of garish colors like religion, nationality, sexual orientation and race to appeal to down-market consumers.

But if we do dare peek out from under our security blanket of denial, what do we see? We are the children of the 20th Century, the bloodiest so far in history. Future historians, if there are any, will see the 20th as an orgy of mechanized mayhem, featuring brutal totalitarian dictatorships, two bloody world wars, aerial bombardment of civilians including nuclear weapons, scientific genocides, and the devastation of vast swaths of the earth. Violence was the epidemic that plagued the last century, and violence threatens to overwhelm this one. Violence got off to a fast start on September 11, 2001 – a tragic pretext for the planet's high-tech military super-power to proceed with plans to invade oil-rich, strategically important countries while cowing its allies. Meanwhile several more unstable states have acquired atomic bombs. A booming trade in conventional arms is fueling all the civil wars, slow genocides and intractable regional crises we inherited from the bloody 20th. And we've nine more decades to go with no peace in sight.

Add this growing epidemic of violence to the all those other destructive tendencies, and one chance in a hundred to get us out of this mess begins to look like generous odds.

Call me an optimist.

A Challenge to the Imagination

For the sake of argument, let us agree that there *is* one chance in a hundred for a livable world in 2100. If that one chance does exist, shouldn't we be able to *imagine* it, as a kind of Sci-Fi story? After all, human beings dreamed of space-travel for centuries, and writers of future fictions imagined it with greater and greater accuracy.[27] So why shouldn't 21st Century humans at least be able to *imagine* a possible future in which Starship Earth is saved from self-destruction?

Let's put our imaginations to work. What kind of realistic salvation scenario can we imagine for a planet in the thralls of a powerful social and economic system which seems inexorably to be leading us to predictable catastrophes? If we exclude divine or extra-terrestrial intervention from our fantasy, then we need to imagine the emergence of some kind of positive revolution in human relations. In other words, we need to envision a radical change in the way

---

[27] As a result, neither the first *sputnik* nor Yuri Gagarin's epoch-making manned space flight came as a surprise to Sci-Fi fans, despite the official secrecy that surrounded the Cold War space programs.

humans work, run things, relate to each other and to other living things, before we can imagine the planet being rescued before it becomes unlivable.

But is the emergence of such a positive revolution in human affairs even *imaginable* today?

The only way to answer to that question is to join with me and accept the challenge of dreaming up imaginary visions of *possible* roads to this Utopia. Only when humans pay attention to their dreams can Humanity awake from the sleep-walk of neurotic denial and the nightmare of capitalist barbarism. If we can put our heads together and realistically imagine such a positive human

revolution succeeding, then our one chance in a hundred exists. So why not dream? Whatever the odds may be, betting on Utopia seems to be our only chance of winning. Let's remember the handwriting on the walls of revolutionary Paris in 1968: 'Take Your Dreams for Realities!' 'All Power to the Imagination!' Indeed, perhaps dreaming together is the most useful thing we can do in the midst of all the conflict and confusion around us: to dream of *possible* Utopias and to imagine materially possible roads to get there.

Translation of above into revolutionary jargon for the benefit of Serious Revolutionaries: Given the propensity of negative tendencies in the contemporary objective situation to converge into critically critical crisis, the spontaneous semi-conscious mental activity vulgarly known as 'dreaming' posits itself as an imperative task that every conscious militant must urgently embrace.

At this point in our discussion I hear parental voices whining: Isn't dreaming up roads to Utopia an impractical waste of time, like playing *Dungeons and Dragons* or *Second Life*? Maybe, Mom and Dad, but what if play is the only way out of the industrious mess you (and your parents) got us into? How can people change the world without a positive vision, a direction, a goal?

The Power of Utopias

In any case, it turns out that the human imagination is a powerful thing, and Utopian thought has been a major influence on human society at least since the Greek philosopher Plato outlined his ideal society in *The Republic* – a two-thousand year-old book which continues to inspire political thought to this day. During the Catholic Middle Ages, Saint Augustine's Utopian *City of God* set the ideal pattern for a Christian polity. In 1516 at the dawn of the capitalist era, the term *Utopia* (the word means *No-place* in Greek) was coined by Thomas

Moore, an idealistic churchman (and later high official at the Court of Henry VIII). Moore saw private property, enforced by legal violence, as the root cause of the poverty and injustice in Tudor England.[28] He spun a traveler's tale of a faraway land where nobody starved because every able person shared in society's work for just six hours day – anticipating the French 35-hour work-week by five centuries. Moore's outspoken idealism later cost him his head (and earned him a sainthood) when he refused to approve of the King's divorce.

QuickTime™ et un
décompresseur TIFF (non compressé)
sont requis pour visionner cette image.

Meanwhile over in sunny France, François Rabelais, the unfrocked monk and medical doctor who wrote the comic novels *Gargantua* and *Pantagruel,* created an anarchistic Utopia in his fictional Abbey of Thélème, a reversal of the oppressive monastic life, whose only rule was Do What Thou Wilt. Utopias based on religious visions of human holiness and wholeness have inspired vast peasant revolutions down through history. In Germany in 1563, the city of Münster was turned into a radical commune by Anabaptists under Jan of

---

[28] England, Moore's traveler observed, was a barbarous land where sheep eat men because the peasants were starving after being driven off their common lands, which were enclosed as sheep-walks, providing profits for the wool industry and mutton for the rich to eat.

35

Lyden; in 17th Century England, the Diggers and Levelers shared out the land and wealth; and in China, beginning in 1851, the Ta'I-p'ing rebels occupied major provinces in China for over a decade. All were led on by dreams of fellowship and equality.

Chinese Utopians. During the Ta'i-p'ing Rebellion of 1851-1864, the rebels conquered and held major portions of China for over a decade before being finally put down by the British General Gordon (henceforth 'Chinese' Gordon). Inspired by a religious sect, the T'ai-pings abjured alcohol, gambling and opium; they practiced complete equality between men and women, equal division of the land, construction of a new social order based on cooperative hamlets of twenty-five families and State granaries as a hedge against recurring famines, which had decimated China in the 1840s.

In the early 19th century, the 'Dickensian' poverty of the dawning Industrial Age provoked a new Utopian response in the socialist proposals of Fourier and Saint-Simon and in the successful colonies created by the philanthropist Robert Owen. These Utopian visions in turn inspired a young German philosopher named Karl Marx, who sought to integrate them with a new political force that he saw emerging under capitalism – workers' social justice movements that took to the streets throughout Europe in 1848.

Marx and Utopia: The difference between the Utopian socialism of Owen, Fourrier and St. Simon and what Marx and Engels (in the Germanic philosophical jargon of their era) called 'scientific socialism,' was this. The Utopians proposed an ideal model society without worrying too much about how it could be realized (except for Owen, who founded actual colonies). Marx rooted socialism in the 'science' of history, as the successful outcome of the class struggle between worker and capitalist. Marx himself published no Utopian blueprints, although he did theorize about socialism and its higher stage communism in letters to his associates. Marx's 'scientific' method was to learn from the actual movement of the workers, whose 'way of knowing' was through engaging in social struggles – like the English workers' campaigns for a democratic Charter and the Ten-Hour-Day. Thus, when the French workers created the world's first workers' government (the democratic, egalitarian Paris Commune of 1871), Marx pointed to the Commune's actual working existence as the practical answer to the theoretical question of how to organize socialism. So Marx did not so much reject Utopia as redefine it as 'the new society emerging from the shell of the old.'

In 1888 the American socialist Edward Bellamy published his novel *Looking Backward* about a dreamer from Boston who awakens in a future society where people live secure, fulfilling lives with no use for money, under a rigorously rational socialist regime. This anti-capitalist best-seller initiated millions of young Americans into thinking along lines that were entirely new to them and radicalized a number of future American socialists like Eugene V. Debs, Daniel de Leon, Charles Kerr, and the great defense lawyer, Clarence Darrow. The novel's popularity spawned socialist clubs all over the country and helped unite splinter groups into a growing nationwide socialist movement in the 1890s.[29]

In England, the poet and graphic artist William Morris, founder of the Arts and Crafts movement, became converted to Marxian socialism around 1880. Morris was uncomfortable with Bellamy's utilitarian Utopia, with its obsessive productivity and state control, and so in 1890 he answered it with his own successful novel, *News from Nowhere*. Morris' dreamer awakes in an idyllic post-revolutionary London, free of industrial pollution, where the inhabitants, handsome, sane and happy, live next to nature and work only for pleasure. This novel had an enormous influence in England.

A half-century later, British socialist George Orwell wrote his satirical anti-Utopias *Animal Farm* and *1984* and opened the eyes of millions of readers to the phoniness of totalitarian Communism's claims on the Utopian dream. During the later 20th Century a number of North American science fiction writers tried out Utopian scenarios. Robert Heinlein, Margaret Atwood, Ursula Le Guin, Marge Piercy, Kim Stanley Robinson, Ernest Callenbach and others have created futuristic Utopias that give us critical perspectives on the present as well as plausible, detailed, brilliantly imagined histories of possible future societies in which everything from ecology to sex has been revolutionized. Translated in many languages, these thought-provoking, prophetic, sometimes inspiring Utopian novels have been read by millions.

---

[29] **Socialism in the U.S.** The half-forgotten American socialist movement had millions of voters and locals in cities and rural areas all over America. Socialists published daily papers in a number of cities as well as 140 magazines in 14 different languages.

Fascist Dystopias

Future fictions can even inspire deeds. In the 1980s the racist right in the U.S. was galvanized by a novel called *The Turner Diaries* by Andrew MacDonald, the leader of the white separatist organization National Alliance. The novel depicts a violent racist revolutionary struggle in the United States that escalates into global genocide, leading to the extermination of all Jews and non-whites. For the author and his fans, this was not a negative outcome, but rather the fulfillment of his dream of a White world.

The Turner Diaries soon became the Bible of the Nazi-Christian armed militias that flourish in the United States. In these milieus, some folks took MacDonald's paranoid fantasies for actual fact. *The Turner Diaries* was the bedside reading of Timothy McVeigh, the young ex-soldier who killed more than 400 people with a bomb of his own making when he blew up the Federal Building in Oklahoma City in 1995. He was apparently inspired by the episode where Turner describes how the Order dynamites the FBI Building. Which goes to show that life sometimes imitates art. (Not to be outdone by the Christian Fundamentalists, bin Laden's Islamists raised the *ante* seven years later and killed 3,000 in New York.)

Since around 2000 the *Left Behind* series of apocalyptic novels have been topping the best-seller lists in the U.S. – a publishing phenomenon that has generated films, and other spin-offs. The novels describe the adventures of a group of evangelical Christians who survive the rise of the Antichrist – plus plagues, judgments, and the final battle of Armageddon (*Left Behind* Vol. 11). These novels have a born-again Christian audience of millions linked by talk radio and fan clubs, where current events are interpreted in terms of the

Apocalypse scenario derived from the 2nd Century Gospel of St. John.[30]

It's a sad commentary that wackos, racists, survivalists and end-of the world fundamentalists seem to be the only subcultures with a vision of the future, albeit a frighteningly negative one. Our strife-torn world cries out for positive visions. We desperately need an *imaginable* Utopia. It isn't enough for good people merely to protest, to struggle eternally *against* the

---

[30] See 'Religion and Repression in the US' in Part II above.

latest outrage. Of course we must resist war, racism, sexism, police-state repression and a host of other evils. But what we most need today is a positive goal, a vision of a *possible* future without which our awareness of the endless evils of this world only makes us passive and cynical.

A Favorable Moment?

Such a vision – at once Utopian and realistic – is needed to strike the imagination and spark hope, without which no positive revolution is possible. One chance out of a hundred isn't a huge hope, agreed. But we know where despair leads: drugs, anomie, religious and nationalist fanaticism. Moreover, the historical moment, although dark, may well be favorable for floating a new revolutionary vision of a more human society for a simple reason: since the collapse of Communism, Social-Democracy, and Neo-Liberalism, there are no more competitors.

During the 90's Communism – more nightmare than dream – transformed itself into Mafia capitalism in Russia and China and lost its appeal. In Europe Social Democracy is definitively discredited as a Left-wing cover for free-market privatization. And since 2001 the American model of free market neo-liberal capitalism has lost its sheen. Once proclaimed as 'the end of history,' the neo-liberal vision is increasingly tattered.

Only yesterday, greed was good and CEOs were gods. Then the dotcom bubble burst, massive embezzling by top management was exposed (remember Enron?), looted retirement funds collapsed and big modern countries like Argentina found themselves bankrupt after submitting to IMF economic therapy. Seven year later, Bear Stearns, Lehman Brothers, Washington Mutual, Wachovia and even Freddie and Fannie Mac gambled themselves out of business. Today, the diehard free-marketeers are hardly more credible than the

39

diehard Communists. The world is waking up from the American Dream with a nasty hangover. Only yesterday, reactionary new philosophers in Europe and neo-con pundits from right-wing think tanks in the US had a monopoly on politically correct thinking. Today they are seen as tiresome, not trendy. Their world is in crisis. We are entering a century of breakdown and contestation. It will either end as a century of Utopias or it will end in catastrophe.

The men in suits who rule the world today have no plan for the future. Their main preoccupation is holding onto their power and wealth. Their perspectives are limited to inflating quarterly balance sheets and winning biennial election campaigns. If they don't see any further into the future, it's also because they unconsciously understand that there will be no future – since they are busy killing it. They are the officers of a ship drifting rudderless toward a rocky shore, busy looting the cargo, locking up the passengers and crew below decks and fighting among themselves for the booty.

Mutiny on Starship Earth

The name of that vessel is Starship Earth. Its only hope is that the passengers and crew can figure out a way to get organized and take over the bridge before it is too late. Mutiny on Starship Earth: great title for our Utopian scenario. Just what we need to start with, *if* we can imagine a plausible one.

That is the nature of the Utopian Bet. Even with the odds against us, it's a bet we can't refuse. Because like it or not, we are the all in the same boat, passengers and crew alike – far out at sea and drifting toward shipwreck. One chance in a hundred may seem like pretty slim odds, but look at it this way: The bad news is that we will soon have nothing to lose but the dismal spectacle of a dying world – made uglier every day by increasing injustice, suffering, and stupidity. The good news is that we have a finite chance to save a beautiful planet with all our friends on board. Nothing to lose against an infinity of life and beauty? Mathematically speaking, it's zero against infinity – pretty good odds in my book.

Talk about a bet you can't refuse!

How to get There from Here:
A Modern Archimedes Hypothesis

*I will raise the Earth! * The Archimedes Hypothesis * The Lever of Planetary Solidarity * Democracy, Internet, Emergence * The Fulcrum of Planetary Consciousness * Our Age of Absolutes * Simple, One-Sided Negation * Utopia, or the Negation of Negation * Connectivity, Complexity, Quantum, and Emergence * An Ecotopian Manifestival * Conclusion*

Supposing then that we do bet on Utopia, our next problem is imagining how we can possibly get from here to there without supernatural or extraterrestrial help? In other words, what are the human (social), material (technological) and spiritual (ideological) elements – latent in globalized capitalist society – that can combine to enable the emergence of the planetary movements capable of stripping the billionaires of their power and creating sustainable post-capitalist societies?

I will raise the Earth!

They say that in ancient times, that bold philosopher and inventor Archimedes boasted: Give me a lever long enough, a fulcrum, a place to stand, and I will raise the Earth! Of course, we know Archimedes' amazing feat was only a hypothesis – a 'thought experiment' that could take place only in the mind. But Archimedes's discovery was no less powerful for being a 'mere' idea dreamed up by a philosopher. In the centuries after Archimedes, inventions based on his hypothesis vastly multiplied the puny strength of human beings so that they were able to circumnavigate the globe and eventually to dominate it – for better or for worse. Can anyone then doubt the ability of an idea – a thought experiment – to multiply human power?

Our problem, if we want to successfully imagine a plausible science fiction scenario with a happy ending, is to think up a similar hypothetical formula for multiplying human power so that our passengers and crew can lift the Earth before it is shipwrecked. Our mutineers will need a lot of leverage to overpower the officers who are fighting among themselves, looting the ship, and steering it toward disaster. How to imagine such a *lever, platform,* and *fulcrum*? History seems to indicate that whenever people are ready to pose new questions, the means of resolving them are already present – if only as possibilities for science fiction.

41

The Modern Archimedes Hypothesis

In our scenario for 'Mutiny on Starship Earth' the three elements are already on board, ready to be configured into a new power strong enough to halt the onrush of global self-destruction and release the human energy to build a new society. I call them: *The Social Lever, The Electronic Platform, and The Philosophical Fulcrum.*

www.internationale-invisible.org

- *The Social Lever* is the vast untapped power of planetary solidarity. Once the billions of passengers and crewmembers aboard Starship Earth unite and act together, no force can stop them. Divided, they are pitiful and weak. United, their power is irresistible.

- *The Electronic Platform* is the World Wide Web. Its emergent technology is tentacular, infinite in its connections, interactive, and indestructible because its center is everywhere and nowhere. As accessible tomorrow as the telephone is today, the Internet provides a place to stand large enough for billions to interact. The Web is a planetary platform where each can speak for her/himself on equal footing, where billions of passengers and crew-members can connect, unite, empower themselves and take initiatives on a planetary scale – the only scale on which it makes sense to confront the power-mad officers of predatory global capitalism.

- *The Philosophical Fulcrum* is planetary consciousness: the awareness that planets are mortal. It is a vision which places the survival of Starship Earth and its inhabitants at the center of all things. It is the affirmation of Life on Earth as a new universal, as the common spiritual and practical basis around which billions can unite.

42

The Lever of Planetary Solidarity

Solidarity is the most familiar of the three powers. As the radical poet Shelley put it: We are many, they are few. We all know that there is strength in numbers, and it's six billion of us against about six thousand billionaires. It follows that united we stand, divided we fall, for in the words of the old song union makes us strong. Solidarity is not merely a realistic tactical, practical necessity; it is a positive social ethic and a fundamental human value as well. The old labor slogan sums up the lesson of all the great religious teachers of the past two thousand years: An injury to one – to the humblest child among us – is an injury to all.

Women and Children First. But what about human nature? people object. To be sure, the aggression, competitiveness and greed exemplified by the brawling, pilfering officers of Starship Earth (and by most of us average folks on petty, personal levels) are based on natural human instincts – traits which capitalist society magnifies both by cultivating and rewarding them. But cooperation and solidarity are also instinctive human survival traits – arguably more essential, if less obvious, because we take them for granted. Yet, without the nurturance and attention of parents, extended families and local societies, no human infant could survive our prolonged helplessness or ever learn to speak. In humanity's long past, solidarity and collaboration have been more effective than competition and aggression for our survival. As Barbara Ehrenreich points out in *Blood Rites: Origins and History of the Passions of War,* early humans – naked, hairless, clawless bands of men, women and children armed with sticks and stones – were easy prey for mega-mammals like the saber-toothed tiger. How then did these early human bands protect themselves and their young when faced with huge ravening predators? Apparently, our ancestors drove them off by forming a chorus line, donning costumes, making horrible noises with voice and instruments and putting on a rhythmic group dance! This is not a joke. Put yourself in the place of a tiger looking to pick off a slow-moving human child for an easy snack and suddenly faced with an organized band of fifty men, women and children all wearing branches on their heads to look ten feet tall, waving more branches like claws on long, outstretched arms, jumping up and down, pounding their feet, agitating their branches and beating on drums altogether in the same rhythm while advancing in a body like a 100-foot Chinese dragon screaming like a banshee. Well, I wasn't *really* in the mood for human child today, anyway. According to Ehrenreich, it would be hundreds of thousands of years before a class of aggressive, male predators armed with hi-tech bows and spears emerged to drive off other predators, call themselves chiefs and dominate society – like the officers of Starship Earth.

In the case of our Mutiny scenario, it is obvious that if the passengers and crew imprisoned below decks in sealed compartments don't find a way to get together and unite, they won't be able to take over the bridge before the money-crazed officers wreck the ship.

If we base our successful mutiny scenario on human history, for the sake of realism, it turns out that the potential power of mass solidarity has shown itself at revolutionary moments from ancient times. Ever since the revolt of Spartacus and the Roman slaves, the poor, the downtrodden, the exploited have shown their ability to unite and use their numbers to win concessions from their powerful oppressors – even to overthrow them. Down through the ages – from the vast peasant uprisings in Feudal times to the mass revolutions of the 18th, 19th and 20th centuries – numbers, united, have overcome armed entrenched power structures… At least momentarily.

Make no mistake. In no time or place have the wealthy ever shared any of their power or privileges without a struggle. It was only by uniting in mass movements, unions, and political parties that ordinary working people won such democratic rights as universal suffrage, freedom of assembly, freedom of association, the eight-hour day, and legislation mandating universal education, healthcare, job safety and social security. Moreover, such reforms – today under attack – were achieved only after generations of struggle and only in Europe, the Americas, and a few Asian and ex-colonial countries.

Today, neo-liberal capitalism is attacking these basic rights on a global scale, even in the wealthy advanced countries. Moreover, in vast portions of the world, the common people still have not won personal freedom, civil liberties or a say in government – in spite of generations of mass sacrifice in the name of revolution and national independence. As a result, their labor is cheap. Globalization allows transnational businesses to exploit that cheap labor, and capital has been flowing from the democracies – where employees can still protect themselves to some extent – to the dictatorships, where they can't. Moreover, authoritarian rule – the business-friendly, security-driven police state – is on the rise even among the traditionally liberal democracies: a contaminated export blowing back to the capitalist homelands along with third world poverty in first world cities.

Solidarity must be international to be effective, as the workers of Europe concluded after the defeat of the Europe-wide 1848 national-democratic revolutions. In 1864 they formed the first International Workers' Association. Nearly a century and a half later, under globalized corporate capitalism, it is all the more obvious that unless the lever of solidarity is extended across borders, it is no longer an effective tool against the profit-driven 'race to the bottom.'

44

Without it, the billionaires – who can move their money electronically and ship their factories cheaply from country to country – will always dominate the billions, who are rooted at home and barred from crossing national borders seeking work in the so-called free labor market. Thus the same ruthless U.S. corporations who moved their operations to impoverished Mexico after imposing NAFTA are now relocating to Asia, where the wages are even more pitiful.

E.POTTIER   DEGEYTER

Why did the advantages won by people-power in the past remain partial and temporary? Largely because they remained isolated. By uniting, the slaves of Ancient Rome were able to win military victories under the leadership of the gladiator Spartacus. But they were eventually hunted down by fresh Roman Legions brought in from other provinces of the Roman Empire. In modern times, the same isolation seems to have condemned every revolution to the same sorry fate. At various times, the common people in France (1789, 1830, 1848, 1871, 1968), Russia (1905, 1917), Spain (1936), China (1911, 1949), Hungary (1956) and Czechoslovakia (1968) have united to successfully wrest power from the hands of feudal, capitalist or Communist overlords. But as long as their revolutions were confined to one country, they were doomed to ultimate defeat – just like Spartacus and the slaves of Rome. These revolutionary moments flash out like solitary beacons across history, illuminating at once the liberatory potential for mass self-organization latent among oppressed people – as well as the seemingly inevitable doom of their struggles when left isolated. Some recent examples:

1871. Following the French Emperor Napoleon III's defeat by King Frederick of Prussia (who thus became the *Kaiser* of the German empire), the workers of Paris took power in the besieged French capital, held out against the invaders, organized elections and took charge of defense, administration and education on an egalitarian basis. But this Paris Commune, isolated from the rest of France, was crushed after two glorious months by the official French Army with the help of the Prussians.

1917. The useless slaughter of the First World War provoked mutinies in many armies, and a wave of mass revolts followed the Armistice in 1918. But the revolutionaries took power first during the War, in backward, impoverished Russia, where there was no basis for building a modern socialist society. Worse still, the Russian people were cut off from the workers of Europe first by the War and then by the intervention of counterrevolutionary armies and expeditionary forces financed by France, Britain, Japan, Poland, the U.S. and other capitalist governments which feared the revolution would spread. Isolated, the Russian Revolution degenerated into a totalitarian dictatorship – thus discrediting the dream of socialism or communism in the eyes of many workers for nearly a century.

1936. Under the Spanish Republic, a fascistic *junta* led by General Franco staged a *coup d'état* against the elected government, but the workers and small farmers rose up in arms and held out for three years, despite betrayal by the liberals and Communist leaders. To crush revolutionary democracy in Spain, Franco had to import troops and weapons from Nazi Germany and Fascist Italy, while France, Britain and the US – worried about their investments under a Spanish democracy – isolated the legitimate Spanish Republic with a one-sided embargo. Ironically, the democracies' abandonment of the Spanish people made Hitler's conquest of Europe inevitable.

1944-45. At the end of World War Two, the leaders of the democratic West, Churchill and Roosevelt (later Truman) turned Eastern Europe over to the tender mercies of their ally Stalin, the Russian Communist dictator, in return for Stalin's promise to call off the Communist-led armed Resistance movements threatening to take power in post-war France, Italy and Greece under the popular slogan: From resistance to revolution! In Greece, the red partisans refused to submit to a British-imposed puppet government, and resisted, in isolation, for several years. In East Europe, Stalin bypassed local Communist-dominated anti-Nazi resistance fighters and imposed loyal (to him)

46

Communist puppets who had spent the war in Moscow. Yet within a few years, East European workers and intellectuals began rising up against the pitiless, slave-driving 'Communist' police state: uniting in a general strike (Berlin 1953); creating Workers' Councils (Hungary 1956); establishing socialism with a human face (Czechoslovakia 1968); and setting up independent Solidarity trade unions (Poland 1981). Russia was able to crush these heroic revolts only because until 1989 they remained largely isolated within individual Communist satellites and took place at different times. And although the Western powers urged anti-Communist resistance *via* Radio Free Europe, they turned their backs on these actual workers' revolutions and allowed the Russian tanks to roll over them without so much as lifting a finger.

In the **1950**s and **1960**s colonial peoples all over Asia and Africa fought their way to independence. But new bureaucratic-military elites – espousing 'nationalist, ''democratic,' 'religious,' or 'Marxist' ideologies – took over the reins of power and instead of realizing the dreams of Pan-African or 'International Socialist' Unity, squabbled among themselves, exploited tribal politics and got rich on sweetheart deals with the former colonist and multinational corporations, who today continue to lay waste to the lands and the peoples of Africa in their greed for petroleum and precious metals.

1968. That year a wave of popular rebellions broke out in a number of countries challenging simultaneously both Russian and Western imperialisms. Yet despite similar goals and mutual sympathies, these revolts remained isolated and were finally repressed by the police and armed forces of the various governments. As I argue above in my essays on 1968 ('Where Are the Riots of Yesteryear?'), these movements certainly inspired each other from Vietnam to Paris to Prague to the U.S. and shared common goals. However, the rebels of 1968 were not connected globally and had no means to coordinate their movements in real time on an international scale – divided as they were by the Iron Curtain and lacking the kind of interactive information and communications systems activists take for granted today.

1989. By the time the Berlin Wall actually fell and the Moscow-imposed dictatorships of Eastern Europe were overthrown, the Utopian spirit of 1968 in the West lay buried under twenty years of capitalist counter-revolution epitomized by Margaret Thatcher's doctrine that 'There Is No Alternative' (TINA). Thus, instead of being greeted by the solidarity of rebel students and workers, the newly freed Russian and East Europeans were overwhelmed by capitalist speculators: AFL-CIO union representatives preaching the gospel of pension plans, neo-liberal 'Chicago boys' preaching 'shock therapy' and Mafia-capitalists privatizing the collective factories and houses they had labored to create and still officially owned under Communist laws – truly the robbery of the century! On the other hand, we can only imagine what kind of

47

world we might be living in now if the Iron Curtain had fallen in 1968, when it seemed like the whole world was rising up and demanding Utopia.

Today, more than ever, the motto United We Stand, Divided We Fall must be understood globally. An injury to one is an injury to all, anywhere on the planet. Movements for justice and equality can never succeed if they are confined to a single country. This lesson becomes more and more urgent as capitalist globalization imposes a 'race to the bottom' of pay and conditions on wage earners in every land. The Lever of Solidarity must be international before it can 'lift the world.'

Thus, if we want our scenario for a successful Mutiny on Starship Earth to be historically realistic, we must visualize something quite amazing: global movements directed against multi-national capital – including, for example, planetary demonstrations for peace; women's rights; environmental and social justice as well as world-wide general strikes supported by consumer boycotts targeting multi-national corporations; all leading to an international wave of uprisings and takeovers broad enough to surround and isolate the billionaires and their reactionary allies.

Is there any real-world evidence for such a visualization? The recent wave of international popular movements sweeping across Latin America, into the Hispanic US and even reaching out to Asia holds the beginnings of a real promise. Even traditional labor unions (often spurred by informal ethnic/community international solidarity groups) are finally moving into cross-border organizing. It is becoming increasingly obvious to all that in a globalized economy, human rights, social benefits and popular reforms must be enjoyed by working people in *all* countries before they are secure in *any*, and that movements for human and environmental rights must be ***planetary*** to succeed. The question remains, how, practically, will the passengers and crew of Starship Earth be able to unite internationally instead of being isolated and repressed like so many revolts of the past? Here we must move on to the technological basis for our modern Archimedes hypothesis, the new material element that makes a successful Mutiny on Starship earth practically possible, a realistic one chance in a hundred.

Patriotism or Planetarism? The idea of 'the nation' as something to which one owed loyalty (instead of just taxes) and from which one derived identity (as opposed to the family, the tribe, the village or town, the trade, and the ethno-linguistic group) is a modern invention, along with total war. Previously, people owed allegiance to a local lord or paid tribute to the capital of some remote, multi-ethnic empire (e.g. Rome). At the time of the French Revolution, which invented the idea of the Nation, few Frenchmen could sing the *Marseillaise* since most peasants (the vast majority of the population) did not speak French and had only the vaguest idea of 'France' (represented only by the annual visit of the tax collector). A hundred years ago, my paternal family lived in Krakow, then a part of a non-existent 'Poland' carved up between the Austrian, Prussian and Russian Empires. At the time, Krakow was incorporated into the relatively liberal, multi-national Austro-Hungarian Empire (whose administrative language was church Latin). My great-grandfather spoke Yiddish at home, studied ancient Hebrew, and dealt with the outside world in Polish, German, Lithuanian or Russian. In those days, passports were only for diplomats and rich travelers; merchants and artisans routinely wandered from country to country plying their trades. Some, like Aaron Greeman, ended up in the U.S., whose most radical Founding Father, Tom Paine, agitated in Britain, America and revolutionary France famously declared: The world is my country!

The Internet as a Planetary Platform

Historically, advances in communication and transportation technology have generally gone hand in hand with advances in popular self-organization. During the democratic revolutions of the 18th Century, cheap printing and the post office (both recent developments) enabled revolutionary committees of correspondence in the American colonies and the French provinces to share local grievances, discuss ideas, organize congresses, inform each other of plots, publish and circulate the revolutionary broadsheets and pamphlets that made the revolutions of 1776 and 1789 possible. In the 19th Century, railroads, steamships, the telegraph and the daily newspaper spread the democratic revolutions of 1848 all across Europe within months. Unfortunately in the 20th Century, radio and later television – organized as one-way, top-down broadcast media – became the favorite tool of totalitarian dictators like Hitler and Stalin, manipulative politicians like Churchill and Roosevelt, and wealthy advertisers whose right-wing commercial media monopolies dominate the airwaves in the so-called free countries...

On the other hand, in the 21st Century, the Internet promises to give the advantage back to people-power. It also may give a new meaning to informational democracy. For the first time in history, this new technology has placed at the disposal of the billions an uncensored source of information as well as a planetary platform large enough and accessible enough for all to participate, decide and act together. With its infinite interconnections, the World Wide Web enables groups in struggle to communicate, exchange information, discuss ideas, work out common programs and coordinate actions on a planetary scale in real time. The technology of the Internet has the potential of creating vast, worldwide assemblies where true international democracy can take form; forums where consensus can be reached on an ongoing basis; platforms where massive planetary actions can be coordinated from hour to hour around the globe. With ever more powerful computers joined together, even problems like translation are being solved. Precisely what the passengers and crew of

Starship Earth will need to break out from below decks and take over the bridge from the squabbling, pilfering officers.

The Web is also a vast 24-hours/day 7-days/week public library where the passengers and crew can find and propagate (among other things) the uncensored information and revolutionary ideas they will need to unite. The collective creation of today's Wikipedia, the ever-expanding, multi-lingual self-correcting information resource, is a model of this kind of Internet emergence. For the first time in history, the storehouse of revolutionary internationalist thinking and the recorded experiences of centuries of struggle is accessible to all. Thus the Web potentially weaves together ideas and planetary communication, connecting the Lever of solidarity with the Fulcrum of planetary consciousness.

Democracy, Internet, Emergence

Before going further, I want to make it clear that I do *not* believe that technology can substitute for active human solidarity and collective organization on the ground. 'Revolutionary' chat rooms can never replace face-to-face workplace and neighborhood organizing; radical Websites are no substitute for popular movements, unions, parties, newspapers, alternative broadcasting, international meetings and other forms of human interaction. Nor do I maintain that the Web is immune to police-state censorship and spying by authoritarian regimes, for example in China, where the authorities are often able to block discussion of subjects like democracy (with the complicity of do no evil Google) and like the Bush administration, mine emails and postings (with the help of Yahoo) in order to arrest and punish dissidents.

On the other hand, hackers in China and around the world often find ways to get around police-state censors and their U.S. corporate accomplices. Indeed, the hacker mentality and the 'freeware' movements incarnate a Utopian spirit in themselves and should be considered as the allies of social movements around the world. Freeware challenges the commodified basis of human creativity and corporate monopolization of collectively developed 'intellectual property' from computer software to South American healing plants. In any case, networked technology is a Pandora's book for the world's would-be censor. Thus, when the Burmese dictatorship shut down the Internet during the monks' rebellion, the demonstrators used their cell-phones – another new form of electronic networking in the hands of the people – both to coordinate their movements and to get photos of the repression to the world press. Granting these limitations, what I am suggesting is this:

1. The Internet is a powerful and increasingly accessible new tool for struggle whose revolutionary potential is beginning to be understood by popular movements around the globe.
2. The Internet's web-like global network, whose 'center' is everywhere and nowhere, may turn out to be a more effective model for the emergence of planetary, democratic and working-class movements than the traditional hub-and-spokes, center/periphery, top down model of centralized parties and 'internationals.'
3. The Internet makes *technically possible* the internationalist dream of a global movement of working people uniting to overthrow the bosses and establish a sustainable, self-governing post-capitalist world.

This is not just theoretical. Far from isolating people in front of their computers, the Internet helps them to get to know each other, to feel less alone, to access information, to mobilize massively for action. For example, beginning in 1998 a piece of software named *meetingtool* developed by the website MoveOn.org allowed potential antiwar activists to find each other in isolated localities. To bring together interested people within a given zip code area, all they need do was to post the location and the date of the first meeting on the site. People out in Idaho who thought they were the only ones opposed to the war suddenly found themselves among a dozen equally outraged neighbors, ready to demonstrate. Fact sheets taken off the Internet gave them the courage to stand up to critics.

Email turned out to be a perfect channel for one-on-one political organizing. As it's generally someone we know – a friend, a relative, a co-worker – who connects us with a mobilization site like MoveOn.org, the personal reference makes us comfortable with the connection from the start. It's not an anonymous ad or flyer. Moreover, visiting a site doesn't obligate you, but offers you different levels of involvement: receiving information, forwarding it to friends, signing a petition, downloading a flyer or poster, distributing it, joining a local group, going to a demonstration. . . It was by these methods that on the eve of the invasion of Iraq, MoveOn managed in six days to mobilize a million people in 6,000 simultaneous demonstrations in 130 countries on March 16, 2003.

Despite it origins as a Defense Department program, the Internet has been eagerly appropriated by global justice movements and proven itself an invaluable tool on the ground. Some examples: the Zapatistas opened the anti-globalization era with their anti-NAFTA rebellion in 1994 and used the Internet to gather global support against the invading Mexican Army; the locked-out Liverpool dockers and their supporters organized a successful international dockers' boycott of scab shipping in 1997; the anti-corporate globalization protesters in Seattle, Genoa, Cancun who eventually crippled the

IMF and WTO, coordinated their movements via Internet as did the global social movements that connected at the World Social Forums; the demonstrators who freed President Chávez from the *coup* plotters in 2002; the millions of demonstrators in 57 different countries who protested invading Iraq in April 2003; the workers and students of the Korean General Strike of 1997; the rebels in China, who reportedly pulled off 83,000 strikes and uprisings against overwork and pollution in 2006; not to mention the many blogs and alternative news sites around the glob that get behind the 'official' story put out by governments and the billionaires' corporate media.

The Web has also enabled and perhaps influenced new types of organization, based on the network model rather than the traditional hub-and-spokes model. In Latin America, the symbolism of the web, powerful yet delicate, had already been proposed by activist women as an alternative to male-dominated, top-down power. In recent decades, new forms of horizontal organizations are emerging there, rooted in urban neighborhoods and rural communities, in factories and on the land, yet networked nationally and even internationally. Self-organized, autonomous groups of peasants and indigenous peoples have been networked all over the Americas since 1992, when the Internet helped bring them together to celebrate 500 years of survival and resistance to colonialism.

Today, these movements network online and at World Social Forums, connect with networks of workers, ecologists, and activists, compare conditions, discuss strategy, and organize global solidarity with similar movements as far off as Asia. In the context of national politics, these autonomous networks are at the base of the vertical power of progressive presidents like Lula, Kirchner, Correa, Chavez, and Morales – pushing these governments to challenge the power of local landowners and the global corporations. Far from being 'historically backward,' these rural communities have successfully appropriated 21st Century capitalist communications technology at its highest level and used it as a weapon for their own emancipation. They are in today's planetary vanguard: challenging capitalism, protecting the land and saving nature from the ravenous corporations.

If the Web model of a network of networks continues to prove effective as a structure for an expansive, flexible, practical transnational organizing, might it not also foreshadow the structure of a future self-organized planetary society? The Achilles' heel of democracy has always been the necessity of delegating authority to representatives, who all too often end up forming a separate political class with its own interests. But what if direct 'town-meeting' type participatory democracy could be organized not only locally, but also regionally, and globally via Internet hookup? What if every citizen of the planet could make her/his voice heard equally with every other, get access to experts' advice and unite with others of the same persuasion? And then *vote* – whether in their own mass assemblies or internationally via a secure Internet hookup? What if the great issues facing humanity could be debated everywhere and then *decided* in global referendums via the Internet? What if the necessary economic planning on a global scale could be combined with worker self-management and maximum local autonomy? What if every individual could participate in decision-making in each of her capacities as resident, producer, consumer and citizen? What if, after centuries of successful revolutions being hijacked and perverted by new bureaucratic elites, the common people were able to control the destiny of a new society as it emerges *from below?*

Back in 1958, when computers were in their infancy, the (then) Marxist philosopher Cornelius Castoriadis was the first to imagine such a computer-connected self-managed society in his essay 'The Content of Socialism. [31] A critic of bureaucratic top-down management as exemplified by Russian Communism and American capitalism, Castoriadis saw socialism *emerging* out of workers' self-activity. A professional economist, he was able to elaborate in concrete detail a complete national economy, free of the waste and coercion of corporate Communist central planning. In Castoriadis' Utopia, 'Planning Factories' produced alternative plans – to be debated and eventually voted by the producers via wired hookups – explaining in simple terms the relative costs and consequences of each proposal in terms of labor time, resources, growth and consumption levels – giving society the choice between enjoying more leisure or working harder for future goals. The concrete images in Castoriadis' Utopian model made such an impression on me a half-century ago that I have never since doubted democratic socialism's practical '*do-ability.*'

Castoriadis' vision derives from the traditional Marxist notions of revolution as evolution in the fullness of time. It recalls Engels' image of the new world emerging out of the shell of the old – adopted by the Industrial Workers of the World (IWW). What was original in 1958 was Castoriadis' appropriation of

---

[31] '*Sur le contenu du socialisme*' by P. Chaulieu (pseudonym for Cornelius Castoriadis) was first published in *Socialisme et barbarie* (Nos 22 and 23, 1957-58) – the year before I joined the group in Paris. Castoriadis' inspiring text was quickly translated and published in England as a *Solidarity* pamphlet by 'Paul Cardan' and eventually in French in 1979 under Castoriadis' real name – which I only learned years later. At that time, Castoriadis, a Greek revolutionary, who was living as a refugee in a France militarized by the Algerian revolution – a cause which *Socialisme ou Barbarie* openly supported. Trained as an economist, he worked under his real name for the Paris-based OCED and knew everything about the world economy (and everything else). It was in conversation with Castoriadis that I first heard about Norbert Weiner (then at Harvard) and cybernetics.

the theories of the socialist-minded mathematician Norbert Weiner, the pioneer of computer science of who explored the feed-back principle and recognized the emergent quality of cybernetics.[32] Today, physicists, biologists, mathematicians, cyberneticists and scientists in other fields are studying and analyzing the emergent phenomena of spontaneous self-organization from below in the context of Chaos/Complexity/Emergence Theory to which we will return below.

The Fulcrum of Planetary Consciousness

The Fulcrum of Planetary Consciousness is the philosophical base on which the Archimedes Hypothesis stands. As such it is less easy to describe than the Lever of Planetary Solidarity (whose basis is historical) and the Web (whose basis is technological). Moreover, like the Internet, planetary consciousness is still in its infancy.

For hundreds of thousands of years, humans' horizons were limited to their immediate environment, to their band or tribe or settlement. If the ancient Greek philosophers were the first to speculate that the Earth is a planet and plot its orbit, only in the last five hundred years have people actually learned to measure it, map it and sail around it. Only very recently – thanks to radio and TV – have the vast majority the earth's human inhabitants become aware of lands and continents beyond their own village or province. Before WWI, according to Graham Robb, many French country folk didn't speak French and had never ventured beyond the next village.[33] And it was WWII that brought knowledge of the outside world to the South Pacific. In the 1960s the transistor radio transformed the world-view of billions of Africans, Asians and South Americans living on the land. And only in our own times have humans actually *seen*, via photos taken from space and viewed by millions, the amazing, cloud-swirling blue-green globe we live on. Today, most of the planet's six billion humans know they are living on a globe inhabited by many other peoples. I consider this a planetary revolution in human consciousness whose power and depth have as yet not been realized.

Tragically, this revolution in planetary consciousness coincides with growing planetary awareness that life on our planet is menaced with extinction. Since 1945 – since Hiroshima and Nagasaki – it has become more and more evident that our survival as a species is threatened by our own ingenuity in inventing machines of unprecedented power and

---

[32] See Norbert Weiner, *The Human Use of Human Beings* (Anchor, NY, 1954).
[33] Graham Robb, *The Discovery of France: A Historical Geography From the Revolution to the First World War*, W. W. Norton 2008.

destructiveness. Since the annihilation of the two Japanese cities – followed by sixty years of nuclear proliferation and stockpiling – intimations of humanity's mortality have slowly been imposing itself on all but the simple, the selfish and the self-deluded. Likewise, awareness of the slower, yet deadly destruction of the natural world, ruthlessly ravaged for corporate profit, is becoming universal. More and more humans are experiencing the palpable effects of pollution and global climate change, and as the massive (Internet connected) food riots indicate, 21st Century peasants and villagers are increasingly likely to attribute these dramatic droughts, storms, floods and epidemics to global causes – indeed to global corporations – than to local gods or spirits. Another revolution in human consciousness as yet unevaluated.

Meanwhile, we humans have already learned to split the atom and manipulate the genome. Overgrown children, we are playing with the very building blocks of matter and of life. We are also breaking them. Our technical abilities have developed far beyond our level of social and political organization, and as a result, atomic power and genetic engineering have been used  exclusively for power and profit: monstrous weapons of war, Chernobyls and Three-Mile Islands built on the cheap; and profitable, patented genetically modified seeds imposed by force and fraud to contaminate traditional crops, turn farmers into corporate serfs and destroy self-sustaining peasant agriculture. Our species, which Victor Serge once depicted as 'intelligent monkeys toiling on a green globe' has become too smart for its own good. Human monkeys have monkeyed around with genome and the atomic structure of matter-energy and unleashed powers they are unable within capitalist society, to control. Thus the planet that emerged out the first Big Bang it is now heading for another Big Bang if we don't take control of our technology, that is to say if we fail to connect up our collective brain before engaging gears!

Awareness of this danger is the next stage of planetary consciousness: stepping out of denial and acknowledging the possibility – increasingly likely – of annihilation in the foreseeable future. Like the proverbial elephant in your living room, there is no getting around the looming specter of extinction, whether it takes the form of Nuclear Winter or of the gradual death of the polluted biosphere. At this level, planetary consciousness is awareness of the unavoidable existential choice between irreconcilable absolutes: People and Profits, Nature and Money, Life and Death.

On the one hand, the likelihood of destruction of life on earth is more and more probable. On the other, there is one chance in a hundred for a positive revolution in human relations leading to a new society based on solidarity and cooperation, rather than greed and conflict. Our unavoidable existential choice is between two absolutes: Life or Death.

Our Age of Absolutes[34]

If planetary destruction is an idea that confronts us as an absolute end, it follows that its opposite – Life itself – must be taken as an absolute end in itself. Thus, the material prospect of universal Death forces us to consider Life – Life on this planet – as a universal. For no other reason than that all other ideas would be unthinkable without it. But what do we mean by Life? The consensus of scientists is that Life develops out a process that began at the Big Bang with particles of swirling gas solidifying into a geological entities – stars and planets – one of which developed a biosphere as proteins and amino acids develop into proto-viruses, form DNA, and reproduce themselves endlessly morphing minerals, air and water into life-forms of greater and greater complexity. Life is thus understood as the ability of matter to reproduce itself according to code – that is to say, information, intelligence – with greater and greater complexity until it achieves animal intelligence and eventually human self-consciousness. Life thus emerges as unity of interacting opposites: spirit (code, information) and matter. Life means spirit actualized in matter, from the earliest proto-virus to the brain of an Einstein.

Intelligent Design? My Leftist friends may jump on me for saying this, but I think that evolution, the process of intelligence emerging through matter, may be usefully described as intelligent design (or rather as 'design by intelligence'). Not of course on the analogy of God the watchmaker with his elaborate preconceived plan and total control of his material, but in the sense that complexity emerges spontaneously out of the interaction of myriad infinitesimal bits of matter imprinted with code. So it is not really a stretch to assert that it was code, information, the *logos,* the spirit, intelligence itself that breathed life into inert matter. 'In the Beginning was the Word.' Evolution can thus be described as the developing emergence of intelligence in matter. Not Nature created *a priori* by a Divine Intelligence of course, but Nature becoming conscious of itself through evolution and human history. This was the view of the Anarchist philosopher-geographer Elisée Reclus. (A materialist Hegelian might call this 'spirit's self-determination in the world').

---

[34] I have borrowed this concept, and the Hegelian-Marxist dialectical logic which flows from it, from the Marxist-Humanist philosopher Raya Dunayevskaya, who in her classic *Marxism and Freedom* (1958) and her more Hegelian *Philosophy and Revolution* (1989) revived the dialectic and humanism of Marx and showed the relevance of Hegelian Absolute Method to our epoch.

What are the implications of this realization? If we understand Life as what a Hegelian would call an Absolute, then we must follow it *through to its logical end*, allowing no other considerations to divert us. Holding fast to our subject – Life on Earth – thus becomes a kind of 'absolute method' – in which awareness of the planet's destiny becomes the crux, the touchstone, the absolute reference for all our thinking. Because outside of planetary survival there is simply nothingness – at least in so far as our species is concerned – survival becomes the prism through which we examine all economic, social and political problems, indeed the basis on which *everything* must henceforth be criticized and judged. Precisely because the 21st Century may be the last century, it is the Century of Absolutes.

Socialism or Barbarism? A half-century before Hiroshima, Rosa Luxemburg had already posed the alternatives facing humanity as socialism or barbarism (the slogan adopted by the group formed by Castoriadis and his comrades following WWII). The barbarism Luxemburg feared would triumph if capitalism were not defeated on a planetary scale following World War One took the forms of Nazi fascism and Stalinism, of Auschwitz and the Gulag, of Dresden and Hiroshima. Following this Second World War, U.S.-Russian rivalry provoked a 40-year global 'Cold' War – based on the barbarous doctrine of 'Mutually Assured Destruction' (MAD) – which kept humanity permanently at the brink of a nuclear holocaust. Today, with nuclear proliferation and the U.S. embarked on an, open-ended global war for single superpower imperialist domination – the so-called 'War on Terror' – we are arguably even closer to the brink. In the 21st Century, with the environment within decades of irreversible catastrophe, Luxemburg's 'socialism or barbarism' has become an Absolute.

Today, any political or moral vision that is less than planetary must perforce be rejected as irrelevant – if not dangerous. The planet can no longer afford the Me-First philosophies of particular nations, religions, corporations, elites, genders and so-called races, each absurdly claiming that God or History or the Right is on its side. These 'Me-Firsters,' who dominate the media everywhere, deafen us with the clamor of their competing self-interested claims for this or that God, this or that state, this or that ethnic identity, economic system, or reigning political class. So loudly do the Me-First ideologues hawk their deadly wares that no one dares point to the obvious fact that their claims cancel each other out.

Indeed, all the competing Me-First brands on 'god-market' use the same advertising slogan: I alone hold the Truth, the Light, the Way. And they all add: Our competitors are all liars and their gods (or nations, or identities, or economic systems) are inferior fakes. (In this alone they are *all* telling the truth.) In fact, the fundamentalist ideologies of the Me-Firsters serve mainly cover the selfish interests of one or another Me-First elite, whether 'free-market' or 'Communist,' Christian, Jewish, Hindu or Islamic, Serbian or Croatian, fair-skinned or dark. Moreover, these competing Me-Firsters ultimately rely on the same intimidating argument: If you're not with us, you're against us. It is an argument which they usually back up with an offer to maim, kill or imprison you if you try to argue.

Simple, One-Sided Negation

Nonetheless, we do argue, protest, resist. But experience shows that it is not enough merely to struggle *against* this or that war, this or that corporation, this or that oppressive policy, or dictatorial regime, although obviously we do and must continue to protest. But we must also remember that simplistic, one-side opposition leads inevitably to one of two fatal fallacies: the Lesser-of-Two-Evils Fallacy (LTEF) and the The-Enemy-of-my-Enemy-is-my Friend Fallacy (EEFF). One-sided opposition to an identifiably evil Me-First politician, party, or policy (e.g. George W. Bush and the neo-cons) leads to the logical trap of choosing the Lesser Evil. This usually means picking the least bad among the competing Me-Firsters and losing touch with the ultimate goal – changing society and saving the planet. By falling into the LTE trap, we not only automatically give our support to an evil Me-Firsters (albeit the 'lesser' one); we also abandon our philosophical ground and accept the ground of our *status-quo* opponents.

The LTEF trap has been the fatal error of many promising mass movements of the past. For example in the U.S. during the 1970s and 80s the movements for a Nuclear Freeze, the Environment and Women's Liberation mobilized millions of citizen activists at the grassroots levels. Through massive demonstrations and persistent non-violent blockading of dangerous facilities, these movements forced governments to listen, to sign a few treaties limiting nuclear weapons, and to pass some legislation protecting the environment and women's reproductive rights.

Unfortunately, the leadership of these movements fell into LTEF trap. In the name of 'practicality' these organizations channeled vibrant grass-roots movements into the narrow electoral and lobbying channels in the hope of acquiring 'inside influence.' Of course the Me-First politicians of the Democratic Party, once elected, took their support for granted and dropped their issues – peace, the environment and women's rights – off their political agendas. As a result, the ultimate goals of the mass movements were lost from view, the activists were demobilized and discouraged, and the organizers were co-opted by the establishment. The practical logic of 'let's get real and elect the LTE' turned out to be 'crackpot realism.'

58

The same sorry scenario was played out a generation later in the wake of the massive, world-wide protests against Bush's invasion of Iraq. In 2004, the U.S. anti-war movement collapsed into the Democratic presidential campaign (remember John Kerry?) and then disappeared after their candidate failed to oppose the war and then lost the election for flip-flopping. Meanwhile Exxon (as in *Exxon-Valdez*) and Montsano (as in *Dioxin*) paraded as Green corporations (the color of their dollars?) along with former Vice-President Al Gore, who helped Clinton sabotage the Kyoto Accords (an inconvenient truth they don't mention about the 'green' Nobel Prize winner). In any case, there is no longer time for LTE reformism, even if it did occasionally result in some temporary incremental gains.

On the other hand, simplistic, one-sided opposition can lead to an equally dangerous logical trap in the opposite direction. As I argued above in 'Who are the Good Guys (if any) in Iraq?' and 'Alice in Imperialist Wonderland,' people can get so outraged by a particularly evil regime that they jump to the conclusion that 'the Enemies of Our Enemy are our Friends' (the EEF Fallacy) and support the other side – however barbarous. If we fall into the EEFF trap, we not only loose sight of our goal – Life, survival, a new society – we actually get dragged into taking sides in the destructive wars among the competing violent Me-Firsters! Yet this is the curtailed logic of many on the Left, who in their rage against the machine have forgotten what every schoolchild can tell you: two wrongs don't make a right.

Utopia, or the Negation of Negation

Our Age of Absolutes demands that we get past simple *againstness* and look to the Second Negation, the Negation of Negation that represents the Positive alternative to the system that is destroying the planet. It also insists on asking the questions: What happens *after* we get rid of this or that Evil we are against? Won't we be stuck again with another successful revolution turned into a new tyranny? It insists for example that the needs of women, of ecology and of oppressed people be made paramount *before and during* the revolution instead of being put off until the day *after* ('Tomorrow never comes.')

The Second Negation grows out of the negation of Life under predatory capitalism. It arises from *within* that alienated society dominated by Mammon-worshipping businessmen who bow down to the graven images they have stamped on the money that is their true idol. From within the contradiction between Life and Money, from within that alienated society where billions toil, suffer and starve to earn profits for corporations, Humanity cries out *Ya basta!* – the Earth is not a commodity to be bought and sold! Life is not a commodity to be bought and sold, I personally am not a commodity to be bought and sold.

Planetary Consciousness means understanding that the same human ingenuity which threatens the planet with destruction *also* holds the promise of a life of abundance, once it is liberated by freely associated human subjects. For if creative humanity manages to unite on a planetary scale, if our species, instead of destroying the planet comes together to save it, if we are able to build a new society based on intelligence and love, balancing community and individual freedom, competition and cooperation, ingenuity and harmony with nature, then we may discover a new, truly 'human' nature and begin true human history – a post-history, a truly 'common era' whose infinite development we can barely imagine. A new society in which humans, liberated from the bonds of fear, greed, competition for survival, solitude, self-alienation, class antagonism, war, hatred, and servitude, will be reintegrated into the biosphere and free to develop the full human potential for creativity, discovery and spirituality.

This final stage of Planetary Consciousness consists in realizing the necessity of a positive revolution in human relations, the emergence of a new society based on solidarity and cooperation rather than on greed and oppression. This planetary consciousness speaks in the new voices now being heard around the planet. Thousands, perhaps millions of people have begun proclaiming in chorus: Another world is possible! By organizing and resisting corporate globalization, by educating themselves and others, these global justice movements are helping to save the planet on a practical level by fighting pollution, forest-destruction, privatization of social and natural resources. In the meantime, these *alter-mundialistas* – like all of us – are searching for alternatives, for a planetary vision of a *possible* better world, for an idea capable of drawing together billions and focusing their power. In other words for Utopia.

Connectivity, Complexity, Quantum and Emergence

This new Planetary Consciousness has great historical potential, but time is short and Starship Earth seems to be accelerating its course toward disaster. Admitting for the sake of argument that my New Archimedes' Hypothesis provides a theoretical basis for a successful Mutiny among the passengers and crew, it is hard to imagine it taking place within the next few years without Divine or Extra-Terrstrial intervention. How will all these billions get together? How will the vast, untapped force of humanity become conscious of itself and emerge before it is too late? To answer these questions, let us return to the Internet, specifically to the underlying scientific principles of Connectivity and Emergence that account for its stupendous growth.

The new factor that makes the age-old dream of humanity rising actual in the 21st Century is connectivity. It has recently been demonstrated that there are on the average only six degrees of separation between each of the six billion humans on the planet. That means that you probably know someone, who knows someone else, who knows someone, who knows someone, who knows someone who knows me – or even more unlikely, who knows a certain peasant in Setchuan, China named Mrs. Wu. These are weak connections, of course, but another of the paradoxes of Emergence is that weak connections are the fabric that makes up the strength of complex network structures like the Internet and the human brain.

Connecting up the cells of the collective brain of humanity is precisely what is needed to save the world from the pseudo-rationality of the corporate profit system that is consuming it like a cancer. The Internet provides the connectivity for the emergence of what can be called 'Planetary Consciousness' – the fulcrum of the modern Archimedes Hypothesis. And although the phrase 'the collective brain of humanity' sounds mystical, recent experiments and research have confirmed what *Wall Street Journal* and *New Yorker* business columnist James Suroweicki's recent book calls *The Wisdom of Crowds*. (Subtitle*: Why the many are smarter than the few and how collective wisdom shapes business, economies, societies and nations.)* It turns out experimentally that the judgment of large numbers of randomly chosen people is often strikingly superior to that of the experts. What is the explanation? The diversity and impartiality of opinions in a freely associated group or random mass apparently combine in positive ways to create this collective intelligence. But it only works when people are free of the kind of hierarchical constraints that produce 'group-think' in committees, hence the pitiful failure of the 'experts' in authoritarian, bureaucratic organizations like the CIA to deliver accurate 'intelligence' (for example about Saddam's WMDs).

This 'wisdom of crowds' can be seen as a wired version of the 'wisdom in the heads of many' we old socialists used to talk about. The creation, by thousands of individual contributors in a dozen languages, of *Wikipedia* the free online encyclopedia, is a splendid example of collective wisdom, far surpassing the long-revered *Encyclopedia Britannica* in scope. As for accuracy, *Wikipedia* is always correcting itself, whereas the elitist *Britannica,* which cost hundreds and rarely revised itself, was full of upper-class prejudice and long neglected the achievements of native peoples.

In any case, there is nothing impractical or unscientific in the romantic image of the collective brain of humanity connecting up its myriad nodes through cyberspace. Or of humanity acting with collective wisdom and strength of billions to take charge of our poor world. 'Only connect!' could be the motto of a modern revolutionary network. Quite the contrary, the concept of Emergence is common to much 21st scientific thought in fields as diverse as Quantum mechanics, cybernetics, and brain physiology. Emergence – the spontaneous creation of order and complexity out of chaos – has now been observed in various natural phenomena which were previously inexplicable in terms of the standard top-down scientific models of cause/effect, leader/follower.[35] For those of us without access to higher mathematics, biology provides a more graphic example of emergence in the slime molds that appear and disappear as if from nowhere in the woods. Under certain favorable conditions, thousands of autonomous cells spontaneously come together and form new, more complex autonomous organism – the slime mold, a goopy vomit-like blob, which emerges, changes shape and moves. Not only that, it *thinks,* sort of. When placed by experimenters between two bits of food, it sent out pseudopods in *both* directions. However, when conditions change, the organism disaggregates into individual cells and seems to vanish. Scientists spent years searching for the 'leader' cell. Only after advanced computer techniques allowed researcher to model this behavior mathematically was its bottom-up nature accepted.

Similarly, scientists long rejected well-documented reports from Asia of thousands of chirping crickets or flashing fireflies suddenly chirping or flashing in unison – just as human concert audiences sometimes start clapping in unison without any leader intervening. Emergence has long been observed in the complex organization of ant and bee 'societies;' it is also visible in the

---

[35] See *The Quantum Society: Mind, Physics and a New Social Vision* by Danah Zohar and Ian Marshall, 1993. Also 'Quantum political economy' by Marxist physicist David Hookes (Univ. Liverpool).

development of the infant human brain, where billions of brain-circuits spontaneously grow out of a few cells and connect into complex networks; we see Emergence as well in the history of the world's cities where people of many trades came spontaneously together, each pursuing his/her own interests, and 'accidentally' produced what we call civilization. Social movements are also a form of spontaneous self-organization from below, as Rosa Luxemburg observed in 1905, the year of the revolutionary mass strikes she analyzed in Poland-Russia. Order and complexity are thus observed emerging out of chaos, based on connectivity between large numbers of free agents following their own paths.[36]

However, for this complexity to emerge, there must be a critical mass of individuals. 'Many is different' is the rule in Chaos-Complexity-Emergence theory. The other critical condition is freedom to communicate and interact 'horizontally' free of distortions imposed by a 'vertical' one-way organizing power, for example by corporate or government bureaucracies which generate group-think. A corollary of complexity theory is that free of such interference, tiny events may trigger huge changes, like the proverbial beat of a butterfly in China provoking a hurricane in Bermuda. Such is the nature of epidemics, fads, and religions, which grow exponentially once they reach the 'tipping point.' Utopia may turn out to be such an 'idea virus,' spreading through the

---

[36] The grandfather of Chaos/Complexity/Emergence theory was probably Blaise Pascal, the 17th Century French mathematician, scientist and religious philosopher – from whose *Pensées* (Thoughts) I borrowed the 'Bet' argument – and who contributed to probability theory, infinitesimal calculus and invented the first mechanical computing machine. In the early 20th Century the Soviet geologist Vladimir Vernadsky developed his theories of the interconnected geosphere, the biosphere and the noosphere (human thought) which seem to be confirmed by modern science. My own highly superficial knowledge of these theories comes from reading the books of Edgar Morin (who was part of *Socialisme ou Barbarie* in the early '50s) and scientific popularizations, often written by practicing scientists. For example Steven Strogatz (Cornell Applied Math), one of world's leading researchers into chaos, complexity and synchronization, author of *SYNC: the emerging science of spontaneous order* (Penguin Science 2003); Mark Buchanan, former physicist and *Nature* editor, author of *Small World: Uncovering nature's hidden networks* (Phoenix London 2002); Albert-László Barabási, (Physics, Notre Dame) *Linked* (Penguin 2003). The best of the science writers is Steven Johnson, whose *Emergence* (2001) is a classic for beginners. See also Roger Lewin, *Complexity, Life at the Edge of Chaos* (Phoenix London 1993); John Gribbin, *Deep Simplicity, Chaos, Complexity and the Emergence of Life* (Penguin 2004); and James Gleick *Chaos, Making a New Science* (Penguin 1987). The same research bolsters Malcolm Gladwell's best-selling *The Tipping Point: How Little Things Can Make A Big Difference* (Little, Brown & Company 2000) which focuses on exploiting the PR potential of complexity theory.

Web and provoking the emergence of planetary consciousness. In any case, the recognition of emergence as a powerful natural phenomenon makes it scientifically plausible to visualize the emergence of a world-wide movement of multitudes of ordinary working people connecting and joining forces to save the planet.

Materialist Spirituality Victor Serge's artist son Vlady Kibalchich ironically referred to his father's 'materialist spirituality.' Indeed, Serge derived his spirituality directly from his materialist scientific worldview rather than from any tendency toward religious belief – i.e. 'superstition.' To be sure, Serge's vitalistic philosophical materialism is closer to Spinoza's materialism, Darwin's Hegelian-Marxist dialectics, Bergson's *élan vital*, Verdnatsky's *noosphere* and Edgar Morin's complexity than on mechanistic positivism or vulgar scientism. The immaterial wrote Serge is not in the least unreal, but on the contrary an essential form of the real (thought) completely unexplainable by yesterday's scientific rules. Indeed, it was after reading two recent books about new discoveries and theories in genetics that he noted: The old materialist schools would wax indignant and yet it is quite evident, however mysterious nature may be, that thought is the product of life, consubstantial with life, and that there would be nothing particularly bold in maintaining that it [thought] is itself life coming to discover and know itself. Fifty years after Serge's death, this kind of planetary consciousness is emerging and propagating itself on the 'material basis' (if electrons are considered 'material') of planetary network connectivity. Now that nearly all of humanity's scientific and intellectual insights are accessible to billions of humans, life is coming to discover and know itself on a planetary scale. Our only hope is that humanity will use this technology to connect up its collective brain and multiply it calculating power like computers all connected together.

Such a visualization requires a major revolution in our way of thinking. The 'vertical' model of top-down organization, whether in society or in nature, has such a hold on our minds that it is difficult for us to think 'horizontally' much less in three or four dimensions. We have all inherited the 17th Century 'scientific' mindset of Descartes and Newton with its discrete atoms and billiard-ball physics. Our social thinking is still based on Adam Smith's 18th Century theories of humans as unconnected individual economic atoms. Our political notions – whether establishment or 'revolutionary' – rely on simplistic top-down models of expert leaders and hierarchical organizations. Our logic is confined to mechanical notions of Cause and Effect and the crude duality of Either/Or, A or Not-A. Yet Quantum mechanics has been telling us for nearly a century that the universe is unstable, elusive, multiple, contradictory, holistic, and that it doesn't work mechanically the way scientists used to think. Impossible? According to Zohar and Marshall, Quantum physics is like the Queen in Lewis Carroll's *Alice Through the Looking Glass*: it asks us to 'believe six impossible things before breakfast.' Quantum logic is based on Heisenberg's Uncertainty Principle, where the act of observing phenomena itself alters them. For example light can be understood either as a particle or a wave, depending on how we measure it, but it can never be observed as *both*. It also turns out that electrons don't spin in orbit around atoms like the stable planets revolving around the sun in Newton's model. Not only do they leap from orbit to orbit for no apparent reason, ghostlike they appear to occupy several potential orbits *simultaneously*. This potentiality is like the mental 'trial balloons' in our minds as we imagine various possible futures. Moreover, not only is the position of electrons indeterminate, apparently *everything* in the universe is interconnected in a holistic system so that particles are observed in 'ghostly' action and reaction over distance and over time. Quantum reality was described by one of its discoverers as 'a vast sea of potential.' Indeed, Quantum systems interact and interpenetrate, retaining their integrity (their 'particle function') while at the same time merging (their 'wave function').

An Ecotopian Manifestival

Physicists have often compared these Quantic interactions to people dancing. As the dancers move together rhythmically (the wave function) they retain their individuality (the particle function) while at the same time creating a new emergent holistic system (the dance itself). Dancers love the feeling of getting 'swept up' or 'lost' in the dance, yet somewhere we are always aware of our own individuality. There is no 'contradiction' between our individual and social selves. The dance itself emerges as we interact with other dancers, mirroring their movements and being mirrored in turn. Like all emergent holistic systems, the dance is a 'whole greater than the sum of its parts' (another 'impossible thing' we were taught not to believe in). Humans apparently crave this kind of creative interaction, according to Barbara Ehrenreich in her brilliant *Dancing in the Streets: A History of Collective Joy.* Ehrenreich shows that ecstatic danced religion – still practiced in indigenous societies – was humanity's earliest expression of spirituality. On the other hand, down the ages organized religious and political authorities have uniformly tried to repress this tradition because of its revolutionary potential. Collective joy has been the enemy of power from Greek King Pentheus' tragic attempt to suppress the worship of Dionysius to Puritanism's suppression of the participatory tradition of Carnival and its replacement by spectacle and individual consumption under capitalism. Ehrenreich, a leading U.S. Socialist, ends her *History of Collective Joy* with a hopeful 'Possibility of Revival,' and I think she's on the right track.

What better metaphor for the potential of humanity's radical Emergence than the image of billions of people dancing in the streets? Instead of a monolithic, militaristic, top-down revolutionary vanguard liberating the Masses, why not imagine multitudes of people everywhere descending non-violently into the streets and dancing up such a storm that even the hired mercenaries of the capitalists put down their guns and join the joyful throng! It wouldn't be the first time that dance epidemics have swept across the world. According to ancient Greek historians Paucities and Plutarch, female worshippers of Dionysius called *maenads* used to abandon their spinning and children and run

65

out into the woods in a frenzy of dance. In the Middle Ages, an infectious 'dance plague' called the *Tarantella* swept from village to village across Italy, irresistibly drawing people into the streets to dance until they dropped. Even in the most repressive societies, women still retain their traditional female circle dances, and I suspect that women – including women of faith – will take the lead in dancing our way out of self-destruction. And if men are irresistibly drawn into the dance, they will have to lay down their weapons before they are allowed to join in. 'The Dance Craze that Saved the World?' Why not, in this age of planetary connectivity where fads, fashions and financial disasters are propagated literally at the speed of light? Instead of organizing a centralized World Party, we eco-revolutionaries should be calling a Party for the Planet, like Dr. Earth, whose new London eco-club *Surya*[37] has shock absorbers beneath the dance floor which convert dance motions into electricity to run the club's air-con system. The club's tables are made out of recycled magazines and the walls crafted from old mobile phones. 'We are now at the 11th hour of a global Armageddon caused by climate change,' says Dr. Earth. 'Clubbing should not be about escapism, alcohol and drugs. It should be about bringing people together in the name of hope, planet Earth and a positive future for mankind.' Right on, Doc!

Party for the Planet! is only one of a number of Mutiny on Starship Earth scenarios consistent with contemporary science that the Archimedes Hypothesis permits us to imagine – perhaps the most pleasant imaginable – as one chance in a hundred. But aren't love and joy more powerful than hate and shame? The world's great Teachers all seemed to think so. To hold fast to such an idealistic planetary vision – I frankly admit it – demands an existential 'leap of faith.' Or at the very least the kind of 'temporary suspension of disbelief' we bring to a good film or novel. At every moment, the headlines seem to undermine our assumptions, while the voices of despair invite us to recline into cynicism and expediency, or to embark on self-defeating dangerous shortcuts. But however much we are tempted to doubt the power of these assumptions, our existential commitment directs us to behave *as if* the assumptions on which survival depends were demonstrably true before the fact. That is the Utopian Bet, and the only way to verify the validity of its assumptions is to play them out to the end. To win the Bet we must start with the assumption that we really *do* have a chance and then bet everything we have on that one chance. What do we have to lose that we aren't losing now?

Conclusion

The Archimedes Hypothesis proposes a theoretical model for visualizing the material-historical possibility of a planetary revolution in our age of globalized

---

[37] www.club4-climate.com

corporate capitalism and planetary connectivity. The power of solidarity has proven itself capable of overcoming tyranny again and again, wherever people have united. The consciousness that a new society is necessary if the planet is not to be destroyed is more and more widespread. Today's Internet technology at last provides a space for people around the planet to connect and take positive action on a global scale. Scarcity is no longer an issue. Modern technology produces such an abundance of food and material goods that overproduction undermines market stability. Inequality, not scarcity, is the cause of want. Utopia may thus be a realistic possibility – however remote it may seem at the moment. At the very least, the Archimedes Hypothesis permits us to imagine realistic science fiction scenarios about successful Mutinies on Starship Earth. It gives us the theoretical right to dream. And if one or more of these scenarios is compelling enough to fire the imagination of people around the world, who knows what may result from these small beginnings when the idea-virus of Utopia reaches the tipping-point and becomes an epidemic?

That, at least, is our Utopian bet. On the one hand, nothing to lose but the dismal spectacle of a dying world; on the other, a chance in a hundred to save ourselves and the beautiful blue-green planet we live on. In any case, it's a bet we can't refuse. In the 18th Century – the age of scientific and political revolutions – radical writers like Voltaire, Diderot, Thomas Paine and the Encyclopedists boldly proclaimed, The pen is mightier than the sword. History proved them right. Feudalism was overthrown. Today in the 21st Century – the age of connectivity and emergence – the Archimedes Hypothesis entitles us to state a claim of our own: The electronic keyboard is mightier than the nuclear missile!

All Power to the Imagination!

P.S. Please join me and my friends at www.wikitopia.wikidot.com and help dream up realistic scenarios for *Mutiny on Stareship Earth.*

The Invisible International

The Franco-Russian revolutionary and novelist Victor Serge[38] coined the phrase 'invisible international' at a dark moment in history. In 1940 he found himself stateless, penniless, trapped in Vichy France, where he was on the murder-list of the KGB and the Gestapo[39]. Serge survived and eventually escaped thanks to the solidarity of what he called an 'invisible international' of comrades around the world. Serge was part of a fraternity of survivors of shipwrecked revolutions who were struggling to stay afloat in the rising tide of fascism. Scattered between Vichy France (a trap), Mexico (welcoming to political refugees and to KGB assassins alike) and New York, they maintained contact by the thin thread of the mail – when Serge could get money for stamps – sending political analyses along with money orders, lending support in the battle for visas in 'a planet without a visa.'[40]

Serge's comrades were themselves persecuted dissident revolutionaries – Spanish Republican refugees of the POUM[41]; antifascist and anti-Stalinist refugees from Italy, Germany, Austria; Russian Left Oppositionists still resisting in Stalin's camps; a few socialists and leftist intellectuals in NY. Serge's comrades were also battling for the survival of their shipwrecked ideals, creating small exile reviews when they could, arguing, exchanging their Marxist 'theses' – even within the Gulag. These independent socialists and revolutionaries had resisted Stalin's hijacking of the Russian Revolution and fought the rise of fascism. Now they wanted to understand their defeats and if possible to trace new perspectives. If they were unable to prevent Communism's betrayal and fascism's triumph, they could at least be lucid and search for the right terms to understand these events theoretically. Forged in the heat of a great world crisis, their analyses remain critical.

---

[38] Victor Serge (1890-1947) Please see "Who Was Victor Serge and Why Do We Have to Ask?" in Part IV below.
[39] As documented in recently opened Soviet Archives. See Susan Weissman, *Victor Serge: The Course is set on Hope*, Verso, London.
[40] The phrase was Trotsky's.
[41] POUM (*Partido obrero de unificacion marxista*): anti-Stalinist party of the Mocialist left mainly active in Catalonia during the Spanish revolution of 1936-1939. While the POUM militia were going up to the front to battle against Franco fascists, the Spanish Communists under the order of Stalin were preparing to destroy them. Driven out of Spain by Franco, stabbed in the back by the Communists, interned in the concentration camps of the French Republic, many fought in the French Resistance. The story of their tragic heroism has been told by George Orwell in his memoir *Homage to Catalonia* and by Ken Loch in his film *Land and Liberty*.

The Historical Invisible International

What if we took the liberty of expanding Serge's phrase historically to embrace revolutionary dissidents of the past and to include what remains relevant in their writings and their example? This Historical Invisible International would be composed of persecuted, marginalized socialist and anarchist minorities, revolutionary heretics like Serge whose critical thought and experience as fighters against the totalitarianisms of the Right and so-called Left still have great value.

Let's imagine this Historical Invisible International as a large virtual meeting hall where stand assembled all the world's radicals and socialists of every clime and epoch. At this assembly, we might encounter old rebels dating back to the Roman slave Spartacus and extending across the planet to every movement from A to Z – from Autonomists to Zapatistas (great!). Imagine if we could listen in on their conversations, even ask them questions: Learn from them whatever there is to know about class struggle down through the ages. Whom would we find in this hall of defeated heroes? Here are the ones I know well enough to point out in the crowd:

- Look, over there, those guys with long bows? That's Wat Tyler, John Ball and the other peasant revolutionaries of 14th Century England; from Europe we see Jan of Leyden and the Utopian Anabaptists; back in England the *Diggers* and *Levelers* of the 17th Century Revolution; from France Babeuf has organized a *Conspiracy of Equals,* radical democrats like Tom Paine and Mary Wollstonecraft active in several countries, Luddites, Chartists, *Canuts* from Lyon *Teipings* from China and of course over in the corner a bunch of Wobblies from Montana hanging out with Joe Hill. . .
- Down in front there I see some great American revolutionaries like Harriet Tubman, Sojourner Truth, Frederick Douglass, Susan B. Anthony, E.V. Debbs, Bill Haywood, Mother Jones and of course Malcolm and Martin...
- Among the Utopians I see jolly old François Rabelais, a somewhat primmer Thomas More, Fourier, Saint Simon, Robert Owen, William Morris and Oscar Wilde arguing about esthetics with Edward Bellamy, as well as friends and contemporaries like Paul Goodman, Starhawk, Ernst Callenbach . . .and, is that Manny Wallerstein over there?
- In the Anarchists circle I've conversed via books with Montaigne's friend La Boétie as well as with Proudhon, Bakunin, Louise Michel, Kropotkin, Marius Jacob, Flores Magon, Durruti, Emma Goldman

(my hero among them all), Voline, and in real life with Marcel Body, Russell Blackwell, Daniel Guérin Sam and Esther Dolgoff . . .

- Among the intellectuals reading in the hall's library, I see critical socialists like Antonio Gramsci, Georg Lukacs, and the skeptical philosopher who famously wrote 'The only thing I know is that I am not a Marxist.' [42]
- Hanging around Praxis in Moscow, one finds modern incarnations of all the repressed Russian revolutionary opposition to totalitarianism: Left Social-Revolutionaries, Anarchists, Left Mencheviks and dissident Communists Workers' Opposition (Kollontai, Shliapnikov), the Left Opposition (Preobrejenski, Joffe, Trotsky, Smilga, Victor Serge), Sapronov and the Democratic Centralists as well as the dissidents of Third International (Balabanova, Bordiga, Souvarine, Sneevliet). . .
- Over there's another group speaking German with the martyred Spartacist leaders Karl Leibnecht and Rosa Luxemburg. Around them I see the Dutch and German Council Communists with Anton Pannekoek, Paul Mattick and Karl Korsch. . .
- And of course there are the post-Trotskyite revolutionaries some of whom I have talked (or debated) with in the flesh as well as in their books: among them Raya Dunayevskaya, Cornelius Castoriadis, Tony Cliff, Hal Draper, Maximilien Rubel, Danel Guérin, Ngo Van, Paul Mattick, and many others. . .

I used to dream that if my comrades and I could enter that imaginary meeting hall and participate in the discussions among these revolutionaries of every era, perhaps we might pick up the red thread that would lead us out of the political labyrinth in which we are lost. Well, *Halleluyah!* Today we can, thanks to the Internet! Today any curious teenager in Vietnam or Vermont can check into an Internt café, hook up to the nets and visit all these historical rebels through Wikipedia and at their sites, often run by active disciples eager to network with new people. Today, revolutionary texts that previously could only be found in the great libraries of Paris, London and New York are two or three clicks away on the Internet. As a student eager to read Victor Serge, I actually had to go to Paris and hand copy his writing at the *Bibliothèque nationale.* Now Serge is on Facebook! Today, our imaginary meeting hall virtually exists, on a platform

---

[42] The author of that phrase was Marx himself, and he said it more than once when appalled by the things self-styled 'Marxists' were saying. If Marx knew what was done in his name under totalitarian Communism, he would turn in his grave. Marx's words 'working people of all nations unite' have about as much in common with Stalinist 'Communism' as Jesus Christ's 'the poor shall inherit the earth' has to do with the Spanish Inquisition and the luxurious Borgia Popes.

wide as the planet itself, with sites devoted to all these visionaries whom we are free to visit as often as we wish.

I've often wondered if a consensus could emerge in this great assembly among rebels of every time and place? Could we imagine these anti-totalitarian revolutionaries evolving some sort of synthesis of their common ideas and social experiences? Could we imagine them agreeing on a minimum program, a Virtual Charter which today's internationalists might find illuminating? What would such a Charter look like? Perhaps like a 21st Century globalized version of the Charter of the International Workers Association (Ist International) or the *Preamble* of the Wobblies (IWW) which was written over a three or four day period in a hall in Chicago in 1905 by an assembly of about a hundred men and women, Marxists, socialists, syndicalists, labor organizers, anarchists and working stiffs? They got off to a good start by agreeing on the following **Preamble**:

The working class and the employing class have nothing in common. There can be no peace so long as hunger and want are found among millions of the working people and the few, who make up the employing class, have all the good things of life. Between these two classes a struggle must go on until the workers of the world organize as a class, take possession of the earth and the machinery of production, and abolish the wage system.

Occult Learning

One thing is sure: if these witnesses to revolution cannot give us infallible formulas for getting to a socialist society in the future, they can by their critical thought put us on guard against *what we must not do* if we want to get there. The lessons, however negative, that they bring us from their defeats, are an unavoidable point of departure. These hard-won lessons constitute a treasure of Occult Learning built up by the working class in its victories and its defeats, analyzed by its best surviving thinkers, distilled in the alembic of historical experience, purified by critical spirit. This knowledge remains 'occult' because it has long been marginalized, forgotten, buried under party lines and official lies. But as Victor Serge wrote, 'nothing is ever lost.' The Occult Learning of yesterday's rebels is still there to discover. Their example and their writings survive. It's up to us to extract its quintessence! So let's begin by looking backward at the three historical Workers' Internationals to see what lessons they might hold for the 21st Century.

The Example of the Multi-tendency IWA

The First International, known at the time as the International Workingmen's Association (IWA) came together in 1863 and fell apart not long after the

71

defeat of the Paris Commune a decade later. I would like to propose the IWA as a model horizontal bottom up worker self-organization with long-term goals and ramifications among organized workers in many lands. Essentially a correspondence network, the IWA served a practical function in keeping workers informed of each others' struggles in the various countries and of organizing solidarity where possible. At the same time, the IWA fulfilled the two functions which, according to the Marx-Engels 1848 *Communist Manifesto,* distinguishes the activities of 'communists' (we should say 'socialists' today) from other participants in the class struggle: 1) in every local struggle, to look out for the interests of the working class as a whole, worldwide 2) in every partial struggle, to look toward the long run, the ultimate historical goal of total worker self-emancipation.

In contrast to the 'vanguard,' 'hub-and-spokes,' 'general staff' models of organization exemplified by the bureaucratic parties of the Second (or Socialist), Third (or Communist) and Fourth (Trotskyist) Internationals, let us look at the structure of the IWA and at the actual practice of Marx himself, who served as its General Secretary. The IWA's Charter stated its purpose was to 'establish relations between the different associations of workers in such a manner that workers in each country would be constantly informed of the movements of their class in other countries.' In other words, the IWA was first of all an international workers' information network with an extremely practical purpose (a purpose I believe can be greatly facilitate by a network which exploits the information-sharing technology of the Internet).[43]

Further, the original IWA was also a socialist organization defined by its Statutes and Congresses and a General Council. Let us recall that membership and voting at congresses were restricted to 'workingmen' which excluded both women workers (regrettably) and intellectuals (perhaps correctly). It was when the organizers couldn't find the right words to express their aims in a Preamble that they appealed to 'the eminent writer Dr. Marx' whose position was that of unpaid volunteer secretary and 'scientific' advisor (through his Addresses to the Council on history, economics, politics). Far from being a 'Marxist' organization, the IWA was a broad, multi-tendency coalition of worker groups reflecting the theoretical level of the organized workers of its time.

In the beginning, the followers of the French socialist Proud'hon were in the majority. The Proud'honists believed in a socialism based on mutual credit, and they opposed strikes, revolutions and women's rights. The IWA did not really take off until the economic crisis and strike wave of 1868, and it was 'not the International who threw the workers into the strikes, but the strikes that threw the workers into the International.' Only then did Marx's ideas win general acceptance. In 1869, Bakunin and his anarchist followers were accepted into the IWA and introduced yet another political current, federalism.

Two years later, the Paris Commune, the first workers' government, was created by French workers and soldiers in the wake of Napoleon III's defeat in the Franco-Prussian War. Although Proud'honists and Internationalists of

---

[43] Contemporary revolutionary groups like Collective Action Notes (CAN) from the U.S. and Echanges et Mouvements from France who are devoted precisely to this vital function of collecting and exchanging information about strikes and worker revolts around the world.

the IWA were members of the Commune, it was an improvised affair rather than the application of anyone's theory. After the Commune's tragic defeat, it was Marx who was assigned by the IWA's London Committee to sum up the basic lesson learned through experience by the Paris workers for future generations of workers. They were 'anarchist' lessons: smash the state and replace it with the armed people governing themselves through elected, revocable representatives paid at workers' wages. Marx was the first to acknowledge that it was not he, the 'revolutionary Marxist,' who created this essential view of the workers' self-government, but the workers themselves through experience. Further, Marx made an important change in his major theoretical work, *Capital,* after observing that the actions of the Parisian workers had 'stripped the fetish off commodities' and revealed their essence. In May 1871, the short-lived Commune was brutally repressed by the French Republic with the help of the Prussians. The capitalist repression spread to every land with massive police repression of workers' associations. Thus, the First International was effectively destroyed as a practical movement, but only after having 'stormed the heavens' with the first practical workers' government.[44]

Rich Lessons of the First International

The first lesson is that collective experience and self-activity, rather than doctrines that lead working people to their revolutionary discoveries. As Marx put it, self-activity is the workers' 'method of cognition' which the

---

[44] **Nothing fails like failure.** It was later, during the repression following the defeat of 1871 – in the midst of the subsequent quarrels and factionalism among demoralized, embittered, exiled revolutionary intellectuals fighting over what remained of the IWA – that the famous split took place between the so-called "Marxists" (Marx famously denied he was a 'Marxist'!) and the anarchists following Bakunin. In this ugly aftermath, the conspiratorial "libertarian" Bakunin maneuvered to raid the moribund rump of the IWA and take over the name. He was outmaneuvered by the wily Marx, who sent the General Council across the Atlantic to New York to wither and die. In retrospect this 'battle of titans' seems like a battle of pygmies revealing the small side of these two bearded, 19th Century patriarchs blinded by national prejudices (Bakunin's anti-Semitism, Marx's fear of Russia). Unfortunately, the split remained permanent between the two great branches of the socialist family, now sharply divided between "libertarians" and "authoritarians". Tragically, all that people remember today about the IWA is the nasty factional split between in a half-dead exile group, rather than the vigorous and suggestive history of this first and highly successful attempt of working people to organize themselves internationally. But the living history of the IWA, rather than its ugly postmortem, remains rich in lessons for workers today who wish to unite in an international network.

revolutionary intellectual can only later formulate, not prescribe. In other words, there is a movement from practice to theory, which precedes the movement from theory to practice. Marx caught it, as did Luxembourg in 1905. Kautsky, the main theoretician of the Socialist Second International, could only see the movement *from* theory and taught Lenin that socialism is imported into the working class by party intellectuals. In reality, what takes place is a two-way road between theory and practice, ending in the unity of workers and intellectuals, as Raya Dunayevskaya demonstrated in her 1958 *Marxism and Freedom.*

The second lesson is that such an international network must from the beginning offer practical advantages by providing facilities for the exchange of information about workers' struggles, the gathering of statistics about conditions of labor, the linking of organized workers for international action. With the Internet, this becomes a practical possibility. The third lesson is that genuine international workers' organizations must be horizontal rather than vertical, multi-tendency and democratic, rather than top-down authoritarian, if they are to leave room for the development of class consciousness through lessons drawn from experience.

Thus, we can be sure that we are on the right track when we imagine the emergence of an international network. But it is equally certain that it is not we, a few thousand *Altermundialistas* but billions acting together, who can create a vast international movement and unleash the human power necessary to uproot capitalism and save the planet if it can be saved. So for the moment let us agree on two main points borrowed from the *Communist* Manifesto: 1) that the emancipation of the working people can only be the result of the activity of the working people themselves and 2) that this emancipation will take place on the planetary scale or it will not take place at all.

Rule of Thumb Internationalism

How then do we as revolutionary internationalists differ from other working men and women in struggle? What do we have to add? What is our role? Certainly not that of chiefs, but perhaps the more modest roles of leaven, helping the dough to rise; of idea-viruses spreading the contagion of revolutionary thought; of memory-cells and teachers in the movement, making the lessons of the past actual in the present. Like the 'Communists' in the 1848 *Communist Manifesto,* our role is two-fold: 1) in every particular, local or national struggle, we pose the question: 'How does this struggle increase international/planetary worker solidarity?' 2) In every partial, limited, immediate struggle, we pose the question: 'How does this struggle advance the historical perspective of the abolition of wage-labor and capitalism?' These are the questions, the historical and the planetary, that we internationalists seek to

75

bring to the fore in every struggle. From this follows a relatively simple rule-of-thumb that can be applied to nearly any situation or movement:

> **The Internationalist Rule of Thumb:**
> **'Every tactic is good that unites us globally, that promotes solidarity among working and unemployed, among men and women of all nationalities.**
> **Every tactic that divides us by race, sex, or nation is destructive.'**

Based on rule-of-thumb internationalism, we see that the failures of the Second (Socialist) International and the Third (Communist) Internationals derive in a large measure precisely from their lack of consistent, thoroughgoing internationalism.

The Mighty Second International Collapses

Sectarians are perennially trying to create new Internationals based on 'revolutionary Marxism.' But ideology is not enough. The powerful Socialist International was officially based on 'revolutionary Marxism,' and it organized millions of workers within a vast network of Socialist parties and trade-unions with a mass press, and important youth and women's sections in Germany, France, Belgium, Holland, Austria, Russia. During the previous international Congress, the revolutionary tendency spearheaded by Rosa Luxemburg had gained the majority over the 'revisionist' faction led by Bernstein, and that the in the event of war, the Socialist Parties were pledge to respond by a general strike. Yet this powerful international Socialist party collapsed like a house of cards in August 1914 when the majority of the German and French socialists supported their capitalist governments at the outbreak of the First imperialist World War – turning millions of workers into fratricidal murderers. The Second International was so firmly based in 'revolutionary Marxism' that at the outbreak of War in August 1914 Lenin himself still looked upon its chief theoretician Kautsky as his 'master' and literally *refused to believe* the press reports of the German Socialists' betrayal. (He preferred to imagine that the reports were 'planted' as part of an Imperial disinformation campaign than admit the truth).

The Third International Promotes Counter-revolution

The same rule-of-thumb exposes the sham internationalism of the Third International, also firmly based on 'revolutionary Marxism.' It, too, foundered on the rock of chauvinism by identifying the interests of the working people of the planet with the interests of the Russian state. Trotsky scornfully concluded that the Moscow-directed Third International or

76

'Comintern' had been degraded under Stalin to the role of 'border guards' protecting the interests of Russia. In fact, the Comintern had become an agent of international counter-revolution. Ken Loach's recent film *Land and Freedom* shows how the Comintern during the Spanish Revolution of 1936 allied itself with the Spanish Republican bourgeoisie and introduced police-state methods to crush the magnificent social revolution of the Spanish workers and peasants whose self-activity was creating a new society and fighting Franco.

Moreover, I think we have all come to realize that the Moscow-centered Comintern under Zinoviev, with its bureaucratized structure and bullying, manipulative methods was tainted from the start. Consider the fiasco of the 1923 Communist *putsch* in Germany, when the Comintern held back the workers' insurrectionary mood of the summer so as to 'order' a German revolution to coincide with the anniversary of the Russian October Revolution. But when October came around, Moscow panicked and gave the order to call off the German uprising at the last minute, exposing the German Party and particularly the workers of Hamburg (who didn't get the message in time and took over the city) to violent repression. But instead of drawing the lessons of this Moscow-directed disaster, the 'revolutionary Marxist' Comintern placed the responsibility on the local German leaders (some of whom had not even been kept informed of the insurrectionary plans!) and purged them. It could be argued that this Russian-engineered disaster of 1923 closed the period of international revolutionary struggle that had opened with the Soviet victory in 1917, and ushered in the era of fascism. This is a practical example of how the 'hub-and-spokes' model of an international network functioned from its inception, well before Stalinism.

The Fourth and 'Fifth' Internationals

Stalin took over Russia and the Third International in 1928, and one of his first acts was to exile his arch-rival Leon Trotsky, who since 1923 had been criticizing the Soviet regime as bureaucratic and nationalistic. During the Thirties, Trotsky attempted to create a rival Fourth International based on 'revolutionary Marxism' from the top down in the absence of existing anti-Stalinist national parties. The result was an ideological sect, which immediately split into two factions and has not stopped splitting since.

Does our imaginary Invisible International include present-day disciples of these mico-parties? Of course – as long as they have not sunk into stagnant and fanatical sectarianisms, as long as they go on searching and asking questions. In spite of the sectarianism that often divides and embitters the factions of the international far left, these groups include many possessors of Occult Wisdom, bearers of revolutionary ideas who continue to defend and expound them. Alas, Dear Comrades, all our efforts for uniting into an ultimate international have

77

sunk into sectarian power-struggles and squabbles over the 'correct political line,' as if any group could have a monopoly on the truth.

Yet the mini-parties and radical sects we devoted ourselves to building and defending over so many lonely and difficult years were not necessarily sterile. We exposed thousands if not millions of young people to revolutionary ideas for the first time. We preserved, disseminated and developed these ideas during a difficult and confusing period when such ideas were basically 'underground' even where they were legal. We were a transmission-belt passing on the Occult Wisdom we received, often by oral tradition, from surviving revolutionaries of Serge's generation who remembered back even further. Our groups were the hard nut-shells which preserved the germ of radical critique of the world through the winter of its defeats.

Today we need to crack open those shells, to liberate the revolution, to join what Marx called the 'actual movement' – not to lead it or to take it over, but to bring to it organizational skills, socialist ideals, a form of analysis based on historical experience, a perspective for another possible world. In other words, to break open the hard shells of our splinter groups and liberate the Occult Wisdom jealously preserved inside. If the Left of the Left remains with its sectarian shell, it will dry up and die. If it has the courage to break out of its shell, it will fulfill its biological function by procreating, something most people find to be fun.

Among such activities, let me propose using our experience and Occult Wisdom in a playful and imaginative mode. Instead of *arguing* about whose political line is more correct, let's hold a contest for the best fictional Path to Utopia that shows us *how* that political line gets us to a new society and what the new society looks like. I've participated in various attempts to form networks, alliances and the like on the basis of some sort of Manifesto, and they have all crashed upon the rocks of sectarian power struggles. After my disappointment at the latest failure to form a 'Fifth' International (the 1997 Capetown, South Africa Conference for International Network for a Socialist Alternative) I came to the conclusion that as long as there was *power* to be had in an organizational structure, people will fight over it and mask their power-hunger with doctrinal differences. It was then that I came across the phrase 'invisible international' in Serge and began to think in terms of a *virtual* Charter. What if we made an online game of it? Each player or player-group picks an identity. I'll be Rosa Luxembourg, you be Bakunin. What if we all met in a virtual meeting hall on a Wiki and try to hammer out a *virtual* Charter, adding on ideas in the open-source spirit rather than treating ideas as private property to fight over.

The Wiki is ready and waiting at http://wikitopia.wikidot.com/

So come on all you Marxists, anarchists, socialists, post-Trotskyists, libertarians, communists, latter-day Sixty-Eighters – to your computers! Let's take time off from collecting signatures, publishing unreadable articles and holding interminable meetings, to think about Utopia! Let's dream, and take our dreams for realities once again! Let's bet on Utopia while there's still a planet to save!

The Workers' Invisible International

This huge Invisible International, still in search of its identity, includes all the workers and poor people across the planet who struggle against the power of the banks, multinationals and governments who stand between them and a living wage. We're talking about the crew-members of Starship Earth. They run all the machinery, clean and repair the cabins, prepare all the food and are made to slave for the officers and serve them. Most of the passengers are their families, deep down in steerage where it stinks, where it's cold and disease is rife and there aren't enough rations to keep everyone alive. They have the most incentive to overthrow the officers. They also have the power to STOP the machinery AND the know-how to run the ship afterwards. They have been the backbone of every previous revolution. The officers know this, and use all their force and guile to keep them down. Yet they rebel:

- In Argentina pickets and assemblies overthrew several governments to protest the IMF- provoked bankruptcy of their economy. Their slogan: 'get rid of the whole lot!'
- Chinese strikers fighting a totalitarian Communist regime that sells their sweated labor for pennies to capitalist American multinationals like Nike. 80,000 revolts requiring armed state intervention were officially reported in 2007.
- Peasants and other citizens of India and Latin America defending their drinking water against the profitable privatizations of Vivendi, Suez and local capitalists.
- Brazilian *seringueros*, tappers of wild rubber defending their living and that of the Amazon forest.
- The 'new' Korean proletariat whose general strikes overthrew the dictatorship of the generals and industrial monopolies like Hyundai and Daewoo.
- Chinese peasants revolting against arbitrary taxes and driving Communist Party profiteers out of their village councils.
- Super-exploited Mexican workers in the *maquiladoras* (free trade zones on the American border) organizing with the help of US unionists.

- The workers and unemployed of Europe and the US struggling against the take-backs, speedups, downsizing, plant closures, out-sourcing, automation, flexi-time, safety violations, degraded working conditions and stress imposed in the name of globalization.

These working men and women are slowly and painfully learning, through frustrating struggles at the local and national levels, that they are facing a formidable global adversary. They are beginning to recognize how their unseizable, ubiquitous enemy thwarts their every effort to improve their lot in one place or another. They are observing how this adversary divides them the better to rule and exploit them. They are experiencing the effects of a globalized 'free market' which defines itself by international borders pried open for the penetration of foreign capital and slammed shut against migrants searching for work.

These workers see the multinationals taking over everywhere. Overworked, underpaid Asian workers feel themselves being squeezed dry by local subcontractors competing to offer the lowest prices to foreign corporations. In the multinationals' home countries, workers are forced to submit to wage cuts, factory closings, privatization of public services, deterioration of their living conditions, their standard of living swept away in a global race towards the bottom of the lowest labor costs – all this justified by the global market and 'foreign' competition.

Similarly, farmers of Africa, Latin America and Asia are seeing themselves ruined by low agricultural prices while the governments of rich countries give gross subsidies to giant multinational agribusinesses like Monsanto. Billions of Africans, Asians and Latin Americans are seeing themselves deprived of schools, hospitals and infrastructures by reductions in social budgets and privatizations imposed by the IMF and World Bank – all in the name of 'free trade'! At the risk of extinction, these folks on the bottom need to organize themselves on the planetary level.

The way will not be easy. National pride, racial and religious prejudices will remain obstacles. Existing trade unions, narrowly focused on local fiefdoms and marginal improvements, will prove unable or unwilling to address their members' most pressing problem: the decline of wages to the worldwide lowest common denominator through globalization. Only international solidarity can possible solve this problem, but the union bureaucracy, locked into the wage-system and the legal system, is unlikely to jeopardize its privileged situation as intermediary between labor, business, and government. It will resist any kind of global activity that might violate sacrosanct labor contracts and labor legislation, subjecting them to fines, etc. Most of the unions will continue to fight losing rear-guard actions, attempting to rescue pensions and a few jobs out of factory closings, locking the barn door after the horses have been stolen. Only a few maverick unions show signs of going global, and the first planetary solidarity actions will have to be organized without the 'help' of the labor bureaucrats, if not over their opposition.

Workers around the globe are reaching out, groping toward international solutions to international problems. For the first time, the Internet gives them the technical ability to do so. Chinese dissidents, Korean trade-unionists, striking British dockers have already made use of the Internet to communicate, organize solidarity, tell the world about their struggles and develop links with other movements. One day working people will be led to organize the first global strike against a multinational, and thanks to the Internet they will be able to bring it off.

On the day when all the employees, subcontractors and subsidiaries of a multinational like Daewoo, Nike or Airbus Industries go on strike simultaneously in every country, the invisible international of the workers will stop being a dream or an 'occult conspiracy.' It will take on the flesh and bones of a waking giant, and its rising will be the beginning of the end of capitalist exploitation – *if* capitalism has not already destroyed the world.

The Invisible International of Global Social Movements

This young invisible international is looking good. Its diversity is its strength. It brings together movements organized around single issues from torture in prisons to the nuclear threat. It speaks many languages and speaks with many voices, including voices heretofore un-heard: feminine, third world, peasant voices. It has answered capitalism's arrogant TINA ('There Is No Alternative') with a loud 'Another World Is Possible.' Not only does it speak, it listens.

Throughout the world it attracts critical spirits and passionate activists, for the most part young, who are looking for a way out of this dying capitalist society. It is present whenever the representatives of global capitalism come together to divide up the world's resources among themselves. In the name of the human community and the biosphere, it dares confront the financial power of multinational capital and the might of the state. It organized the world's first global antiwar demonstrations, massively supported in many countries. Its struggle to save the planet from destruction is historic.

This young invisible international possesses its own Occult Learning. Many of its people grew up with the computer and the Internet, and they have made marvelous use of them to inform themselves and to weave their networks. The skill of its researchers, its access to facts, statistics and studies is impressive.

Its use of the Internet as an organizing tool has opened up new possibilities for global action. Like the Internet itself, it takes the form of a sprawling web linking individuals, local groups, political organizations, and various networks organized around issues like ecology, war, AIDS, hunger, human rights, capitalist globalization. Along that web, information is exchanged to fertilize discussions; international encounters are planned.

The 1999 anti-IMF protests in Seattle surpassed all expectations and drew the attention of the whole world to the problem of capitalist globalization. Seen marching there side by side for the first time were timber-industry unionists and tree-hugging ecologists, bare-breasted feminists and members of religious orders, anarchists and professional societies. Subsequent meetings in Rio, Porto Alegre, Genoa and elsewhere brought thousands of militants and thinkers in struggle and dialogue. Among them: ecologists, native peoples, trade unionists, anti-nuclears, feminists, gays, human rights militants, peasant and ethnic communities, enraged scientists, radicals and protesters of every stripe. The World Social Forum, which met for the first time in Porto Allegre, Brazil in 2001, has become an annual event bringing together activists from social movements around the globe, a kind of 'movement of movements.' They go to forums to learn, to pose old questions in a new way, to develop original forms of collective action, and especially to weave ties among people of other countries, other movements.

Nobody dominates. No party line is imposed. No petty dictators pass down orders from on high. Rather, a highly organized chaos of organizations, websites, networks. Sites loaded with detailed information on each issue intertwined by an infinity of links with other sites. A proliferation of projects and ideas. A discussion open to all. A circle, a web instead of an authoritarian center handing down information and commands down to the rank and file. Enough to drive old politicos and disciplined militants to despair. But when it comes to mobilizing – what boldness! What initiative!

In 2002-2003, faced with the threat to the peace posed by the aggressive arrogance of the Bush administration in Iraq, this new movement mobilized millions in the first global demonstration in history. The *N.Y. Times* spoke of the birth of a 'second superpower': global opinion. In another dramatic development, from the heart of a US still in the grip of post-11 September 2001 patriotic hysteria, a million Americans poured into the streets, braving FBI cameras, Army helicopters and police charges to show their opposition to the war and demand regime change in Washington. We could not stop the war, but we recognized our strength, our identity as a planetary movement, an invisible antiwar international.

For many, Internet contact with this new invisible international represents the first experience with organized protest. Caring about the earth, about peace and social justice, in love with a simple, sane life, its members seek a way out of a

82

cruel, destructive, and irrational system. This new invisible international cannot help being anti-capitalist. The same multinationals block the way forward of every reform desired by its constituents, be it preventing war, eliminating poverty, saving the environment, protecting human rights, or blocking the capitalist privatization of the planet's resources. 'The World is not for sale' is its motto. Its slogan is at once Utopian and revolutionary: 'Another world is possible!'

At the latest meeting of the World Social Forum at Belem, Brazil (February, 2009) the members of the **Assembly of Social Movements** spelled out their aims in the following **Declaration** which deserves the widest attention:

We the social movements from all over the world came together on the occasion of the 8th World Social Forum in Belem, Amazonia, where the peoples have been resisting attempts to usurp nature, their lands and their cultures. We are here in Latin America, where over the last decade the social movements and the indigenous movements have joined forces and radically question the capitalist system from their *cosmovision*. Over the last few years, in Latin America highly radical social struggles have resulted in the overthrow of neoliberal governments and the empowerment of governments that have carried out many positive reforms such as the nationalisation of core sectors of the economy and democratic constitutional reforms.

In this context the social movements in Latin America have responded appropriately, deciding to support the positive measures adopted by these governments while keeping a critical distance. These experiences will be of help in order to strengthen the peoples' staunch resistance against the policies of governments, corporations and banks who shift the burden of the crisis onto the oppressed. We, the social movements of the globe, are currently facing a historic challenge. The international capitalist crisis manifests itself as detrimental to humankind in various ways: it affects food, finance, the economy, climate, energy, population migration and civilisation itself, as there is also a crisis in international order and political structures.

We are facing a global crisis which is a direct consequence of the capitalist system and therefore cannot find a solution within the system. All the measures that have been taken so far to overcome the crisis merely aim at socialising losses so as to ensure the survival of a system based on privatising strategic economic sectors, public services, natural and energy resources and on the commodification of life and the exploitation of labour and of nature as well as on the transfer of resources from the periphery to the centre and from workers to the capitalist class.

The present system is based on exploitation, competition, promotion of individual private interests to the detriment of the collective interest, and the frenzied accumulation of wealth by a handful of rich people. It results in bloody wars, fuels xenophobia, racism and religious fundamentalisms; it intensifies the exploitation of women and the criminalisation of social movements. In the context of the present crisis the rights of peoples are systematically denied. The Israeli government's savage aggression against the Palestinian people is a violation of international law and amounts to a war crime, a crime against humanity and a symbol of the denial of a people's rights that can be observed in other parts of the world. The shameful impunity must be stopped. The social movements reassert their active support of the struggle of the Palestinian people as well as of all actions against oppression by peoples worldwide. problem and progress as fast as possible towards the construction of a radical alternative that would do away with the capitalist system and patriarchal domination. We must work towards a society that meets social needs and respects nature's rights as well as supporting democratic participation in a context of full political freedom. We must see to it that all international treaties on our indivisible civic, political, economic, social and cultural rights, both individual and collective, are implemented. In this perspective we must contribute to the largest possible popular mobilization to enforce a number of urgent measures such as:

Nationalizing the banking sector without compensation and with full social monitoring
Reducing working time without any wage cut
Taking measures to ensure food and energy sovereignty
Stop wars, withdraw occupation troops and dismantle military foreign bases
Acknowledging the peoples' sovereignty and autonomy ensuring their right to self-determination
Guaranteeing rights to land, territory, work, education and health for all
Democratize access to means of communication and knowledge.

The social emancipation process carried by the feminist, environmentalist and socialist movements in the 21st century aims at liberating society from capitalist domination of the means of production, communication and services, achieved by supporting forms of ownership that favor the social interest: small family freehold, public, cooperative, communal and collective property.

Such an alternative will necessarily be feminist since it is impossible to build a society based on social justice and equality of rights when half of humankind is oppressed and exploited.
Lastly, we commit ourselves to enriching the construction of a society based on a life lived in harmony with oneself, others and the world around (*el buen vivir*) by acknowledging the active participation and contribution of the native peoples.

We, the social movements, are faced with a historic opportunity to develop emancipatory initiatives on a global scale. Only through the social struggle of the masses can populations overcome the crisis. In order to promote this struggle, it is essential to work on consciousness-raising and mobilization from the grassroots. The challenge for the social movements is to achieve a convergence of global mobilization. It is also to strengthen our ability to act by supporting the convergence of all movements striving to withstand oppression and exploitation.

Part II:

Dissecting our Decadent Decade

Dangerous Shortcuts and Vegetarian Sharks [1997]

Original contribution to the **Encuentro Intercontinentàl**
'Against Neo-Liberalism and for Humanity,'
(Barcelona, Spain, August 1997)[45]

Neo-Liberalism or Capitalism?

Compañeros, as someone who as been an activist since the late 1950's, I find it both inspiring and refreshing to participate in this *Encuentro* organized at the suggestion of the Zapatistas in an attempt to 're-invent' a politics of resistance in an atmosphere of inclusiveness, mutual respect and humanism. Here at the *Encuentro* I have been hearing many interesting ideas put forward about alternative economies, new forms of resistance and ongoing attempts to resist globalization and the commodification of life. However, I have also sensed a good deal of confusion over the fundamental question of whether we ('Humanity,' our movement) are supposed to be just 'against neo-liberalism' or against capitalism itself. I am beginning to worry that using the phrase 'neo-liberalism' as an ideological short-cut to designate the global economic system may prove in the end to be imprecise if not dangerously misleading.

First, let us ask ourselves what is the difference between neo-liberalism and capitalism? Strictly speaking, the term 'neo-liberalism' refers either to an economic *theory* or to a *policy* based on that theory. The word 'capitalism,' on the other hand, designates an actual economic reality: the profit system we live under.

---

[45] Parts of this text were originally published in French as *Dangereux raccourcis et requins végétariens: Zapatisme et néolibéralisme* in Oiseau-tempête printemps 1998. Also, more completely, in *Temps critique* No. 11, hiver 1999

What Is Neo-Liberalism?

Neo-liberal economic *theory* is market fundamentalism based on Adam Smith's *The Wealth of Nations,* published in 1776. Smith's *laissez-faire* free trade liberalism was updated (hence the 'Neo') by Milton Friedman and his disciples at the University of Chicago – the famous 'Chicago Boys' who so disastrously advised Pinochet and Yeltsin in the 80s and 90s. It states that the 'invisible hand' of the market will, in all circumstances, inevitably lead to maximum happiness ('the greatest good of the greatest number' through capitalist competition unbridled by government regulation).

Market fundamentalism fell into disfavor after the stock market crashed in 1929, and in the 30's it was supplanted by Keynesian theory as exemplified by Roosevelt's New Deal and the post-war European Social Contract. Under the influence of Keynes and his disciples, the welfare state, government regulation of markets, and government investment in infrastructure were implemented in order to enable capitalism to survive the Depression, win WWII, reconstruct capitalist Europe and win the Cold War. However, in the 1980's, neo-liberal *policies* were re-introduced by Margaret Thatcher and Ronald Reagan in order to smash the power of trade unions, dismantle the welfare state, de-regulate markets, privatize basic industry, privatize social services and impose the same 'reforms' on the rest of the world through the international financial institutions like the IMF and World Bank.

Although today's neo-liberal theorists parade as throwbacks to Adam Smith and John Locke, true liberals who criticized royal monopolies, attacked censorship and other unfair restrictions, in fact the *Neos* have twisted their predecessors' 18th Century progressive liberal ideas about fair markets and free trade into justifications for imposing the interests of monopolies (transnational corporations) and for wiping out small producers everywhere in the world. The only markets the *Neos* worship are the financial markets. (Don't think 'farmers' market' think Chase Manhattan Bank.) Government intervention is 'bad' (welfare corrupts the poor and distorts the labor marker) except when it comes to bailing out failing companies and giving out no-bid contracts (corporate welfare. National markets in poor lands must be 'opened,' but only to capital hungry for cheap labor. As for hungry laborers looking for work, the 'open' market stops at the border of the rich capitalist countries.

Market fundamentalism has become unquestionable dogma in the media and the universities. None dare dissent from Margaret Thatcher's famous proclamation 'There is no alternative' (TINA) to market capitalism. Designed to raise the rate of profit, neo-liberal *policies* have been highly successful in increasing the wealth of investors at the expense of workers and the environment. The mushroom growth of de-regulated capital has now reached 1929 proportions, and one wonders when this speculative bubble will burst.

What Is Capitalism?

Capitalism (*aka* Free Enterprise or the 'profit system') is not a *theory* or a *policy* but an economic system – one that has been around for hundreds of years. Capitalism was global from its inception five centuries ago, as we were reminded in 1992 by the protests of the indigenous peoples of the Americas at the celebration of their disastrous *Encuentro* with Columbus in 1492. The capitalist *system* is defined as commodity-production based on the exploitation of wage-labor and nature. Throughout its history, various *theories* have been advanced to explain the origin of capitalist wealth and capitalism has adapted a variety of *policies*. These have ranged from mercantilism, free-trade, protectionism, monopoly-trust imperialism, welfare capitalism, to state-capitalism (with variations as diverse as Japanese feudal-trust capitalism, Stalinist 'Communism' and Nazi fascism) and now neo-liberalism. None of these *policies* changed capitalism's essence: the self-expansion of capital through the exploitation of nature and the extraction of unpaid labor-time from workers.

The danger of focusing exclusively on the apparently 'new' characteristics of 21st Century high-tech capitalism is that we tend to neglect its essential nature as the *system*; a *system* where profit derives exclusively from capital's 'theft' of unpaid labor (surplus value) and from the pillage of the land. Slogans like 'Against Neo-Liberalism' tend to distract from capitalism's systematic nature and focus peoples' energies on opposing the most recent *manifestations* of capitalism – corporate takeovers, downsizing, conglomeration, restructuring, integrated global systems, free-trade dogmatism, globalization. As if we could somehow turn back to a 'kinder, gentler capitalism.'

> **If sharks were men, they would build enormous boxes in the ocean for the little fish, with all kinds of food inside, both vegetable and animal. They would take care that the boxes always had fresh water, and in general they would make all kinds of sanitary arrangements. If, for example, a little fish were to injure a fin, it would immediately be bandaged, so that it would not die and be lost to the sharks before its time. So that the little fish would not become melancholy, there would be big water festivals from time to time; because cheerful fish taste better than melancholy ones.**
> **– Bertolt Brecht**

In any case, none of these neo-liberal manifestations is really new. Consolidation (big capital eating little capital) has always been the rule in the marketplace. The practice of downsizing to cut labor costs was seen by Marx as the 'absolute law of capitalist development' leading to a 'permanent reserve army of unemployed workers' at the disposal of capital. As far as 'globalization' is concerned, gold and silver stolen from the Native Americans financed the initial development of European capitalism in the 16th Century. By the 18th Century, British imperialism had developed enormously profitable integrated global chains of production and distribution (examples: Indian cotton woven in England for sale in India; the Atlantic triangular trade of sugar, slaves, guns and rum). And by 1900, Asia was producing fully 29% of the world's commodities, with Japanese ceramics flooding the Western markets.[46] By contrast, in 1996 Asia's share was only 22%. No wonder they call it 'Neo-liberalism'.

Substituting 'neo-liberalism' for 'capitalism' is not only imprecise, it may also be downright misleading – dangerously misleading for our Zapatista-inspired world social movements. If we are against neo-liberalism only, won't we be tempted to adopt a strategy of pressuring the powers-that-be to choose *another theory* (e.g. neo-Keynesianism) or *another economic policy* (e.g. protectionism)? Won't we be tempted to hope that under more benign policies the oppression of Humanity and the destruction of Nature would be checked or at least significantly diminished? Won't we be temped to tame the beast rather than to destroy it?

If such a reformist strategy were successful, it would certainly be a neat short-cut, and we wouldn't need to think about more frightening alternative scenarios. Most people would prefer to imagine that a harmless panacea like a Tobin-type tax on international finance would save the world – rather than focus on scarier prospects like living through the final crisis of the global capitalist system and facing the necessity for humanity to uproot it and build a new world on its ruins. Hoping for reform is surely more reassuring than thinking about some kind of planetary revolution, with all the upheaval and suffering such a prospect necessarily entails. But is it realistic?

Reformist Shortcuts and Vegetarian Sharks

Alas, *compañeros,* I am afraid that such reformist 'shortcuts' are based on a

---

[46] Personal disclosure: in 1900, Louis Greeman, my paternal grandfather, (also Jewish) worked as a wholesale salesman for a Tokyo porcelain manufacturer exporting Japanese 'Chinaware' to U.S. department stores; it was a good job, and in those days the British and U.S. firms in N.Y. wouldn't hire Jews.

dangerous illusion. They all tacitly assume that capitalism can be reformed. However, in my experience, trying to make capitalism change its nature makes about as much sense as trying to convert a shark to vegetarianism. It is also about as safe. By its nature, capitalism is no more capable of giving up the ruthless exploitation of humans and nature than the shark can give up blood and flesh. Just as a vegetarian shark would eventually starve to death, a capitalist corporation or nation that failed to pay its workers the minimum and extract the maximum would be eliminated by the competition of more ruthless 'sharks' in the world market. So would a 'green' capitalist who actually spent the necessary money to clean up his industrial wastes and raised his prices accordingly. I realize how scary it is to accept the fact that the only way out for humanity is to totally uproot the capitalist system. Taking the shortcut of being 'Against Neo-liberalism' is much easier and more popular. But is it fair to invite people to join us and dive into the troubled sea of social struggle without posting the warning: '*Danger! Shark-Infested Waters!?*'

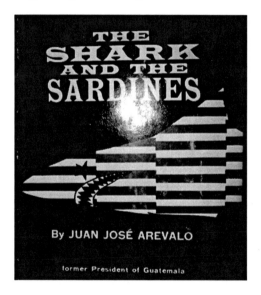

One of my first political memories dates from 1954, when I heard my parents talking about how the CIA overthrew the democratically-elected reformist government of Guatemala. What were Guatemala's crimes? A law recognizing workers' right to organize and strike and a proposal to buy up unused land at declared tax value and distribute it to the landless peasants. Unfortunately for the Guatemalans, the country's biggest employer, the United Fruit Company (Chiquita Banana), owned 85% of the land and had friends in Washington. So suddenly 'freedom' was at stake. After the CIA-directed *coup*, Guatemalan ex-President Juan Jose Arevalo published *The Fable of the Shark and the Sardines* concluding: 'Sharks will eat sardines forever and ever. But they should eat them plain, without doctrinal oil, without legal jelly, without the cellophane wrapping paper' of democratic ideology. I was too young to read his allegory at the time, but the cover image of a big U.S. shark eating little Latin American sardines has remained in my head to this day.

The next sardine I saw gobbled up was the Dominican Republic, which after years of dictatorship had elected a grandfatherly social-democrat named Juan Bosch. In 1965, Lyndon Johnson invaded the Dominican Republic with very little protest from the U.S. Left, already fixated on Vietnam. Yet all these tragic disasters didn't stop Chile's reformist President Salvator Allende from taking the same reformist shortcut a few years later. Only weeks before his government was overthrown in a bloody CIA-backed *coup*, Allende went on the radio urging Chileans to trust Chile's 'democratic army' and its chief of staff, General Pinochet, begging the organized peasants, workers' unions and militant students *not* to organized for self-defense. This time, *compañeros,* I was old enough not to believe in vegetarian sharks like 'democratic armies' and 'republican generals.' So it was with mixed feelings that I watched, impotent, when the inevitable army *coup* overthrew Allende in 1973. What to think about well-meaning reformist politicians whose tragic illusions consigned thousands of Chilean workers and intellectuals to decades of suffering under torture regimes?

The Welfare State

Some reformist opponents of neo-liberalism argue for a return to the welfare state as a goal for our Zapatista-inspired movements. They have an argument. During the Cold War period, Western capitalism developed the welfare state as a way of stimulating consumption while building a bulwark against Russia and attempts by Communists in the West to exploit worker discontent. This 'social contract' was at the same time an historic victory for workers in the West. Unemployment insurance, retirement, the right to organize, public schools, health and transportation were granted only after the huge strike waves of 1936 and 1946. But the social contract in the West was guaranteed (or rather enforced) by the threat of 'Communism' in the East. Although the state-capitalist regimes in Russia and China were internally exploitative, they did represent an alternative to the Western profit system - an alternative which remained attractive (at a distance) to many Western workers and oppressed minorities, like Jews and Blacks in the U.S. Indeed, the imperialist Kennedy-Johnson regime was forced to grant voting rights to 'Negroes' because their protests (and the racist violence they uncovered) were 'helping the Russians' by making Amerikkka look bad.

Thus, thanks to the New Deal and welfare capitalism, it seemed logical to see the national state itself as a 'progressive' and protective institution for more than a half-century. However, once the threat of Communism collapsed in 1989, Western capitalists felt free to resume naked exploitation as in the pre-1917 period. Neo-liberals like Thatcher (the 'milk-snatcher') immediately proceeded to dismantle the welfare state, thus increasing the rate of profit by cheapening the price of labor and making workers more vulnerable. Historically speaking, today's neo-liberalism is capital's counter-offensive against labor in the class war. It is an offensive aimed at turning back the clock and wiping out the historic victory of European labor and returning to the long hours, dangerous work, low pay and crying poverty described by writers like Dickens and Engels in the early 19th Century.

This counter-offensive must be fought at every turn, and in every land. U.S. wages can never rise until Mexican wages rise. We must fight it - as the Zapatistas have been fighting since the introduction of NAFTA - through movement struggle, and without any illusions about the 'welfare state.' The Zapatistas certainly have no illusions about their adversary. Mexico is the world's oldest welfare state, ruled for generations by the dictatorial Institutional Revolutionary Party. The *PRI*'s power is based on a police state and a corrupt welfare patronage system. Rather than succumbing to the insanity of trying to work *within* the Mexican government system or even pressuring it to change its shark-like nature, our *compañeros* and *compañeras* in Chiapas have sanely chosen to *ignore* it, while concentrating on grounding their movement in *themselves* and inviting others – ourselves – to do likewise! An original strategy and a promising one that some of us are trying to model in very different circumstances.

Nationalist Shortcuts

Unfortunately, reformism and the welfare state aren't the only vegetarian sharks on the 'neat shortcuts' market. We also have protectionism. To the extent that 'Neo-Liberalism' is synonymous with free market globalization, the slogan 'Anti-Globalization' misleadingly suggests that humanity might be better off under some form of *national* capitalism. This strategy looks very good on paper. But tactically, it is an open invitation to local activists in each country to form political alliances with protectionist elements among the 'patriotic' owning classes – who are also opposed to the penetration of 'globalized' capital. Such allies would include local exploiters defending their turf like landowners, businessmen, factory-owners, managers of state enterprises, religious leaders and military officers. All of the above groups have their own reasons to oppose multinational penetration (as well as to collaborate with it when their interest dictates). All are enemies of the rural poor, the workers and radicals like us.

The problem is that such protectionist or nationalist alliances in the name of 'Anti-Neo-Liberal-Globalization' can serve to camouflage the fundamental conflict between rich and poor within each country. For example, when my *compañeros* in the Detroit auto factories were attempting to organize solidarity with Japanese and Korean auto workers, the corporations together with officials of the United Auto Workers Union were urging workers to 'Buy American!' This patriotic frenzy did nothing to slow plant closings. Instead, it encouraged racism and war-mongering and led to the senseless vandalizing of Japanese cars in the workers' parking lot. Small wonder the most consistent protectionist opponents of globalization today are semi-fascist nationalists like France's Le Pen and Amerikkka's Pat Buchanan, who is apparently courting anti-globalist NGO's with some success. Like these NGO's, the super-patriotic racist reactionaries are *also* fighting against Neo-Liberal Globalization in the name of 'national sovereignty.' People always say 'politics makes strange bedfellows,' but do we really want to go to bed with these racist sharks?[47]

> If sharks were men there would be an end to all little fish being equal, as is the case now. Some would be given important offices and be placed above the others. Those who were a little bigger would even be allowed to eat up the smaller ones. That would be altogether agreeable for the sharks, since they themselves would more often get bigger bites to eat. And the bigger little fish, occupying their posts, would ensure order among the little fish, become teachers, officers, engineers in box construction, etc. – Bertolt Brecht

Illusions about the national state can also be dangerous. Since every *national* capitalist economy competes with every other, the rich in each country will inevitably try to mobilize the poor for fratricidal slaughter in 'democratic' or 'patriotic' wars against the 'imperialist aims' of another *national* capitalist group. World War I was sold as a war to 'save democracy' from *German* imperialism. In fact, millions died to protect J.P. Morgan's British investments

---

[47] *Update 2007.* Ten years later, there is no shortage of strange bedfellows on the political scene: Who, a few years ago, would have dreamed that Lula of the Brazilian PT would end up in bed with George Bush or that Venezuela's Bolivarian President Chavez would be seen cavorting in Teheran with Ahmadinejad, the reactionary President of the Islamic Republic of Iran?

from German competition. During the 1930's, Hitler's NAZI's (*'National Socialist Workers Party'*) used xenophobic propaganda to mobilize the *volk* against the 'stranglehold' of international *Jewish* capitalism and *British* imperialism. During the same period, Japanese capital militarized to fight the penetration of Asia by *white, European* capital. In 1949 Mao-Tse Tung's 'Communist' Chinese regime was established on the basis of yet another neat shortcut: Mao's theory of the 'block of four classes' which united the workers and peasants behind the *'patriotic* landowners' and the *'nationalist* bourgeoisie' in the fight for *national* sovereignty against the foreign capitalists. The workers never got their rights under Mao, and today's 'Communist' China invites the foreign capitalist in to exploit them while the Party assures 'national sovereignty' in its claims on Hong Kong and Taiwan.

Jaws

Can we count on the nation-state as an ally for our new social movements? The day I see the state protecting strikers from goons and shielding demonstrators from fascists is the day I will start believing in *that* particular vegetarian shark. The state's main function down through history has been the repression of the poor majority in the interests of the rich minority. On this point Anarchists, Marxists and even 'realist' political scientists are all agreed. The nation-state is the capitalists' ultimate weapon in the class struggle. Its essence is the monopoly of violence in a given (or contested) geographical area. If capitalism is a shark, the state represents its jaws – the jaws with which it rends the flesh of its prey in order to devour them. The modern state's jaws are double-lined with razor teeth, row upon row of police departments, prisons, oppressive administrations, standing armies and secret armies like the CIA.

Appealing to existing nation-states to save us from the depredations of neo-liberal policies (for which it is the chief enforcer both at home and abroad) is truly asking the capitalist shark not only to turn vegetarian but to have his teeth filed down as a sign of good will – especially as national states are becoming more and more violent and repressive. On the other hand, if the majority of working people in a given country were to win the battle of democracy and gain power over the state, new opportunities might appear. But only on two conditions: 1. that popular democracy spreads quickly to other lands and breaks down national borders; and 2. that the mass movement quickly dismantles the permanent apparatus of regular police, armies and prisons and replaces them with people power. Otherwise, the dangers of corruption, militarization and bureaucratization are apparently irresistible, as the tragic examples of Russia, China, post-colonial Africa, Vietnam and even Cuba seem to indicate.

Dangerous Shortcuts of the Past:
Anti-Imperialism and Anti-Fascism

The danger of national revolutions turning sour after conquering state power reminds me of a shortcut which mislead my own political generation: the anti-imperialism of the 1960's. Since our anti-war and anti-imperialist movements never focused on the capitalist system as the root cause of war and racism, they ended up getting lost in every imaginable short-cut. Some of us got sidetracked into supporting capitalist 'peace candidates' like U.S. Senator 'Clean-for-Gene' McCarthy. Others ended up cheer-leading for state-capitalist dictators like Enver Hoxa, Mao Tse-tung, Kim Il Sung, Colonel Quadaffi and Ho Chi Minh among other *bona fide* anti-imperialists. During those heady days of campaigns, marches and red brigades, no one had time to listen to the minority among us who had understood that 'imperialism' is not a *policy* but the *essence* of capitalism. No one heeded the voices of the anarchists and critical Marxists who had understood that so-called 'Communism' was merely another name for totalitarian, bureaucratic state-capitalism and who saw that 'national liberation' might mean fighting and dying to replace a foreign oppressor with a native one.

Today, the 'anti-imperialist' rulers of liberated Vietnam and 'Communist' China whose pictures some of us carried in demonstrations are busy getting rich by shamelessly luring foreign capitalists to come over and exploit their workers under hideous sweat-shop conditions: conditions that vanished from the major industrial countries nearly a century ago. These profitable (for capitalism) conditions are held in place by a 'revolutionary' one-party-state – celebrated by the editorialist of the *NY Times* under the headline: 'Long live Mao's legacy and Merrill Lynch!'[48] To be sure, 'anti-imperialism' was easier to explain than 'anti-capitalism.' For my generation, Ho Chi Minh was the George Washington of Vietnam and Mao the Great Helmsman – even when he undermined the Vietnamese resistance by cutting a deal with Nixon and Kissinger. Some shortcuts!

---

[48] *N.Y. Times*, June 3, 1997. Merill Lynch was one of the biggest traders on Wall Street until the Crash of 2008.

The Popular-Front anti-fascism of my parents' generation, which I grew up on, also turned out to be a dangerous shortcut. Why did the anti-fascists fail to stop fascism in Spain (or elsewhere in Europe) in 1936-39? Why did the French Resistance lead to the re-establishment of French capitalism and the French colonial empire? Was it not in part because they took a short-cut, the co-called Popular Front? This anti-fascist alliance of Stalinist Communists, Social-Democrats and liberal-democratic capitalist parties, was broad, powerful and impressive. It mobilized mass trade-unions, youth and cultural organizations. But after all the wonderful folk-songs were sung and the stirring rallies rallied, Pop Front 'anti-fascist' European socialists like French Socialist Premier Leon Blum sold out the Spanish Republic when General Franco (backed by Hitler and Mussolini) launched his fascist *coup*. Even the leaders of Spanish Anarcho-Syndicalism (CNT) and Anarchism (FIA) succumbed to the Communist-dominated United Front Against Fascism and betrayed their principles by becoming government Ministers, abstaining from all criticism, and printing pro-Russian propaganda in their newspapers – much to the dismay of the Russian-American Anarchist, Emma Goldman. Meanwhile, the workers and farmers of Spain were heroically combating both fascism *and* capitalism, only to be stabbed in the back by the Stalinist Communists.[49] Two years later the French, demoralized by Republican Spain's defeat, caved in to Hitler at Munich. Finally, even the Communists abandoned anti-fascism when Stalin signed his infamous military pact with Hitler in 1939.

If sharks were men, they would, of course, also wage wars against one another, in order to conquer other fish boxes and other little fish. The wars would be waged by their own little fish. They would teach their little fish that there was an enormous difference between themselves and the little fish belonging to the other sharks. Little fish, they would announce, are well known to be mute, but they are silent in quite different languages and hence find it impossible to understand one another. Each little fish that, in a war, killed a couple of other little fish, enemy ones, silent in their own language, would have a little order made of seaweed pinned to it and be awarded the title of hero. – Bertolt Brecht

---

It took five years and 20 million dead in WWII to stop Hitler. After the war was won, the majority of French capitalists could and should have been expropriated (if not shot) for collaborating with the Nazi German occupiers. But thanks to a new Popular Front alliance, de Gaulle and the Communists took over the workers' and peasants' Resistance, substituted patriotism for the

---

[49] Ken Loache's 1995 movie *Land and Freedom* tells that tale most accurately, as did writers at the time like George Orwell (*Hommage to Catalonia*), Emma Goldman (*Vision on Fire: Emma Goldman on the Spanish Revolution*) and Victor Serge (*Memoirs of a Revolutionary*); but who listened?

slogan 'From the Resistance to the Revolution,' and laid the basis for the post-war capitalist reconstruction of France and the re-conquest of France's colonies. Capitalism itself was never called into question. As a result, the revolution was put off to *mañana,* the French CP and SP voted to send French troops to Indochina and Algeria, and government officials with the blood of deported Jews on their hands made an easy transition from Vichy France to high office in the IVth and V[th] French Republics. Today, fascism and racism are on the rise again in Europe - in both France and post-Soviet Russia. Anti-fascism: some great shortcut!

Avoiding the C-word, the M-word and the R-word

Compañeros, I understand how the slogan 'Against Neo-Liberalism' – translated from a Latin American context rich in cultural resonances – came to be adopted by our new social movements in a new global context. I also sympathize with the desire of our movement to appear non-sectarian and to avoid ideologically 'loaded' expressions like 'proletariat,' 'class struggle' and 'capitalism.' On the other hand, I wonder why so many activists should resist using the correct term, capitalism, when even bourgeois economics text-books and conservative editorial writers are not afraid to use the C-word to designate the profit system we live under. Why should we be afraid to talk about 'capitalism' and 'class' when the *Wall Street Journal* screams 'class struggle!' every time the Democrats even consider taxing profits and when the most influential business magazine in the U.S. cheerfully advertises itself as '*FORBES: Capitalist Tool*?'

One explanation for the near-phobic avoidance of C-words like capitalism and class is that a certain Karl Marx used them, and we don't want to be labeled as 'Marxists.' Neither did Marx himself, who famously wrote: 'If I know one thing, it is that I am not a Marxist.' To be sure, many people today react to Marxist terminology as ideological, tainted, and worst of all *passé.* So we are forced to re-invent the wheel of 'capitalism' and awkwardly rename it 'that neo-liberal round thing that rolls.' If we continue to follow this politically correct logic, we will end up unable to refer to other basic realities like 'evolution,' 'the unconscious mind,' and 'gravity.' After all, Darwin, Freud and Newton are also ideological, tainted and *passé.* And we don't want to exclude or offend creationists, Pavlovians, and flat-earthers – much less appear 'elitist.'

98

Kidding aside, to me the worst kind of elitism consists of talking down to people and sugar-coating unpleasant truths. I still remember the fellow-traveling French existentialists of the 1950's hiding the truth about slave-labor in the Russian *gulag* from the French workers so as 'not to lead Billancourt [the big auto factory near Paris] to despair.' Maybe if the Left intellectuals of the 50's had had the honesty to tell the truth about Stalinism, Billancourt workers wouldn't be voting for Le Pen's National Front - as many do precisely out of despair - and we wouldn't have the neo-liberal Parisian 'new philosophers' dominating the intellectual scene. Today's post-modern generation is justified in remaining highly suspicious of totalizing ideals and grand narratives inherited from the 18th and 19th Centuries. Concepts such as rationality, science and 'progress' have served to justify untold horrors under both free enterprise and Communism. The 20th Century, with its murderous eugenics, its totalitarian police states, its mechanized mass destruction of civilians, cities and whole peoples has revealed where such totalizing concepts can lead. Let us therefore remain suspicious, vigilant, critical, unafraid to analyze and deconstruct all such absolutist notions. But let's not throw out the baby of clarity with the bath water of long-dead totalizing ideas and grand narratives, tragically accepted at face value by earlier generations.

If sharks were men, there would, of course, also be schools in the big boxes. In these schools the little fish would learn how to swim into the sharks' jaws. They would need to know geography, for example, so that they could find the big sharks, who lie idly around somewhere. The principal subject would, of course, be the moral education of the little fish. They would be taught that it would be the best and most beautiful thing in the world if a little fish sacrificed itself cheerfully and that they all had to believe the sharks, especially when the latter said they were providing for a beautiful future. The little fish would be taught that this future is assured only if they learned obedience. The little fish had to beware of all base, materialist, egotistical and Marxist inclinations, and if one of their number betrayed such inclinations they had to report it immediately to the sharks.   – Bertolt Brecht

---

Calling things by their true name: that, in my opinion, is the beginning of wisdom and honesty, whether we're talking to our children about death and sex or to people in struggle about capitalism and revolution. In either case, there is no such thing as 'non-ideological' vocabulary. Every phrase betrays its underlying ideological context - religious or political. The dominant ideological dogma today is TINA: 'There Is No Alternative' (understood: to *capitalism*). This ideology is so pervasive as to be nearly invisible in the mainstream media and academic discourse, where alternative ideas are broached only to be ridiculed as 'Utopian.' This stifling context demands that we avoid such 'ideological' and *passé* words as 'capitalism,' 'class' and 'revolution.' So we talk about post-modernism, post-industrialism, post-Fordism, identity, subaltern groups, globalization, and neo-liberalism. Even those of us who consciously seek to create alternatives often unconsciously limit ourselves to alternatives *within* capitalism. But is it possible to cure the symptoms of neo-liberalism without attacking the disease – capitalism?

What Did Marx *Really* Say?

So let's let down our ideological guard for just a moment and take a quick look at what Marx (rather than his enemies or his degenerate disciples) actually had to say about capitalism and revolution. In 1867, Marx published his famous and unread book on *Capital*. In the first volume, Marx picked up the analysis of capitalism where the neo-liberals' idol Adam Smith had left off in 1776. Marx's only original addition to Smith's description of the capitalist market place was this: human labor, unlike its material products, is a living, feeling, creative being, not a commodity. Although in a fair marketplace, all commodities are ideally exchanged at their value, human labor is not a fixed, lifeless object like other forms of merchandise. Not only does human labor feel and suffer, it also creates new value in the process of being 'consumed' by its purchaser, the capitalist, who gets to keep that new value created by the laborer. A day of human labor may routinely produce commodities worth two, three or twenty times more value than the value of the wage the boss paid the worker for a day's work. Put another way, in the first two or four hours of her working day, the sewing machine operator creates a quantity of blue-jeans equivalent to the values her day's pay allows her to consume in food, heat, rent etc. For the rest of the day, which may be extended to eight or ten or twelve or more hours, she works free for the boss.

Marx identified this 'surplus' value as the true source of the capitalists' profit (assuming that the capitalists have already seized the land and are able to exploit nature at will). The search for surplus value is the reason why the capitalists are always trying to squeeze more labor out of their workers through mechanization, automation, longer hours and speedups; why they are constantly scouring the planet for new sources of cheap labor to exploit. Unlike his command-economy Communist disciples, the real Marx had no problem with markets (where he bought his vegetables when he could afford them). What he rejected was the *labor market*, in which human creative activity (labor) is degraded into an object to be bought and sold for profit like a cup or a cabbage; what enraged him was capitalism's 'werewolf hunger' for cheaper and cheaper labor, including women and young children, which he saw devouring the European poor in his day as it devours the global poor in ours.

So when we chant 'I am not a commodity' or 'the world is not a commodity' we are mouthing Marxist slogans without realizing it. Nor is there anything in Marx's economic analysis of *Capital* that Anarchists and other libertarians should object to. After all, didn't Marx's arch-enemy, the famous anarchist Bakunin, translate *Capital* into Russian? In the later volumes of *Capital* Marx went on to analyze 19th Century capitalism's basic laws of motion: capitalism's need to constantly expand production and seek new markets; its ever-increasing concentration of wealth into fewer and fewer hands, the spread of poverty and inequality, the permanence of mass unemployment ('the absolute general law' of capitalist development). Do any of these economic tendencies still sound relevant today?

Moreover, before he died Marx saw the rise of huge powerful trusts and realized that market capitalism might transform itself into its own opposite! If competition could turn into monopoly, if national rivalry could turn into international cartels, then theoretically, market capitalism could turn into a single capitalist economy *without changing its exploitative essence.* This 'state-capitalism' is precisely what developed in Russia in the 1930's after the 1917 Revolution, isolated and besieged, succumbed to the dictatorship of a brutal self-serving bureaucracy which had usurped the title 'Communist.' Stalin and his successors 'applied' Marx's original ideas the same way the Spanish Inquisition 'applied' the preachings of the historical Jesus. Today's right-wing billionaire evangelists *claim* to be Christians in order to bilk the poor, dictators of every stripe will often *claim* to be Marxists in order to fool the poor into supporting them. Should we blame these travesties on Jesus and Marx?

Marx and the State

Far from being the prophet of the totalitarian state, Marx's analysis of politics led him to the same conclusion as the anarchists – that the essence of the state (whether parliamentary or dictatorial) was class violence. He defined the state as consisting of 'special bodies of armed men, prisons, etc' organized for the purposes of repression in order to maintain the status quo in favor of the rich. Today, we face a new proliferation of such armies, police forces, militias, prisons and other repressive apparatuses multiplying in every land. In our age of increasing inequality, these 'special bodies' are necessary to protect the billionaires from the billions. Marx saw socialism as full democracy, spread to the economic sphere. He saw 'democratic' capitalist government as a kind of 'central committee' of the bourgeoisie, ruling in the interest of capital and arbitrating its inner quarrels via parliaments. Today, big money, in the form of huge political contributions and media ownership, more and more dominate 'democratic' politics everywhere, while 'reforms' always end up making the rich richer and the poor poorer.

The War of the Classes

Finally, in his political writings (beginning with *The Communist Manifesto* of 1848) Marx developed the historical observation that the struggle between classes (masters *versus* slaves, landlords *versus* peasants, aristocrats *versus* bourgeois, capitalists *versus* workers, etc.) may, when the times are ripe, result in revolutionary changes in society. (He also noted that theses struggles may also lead to mutual destruction.) Reviewing the historical transitions from ancient slave empires to feudalism and from feudalism to capitalism, Marx observed that each of these social systems, however 'natural' 'permanent' or 'given' they may have appeared to their contemporaries, was in fact transitory. From this he concluded that capitalism, too, should be considered transitory and that hence, 'another world' was not just desirable, but historically *possible*.

As an activist, Marx devoted himself to the practical job of helping workers from many countries to organize themselves *internationally*. Precisely because he saw capitalism as a *global* system, he made 'Working people of all countries unite!' his motto. Like most 19th Century radicals, Marx saw cooperation and mutual aid as the principle of the emerging new society, which was commonly known as 'socialism' or 'communism.' Marx did not invent the terms nor did he ever propose a blueprint, leaving that to Utopians like Owen, Fourier and Saint-Simon. *Internationalism* was the essence of his teaching, *criticism* that of his method. Opposed to all sectarianism, he rejected the label 'Marxist' (invented by his opponents) and feared having his ideas distorted and dogmatized by his 'followers.' For these reasons, he and Engels never tried to form a 'Marxist Party.' It didn't bother them that the vast majority of the members of the *International Workers' Association,* the organization to which Marx devoted his energies as Secretary, were followers of his rival, the French anarchist Proudhon. So indeed were most of the Communards of Paris, whom Marx hailed in 1871 as the creators of the first socialist society. For Marx it was not doctrine that counted, it was the *'actual movement'* of the masses creating a new society in their own image.

Capitalist Crisis and Revolutionary Emergence

Marx saw the new world *emerging* from the ashes of the old – as bourgeois capitalism had emerged from the ruins of corrupt, decadent, bankrupt aristocracies. According to Marx, capitalism was a bloated system doomed to die of indigestion – that is to say, of overproduction. For Marx, capitalism's essential need constantly to expand production is in direct contradiction with its other essential need: to keep wages as low as possible and to eliminate 'surplus' workers in order to increase the rate of profit. But if there are fewer and fewer workers with money to spend, who is going to buy up all those mountains of commodities (most of them useless) the capitalists keep churning out? Marx saw depressions and wars as capitalism's way of getting rid of all those mountains of un-saleable commodities in order to wipe the slate clean and begin a new cycle of production. Not only is capitalism transitory, Marx believed, it is also in permanent crisis. Capitalism was therefore doomed to collapse as a result of its own inner contradiction, under the pressure of the emerging new society. It would be overthrown by the revolt of the oppressed - culminating in the global uprising of the true producers of social wealth, the working men and women of the world. Such was Marx's vision.

It is true that Marx saw the growing class of wage-workers created by capitalist expansion as capital's natural antagonist and its eventually 'grave-digger.' However, near the end of his life Marx began to feel that the attachment of pre-capitalists peoples to their communal culture and economy (for example the Russian peasants' *mir* or communal village) represented both a form of resistance to capitalism's degradation and – along with the organized workers – an embryo of a future society. To me, today's Zapatista movement represents just such an embryo.

The problem is that Marx (like ourselves) had no way of knowing *when* capitalism's collapse (and humanity's emergence) might occur. On the one hand, Marx assumed that the final crisis could come quickly, especially as capitalism's periodic boom and bust cycle seemed to be getting more severe as the 19th Century drew to a close. On the other hand, Marx's theory indicated that global capital would never stop expanding until it had taken over the whole earth, enclosed all the open lands, uprooted the last independent farmers and turned every human into a dependent consumer of commodities - whether as a wage-slave or a member of the 'unemployed reserve army.' For as long as capitalism can keep expanding and overproducing, it can compensate for the tendency of the *rate* of profit to decline, by an ever-increasing *mass* of profits.

As a revolutionary, Marx *hoped* that the workers would put an end to capitalism long before it devoured the whole planet. Unfortunately during the 20th Century, as capitalism careened from world war to depression to world war, the ultimate goal got lost while 'revolutionary' leaders (many of them self-described 'Marxists') led humanity into dangerous shortcuts like nationalism, reformism and state-capitalism. Will the coming 21st Century be able to stop capitalism before it devours the earth and its peoples? Not if we fail to call it by its name. Not if we keep on taking dangerous shortcuts and convincing ourselves that the capitalist shark can be converted to vegetarianism.

Back to 'Neo-liberalism' vs. 'Capitalism'

Although Marx's name remains anathema, his analyses seem more and more relevant (and are generally followed in practice by capitalists and stock market analysts!). So powerful is this anathema that even Sub-Commander Marcos, in his recent manifesto 'The Fourth World War Has Begun: Six Pieces of a Puzzle'[50] expounds precisely the six Marxian points outlined above (unemployment, pauperization, concentration, accumulation, and globalization of capital) without once alluding to Marx or his theories. As a result, when the reader gets to the conclusion – the 'Seventh Piece' of the 'Puzzle' – we are no longer sure whether the 'Fourth World War' Marcos has declared is the war between the rich and the poor or the war between 'Globalization' and 'National Sovereignty.' This ambiguity remains a point of tension in our movements. To be sure, concepts like Globalization and Neo-Liberalism are illuminating and useful in describing aspects of our modern condition. But we must not allow them to become substitutes for its essence, capitalism, lest we be unconsciously led into ideological shortcuts like reformism, protectionism, the welfare-state, anti-fascism and anti-imperialism. Such shortcuts usually turn out to be roads to Hell, which, as George Bernard Shaw remarked, are always 'paved with good intentions.'

---

[50] *Le Monde diplomatique* August 1997

Good Intentions

Our burgeoning Zapatista-inspired movements have already understood that 'the world is not a commodity' to be bought and sold. What needs to be understood next is that the commodity-culture cannot be overcome until wage-labor, the alienated human activity that produces commodities, is abolished. Only then can we live like human beings, as the Indigenous of Chiapas are attempting to do against terrible odds. This humanism contrasts with previous movements (Social-democratic, Communist, etc.), which often got stuck inside the capitalist game by simply demanding *more* for the workers or by assuming that if only the *state* would replace the market, capitalism would be different. In this respect, our Zapatistan analysis – based on the humanist philosophy of *pre-capitalist* indigenous people whose revolt is a refusal of wage-labor commodity society – is a thousand times closer to the original ideas of Marx than the analysis of most of the self-designated 'Marxists.' And we are light-years ahead of all the welfare state-ists, social-democrats, nationalizers and 'communists' with their bureaucratic panaceas.

The Chiapans have understood, as Marx himself did, that capital is not a *thing* but a *human relationship* – a power relationship which enables one person or class first to steal other peoples' land, then to steal their labor, and finally to disguise this theft under the 'free and fair exchange' of money for labor power. Like the original Marx, they understand that this perverted, money-mediated relationship must be uprooted and replaced by *new human relationships* based on equality, cooperation and community. But can humanity accomplish this task without using the *name* of the beast we must face and conquer – capitalism?

105

Jimmy Carter's Imperial American Peace Prize [2002][51]

Ex-President Jimmy Carter deserves the Nobel Peace Prize for 2002 for at least one reason: his name isn't George W. Bush. And because he finally expressed his tactical hesitations about the latter's mad march toward war in Iraq. But let's look behind the mask of this champion of humanitarianism who has been criss-crossing the globe for the last twenty years that he's been out of work. If we examine the essence, his record as President in office, what do we find? An efficient and unscrupulous defender of the interests of the American Empire.

Carter's Background As a career officer in the U.S. Navy, Carter served the Empire as the Commander of nuclear submarines armed with atomic missiles – the weapon of terror *par excellence.* They give the U.S. the capability of launching a surprise 'preventive' nuclear attack from the enemy's coastline. A few minutes later and their cities and military sites are incinerated. Nuclear subs, which can survive under the oceans during a victorious enemy attack, also provide Mutually Assured Destruction (MAD) as a deterrent. After the Navy, Carter went into politics and got himself elected Governor of the State of Georgia, where the wages were among the lowest in the South, thanks to racism and union-busting.

Carter the Internationalist. But Jimmy Carter was not a Neanderthal. He learned all about how the world runs while patrolling it as an officer of the Imperial American Navy, famous for its 'gunboat diplomacy' and its Marines

---

[51] Translated from the French, *Jimmy Carter: Prix Nobel de la paix impérialiste américaine* published in 2002 in *Herault du Jour,* Montpellier.

106

– always at the ready when it comes to overthrowing foreign governments disloyal to U.S. banks and corporations. The peanut farmer became an internationalist. He participated in seminars at the Trilateral Commission, a semi-secret elite society presided by Nelson Rockerfeller, the billionaire Governor of New York. Rockerfeller had made several tries at running for President and always come a cropper. He made Carter his *protégé*. This humble son of Dixie, with his peanut farm, could actually get elected to the White House, whereas the great representative of finance capital never could himself, for all his billions. Once elected, Carter proclaimed 'human rights' as the motto of his Presidency. But he remained faithful to his Wall Street patrons and defended their global interests around the world. Some examples:

Carter Organizes the *Contras*. In 1979, the Nicaraguans succeeded in overthrowing the bloody dictatorship of the Somosa family, in power since 1934. The Marines under President Roosevelt had imposed the rule of Anastasio Somosa, the Chief of the infamous National Guards and murderer of the agrarian rebel, Sandino, after whom the rebels of 1979 named their revolution. At last democracy triumphed after forty years of ferocious repression. The rebels were young, democratic, liberation Catholics, home-grown *Sandinistas*. None of them were even Communists. What did Carter do? He demanded that the bloody National Guard retain their power to maintain imperialist "order." Then the CIA, under Carter's orders, regrouped exiled National Guards into a terrorist army and sent them back to Nicaragua to destroy the new government, which contemplated sharing out the lands of Somicista *émigrés*. They call this terrorist gang the *Contras*.

I saw them at work in Occotàl and Léon [Nicaragua, in 1984]. They were systematically torturing and murdering nurses, agronomists, volunteer alphabetization teachers and cooperative leader. One day, a copy of an actual CIA manual teaching this method of "targeted assassinations" was found on the body of a fallen *Contra*. (It was also known that the CIA had brought in former Argentinean torturers as their instructors). The CIA manual was explicitly designed to particularly target humanitarian workers so as to kill the idealism of the Nicaraguan people, nullify their progress in health, literacy, agriculture, and undermine their democratic revolution. That was humanitarianism *à la Carter.*

Carter Supports the Salvadoran Death Squads. In El Salvador, Carter supported the government based on right-wing death-squads *escuadros de la muerte*. He proclaims this government 'democratic' after a show-election held at bayonet-point. In 1980, this government massacred 10,000 peasants, trade unionists and resistors thanks to millions in military aid, munitions and advisors sent by Carter. Carter was unshaken by the murder of Oscar Romero, the Archbishop of San Salvador, in his Cathedral or the machine-gunning in the Cathedral Square of hundreds of his followers at his funeral. Only when four U.S. nuns were raped and murdered by Salvadoran soldiers was military aid suspended and replaced by 'humanitarian' aid to the government of assassins. More humanitarianism *à la Carter*.

Carter's Humanitarianism in Asia. In South Korea in the Spring of 1980, workers and students organized huge demonstrations against the military dictatorship of Chun Doo Hwan. Carter's Ambassador advised the South Korean generals to crack down on them. A thousand demonstrators were massacred on May 17 at Kwangju. Similarly, let us recall the *Khmer rouge* mass murderers in Cambodia with their pyramids of skulls. After they weredefeated by the North Vietnamese, Carter intervened to offer them 'humanitarian' support (poor things!) to get them back on their feet and ready to fight. Carter also sent military aid to Indonesia, whose bloody military dictatorship had just brutally annexed East Timor, the newly independent former Dutch colony. They slaughter thousands while Carter's Ambassador organized a cover-up.

Carter in Afghanistan and Africa. And guess what U.S. President began the secret CIA operations in Afghanistan? Guess who first supported the fundamentalist *mujahedeen* against the pro-Soviet government and built the networks that eventually included Osama bin Laden? I admit that the Communist Afghani government, which educated women to be doctors, teachers, and technicians didn't support 'human rights' *à la Carter*. So Carter was forced to impose a regime of raping, plundering, opium-trading, fundamentalist warlords over the Afghani women. And it was Carter again who, before Reagan and Bush, boycotted the UN Special Conferences organized in 1978 and 1980 to redress North-South inequalities and confront racism, thus sabotaging the hopes of a whole period of decolonialization. So it was in the name of the humanitarian neo-liberalism promoted by Carter that they began to dismantle social services and public infrastructure in Africa, ushering in the period of famines and epidemics he now runs around trying to cure through charitable works.

Carter and the Shah. In 1979, a popular revolution overthrew the dictatorship of the Shah of Iran and his terrible secret police, *Savak*. Remember that during its first year, this revolution remained in the hands of democratic moderates. It was a revolution of unionized oil workers, Air Force non-coms and technicians, Marxist students and young feminists as well as that of *bazaar* merchants and Ayatollahs organized behind Khomeini. Democracy was possible, a new edition of Prime Minister Mossadegh's democracy, overthrown by the CIA in 1953 to place the Shah and his torture regime back in power.

What did Carter do? First, he offered his Presidential protection to the Shah – the Rockerfeller's close friend – in the name of 'humanitarianism.' Then he rebuffed the overtures of the government of moderates, thus opening the doors to the fundamentalist dictatorship of Khomeini. But Carter also knew how to divide and rule. He sent arms to Saddam Hussein, dictator of Iraq and former

CIA 'property,' who felt his own power threatened by the contagion of the Iranian revolution. Thanks to U.S. support, Saddam was able to continue the war against Iran for eight years, with a total of about three million slaughtered.

The End of Carter's Presidency But Carter's Iranian adventure destroyed his Presidency when Iranian *mujahedeen* made hostages of the personnel of the U.S. Embassy. For it was presidential candidate Ronald Reagan who, more wily than Carter, made a secret deal with the Ayatollah to prolong the crisis until the 1980 election, which Reagan won easily. This tricky maneuver has gone down in history as Reagan's October Surprise. So if, today, Carter is laudably expressing his reservations about Bush Jr.'s plan to make war on his poor ex-agent Saddam, it is for purely tactical reasons. U.S. troops run the risk of getting bogged down in Iraq, while terrorism spreads out of it. Moreover, a war could destabilize the shaky world economy to the detriment of Wall Street interests. So by criticizing the policy of the Texan adventurist Sheriff George W. Bush Commander Carter, Rockerfeller's *gendarme,* remains faithful at his post.

Glory to Wall Street's humanitarian mercenary! Like his predecessor, the U.S. war criminal Kissinger, Carter well deserves the Nobel Prize for Imperial American Peace!

A Bit of Political History: American society has always been torn between its progressive, libertarian, democratic traditions on the one hand, and its decadent, violent, reactionary slave culture on the other – an idea we develop below in "Religion and Repression in the U.S." In terms of electoral politics, the majorities of the progressive Democratic Party of Wilson and Roosevelt were based upon a tacit alliance between immigrant workers and the educated middle class in the Northern cities, and the "Dixiecrats" of the apartheid Southern states where only Whites could vote and the Democrats ruled as the only political party on the local level. But in 1968 this coalition was shaken apart by Black rebellion and Democratic President Lyndon Johnson's support of civil rights and racial equality. In reaction, the Dixiecrats deserted to the conservative Republican Party, thus tipping the Southern vote to the reactionary presidency of Richard Nixon (Nixon's famous 'Southern strategy'). This New Right now dominates the American political scene. Nixon, then Reagan, waged a cultural war against the gains of the 1960's (the right to abortion, sexual freedom, anti-racism), a crusade in which Bush II is the new Christian knight-in-shining-armor. But the two Democratic presidents, Carter and Clinton, (both former governors of Southern states) remained within this neo-liberal and warmongering framework, despite a lot of fancy words about "human rights."

As we have seen, Carter of Georgia turned a blind eye to the right-wing death-squad murder of the Archbishop of El Salvador, and it was Clinton of Arkansas who first bombed Afghanistan and the Sudan and set forth the new doctrine of American military unilateralism which Bush of Texas picked up to justify his war on Iraq. My French readers may not be aware that Carter's Georgia is in the running with Trent Lott's Mississippi, George W. Bush's Texas, and Bill Clinton's Arkansas for the Poverty Prize, the Ignorance Prize and the White Supremacist Prize. The reactionary powers of 'Dixie' – the geographically small region made up of former secessionist slave states – more or less dominates U.S. politics. Senators from Dixie still dominate the Federal Congress through control of the committee system, and more than half of U.S. Presidents, among them Johnson, Carter, Clinton, and Bush hail from Dixie. So do the majority of ranking officers in the U.S. military. Two other modern Presidents, Nixon and Reagan, came from Southern California (settled by white Southerners) and won office by appealing to the formerly Democratic South. Dixie still harbors powerful racist and Christian Right organizations, not to mention more or less fascist militias.

Iraq: Who are the 'good guys' (if any)?

The U.S.-led war in Iraq has now been going on for almost as long as WWII. The U.S. is still dropping tons of cluster-bombs (banned by most civilized nations) on areas populated by civilians – killing and maiming thousands of children in the areas the occupiers are bound by international law to protect. All the polls show that the vast majority of Iraqis – and of Americans – want the U.S. *out.* Ending this obscene war ought to be the top priority of every decent American. Yet the U.S. anti-war movement – having banked its hopes with the Democrats in 2004 (remember Kerry?) and 2006 – remains for the most part somnolent.

Baghdad burning

Sadly, the tens of thousands of activists who braved the winter cold to demonstrate in D.C. and other cities in January 2007 got almost no press, while the anti-war liberals sat in front of their TV's waiting for the Democrats to pass some wimpy non-binding resolution while voting billions for Bush's new surge. Every time I forget why I *hate* liberals (our main enemy in the Vietnam 'Sixties) they do something like that to remind me.

So the burden of resisting the war has fallen on the shoulders of the soldiers and their families, who are increasingly outraged at being sacrificed in a rich man's war fought by the poor. It takes courage to defy the Green Machine while in uniform! Meanwhile, the Military and Veteran's Administration (its budget slashed by Bush in the first weeks of the war) are turning away wounded vets on the pretext of non-existent 'previous conditions' while the Dems, like the Republicans, claim to be 'supporting our troops.' Alas, the self-appointed vanguards of the Left, instead of capitalizing on this scandalous situation to arouse the populace, are as usual engaging in ideological faction

111

fights. Their manipulative tactics and efforts to dominate the broader anti-war coalitions, succeed in bringing division and demoralization to a movement which seemed so promising in 2003, when it mobilized millions both before and after the actual U.S. invasion. What's the problem here?

The Occupation

As we are all aware the occupation, far from instituting democracy in Iraq, has brought its people nothing but death (a hundred thousands civilians), millions of homeless refugees, and the near-total destruction of the social fabric and of basic infrastructures like water, electricity, transportation and schools – the latest targets of sectarian violence according to the *NY Times*. What the *Times* doesn't say is that the US occupiers, under Bremer's cynical 'divide-and-rule' policy, were largely responsible for establishing a reactionary sectarian system of ethno-religious parties (each with its own militia) as a substitute for the promised secular democracy, which would have put the majority – secular women, organized workers, middle-class doctors, teachers, engineers – in the saddle. A recent front page article told of a young teacher raped and murdered, her body hung up in front of her pillaged elementary school as an example. Another of a 17-year old girl stoned to death for dating the wrong boy. Those articles left me sickened. I could not help but feel responsible as a U.S. citizen and as a (hopefully) decent human being living in relative comfort and peace. Yet, how to help? How to become part of the solution rather than (involuntarily) part of the problem? That is the dilemma for many of us who feel awful about the situation yet remain paralyzed.

A choice of barbarisms

In desperation, some of my old socialist friends are supporting something they call 'The Iraqi Resistance.' As far as I'm concerned, in that way lies madness! For their idea of 'The Resistance' includes the very Islamic parties and militias

112

who are terrorizing and assassinating the civilian population in their sectarian power-struggles over control of neighborhoods – and eventually power and oil. In any case, socialists and democrats have no business trucking with violent, authoritarian, reactionary, religious and clan-based movements who systematically oppress women and suppress trade unions. Yes, it is true that these fratricidal militias also fight against the U.S.-led troops (curiously, less and less). The error of these erstwhile socialists is to conclude from this that 'the Enemies of our Enemies are our Friends' (the EEF Fallacy). Their error is all the more tragic in that during the Cold War, some of these same comrades had the independence to denounce *both* the totalitarian (state-capitalist) Communist system *and* aggressive U.S. imperialism. Sadly, another group of friends – formerly decent 'third camp' socialists like Christopher Hitchens, a great fan of Victor Serge – have also fallen into the EEF trap and now support the barbarous U.S.-led invasion as the best defense against what Bush calls 'Islamo-fascism.'

To my mind, there is no denying that the U.S. led occupation is the root cause of the tragic situation in Iraq. From the very beginning the Coalition turned its back on the secular democratic forces and based itself exclusively on the most reactionary religious and clan-based elements (as it did in Afghanistan). The corrupt Halliburton clones in charge of the occupation totally neglected reconstruction and the restoration of public order while attempting to rule by manipulating the factional rivalries among Kurds, Ba'athists, Sunnis and the various Shi'ite parties. The inevitable result has been chaos, civil war, the takeover of parts of the Army and the Police by rival murderous militias and a U.S.-financed 'government' of double-dealing opportunists squabbling over the spoils. Meanwhile the civilians cower in their homes without jobs, schools, water, electricity, safe streets or elemental human rights.

So who are the 'good guys' (if any)?

Quite simply the normal men and women like you and me: teachers, students, health-care professionals, office and factory workers, trade-unionists, civil servants, and homemakers trying to nurture and protect their children against the double terrorism of G.I.'s breaking down their doors and Islamicists blowing up their markets. Remember that before the U.S.-led invasion, Iraq was a modern society with women occupying more than half the civil service jobs and working as doctors, lawyers and professors (even under the horrid Ba'thist dictatorship). Since the beginning of the U.S.-led occupation, they have been courageously organizing themselves into women's organizations, trade-union federations, democratic and secular societies. Operating below the radar of the media and acting in defiance of terrorism committed by both occupiers and local reactionaries, these democratic, socialist and feminist activists have been quietly building battered-women's shelters and networks of women, unemployed and employed workers. They form the true 'Iraqi resistance' which decent people ought to support.

Some readers may be old enough to have participated in or sympathized with the Central America Solidarity movements of the 1980's. Back then, non-violent activist organizations like Plowshares, Pledge of Resistance, Nicaragua Network, CISPES, Witness for Peace and local Sister City groups brought direct material aid to people struggling against U.S.-backed death-squad regimes in El Salvador, Nicaragua and Guatemala. Along with lobbying our Congress people (successfully!) to withdraw U.S. support to the *Contras* (CIA-backed right-wing militias), we sent delegations bringing desperately needed medical supplies, we embarrassed the U.S. by getting shot at, we helped build schools and clinics in contested areas and we invited Central Americans to speak in the U.S. It is time to form similar networks with our counterparts in Iraq.

114

http://www.ifcongress.com/English/index.htm

The Iraqi Freedom Congress

Last year, Iraqi anti-occupation activists organized an umbrella organization, the Iraqi Freedom Congress (IFC) with the express purpose of seeking similar types of support abroad for battered women and persecuted trade-unionists. A recent IFC tour among U.S. and Canadian trade unions and IFC efforts in Japan have had considerable success. Chapters are now forming in the U.S. and Great Britain. I urge my friends and readers to go to the IFC website, click on 'Make Donation' and give generously through the Pay Pal link. Alternately, click on the link below and give to U.S. Labor Against the War, which supports free trade unions in Iraq. You may feel a little better tomorrow morning when you open the paper and read about the latest U.S.–provoked mayhem in Iraq.

http://www.uslaboragainstwar.org/

Religion and Repression in the United States: A Case of Political Pathology [2005] [52]

The Christian Right currently in power in the United States has for some time been waging – along with its 'wars' on vague but threatening abstractions like 'drugs' and 'terrorism' – an increasingly open war against reason itself. The latest frenzied episode in this war (April 2005) is the campaign of religious hysteria set in motion ostensibly to 'save' Terry Schiavo, the unfortunate young Florida woman kept alive against her wishes for fifteen years in an irreversible coma. Indeed, in the months since the contested electoral 'victory' of George W. Bush in November 2004, America seems more and more in the grip of a kind of religious psychosis.

In every sphere of American society, rational thought and science appear to be on the defensive, while superstition and magical thinking are routinely accepted as fact. Invisible WMDs in Iraq, imaginary conspiracies between arch-rivals like Osama bin Ladan and Saddam Hussein, fictitious military victories ('Mission Accomplished') and 'Creation Science' are passed off as factual. 'We create our own reality,' is the motto of the regime in Washington. Indeed, media-transmitted official lies and half-truths increasingly replace objectively verifiable realities in public discourse as well as in the news reporting that uncritically parrots it. Emperor Bush is visibly naked, but under a tacit agreement no one – neither the Democratic 'opposition' nor the mainstream media – is supposed to notice.

From a psychological perspective, this phenomenon can only be seen as a form of mass political pathology. If this be the case, can Psychoanalysis and Political Psychology help us understand the origins, etiology, inner dynamics, and eventual resolution of this American social disease?[53] I would like to begin this inquiry by proposing a paradigm borrowed from the field of family therapy: domestic abuse.

The most common syndrome revolves around an abusive parent, usually the father, who may be addicted to alcohol, drugs, gambling, stealing, violence,

---

[52] Translated from the French, *Religion et Répression aux Etats-Unis*, originally a series of articles I wrote for the Montpellier leftwing daily *L'Herault du Jour*.

[53] The psychoanalyst Wilhelm Reich, a former member of the Freudian circle in Vienna and an active Marxist, is considered to be the pioneer of political psychology with his analysis of the rise of Nazism. See his 'The Mass Psychology of Fascism.' (By contrast, the apolitical Freud ignored politics to such a degree that he found himself trapped in Vienna in 1938 after Hitler's takeover of Austria.)

incest or other shameful behaviors and who typically suffers from low self-esteem. Such individuals dominate their families through overt or threatened violence and instrumentalize that domination to exploit family members (sexually, financially, emotionally) and to protect themselves both from outside criticism and from crippling self-awareness. In other words, such bullies hide their secret shame (from themselves and others) behind a false front which they maintain by seduction and intimidation.

The abuser typically rationalizes his denial of his obvious (to others) shameful behavior (e.g. his drinking, violence or incest) by means of an ideological front-story, which he uses to smother his own inner doubts and justify his domination of the family. Authoritarian religion and the image of a stern but loving parent (who only punishes the family members for their own good) are convenient ready-made ideological front-stories, but each abusive family has its own – often bizarre – rationalizations. Furthermore, the continued success of the abuser's defense-system of denial depends on closing off the family unit to outside influences. The abuser's inner shame, fear and violence are typically projected on the outside world, viewed as menacing and hostile to the family unit (when in fact it is only menacing to the abuser's front-story and to his domination of the family).[54]

As family therapists and social workers are so painfully aware, the first problem in such cases is overcoming the tacit conspiracy of denial on the part of the abuser and his victims. Both the abusers and their victims themselves will routinely deny that a problem even exists. It's the old story of the elephant in the living-room. Whether the pathology takes the form of incest, alcoholism, kleptomania, gambling or violence, the family affected – or in our case the affected society – is intimidated by the abusive parent and becomes his/her accomplice through denial of the problem. The family members feel obliged to participate in the

---

[54] My paradigm is based on the work of Dr. James Gilligan M.D. of Harvard Medical School. As head Psychiatrist of the Massachusetts prison system he was able to reduce inmate murders and suicides by 80%. He is the author of an accessible, humane and totally remarkable book which I recommend to one and all: *Violence,* Putnam and Sons, 1997.

abuser's irrational world and to accept his lies and rationalizations in order to avoid confrontation; thus they often end up internalizing the abuser's oppressive pseudo-reality, which becomes the 'reality' they are forced to live in – repressing their own rationality in the process. The abuser may also maintain his false front with the help of 'enablers' (e.g. favored family members, cronies, neighbors, hirelings, even constituted authorities) who are complicit with the abuser and accept his rationalizations – sometimes out of intimidation and sometimes out of sympathy and perceived self-interest.

Now let's us see if this commonly-understood domestic abuse paradigm can serve as a useful lens through which to examine the pathology affecting what many recognize as our 'sick society.' If we extrapolate from the family to society, the role of the abusive father will perforce be played by the people in power – personified by the President and his Party. Let us note in passing that the current occupant of the White House, George W. Bush, has a typical abuser profile. Underachiever, dyslectic son of a successful father, bully in school, cocaine and alcohol addict, draft dodger/deserter, business failure, sadist who as Governor of Texas admitted taking satisfaction in signing death-warrants (he set a new record); George W. Bush is also a highly effective manipulator and a successful politician.

I am not arguing here from the point of view of a certain type of Psychohistory in which the personality of a leader (e.g. Hitler) becomes the key to historical events, although it is certainly poetic justice that a man like George W. Bush has become the incarnation and political representative of the American corporate class.[55] More to the point would be to compare the personality structure of the members of that class to that of the corporation itself, as was recently done in the film *The Corporation*. After studying the objective behavior of those 'legal persons' known as Corporations, the documentary concluded that if they were actual persons, they would be diagnosed as schizophrenic. Although George W. Bush's personality is a convenient symbol for the societal abuser in our domestic violence paradigm, it is the class he represents (both politically and metaphorically) that profits from exploiting nature and abusing people in order to maintain its domination over society.

Continuing with our paradigm, the role of the abuser's 'enablers' (e.g. favored family members, cronies, hirelings, even constituted authorities) would be played by the corporate media, the Democratic Party and Religious Right. Whether out of fear, out of self-interest or in return for favors, out of

---

[55] I know the type personally, having attended Yale College in the years between the two Bushes.

identification with the abuser, political enablers back up and perpetuate the abusive regime's face-story, ideology and rationalizations. These enables thus perpetuate and reinforce the state of denial in which the 'family' of American society is immersed. As for the ungrateful role of the 'abused family members,' we, the people, get stuck with that one. Like the members of regular families, some members of our societal 'family' identify with the abuser, buying into his rationalizations in order to seek his favor. Other members criticize him and may suffer his ridicule, ostracism and violence. John Kerry's war record is trashed by a bogus Swift Boat Association; Administration dissenters and their relatives are persecuted (the outing of CIA operative Valery Plame); peaceful citizens are subject to illegal wire-taps; legal demonstrators are beaten and jailed.

The division (between those who identify with the abuser and those who rebel) keeps us 'children' fighting among ourselves and assures the continued domination of the abuser – and the perpetuation of our own exploitation. Official statistics indicate that most working class and middle-income people in the U.S. – whether Dems or Reps, born-again or atheistic, native or immigrant, male or female, Black or White, gay or straight – are working longer hours, earning less in real dollars, commuting longer distances, paying more for poorer healthcare. We are also experiencing a decline in our quality of life (pollution, decaying cities, cuts in education and public services) and wide-scale psychological depression (indicated by the boom in anti-depressant sales). Meanwhile, we the people pay the income and property taxes while skyrocketing corporate profits and executive pay get big tax breaks or hide their profits in off-shore tax havens.

A single example may serve to illustrate this general trend. Why ask why N.Y. public schools are in trouble? When I went to public high school, corporations paid 80% of the taxes. Today their contribution is in the low single digits, and some corporations get away with the 1.5% minimum tax. Instead of money for books and teachers, we get sermons, endless testing and blaming of the victims – children from 'substandard' homes, 'incompetent' teachers. No Child Left Behind actually cuts funding for schools that 'fail' these tests, thereby taking money away from the students and teachers who need it the most. Many districts and principals willy-nilly buy into this ideological false front, even though the payoff (Federal Funding) is in many cases insignificant.

Returning to our paradigm, we must now ask what kind of ideology best rationalizes and sustains the front-story of these societal abusers and enablers. Unreason, religious and patriotic hysteria are the Bushies' weapons of choice. As for denial of the social and economic crises facing most Americans, 'We create our own reality' should be the Administration's logo. On the other hand, objectivity, critical thinking and rational analysis are obviously deadly enemies to the abuser's system of domination, and he will attempt to discredit them at all costs in order to maintain his power over the victims. In the family, the

119

abuser will dismiss Freud and psychology as 'hooey,' and claim the therapist is 'out to get us.' In society, Marx and Darwin are dismissed as 'hooey,' and critics of the system are treated as akin to terrorists. Here we encounter a second level of denial. In order to remain lucid and effective, the investigator/therapist needs to ignore the patients' denial defenses and stand outside of the family's accepted rationalizations - which is paradoxically perhaps easier for us here in Europe than for Americans living within the 'abusive family' itself. But mere objectivity isn't enough. The political psychologist also needs to understand the symptoms *as part of a whole self-perpetuating system* in order to conceptualize the history, inner dynamics and internal contradictions of the pathology - as we shall attempt to do here.

Is the earth flat?

But first, let us take a closer look at some of the symptoms. To outside observers, a wave of unreason seems to be unfurling over American society, affecting religious, political, and even scientific life. The same week that featured the Schiavo scandal, American newspapers reported a variety of other disturbing symptoms of politico-religious delirium. For example, the *N.Y. Times* indicated that many IMAX theaters (3-dimensional cinemas, some of which can be found in science museums) are now refusing to show films about evolution, the Big Bang'Theory - indeed about any of the earth sciences which go against the Biblical story of Creation – for fear of drawing protests from Christian fundamentalists.[56] Meanwhile, in a number of states, high school teachers are being coerced into teaching evolution as 'just a theory' or to teach it along with 'Creation Science' and 'Intelligent Design' (the belief that the complexity of nature proves that there is Divine Intelligence behind it). Even the very distinguished *National Geographic Magazine* recently bowed to the trend by coming out with a special issue entitled 'Was Darwin Wrong?' (In fairness, the answer turned out to be a qualified 'no.') The *Geographic*'s questioning of accepted scientific data inspired a hilarious April Fool parody issue of *Scientific American* with articles such as 'Is the Earth Flat?' 'The Myth of the Atom,' and 'Let's Ignore CO2.'

Alas, the false science promoted by the U.S. Government and the Religious Right is not just a bad joke. It permits the White House to reject as 'unproven' conclusions arrived at by respectable scientific watchdogs and by its own Environmental Protection Agency. Thus denial of the influence of industrial pollution on climate change paves the way for deregulation and legislation designed to favor the polluting auto and petroleum industries. And since the conclusions of science and rational thought contradict the need of American capitalism to remain competitive by externalizing ecological costs, a war on Science and Reason becomes *de rigueur*. Right-wing loyalists are appointed to run government agencies (protecting the environment, protecting workers'

---

[56] *N.Y. Times,* March 19, 2005.

health, housing the poor, regulating financial markets) whose very purposes they oppose, while dissenting scientists and administrators are systematically fired or demoted. Thus, the government succeeds in promoting bogus science along with bogus politics, while the big corporate media tend to legitimize such symptoms of political manipulation and religious hysteria as respectable discourse.

In the health field, the U.S. government openly practices religious censorship. Regulations forbid all personnel working for any Federally-funded organization or institution, including those on foreign soil, even to *talk* about abortion or contraception. The regime also promotes religion by financing parochial schools (disguised as 'charter schools') and supporting evangelizing charities with public funds (as a substitute for social welfare). All these activities are in flagrant violation of the First Amendment to the U.S. Constitution which clearly states 'Congress shall make no law respecting an establishment of religion.'

ACTUALITÉS

L'Ours du nord, le plus désagréable de tous les ours connus

Moreover, the violent fanaticism of self-proclaimed Christian terrorists is not a joke for its human victims: doctors murdered for practicing abortion, women's health clinics bombed with impunity. Even the elderly state appeals judge in Florida who finally allowed Schiavo to die felt the sting of right-wing terror. Himself a devout Christian, he was harassed and threatened with death by Christian fundamentalists and had to be sequestered for his own protection. Yet no one was arrested. In the terror-obsessed United States where the F.B.I. and the Red Squads (subversive investigation units) of local police departments routinely infiltrate non-violent social movements and pacifist organizations, the police tend to look away when faced with manifestations of Christian terrorism. Remember that Christian terrorists, not Islamicists, set off the bomb at the Alfred P. Murrah Federal Building in Oklahoma City. This act of terrorism caused 168 deaths and more than 800 serious injuries – yet there were no conspiracy charges or attempts to investigate the convicted terrorists' associations among survivalists, Christian militias, and neo-Nazis who thrive in nearly every state of the union.

In contrast, the attack on the Twin Towers in New York which caused 3000 deaths was manipulated to justify a domestic witch-hunt and launch an open-ended world-wide crusade against a billion or so Moslems (most of them peaceful non-Arabs). The oppressive violence of the 'abusive parent' (the Christian Right) is denied, only to be projected on an outside enemy (Moslem hordes). Thus the unity of the family unit is cemented in the vicious cycle of abuse, denial and projection. The unit (family/society) turns in on itself; the reasonable protests of rational family members (critics and dissenters) are considered as 'treason' while the advice of family friends (European allies) is ridiculed. It becomes difficult for family members (citizens, politicians, media members) to hold onto to their own sense of reality within such a closed system, especially when the abusive parent is righteously clothed in the double authority of government and religion (and is known to be violent and vengeful).[57]

The spectacle of right-wing fundamentalism invading the media, stifling the political life and public dialogue of the nation is disturbing. The bullying tone is set by openly racist shock jocks, who thanks to deregulation and monopoly, now dominate the radio airwaves. On television, the slightly more respectable right-wing FOX network provides the secular cover for the Christian Right as do commentators like Bill O'Reilly, Rush Limbaugh and Anne Coulter.

Academia and the New McCarthyism

The pathology of denial has not only infected the media, it has also engulfed America's universities (which to their shame had cooperated with the red-baiting loyalty purges in the 50's). Yet remarkably in the 60's, the first wave of opposition to the Vietnam War came from U.S. universities. On hundreds of campuses, professors of Asian history, foreign policy, military history and other relevant subjects participated in nation-wide Teach-ins and shared their specialized knowledge with assembled students and the public. They explained in laymen's terms what the U.S. was doing in Vietnam and why.[58] Some of the big Teach-ins were televised and rebroadcast all over the country. And that was in 1965, *before* the U.S. advisory mission in Vietnam escalated into a full-scale war. Alas, the right wing in the U.S. has spent the last forty years purging and punishing American scholars for their moment of courage and public-spiritedness in the Vietnam years.

In the wake of the so-called 'culture wars' (in fact one-way attacks on largely inexistent 'liberals' dominating the media and phantom 'Marxists' dominating the university) leftist academics have tended to retreat into the Byzantine

---

[57] It is interesting to note in this regard, that the actual mastermind of the 9/11 attack, Bush's violent and vengeful Saudi twin Osama Bin Laden, remains, at the time of this writing, blissfully at large.

[58] For example, as a young French instructor at Columbia University I talked to student rallies about the French defeat in Indochina and my experiences with the student anti-draft movement in France during the Algerian War.≈

obscurantism of postmodernism, with its incomprehensible meta-linguistic jargon and amoral relativism. Thus professors no longer feel called upon to fight for reason, rationality, and scientific objectivity because according to postmodern dogma, these very concepts must be 'contested' as 'totalizing' (read 'totalitarian') abstractions. Similarly, history and systematic political-economic analysis (for example of capitalism) are shunned as 'grand narratives' leading inevitably to totalitarian ends. So no more vulgar class struggle, no more *passé* socialism. Instead give us 'identity' studies and chic 'identity politics' to hide our intellectual nullity, and build new departmental divisions to further isolate and divide us.

Moreover, since the much-vaunted 'death of the subject' no one can be held responsible either for what they write or what they do. How convenient for Bush and Co., who are no longer responsible for the 'collateral damage' when they bomb civilians! How convenient for deconstructionists like Yale Prof. Paul de Man, who hid the fact he wrote pro-Nazi articles in occupied Belgium during WWII. How convenient for university administrators, whose funding depends on massive contributions and lucrative contracts from the government, the military and the big corporations! How convenient for professors, who know they will never get tenure if they criticize the corporations or attack the government. How convenient for the establishment that the *truth* itself should become a 'contested concept' in academia while the biggest liars in the world (Bush and his billionaire televangelist buddies) spell it with a capital T and brandish it like a club over the heads of doubters and critics.

But enough of discourse about discourse about discourse! Haven't the big U.S. graduate schools historically submitted to the corporations that created them in the 1880's, spewing forth racist historiography, elitist sociology, and the biology of eugenics from the corporate-funded ivory towers of Columbia, Harvard and John's Hopkins? As Victor Serge was fond of saying, 'The trouble with searching for the truth is that you find it.' By which he meant that the truth (for example about oil spills) is often dangerous, threatening, and subversive to the powers that be (for example the energy companies that finance most graduate Geology departments). Hail then to the dissidents in the academy who, like the whistle-blowers in the government, have the courage to speak out and suffer the consequences.

Censorship and Propaganda in the U. S.

As we have seen, the painful daily realities lived by millions of poor and middle-class Americans do not correspond to the bogus 'reality' proposed on a

 daily basis by the Bush administration and openly or tacitly endorsed by the mass media. Among the exceptions to generalized complicity in this cultural denial is the celebrated columnist Maureen Dowd, who recently exposed in detail how the White House manipulates the media.[59] First of all, she points out, the Administration does not tolerate criticism. For example, it forced Dan Rather, dean of national television news anchormen, to take an 'early retirement' after he quoted a document from an unconfirmed source concerning the military service of George W. Bush during the Vietnam War. And yet, the information was correct: no one denies that Bush went AWOL for a long time from the Texas Air National Guard. Bush's absence was all the more disgraceful considering that he secured his coveted place in the TANG through favoritism, so as to avoid being sent to Vietnam (this unit could not be deployed overseas).[60] As for Dowd herself, the glamorous veteran White House reporter during four administrations, has simply been banned from presidential press conferences for asking too many pointed questions.

On the other hand, Bush press conferences did include a phony 'journalist' hired by the White House to ask softball questions in front of the cameras.[61] Furthermore, the Bush administration has ended up admitting that it systematically procures favorable articles from hired journalists, and that the

---

[59] *New York Times*, March 18, 2005.
[60] James Goodale, 'Report of the Independent review Concerning President Bush's Texas Air National Guard Service,' *New York Review of Books*, April 7, 2005.
[61] A photo of this fake journalist was eventually found on a web-site offering his services as a male prostitute serving gentlemen as well as ladies!

U.S. Treasury had paid out large sums of money to a score of advertising agencies to create fake 'news reports' which were routinely broadcast as real ones by regional television networks. Little did it matter: the Justice Department ruled that these fake news stories are perfectly legal 'as long as they are based on facts and are not partisan' (!) Dowd calls this a 'Soviet-style propaganda campaign.' It also reminds me of Orwell's *1984* with its 'Ministry of Truth.'

'We Create Our Own Reality'[62]

In any case, the regime has created a system of lies and hallucinations in which any relation to verifiable reality is quickly lost. An unnamed Bush official was quoted by a reporter as denigrating 'the reality-based community.' He explained: 'We are an Empire now. We create our own reality.' American television projects an imaginary Bushland inhabited by merry billionaires. In the place of socially realistic 1970's shows like 'Good Times,' 'M*A*S*H,' and 'All in the Family,' we have 'Lives of the Rich and Famous,' 'Dallas,' and 'The Evening News.' There, peace and democracy are being established in the Mid-East thanks to Bush's victory over Evil Saddam. In that wonderful Bushland the economy is picking up as a result of the tax exemptions which enable the rich to create jobs. So what if the facts indicate otherwise? Just ignore

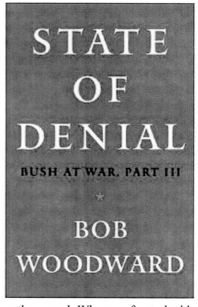

the facts, and Bingo! – they are deleted from the record. When confronted with the absence of   Saddam's Weapons of Mass Destruction and links to September 11 attacks, a Bush advisor announced: 'We create our own reality.' This is what psychologists call 'magical thinking.' Alas, he knew what he was talking about: according to polls, nearly half of all American voters still

---

[62] See 'Without a Doubt,' *NY Times,* Oct. 17, 2004, by Ron Suskind. The Administration's anonymous spokesman went on to deride the impotence of the 'reality-based community' meaning people who 'believe that solutions emerge from your politically discernable reality [...] That's not the way the world really works anymore... We're an empire now, and when we act, we create our own reality. And while you're studying that reality –judiciously, as you will – we'll act again, creating other new realities, which you can study too, and this is how things will sort out. We're history's actors, and you, all of you, will be left to just study what we do.'

believed in these two myths at the time of the 2004 election. Wasn't it Joseph Goebbels, Hitler's propaganda minister, who proclaimed: 'If you repeat a lie often enough, people will believe it?' Indeed, the Big Lie can be effective, but only when the speaker has the power to subjugate the mass media, silence or marginalize critics, cast doubt on empirical reason, and impose an ideology of illusion. Still, let us keep in mind that reality has a way of sooner or later blowing back on the self-deluded who blind themselves by denying it. After all, the 'Thousand Year *Reich*' (Empire) of Hitler's demented dreams lasted only thirteen years.

Elephants in the Living Room

How do people 'create their own reality?' The shameful behaviors of the alcoholic, the incestuous father, the physical abuser are like elephants sitting in the middle of the family living room. They are apparently invisible because the abuser has the power to enlist the complicity of the entire family in his denial of his secret guilt. The biggest of the elephants brought into the White House by Bush, Cheney, Rice, Rumsfeld, and Wolfowitz is called 'Iraq.' People still pretend not to see it but they can't help smelling it as Washington's living room mysteriously fills up with elephant droppings. The Iraqi and U.S. casualty figures increase daily. The U. S. Armed Forces are bogged down with no end in sight. The American troops are demoralized, poorly equipped and stretched to the limit. Intelligence is false or falsified. There is the torture scandal, the runaway costs, the astronomical debts, the obscenely high profits of cronies like Halliburton, etc. The list could go on and on. The mass media and the Democrats hold their noses in silence. A few audacious souls may ask 'What's that smell?' But who within the Beltway dares talk directly about getting rid of the elephant and stopping the ill-conceived, unwinnable, brutalizing war *now*? It's safer to talk about private morality and God. In any case, the existence of the elephants is 'unproven' and zoology is 'just a theory,' and for clinchers, there are no elephants in the Bible!

Abusers tend to project or transfer their inner violence onto symbolic enemies in order to justify their tyranny. In the case of a social psychosis, an abusive government declares an endless war against abstract, invisible, and elusive enemies: 'Communism,' 'Drugs,' 'Terrorism,' 'Evil.' Frustrated, the failed strategists of the failed War on Iraq declare permanent war on the rest of the world. In order to intimidate their own citizens, their allies, and their adversaries, they officially authorize themselves to bring about 'regime change' in any nation which they might judge to be 'friendly to terrorism' or who might be part of an imaginary 'Axis of Evil.' It is sheer madness. According to Pew Research polls, the world is more afraid of Bush than of Osama bin Laden, but no leader, not even France's Chirac, dares to protest.

Citizens and Allies Intimidated

Washington's unilateral warmongering isn't aimed at frightening only the nations labeled 'rogue' by the rogues in the White House; it's also aimed at our allies. Washington is bent on bullying and intimidating rival imperial powers such as France, Russia, and China, who had dared question the American war in Iraq at the United Nations in 2002. Today, Bush shows his contempt for U.S. allies by naming John Bolton, a sworn enemy of the United Nations, as his U. N. ambassador, and in appointing the right-wing ideologue, Paul Wolfowitz, the architect of the War in Iraq, to head the World Bank.[63] Formerly in charge of the reconstruction of Iraq (where he fixed nothing and privatized almost everything), Wolfowitz will now be managing the development of the Third World. A scandal? No allied government dares challenge these imperial nominations, which are nevertheless a direct slap in the face from Bush. Like the Democrats in Congress, America's allies are frightened into submission. Wolfowitz is a monster, yet German Chancellor Gerhard Scroeder and Hillary Clinton both reacted to the scandalous nomination by singing his praises.

 Domestically, our bully of a President has set in motion a police state in which civil liberties are being wrested away. The right to assemble and protest exists only in designated, wire-enclosed 'Free Speech Areas' where no one can see or hear the protesters. The abusive police beating and arrest of non-violent demonstrators is now routine. With the Patriot Act, even individual citizens are no longer protected from government abuse. The Executive Branch can unilaterally designate any citizen or non-citizen ('alien') as a suspect in order to spy on, imprison, secretly detain, even torture such individuals - without answering to any court or public tribunal, indeed without revealing the suspects' names. In order to prevent any recourse to justice, Bush has named as Attorney General Alberto Gonzales, the infamous author of the executive memorandum authorizing torture at Guantanamo and at Abu Ghraib. 'The White House now has its own Gulag' wrote Maureen Dowd.[64] In fact, the United States, whose prisons are overflowing with more than 2 million detainees, surpasses both Russia and China as a prison society.

The Ideological Bunker

Politically, the occupants of the White House are more and more isolated in the ideological bunker of their 'neo-conservatism.' They have no tolerance for contradiction or complexity – even on the part of their own intelligence agencies, and they demand (and reward) blind loyalty above all other qualities.

---

[63] Formerly Deputy Secretary of Defence, this Bush protégé not long ago expressed utter contempt for the 'Old Europe.' It is 'Wolfie' who declared in 2002 that the Iraqis would welcome the Americans 'with flowers' and that the costs of reconstruction would be 'covered by revenues from Iraqi oil.'
[64] *New York Times*, March 18, 2005.

Thus, after a presidential commission of inquest on intelligence stated that the reasons given for the war in Iraq were 'completely erroneous,'[65] the architects of the war, Rice and Wolfowitz, were given promotions, moderates were dismissed (Colin Powell), and the critics hounded and persecuted.[66] The new Masters of the Universe are, like Bush himself, uncomfortable with complexity and have little curiosity about those around them. Many of them are provincial, more or less lacking in culture and foreign language skills, who barely speak proper English and who have little or no foreign experience outside of the business world or American university contacts. The more cosmopolitan Colin Powell, whom they ridicule, was their diplomatic cover. They no longer need him. They have chosen the simpler solution than diplomacy: naked force.

Outside of the United States, their true allies are not the rival capitalist democracies, but reactionary dictatorships which protect their investments and to whom they sell weaponry at a very high profit. Tyranny is reassuring to right-wingers in power. Democracy, with its complexity is threatening. Bush, having looked into the ice-blue eyes of Russia's new Czar Vladimir Putin, dubbed him 'my friend Vladimir.' Let us recall that Vice President Cheney, when he was CEO of Halliburton, sold weapons to Saddam, with whom he was notoriously photographed at the time of the Iran-Iraq war; that Osama bin Laden's Islamic crusade was originally financed by the U.S.; that Washington supports foreign tyrants who terrorize the multitudes of poor people in their native lands. These are the fierce guard-dogs who protect U.S. interests, but who also frighten their masters. They have a tendency to turn on them and bite, as both Saddam and bin Laden certainly did. Indeed, the only 'link' between those two mass murderers is that they both received subsidies from the CIA. Today, the Masters of Washington instinctively prefer to align themselves with the Islamist Pakistani military dictatorship (Godfather of the Taliban and provider of nuclear secrets to North Korea) than to the capitalist democracy India (seen since Nehru's neutralist days as soft, unstable, and pro-communist).[67]

The Religious Right

Returning now to the example of the campaign to 'Save' Terry Schiavo, we are able to contextualize it as the latest skirmish in an ongoing battle against

---

[65] 'Dead Wrong' See the *International Herald Tribune* of April 1, 2005.

[66] Apparently, the White House even went as far as to reveal the name of Valerie Plame, a secret agent of the CIA in order to get even with her husband, Joseph Wilson, an ex-ambassador, who had unmasked the lie about Iraqi purchases of nuclear materials in Africa.

[67] In the same way, they support right-wing paramilitary narco-terrorists in Colombia and turn their backs on the labor government of Luiz Inacio Lula in Brazil, whose policy is nonetheless perfectly compatible with U.S. neo-liberalism.

rational thought. Fundamentalist preachers and politicians attempted to exploit the human drama in Florida by instigating a wave of religious hysteria in the name of the right to 'life' – however artificial and vegetative. Heading up the campaign was George W. Bush himself (who claims to have been 'personally saved' by Jesus Christ), followed by his brother Jeb Bush, the Governor of Florida, who had been meddling in the Schiavo case for years. These two Christian knights were backed up by the Republican leaders of Congress and the millionaire televangelists, with the complicity of the mass media and of congressional Democrats who voted for special legislation to 'save' the brain-dead woman.[68]

Nonetheless, this noisy campaign to bamboozle the American people eventually flopped! The little old Florida county judge made his decision on the evidence, and the public refused to be fooled, hoodwinked or deceived. As Abraham Lincoln put it, 'You can fool some of the people all of the time, and all the people some of the time; but you can't fool all of the people all of the time.' According to the March 23 CBS poll, 82% of Americans were on principle opposed to these politicians' and preachers' extra-legal interventions, and 74% saw them as nothing more than opportunistic political ploys. Thus the campaign of religious hysteria unleashed by the government was blocked by the rationality of the American people. Nonetheless, 80% to 90% of Americans see themselves as religious and are affiliated with a church, synagogue, or mosque. How does one explain this paradox?

To be sure, the shameless abusers in power in America have harnessed religion as their face-saving ideology, and it would be difficult to exaggerate the influence on American society of right-wing religious sects and the conservative Catholic hierarchy. With millionaire backers and millions of followers, they constitute wealthy and powerful lobbies which are increasingly able to censor personal morals and impose their reactionary ideology by intervening aggressively in the political, sexual, and even scientific life of the nation. This religious smokescreen allows the government of the super-wealthy to evade social issues (*i.e.* class issues) by replacing them with 'moral' ones. Indeed, European readers have a hard time grasping that the term 'social issues' in American media parlance no longer designates traditional social questions such as poverty, unemployment, poor housing and delinquency but rather personal moral issues such as abortion and gay marriage.

---

[68] Not to mention help from another living-dead celebrity, Karol Wojtyla, the grand ayatollah of an international sect which proclaims itself 'Holy, Apostolic, Roman, and Catholic?' His Holiness also intervened to 'save' Schiavo before himself being mercifully permitted to die. Nonetheless, Wojtyla's not-unexpected demise unleashed a wave of equally putrescent religiosity in Europe, where his funeral was staged as a media orgy of unwholesome false piety.

The Religious Right in the US is extremely media savvy. Christian broadcasters pioneered the use of radio, T.V. and the Internet to spread their ideas and consolidate their political base. Back in the 1930's, Father James Coughlin, a populist Roman Catholic, was the principal spokesman for fascism in the U.S. His weekly half-hour broadcasts had a big audience, but he remained marginal – especially after he was silenced by the hierarchy shortly before the US entered WWII. Today hate-mongering televangelists like Pat Robertson and Jerry Falwell (who memorably described 9/11 as God's punishment on the U.S. for tolerating gays) have their own daily TV shows and routinely appear as guests on other networks and as advisors to Presidents and politicians.

The fundamentalists have also created alternative cultures, with their own radio networks playing Christian Rock. In the literary field, a series of apocalyptic novels called *Left Behind* has been topping the best-seller lists in the US – a major publishing phenomenon generating films and spin-offs. The *Left Behind* novels recount the adventures of a group of evangelical Christians trapped on Earth – having missed the first cut for Heaven on Judgment Day. They may still be saved, but first they must face the rise of the Antichrist, plus plagues, wars, earthquakes and the final battle of Armageddon (*Left Behind* Vol. 11). This will occur when the Jews re-conquer the biblical Holy Land. These novels have a born-again Christian audience of forty millions linked by talk radio and fan clubs, where current events are interpreted in terms of the Apocalypse scenario allegedly derived from the Bible. The series' author, Tim LaHaye, is a right-wing militant who, with televangelist Jerry Falwell, co-founded a powerful lobby, the Moral Majority.

Taken up by fundamentalist sects and certain Republicans close to Bush, LaHaye's hallucinatory scenario serves as rationalization for the government's policies. The enemy is at the gates. The 'clash of civilizations' between American democracy and politicized Islam may pass for conventional wisdom in Washington, but it looks more like a clash of fundamentalisms to us over here in Europe. Indeed, the politicized Christianity of the Bushies and the Zionist Judaism of Sharon are a match for the politicized Islam of the Ayatollahs… Which makes for more 'strange bedfellows.' With regard to Mid-East policy, the traditionally anti-Semitic Christian Right now supports the Jewish State. Formerly, the Christian Knights of the Ku Klux Klan lynched Blacks and Jews without distinction and with equal fervor. Today they are allied to the Zionist lobby and the oil lobby in Congress, while Senator Lieberman openly associates with fundamentalist Christian sects. According to their common religio-political scenario, Israel will vanquish the Arab-Islamic Anti-Christ while Bush and his oil-rich clique grab the Evil One's oil reserves…. Concerning the environment, the neo-liberal Christian Republicans apply the same kind of teleo-'logic:' it is pointless to preserve our heritage of nature's wealth and beauty, since the End of the World is nigh. Thus, our pious politicians hand over the national forests for clear-cutting to enrich their friends in the lumber industry, remove restrictions on pollution to enrich auto and coal industry billionaires, and seek to open up the vast untouched tundra of Alaska to the greed of the oil industry.

Southern Trees Bear Strange Fruit

There is no dearth of right-wing sects in the United States. We have a vast array of fundamentalist evangelical churches, reactionary Catholic bishops, Orthodox Jews, Southern Baptists, Mormons, Christian Knights of the Ku Klux Klan, apocalyptic survivalists, christo-nazi militias, you name it. These faithful comprise the shock troops of the billionaire regime in power in Washington. Most of these sects are steeped in a culture which originated in the Deep South and which today encompasses many working- class Whites, whose economic and social standing depends in part upon their superiority in relation to Blacks. Back in slavery times, plantation owners depended on this class of uneducated, superstitious, and violent Whites to manage and suppress their slaves. This same class of bullies is glorified in Westerns chivalrously protecting the sacredness of White womanhood by lynching Blacks and practicing genocide on the 'Indians'. Today, our regime of predatory billionaires uses them to intimidate secular civil society and to silence its critics. And just as the majority of officers in the pre-Civil War U.S. Army came from the South (and joined the Confederate Army), so today's professional officer corps. Ironically, right-wing poor Whites are often just as destitute as their Black neighbors, competing with them on the labor market at the bottom of the social ladder.

But racism allows them to sublimate their humiliation by identifying themselves with the masters – slave-owning plantation owners or billionaire capitalists – by projecting their shame on Blacks, whom they hold in contempt and terrorize more or less with impunity. And now we have Arabs ('towel-heads') to feel superior to. In Germany, the unemployed *lumpen* of the Nazi Party imagined themselves to be Supermen (*übermenschen*) descended from a master race (*Herrenvolk*), and Hitler gave them the opportunity to take out their humiliation on Jews and other 'inferior' races. In Texas, where Governor Bush set a modern record for executions (88% of which were Blacks), Blacks and gays are still lynched. Christian fundamentalism is the ideological glue which holds this alliance between poor Whites and cynical or superstitious right-wing billionaires together.

An Intimidating Mass Party?

Viewed through the psychological paradigm of the dysfunctional family, these fundamentalists correspond to the children of a violent father who repress their own humiliation, fear and rage; only to project them on alien others. Wilhelm Reich, in his Marxist phase, had already analyzed this character type in his observations on mass psychology of fascism in Germany. Such children tend to embrace their own repression by internalizing the 'reality' of the abusive father, who is seen as representing rightful authority. It has been observed that battered sons tend to become aggressive and project their own fear and violence on those around them... All to keep their shameful secret within the family. Indeed, these children often see themselves as victims who are 'protecting' themselves. Their character structure becomes rigid and their

132

behavior becomes aggressive.[69] They make good policemen, good soldiers, good torturers and good terrorists.

Such are the shock troops of the 'Republican Revolution.' They add a key fascist-type element to the increasingly repressive imperial regime of George W. Bush. Historically, it has been observed that Mussolini, Hitler, Stalin, Saddam Hussein, Khomeini and the rest depended on five indispensable elements in order to establish and maintain their totalitarian regimes:

1. An irrational ideology including xenophobic hysteria,
2. State power,
3. Control of the mass media,
4. A social-political crisis,
5. An intimidating Mass Party.

Today the American regime of George Bush is close to having all five of these elements at its disposal, and this is a very serious matter. For the first time in my life, I see the spectre of an *imaginable* 'American fascism' – too often carelessly bandied about by hysterical Leftists in the past. Historically, native fascism, although threatening, lacked a mass following in the 1930's and was checked by a highly organized Left of militant trade-unions and political activists. In the 40's and 50's, the bi-partisan 'McCarthyite' witch-hunts – like their post-WWI predecessors – coincided with eras of relative peace, prosperity and high employment, offering no major crises for fascism to exploit. Today, with U.S. imperialism's hegemony nearing crisis, the Religious Right in power has behind it a whole network of fundamentalist shock-troops, many of them violent, allied with the gun-freaks of the NRA. Not, perhaps, a disciplined mass party, but quite an intimidating terror force which had long been tolerated and allowed to operate with near impunity. It is impossible to predict at what point U.S. society may step over the borderline from neurosis into psychosis. And although the U.S. still retains many checks and balances, the theoretical *possibility* – however remote – is indeed frightening.

The Paradoxes of American Religion

Fortunately there are still some sane and healthy social forces in the United States, believers who are resisting the ideological offensive of the Christian Right. This is both because the country is deeply divided, and because the religiosity of American society is itself paradoxical. Paradox number one: politics in the U.S. is traditionally secular. Let us recall that the Founding Fathers of the American Republic (Washington, Jefferson, Adams, Franklin, Paine) were 18th Century deists, if not outright atheists. The word 'God' does not appear in the U.S. Constitution, which makes provision for a separation of Church and State even stricter than the '*Laïcité*' practiced in France. Great

---

[69] See *Violence*, by Thomas Gilligan, M.D. *op. cit.*

readers of Montesquieu, the Fathers' true religion was the strict separation of executive, legislative, and judiciary powers. Religion itself they considered useful to calm the poor and uneducated, as long as it was kept out of politics.

Thus, even today, the Constitutional independence of a Florida Appellate judge (something unheard of in centralized France) under pressure from the President and the Congress remains more sacred than the Bible. In fact, our imperial President, his brother the Governor, and dozens of fundamentalist Congressmen, made fools of themselves by trying to defy the decision of the Florida Superior Court. Simultaneously, a recent ruling by the Supreme Court forbade the placing of a stone with the Ten Commandments in front of a courthouse by a fundamentalist judge in the State of Georgia.

Paradox number two: ecstatic, evangelical Christianity is not necessarily reactionary. Around 1830, Alexis de Tocqueville spoke of the great religiosity of American civil society (which he saw as part and parcel of its narrow-minded, hypocritical, and mercenary spirit). In the Southern states, Tocqueville heard the 'biblical proofs' of the inferiority of Blacks from the mouths of his sanctimonious slave-owning hosts. But he did not see that, a generation later, the Christian radicalism of Black Abolitionists like the former slave Sojourner Truth and the White Abolitionist John Brown would precipitate a Civil War.

So today, it is important not to confuse the religious fanaticism of the right-wing fundamentalist sects which form the electoral base of George W. Bush's' Republican Party with the liberal parishioners and the liberal theology of the traditional Protestant churches - nor with the Black church and a growing number of socially-conscious White and Hispanic Evangelicals.

The Liberal Churches

The faithful among the Episcopalians, Congregationalists, African Methodists, Unitarian-Universalists, Quakers, Reformed Jews, and Liberation-theology Catholics, are generally anti-racist and increasingly accept women or even openly gay people as pastors. At the time of Martin Luther King and of the Vietnam War, many of these churches became involved in movements for peace, social justice, and racial equality. Throughout the next decades marked by anti-nuclear, human rights, and Central America solidarity movements, church people were very much present and visible in demonstrations and in non-violent direct action. They frequently lent their recreational rooms and parish halls to movement organizations for free, and they often served as meeting-places for anti-war and anti-racist organizations - including even the

Marxist *groupuscules* I frequented. These people of faith and conscience still cling to their principles in a country mired in self-centered consumerism and the every-man-for-himself religion of individual salvation.

Other religions, while not strictly 'liberal,' have little in common politically with the Religious Right. For example, while morally conservative, the Jehovah's Witnesses' politically neutral stance means that they do not support right-wing agendas. Furthermore, their refusal to salute the flag or engage in warfare has legally, through the American court system, won any American citizen the right to do the same for reasons of conscience. Similarly, in wartime the humanitarian-oriented Seventh-Day Adventists refuse to engage in active combat, preferring medical roles. Historically, both denominations have chosen to suffer for their beliefs: in WWII, they were sent to Nazi concentration camps - especially Jehovah's Witnesses, who were assigned the purple triangle.

Liberal churches (like their right-wing counterparts) are also human communities which allow American families to shield themselves from the anonymity of a fragmented society. They serve as havens of solidarity and mutual aid against the harshness of American life under neo-liberal capitalism; they compensate for the near total absence of what the French call '*le social*' and '*la vie associative*,' *i.e.* of a basic social safety net or even of regular social contact between people. Leftists and Europeans have trouble accepting the fact that the large majority of Americans practice their religion to some degree and should not be scorned for this. A great number of the 500,000 Americans who demonstrated against the Republican Convention in New York and who voted in record numbers for the Democrats in 2004 came from the ranks of the liberal churches. As we have seen, 82% of those Americans expressed anger at their government's meddling to 'save' a brain-dead woman. As Karl Marx so eloquently put it, they represent 'the soul of a soulless world.' [70]

Democratic Enablers

It was the Republican Right, beginning in 1968 with Nixon's racist 'southern strategy,' who injected religion into U.S. politics by making a 'social issue' out of the 'rights of the unborn.' Alas, today's Democratic Party is playing out its role as 'enabler' by embracing and pandering to religious fundamentalism. Let us recall that in 2004 the Republican Party won its very slim (and contestable) majority by playing the religion card. The Right ran a 'social issues' campaign designed to mobilize poor White fundamentalist voters against a domestic Axis of Evil composed of homosexual marriage, abortion, and moral laxity. Their tactic was to pin the label of godlessness on the traditionally liberal, secular,

---

[70] This is the near-forgotten phrase that completes Marx's famous remark about 'the opium of the people' in the *Manifesto*. In Marx's day, the rich could buy opium in pharmacies, like today's anti-depressants. The poor had only their faith

tolerant, and humanistic Democratic Party and to portray the Democrats as impotent in the face of Mexican and Muslim hordes preparing to invade the Homeland. In the wake of their marginal defeat, the mainstream Democrats have hypocritically gone over to the camp of the Religious Right instead of regrouping their mass base by defending the social-liberal values of civil society and citizenship.

Only a handful of Congressional Democrats voted against the special legislation to maintain the living death of Terry Schiavo. That same week, Hillary Clinton, a probable presidential candidate in 2008, revealed that she has 'always' engaged in daily prayer and declared that the Democrats should 'talk more about their faith.'[71] Note that both Hilary Clinton, a self-proclaimed feminist, and her wayward husband are members of the Southern Baptist Convention, which, in its annual Council in 2000, re-affirmed the doctrine that according to the Bible: 'A woman should obey her husband.' This convenient hypocrisy also allows the billionaire-backed Democratic enablers to avoid talking about down-to-earth problems: like the American quagmire in Iraq, the Enron and Halliburton scandals, the torture scandal, the health care crisis, industrial pollution, the tumbling dollar, runaway factories, unemployment, economic insecurity and homeless families. Neither will they discuss tax exemptions for the ultra-rich, not to mention the astronomical national debt which is used to justify dismantling Social Security, education, and other social services like aid to indigent women and children. These are the painful realities lived by the abused children of our collective abusive parent: realities that must be denied if the abusers are to continue holding power and making money. They are the political, social and economic realities that both major billionaire parties need to avoid discussing; realities that must be subjected to the censoring mechanisms of *denial* of which pie-in-the-sky-when-you-die religion is one component... But not the only one.

Decadence and Retrogression

Since the November 2004 election, the reactionary Bush coalition apparently no longer bothers to conceal its decadent racist roots or temper its hallucinatory and regressive world-view. How to explain this backward leap into decadence and regression in American society, once considered the model of democracy and progress that many Europeans sought to emulate? In the liberal 18th century, American capitalism stood for rationality, tolerance, and science against superstition and despotism. Today, in the neo-liberal 21st century, American capitalism is fighting *against* rationalism, tolerance, and science while promoting superstition and despotism. If the imperial rulers in Washington are behaving more like Nero or Caligula than like Wilson or Roosevelt, it is because the already decadent US Empire – though triumphant

---

[71] *International Herald Tribune,* March 18, 2005

in 1918 and 1945 – is losing its grip, hollowed out by internal and external debt and sapped by increasing inequality.

As we have seen, the billionaire Right uses the masses of fundamentalist poor Whites – including violent and racist elements – both as an electoral base and as shock troops. But this profitable alliance between CEOs and fundamentalist preachers is not just a marriage of convenience. There is a profound affinity, a spiritual one so to speak, in their perception of the spirit of the times and their view of the world. Indeed, the delirious scenario of a universal Apocalypse imagined by 2nd century Christians corresponds fairly accurately to the catastrophes with which people are faced at the beginning of the 21st : wars and widespread epidemics, climate shifts, the breakdown of the social fabric, famines, droughts, the destruction of cities, pervasive fear and dread, dissensions, violence. Now if God isn't the cause of these catastrophes, who is? People might be tempted to blame the government and the wealthy. Alas, the millions of fundamentalists who suffer from chronic unemployment and the failure of small businesses in the United States, suffer no such temptation. They have been taught to deal with the social crisis by retreating into the fantasy that they belong to a special tribe of Chosen Ones who will be saved. Provincial, ignorant, and xenophobic, terrified by the vision of a hostile world which they see in the sensationalistic mass media, they are haunted by the racist nightmare of an uprising of angry Blacks, swarming Mexicans – and now hordes of Arab invaders envious of the 'American way of life.'

Fortunately, Bushland is not the only America. There is another America, democratic, idealistic, and tolerant, for whom religion and personal morality are private matters and the rights of the individual are sacred. There are the four Americans in five who defended Terry Schiavo's right to die with dignity and understood the religious and governmental propaganda media blitz as opportunistic political propaganda.[72] Today, these peaceful, tolerant Americans are on the defensive. They feel betrayed by the Democratic Party, born again as the Party of
Prayer. Largely unrepresented in the media, dumbfounded by the government- and media-driven wave of religious psychosis, they are reeling under the blows and seeking new bearings. Meanwhile, the elephant of the Iraq war continues to infest the living-room. At the moment, the lead in denouncing this stinking, rotten war is being taken by the courageous dissident soldiers and their families. No one dares question their patriotism. Behind them, the U.S. anti-

---

[72] *The New York Times*, March 24, 2005.

war movement is hopefully regrouping.[73] In the 1960's it succeeded in changing public opinion, provoking a crisis in the government, and forcing the withdrawal of American troops from Vietnam. Today, Bush's imperial policy is quagmired in Iraq. The last word has not yet been spoken.[74]

What are they afraid of?

In the meantime, the regime in Washington is hardening up. Permanent war, censorship, campaigns of hysteria, special legislation, despotic allies, overflowing prisons, torture. One may well ask: Why there is so much repression in an opulent consumer society which seems to be stable and which rules the world as an uncontested military and economic superpower? The question is well put. Wasn't Freud's original discovery of the unconscious derived from his observations of the mechanisms of repression? In psychoanalysis as in politics, it is safe to assume that where there is smoke there is fire; where there is repression, there is an equally strong force which is repressed. Freud saw our repressed desires and passions 'returning' in dreams, accidents and dangerous fits of irrationality. Of what societal 'return of the repressed' are the occupants of the White House and their corporate cronies so afraid?

Let us keep in mind that Bush, Cheney, Wolfowitz, and Co. all experienced the 1960's as a traumatic event. First they faced the risk of military service in Vietnam (which they all succeeded in avoiding) and then the deep shock the American superpower's defeat by under-armed pajama-clad Vietnamese revolutionaries. At the same time, these ambitious young conservatives were thunderstruck at the unimaginable spectacle of American society torn apart by resistance to the war, by the Black revolt, by riots in the great cities, by college campuses occupied by rebellious students, by women asserting themselves, by the sexual and cultural revolutions. They heard the word 'revolution' repeated so much that they feared for their privileges and even for their own precious persons.[75]

Schizophrenic Masters of the Universe

Today these 1960's Young Conservatives find themselves swept into power by their generation of conservative billionaires. On the one hand they can only

---

[73] Karen Houppert, 'The New Force of Protest' in *The Nation,* March 28, 2005.

[74] *Update, Nov. 2005.* Since this was published last April, we have seen gold-star mother Cindy Sheehan flush our playboy President Bush out of his Texas ranch and pursue him to Washington accompanied by other military families and a huge (300,000?) anti-war demonstration – totally ignored by the media.

[75] By 1968, the idea of 'revolution' was so popular that advertisers recycled it. For example, the slogan 'Dodge Revolution'— which Black workers at the Dodge plants in Detroit famously parodied with their 'Dodge Revolutionary Movement.'

imagine themselves as the 'Masters of the Universe' free to do whatever they choose. And indeed, for the time being they have been able to construct their own reality and force us to live in it. They have gotten away with enriching themselves, their cronies and the billionaires who finance their political campaigns by exempting them from taxes, giving them extravagant contracts and exorbitant subsidies. More, they have succeeded in making war *profitable* –as well as necessary to their mutual goal of controlling the resources of the planet – all the while passing on the overhead costs in blood and treasure to the working payroll-tax-payer.

The key economic notion of their neo-liberalism is a form of magical thinking in which the United States (and the consumer) can continue to borrow and spend indefinitely without ever having to pay back. Never mind that American predatory capitalism is no longer productive, that almost all 'American' cars and all of the televisions purchased by American consumers are imported, that the United States exports almost nothing anymore except for weapons, garbage, and the dumping of subsidized agricultural surpluses. In the magical thinking of speculators of 2005 (as with those of 1929), this economic boom should continue forever.[76]

But the new masters of the world are schizophrenic, because behind their arrogance, there is fear. They are afraid of the multitudes of people who teem about the Earth – all of the poor people, the aliens, the unfamiliar and incomprehensible races and cultures that they dominate and exploit. They are afraid of their envy and desires, of their latent anger, of their capacity to rebel once again as during the traumatic 1960s. For if the Left has forgotten the power of that revolutionary wave which shook many regimes in 1968, the privileged Right has not forgotten their fright – or the suddenly-revealed fragility of political power.[77] That is their nightmare. The more fearful they were, the more they strive to repress it and to escape into magical thinking.

However deluded by their own propaganda and wish-fulfillment, the predatory billionaires in power in Washington understand all too well that they are only a handful compared to the billions of human beings whom they are pillaging. That widening chasm separating them from humanity must surely make them dizzy, as it yawns ever deeper – recalling the terrifying volcanic eruptions of the 1960's. Indeed, with the *Zapatista* revolt in Chiapas, and with the sieges

---

[76] Nonetheless, as a precaution against a major depression, the U. S. Congress is preparing legislation to prevent consumers from declaring personal bankruptcy but which lessens the liability of corporations in case of failure. If the bubble bursts, the CEOs will not lose their shirts, while their employees will have to work like slaves to pay off their credit cards and mortgages.

[77] Let us remember that President DeGaulle of France fled to Germany, during the May 1968 student-worker rebellion and that a few months later U.S. President Johnson 'resigned' by turning down the nomination to a near-guaranteed re-election.

led by anti-capitalist demonstrators against the World Trade Organization in Seattle, Quebec City, Cancun, and Genoa, the whole world knows their dirty secrets. And now they hear from the four corners of the globe a new generation calling out: 'The Earth is not for sale!' and proclaiming 'Another world is possible!' A formidable return of the repressed.

Alice in Imperialist Wonderland[78]

Lewis Carroll, the creator of *Alice in Wonderland* and *Through the Looking Glass,* satirized the colonial rivalry between England and France *circa* 1870 in his delightful 'nonsense' poem 'The Walrus and the Carpenter.' Every child recalls how the two friends lure out a band of young oysters to join them for a stroll on the beach and then – as shown in the delightful Tenniel illustrations below – sit down and devour them all.

The Walrus, who symbolizes hypocritical, perfidious Britain, weeps for the unfortunate oysters, who represent the newly subjugated peoples of the colonies:

> *With sobs and tears he sorted out*
> *Those of the larger size,*
> *Holding his pocket-handkerchief*
> *Before his streaming eyes.*

Alice, indignant, declares she likes British Walrus better than the French Carpenter because at least the Walrus felt sorry. But when she learns that the Walrus, hiding his huge mouth behind the hypocritical handkerchief of British sentimental moralism, had secretly eaten the most oysters, Alice decides she likes the Carpenter better. Alas, the latter ate 'as many as he could.'

This ingenious parable illustrates the hypocrisy and cynicism which continue to mask inter-imperialist rivalries - for example between the US and France -

---

[78] A shorter version of this text appears in the Summer 2007 issue of *New Politics* under the title 'Alice in Imperialand.'

in our own day. The Carpenter continues to defend tooth and claw his spheres of influence among French ex-colonies and ex-protectorates in Africa and the Middle East, while the US, having replaced Britain in the role of the moralistic Walrus, hypocritically supports the 'rebels' against pro-French corrupt dictatorships in the name of 'democracy.' The result has been a generation of bloody and never-ending civil wars which have devoured hundreds of thousands of Oysters – I mean of dark-skinned men, women and children. Yet such proxy wars – from Algeria to Central Africa – are generally portrayed in the media as inexplicable mayhem rooted in 'age-old ethnic or religious rivalries.'

Anti-imperialist Alices

Unfortunately, many intellectuals on the Left are quite as naïve as Alice when it comes to understanding the nature of these inter-imperialist conflicts which continue to bloody the planet. For some, the one and only imperialist is the American Walrus, the one who eats the most Oysters (while throwing a few to his faithful imperialist lapdog, Britain). Thus for many anti-imperialists and Third World supporters on the Left, the word 'imperialism' has become synonymous with 'US superpower.' Anti-imperialist internationalism is thus reduced to simple anti-Americanism.

This confusion is very convenient for French neo-colonialism which literally gets away with murder, for example in the Ivory Coast today. Like Alice, many intellectuals in both France and the U.S. are naïvely unaware that the little imperialist Carpenter is still devouring 'as many (African and Asian) oysters as he can.' They forget that 'little' French imperialism – personified today by the slightly ridiculous pointy-nosed Carpenter Chirac – counts among his ancestors Louis XIV, the two Napoleons, Clemenceau 'the Tiger' and Charles de Gaulle. They forget that France's current prosperity is in large measure based on its privileged relationships with the French-supported cleptocratic dictatorships which have replaced the former French colonial administrations (thus keeping the profits while reducing administrative costs). However, the imperialist rivalry between the Franco-American allies becomes obvious once we look behind the handkerchief of humanitarian propaganda which masks the genocidal civil wars ravaging central Africa today - as they ravaged Rwanda a decade ago.

Genocide in Rwanda

Indeed, the scandal of Western responsibility in the Rwandan genocides is once again back in the headlines – at least in France. On the one hand, Paul Kagame, the pro-American President of Rwanda, has correctly accused the French government of having supported and armed the genocidal 'Hutu' militias both before and during the massacres of Summer 1994. This complicity had already been exposed in *Le Monde diplomatique* as early as

142

March 1995.[79] On the other hand, a French prosecutor has counter-attacked by accusing Kagame of having plotted the murder of the former President, the pro-French Hutu Habyarimana, in April 1994 – thus provoking the massacres. The prosecutor's case is quite convincing.

The point is that during this sordid imperialist proxy-war between the colossal American Walrus and the small French Carpenter - 500,000 African oysters were being cruelly murdered while the Western media prattled on about 'ancestral ethnic hatreds.'

In fact, the words Tutsi and Hutu refer to two castes of a single ethnic group who for the past hundred years have been turned against each other first by the Belgian colonial regime (who created these legal identities) and then the French. Divide and rule, the oldest trick in the imperialist book. Nowadays, we have the American Walrus cynically backing the ex-'rebel' President Kagame in order to squeeze the French out of their spheres of influence in Central Africa. Nonetheless, today's naïve intellectuals, Alice-like, always seem to feel the need to back one imperialist side over the other. Thus the French section of the NGO Doctors Without Borders 'were eager to intervene [in Rwanda] on the side of the French Army, which the other sections [of DWB] categorically refused.'[80]

---

[79] According to the *Monde diplomatique* '... France massively equipped the Rwandan Military Forces (FAR); France introduced them into the camps where torture and massacres of civilians was taking place . . . From April to June 1994, during which period the massacres continued and 500,000 Tutsi's were murdered with *machetes,* part of the French Army had but a single obsession: continue to re-supply the FAR.'
[80] See '*Retour sur le génocide de 1994 au Rwanda,*' in *Révolution internationale* No 375 Jan. 2007. www.internationalism.org

More recently we saw another instance of this naivety in the buildup to the Iraqi War during 2002-2003. Then the French Carpenters Chirac and de Villepin appeared as veritable anti-imperialists for attempting to block the bloated Walruses Bush and Blair who were preparing, for humanitarian reasons, to devour Iraq's oyster reserves - I mean 'oil reserves.' Yet the anti-imperialist Alices had no clue that Carpenter Chirac was only doing his imperialist duty bravely defending the interests of the French oil cartel Elf/Total, long implanted in Saddam Hussein's Iraq, against the pretensions of the nasty Walruses (Bush/Exxon and Blair/BP) who were trying to gobble them up.

Liberal and Social-Democratic Alices

Fortunately, liberal and social-democratic Alices like Christopher Hitchens were around to reassure us that the tender-hearted Anglo-Saxon Walruses were only intervening in Iraq to save us from non-existent WMD's. Or was it to save us from Islamic terrorism (after having subsidized it in Afghanistan)... Or to free the Muslim womenfolk (by imposing Sharia)... Or to bring democracy (in the form of Islamic militias)? Cynical or naively patriotic, these pro-intervention Alices failed to see that the hypocritical super-armed Walrus likes to hide his ravenous appetite for oysters behind ideological handkerchiefs like 'humanitarian intervention,' 'defending democracy,' and never-ending crusades such as the 'war against drugs' and the 'war against terrorism.' So they support imperialistic interventions 'from the Left,' all the while criticizing the excessively brutal, greedy and sloppy table manners of the Walrus devouring his prey.

Both groups of intellectual Alices - the 'anti-imperialists' and the 'humanitarian interventionists' - commit the same logical fallacy as Carroll's original. Former children will recall that Alice, who as an English school-child believed in Fair Play, waxed indignant at the sniveling hypocrisy of her compatriot, the Walrus, hiding his greed behind tears. So Carroll's Alice instinctively transferred her sympathies to the Carpenter - equally rapacious, but smaller. We find the same naïve reaction among sincere (or cynical) Leftists who, revolted by the hypocritical barbarism of the Western imperialists in the Middle East, turn around and support the frank barbarism of reactionary Islamist militias. I call this common error in reasoning the EEF fallacy: 'the Enemies of our Enemies are our Friends.'

According to this EEF logic, progressives must now consecrate violent, reactionary Islamists under the noble title of 'the Iraqi Resistance.' Never mind that these bloodthirsty sheiks, mullahs and sectarian militias massacre civilians in internecine warfare, blow up elementary schools, rape and murder unveiled women and break up trade-unions. In the writings of my old friends Alex Calinicos and Chris Harmon and their co-thinkers in France and the US these Islamists, dialectically cleansed of such venial sins, emerge as saints. What is

144

the proof that fanatical religious militias are truly 'progressive?' When not murdering each other and preying on civilians, the Islamists *also* fight against U.S. and British troops! Lewis Carroll, who in his day job was a Professor of mathematics and logic at Oxford University and delighted in pushing such illogic to its logical conclusions in his *Alice* books, would have died laughing. But what is truly sad is to see former Marxist internationalists – who during the Cold War had the clear-sighted courage to reject *both* Western capitalist imperialism ('Democracy') *and* Eastern state-capitalist imperialism ('Communism') – fall opportunistically into this EEF trap in Iraq.[81]

But how are we to avoid the trap of taking sides between the imperialist Walrus and his equally rapacious little buddy, the Carpenter? How to escape the false logic according to which one is inevitably obliged to choose between Uncle Sam and smaller rivals like France, Russia, China, Iran, India and Brazil? Or between the Great American Satan and reactionary nationalist-religious forces striving for dictatorial state power in places like Iraq, Lebanon and Israel/Palestine? 'That,' said Hamlet, 'is the question!'

Dustups in a Gentlemen's Club

Engrossed in this dilemma, I decided to address myself to the professional Marxist scholars who publish the journals *ReThinking Marxism* (U.S.), *Historical Materialism,* and *The Socialist Register* (G.B.). Two international conferences organized by the editors last Winter – one at University of Massachusetts (Amherst) and the other at the University of London – provided the occasion. During my sojourn in these postmodern academic paradises, I was heartened to learn that in today's globalized world inter-imperialist rivalries no longer existed (or had been reduced to mere vestiges of former times, like your Correspondent). This excellent news was systematically presented by the keynote speakers – highly respected specialists - at the London plenary session on International Relations. For them, world capitalism is 'a club' (exact quote) whose only problem is to choose new members with prudence. (Is China 'clubbable' yet?) For a moment I thought myself transported back to the 19th Century Oxbridge world of Carroll and Wilde.

Courteously, these Marxist clubmen explained to me that today, with a globalized economy, something called 'international capital' (the club) had emerged. This mysteriously ubiquitous capital apparently has no denomination, no nationality, no home port; and its club has been ruling for the past century over a relatively stable, peaceful world. Naïvely, I asked them 'but

---

[81] This fallacy has led these would-be revolutionary internationalists to some wonderfully absurd deviations like 'Islamic feminism,' presented by the Socialist Workers' Party and Tariq Ramadan at the World Social Forum in London in 2004. See Caroline Fourest, *La tentation obscurantiste*, (Paris, Grasset 2005), pp. 131 ff.

what about the two World Wars?'[82]   These were merely 'dustups' (exact quotation).[83] This last explanation provoked groans from certain members of the otherwise respectful and attentive audience. However, calm returned when another lecturer provided conclusive evidence that the capitalists of every land indeed belong to the same international club. Using slides, he demonstrated that corporate advertisements and government campaign posters promoting higher efficiency through competition were virtually identical whether produced in Britain, Europe, Taiwan or Indonesia. From this it follows that international competition, far from dividing, actually unites all the members of the club by providing each and all with incentives to increase their productivity.[84] Conclusion: inter-imperialist rivalry cannot exist. The Walrus and the Carpenter – like the Limeys and the Gerries, the Yanks and the Japs, the Frogs and the Boches –are members in good standing of the same club, where competition is confined to the tennis court and war to the chessboard.

By now, it had began to dawn on me that these British Dons, like Don Quixote before them, had lost their reason from reading too many books – for example by reading postmodern Romances by legendary authors with foreign-sounding names like 'Negri-and-Hardt.' Reading these Romances, they imbibe tales about Multitudes of revolutionary knights-errant tilting at a huge windmill marked 'The Empire of International Capital.' Meanwhile in the real world, giants of various sizes and nationalities (Russian, American, Iranian, French, Chinese) are busy dividing up the world and fighting over the spoils.

---

[82] Wars which, according to the *passé* Marxism of Luxemburg, Lenin, Kautsky, Hilferding and Trotsky, resulted from so-called 'inter-imperialist rivalries').

[83] Quoted from Prof. Peter Gowan: 'One Logic or Two in Capitalist International Relations and the Possibilities of Transcending the Inter-state System.' Paper presented at the *Historical Materialism* international conference, University of London, Dec. 2006.

[84] As demonstrated by Paul Cammack in his paper 'Governance of Global Capitalism,' at the London conference. Q.E.D. again!

Always practical and curious like Alice, I decided to test these charmingly deranged Dons by asking them to explain to me – without reference to the interests of national capital – how it was that my comfortable teachers' pension, paid in deflated U.S. dollars, was no longer adequate enough for me to stay in a London Hotel ($200) or buy them a round of British beer (at twelve bucks a glass). Like true gentlemen and true socialists, these generous colleagues immediately invited me to be their guests – but no one came up with the obvious explanation for this devaluation, to wit: Uncle Sam, that scheming old Yankee Walrus, was in debt up to his ears having borrowed billions from the Chinese. He solved the problem by cranking up presses and printing cheap dollars. That way he can pay back the poor benighted heathen in devaluated paper (all the while yelling 'unfair!' at the devious Chinese for keeping the *yuan* at an 'artificially low' exchange rate).

What is International Capital?

By this time I began wondering about this *international capital* about which I had yet to hear a precise, operational definition. Is it merely a statistical abstraction (the sum total of all the capital invested in all the world's banks and stock exchanges)? Doesn't it go home some place at night? Or is all this wealth running around the world like a dog without a master? Call me 'insufficiently theorized,' but I always imagined that capital (or rather peoples' individual capitals) had to be parked somewhere, denominated in one or another fluctuating *national* currency ('a mark, a yen a buck or a pound'). I also thought that capital had to be invested in corporations (however extensive their transnational or foreign holdings) chartered by one or another *national* state and traded on one or another *national* stock market.

Moreover, my occasional reading of the *Wall Street Journal* and *Forbes: Capitalist Tool* gives me the impression that these corporations based in one state are always competing with corporations from another, seeking new markets and investment opportunities in order to repatriate their profits to their

147

stock-holders back home. Furthermore, these corporations are generally able to count on the support of their national governments, which they influence through media control and political campaign contributions. In return they receive not only tax breaks and bailouts but also diplomatic and military support in their international operations. Always 'in the national interest' to be sure. From a practical businessman's point of view, the abstract *international capital* of the academic theorist appears like a creature out of Carroll's Looking-glass World.

Take one example: the U.S. multinational corporation *United Brands* (formerly the *United Fruit Company* of Chiquita Banana fame) owns half of Guatemala, including the railroads and other essential infrastructures. This corporation's purpose is to enrich its U.S. investors, and it depends on the U.S. government to keep Guatemalan labor costs low – for example by using the C.I.A. to overthrow Arbenz's reformist government in 1954 and by supporting and arming a horrendous series of death-squad dictatorships ever since. And speaking of bananas, the business pages of my *International Herald Tribune* are full of stories about the diplomatic trade-war between France and America over whether the U.S. has the right to dump cheaply-produced Guatemalan bananas on the European market - a market heretofore dominated by French banana companies implanted in Africa. Like the 2003-04 diplomatic conflict between Bush/Exxon and Chirac/Elf-Total over Iraq, today's banana wars are a clear case of imperialist rivalry between national capitals invested in globalized multinational corporations. How to explain this apparent paradox?

The Unified Actor Fallacy

It goes without saying that all bourgeois capitalists (and the governments they control) agree that they should pay their workers the minimum possible salary, extract from them the maximum amount of labor and send for the police when they go on strike. Small wonder that their 'competitiveness means productivity' propaganda should be nearly identical from Indianapolis to Indonesia.[85] Their bourgeois class interests are complimentary. But that doesn't stop the different national bourgeoisies from competing to attract new capital and to dominate markets or from eating each other up in hostile takeovers, trade disputes or even armed invasions - the ultimate in contradictions.

Even little Alice finally got behind the apparent paradox that the Walrus and the Carpenter were 'friends' (or accomplices) when it came to luring the naïve young oysters onto the beach, but 'enemies' (or rivals) when it came to dividing the spoils. An old-fashioned Marxist (if there were any left) would

---

[85] And were Stalin's Stakhanovite productivity campaigns in favor of 'socialist emulation' any different ?

have patiently explained to her that this friendship is a dialectical relationship, at once complimentary and contradictory.

So how come our London International Relations specialists, all good neo-Marxists, failed to identify such blatant examples of inter-imperialist conflict as World Wars I and II? I can only imagine that our good Dons' Negri-sotted brains became fixated on the chimerical vision of a unitary *'international capital'* as a sort of Unmoved Mover or Invisible Hand. In consequence, the deluded Dons were forced to conclude (erroneously of course) that their own febrile abstraction was the necessary and effective cause of every political-economic effect in the real world, from the World Wars to the price of beans in Bengal. Some people call this kind of logical error the Unified Actor Fallacy (UAF). It consists of treating a plural subject ('immigrants,' 'sports fans,' 'the Jews') as if it were singular. Once we accept the assumption of *international capital* as a single, all-powerful Unified Actor running the world, it follows, like night follows day, that such an ideal world must be harmonious and WWII a mere 'dustup.'

'International Capital': an Anti-Semitic Myth?

Here, please allow me a personal aside. Personally, it is hard for me to conceive of 'International Capital' other than as a kind of imaginary conspiracy, like the 'Jewish capital' that the anti-Semites I grew up among were always raging about.

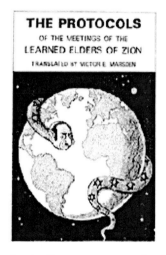

And sure enough, whom do we find today trumpeting their opposition to globalizing 'international finance capital' but our old friends the anti-Semites? For example, that hoary fabrication of the Czarist secret police, the alleged 'Protocols of the Elders of Zion' is now back in circulation not only in Czar Putin's Russia, but translated into Arabic by the Moslem Brotherhood. 'The Jews own the world, they are the Enemy; the international Jewish conspiracy battens on impure, unproductive, international finance capital, trampling on the rights of honest native, racially pure, productive national capital. Worse still, Jews ritually drink the blood of Christian children every Passover.' A crude fabrication, but it worked well enough for the Czars, not to mention Hitler in his day.

The time-tested anti-Semitic 'conspiracy' myth is of great utility to today's super-rich fundamentalist Sunni oil-sheiks and billionaire Shi'ite mullahs, not to mention secular dictators. While these national potentates batten on an oily

149

diet of Oysters Rockefeller, the impoverished populations they exploit and oppress are mobilized against the Enemy Other – international bankers, Israel, the rich Jews in N.Y. and Washington.

Closer to home, we find Hitler-admirer Pat Buchanan jumping on the anti-globalization bandwagon, warring against international finance capital, opposing NAFTA and joining the anti-WTO protests in Seattle in the name of 'America First.'[86] In France, the neo-fascist Le Pen made common front with the far-left to block the European Constitution as did the near-Nazi Haider in Austria. In the Russian Federation, President Putin has adopted the nationalist politics of the openly anti-Semitic 'Brown/Red' neo-Stalinists like Zhirinovsky while merrily squeezing all the oil, blood and money out of the billionaire Jewish oysters – I mean Jewish oligarchs. Anti-Semitism is the glue that bonds the International of right-wing populists, nativists, racists, nationalists, xenophobes, proto-fascists and Nazis of all countries in their opposition to globalization. Whatever their nationality, today's anti-Semitic demagogues speak a common language where code-words like *'international finance capital,' 'American'* (i.e. N.Y. Jewish) or *'multi-national capital'* are used to define the Enemy Other as by nature foreign, alien, conspiratorial – ultimately Jewish. The politics based on attacking *'international finance capital'* rather than capital *per se* is a politics that makes for some very unsavory bedfellows.

Bloody Handshakes

Having exploded both the EEF and the UAF fallacies, we are now able to return dialectically to the paradoxical 'friendship' between France and the United States. As we know, the French Carpenter and the American Walrus have been great Allies since the 1770s when Louis XVI supported George Washington's War of Independence in order to undermine his rival, King George of England. In the 20th Century, the American Republic supported the French Republic during two World Wars ('Lafayette, we are here!') Yet this unity between the world's two oldest republics also contains its own dialectical contradiction, as I discovered during the 50th Anniversary celebrations of the U.S landings in Normandy when the French papers were full of interesting historical information.

It transpired that in June 1944, General Eisenhower landed in Normandy planning not to liberate France but to *occupy* it (like Iraq today). In his baggage train, 'Ike' brought cases of printed bank notes intended to replace the *franc.* Far from planning to free Paris from German occupation much less supporting de Gaulle, the Anglo-Saxon commanders' plan was to abandon the Parisians to

---

[86] See 'Anti-Globalization: Buchanan, Fulani & Neo-fascist Drift in the U.S.' by Tom Burghardt in *My Enemy's Enemy* Kersplebedeb Publishing, Montreal and online at www.kersplebedeb.com/mystuff/books/myenemy.html

their fate and head straight toward Berlin (as we learned from the popular book and film *Is Paris Burning?*) Roosevelt's unspoken goal – pursued by all of his successors – was to take control of France's rich colonies in Africa and Indo-China. On the other hand, the underlying objective de Gaulle's Free France, based in France's overseas territories, was always to preserve these colonies for the benefit of the French bourgeoisie, which had lost its legitimacy by collaborating with the losing side (Germany and Japan).

However, it must be born in mind that this Franco-American rivalry was ever and always subordinated to their Alliance against the Axis and against the Communists. Thus, for example, in 1954 Eisenhower and Dulles were seriously considering dropping an atomic bomb to save the French colonial troops pinned down by the Vietnamese Communists at Dien Bien Phu. Which didn't stop the friendly American Walrus from replacing France as imperialist overlord in Vietnam and suffering his own prolonged 'Dien Bien Phu' in 1965-1975. Nor did it stop the American imperialists from encouraging anti-French rebels in Algeria, Morocco and Tunisia in the name of 'anti-colonialism.' In 1993-94 as we have seen, the two imperialisms fought a kind of proxy war in Rwanda using the 'Hutus' and Tutsis' as pawns just as in 2003-04 they had a big falling out over Iraq and oil.

But that story had a happy ending in 2004 when the Presidents of the two Republics collaborated in overthrowing the elected government of the world's third oldest (and only Black) Republic: Haiti. After kidnapping its legitimate President Aristide, occupying the island (for humanitarian reasons), supporting the terrorist *Tontons Macoutes* and promoting the cronies of the former dictator, 'Baby Doc' Duvalier, Bush and Chirac finally shook hands. And here we are in 2007, with the French and American military advisors (not to mention the Chinese) once again murkily involved in murderous maneuvers in Chad, Central Africa, Darfur and Somalia with more massacres in sight.

"Shouldn't we find out more about
their policies before following them?"

Conclusion: Oysters of the world arise! Oysters have no Fatherland! Don't heed the siren songs of imperialist Walruses and Carpenters! We must unite globally before they gobble us all up! We have a world to win (if global warming doesn't get us first)!

Part III:

Where are the Riots of Yesteryear?

'What Did YOU Do in the 1968 War, Dad?'

Telephone Interview between Richard Greeman and Jenny Greeman
[April, 2008]

Jenny (in N.Y.): So, Dad, the 40th Reunion of the Columbia Strike is coming up, and I'm going to the festivities with Mom. To set the scene for this interview I want to state that Columbia is right up the hill from where I live here in Manhattan Valley.

Richard (in France): Back in 1968 when it was a slum called Manhattanville, I used to borrow your mother's Polaroid camera to take court photos of holes in the plaster and rat-bitten kids for members of tenants associations which we helped organize through CORE [Congress of Racial Equality] and the West Side Block Association. Polaroids were acceptable evidence in land-lord/tenant cases because they couldn't be faked.

Jenny: My husband and I now complain about all the students running around the neighborhood as if we were townies! Anyway, we've got some great pictures here from April 1968, even the cover of *The NY Times*. That strike was a big deal!

Richard: I think the issues at Columbia crystallized the major problems that were national – even international – questions of racism, the imperialist war in Vietnam, and what became known as the youth revolt or student rebellion. But of course the Columbia revolt was far overshadowed by the student-worker near-revolution in France, which broke out a week later. At the time, the Columbia Strike Committee asked me to telegraph, in French, their greetings of solidarity to the students occupying the Sorbonne. The text was later reprinted in French in a book about the *Situationnistes.* If you remember, I quote that group in 'The Permanence of the Paris Commune.'

Jenny: Getting back to Columbia, let's start our interview by going through these old copies of the *NY Post*. The first headline reads 'STUDENTS TAKE DEAN HOSTAGE.' What were you doing, Dad, on that fateful day of Tuesday, April 23rd when all of this began?

Richard: That day, as usual, I taught some French classes in the morning; then at noon I turned out to the SDS rally at the sundial in the middle of the campus, where I had often spoken about the War in Vietnam, based on my knowledge of France's imperialist failure there. A good-sized crowd had gathered and was hesitating about whether or not to do an 'action.' Participatory democracy in practice. Everyone was frustrated because our attempts to negotiate with the administration over the construction of the Jim Crow gym had failed. With my prompting Mark Rudd, the leaders of the SDS 'action-faction' and good friend of Mom and me, decided to lead the group over to Morningside Park, which had just been blocked off by a chain-link fence and where Columbia had already started excavating.

Jenny: The gym.

Richard: Yes, Columbia was planning to take over Morningside Park; to rip up this public park to build a private gym and there was outcry in the neighborhood and on the campus about this.

Jenny: Just to get our bearings here, Morningside Park runs from W. 110th Street to W. 125th street in the valley between Columbus Avenue and Harlem Proper. This is my neighborhood. There's now a fountain and pond with geese at the excavation site and a very popular baseball diamond. Remember, we celebrated last July 4th there with a live band playing patriotic music and the whole neighborhood having picnics and cook-outs.

Richard: Yes. It was a beautiful moment for me. I really believe we saved that Park and it's wonderful that you and your friends are enjoying the fruits of our labor.

Jenny: If you guys hadn't knocked down that fence, we wouldn't have been sitting there…. What happened next?

Richard: After some pushing and shoving with cops, we finally filtered back to the campus and ended up in the lobby of Hamilton Hall, where I had my office and was supposed to teach a mid-afternoon class in Humanities. This was the 'Great Books' course that Columbia had put into the curriculum at the time of WWI so that young ROTC's who would then go off and fight for democracy would know the canon/tradition for which they were laying down their lives… We read everything from Homer and Plato through Old and New Testaments and on through Montaigne and Voltaire (my specialty). Enough culture to give a sense of superiority and help breed a native American officer class. But the canon can also be read against the grain.

Jenny: What do you mean, Dad?

Richard: Today they call it 'deconstruction.' Back in 1968, I had a whole back row of Navy ROTC students (Columbia was all-male) who regularly came to class in beautiful navy blue and white uniforms. In the next row I had young orthodox Jews in the class who knew the Old Testament 10 times better than

156

their bearded (to look older) professor. In fact I was barely 6 years older than the freshmen and only 3 years older than the seniors who were taking the course late. With these guys we read Thucydides' account of the war between Athens and Sparta in which Athens (a democratic, but imperialist power) sent an army over across the water to Sicily to conquer Sparta's ally, Syracuse – just like the US invading Vietnam in the long war with Russia. Of course, the Athenians ended up losing both their army and their democracy. These were very bright NY students. The young officer candidates were well aware of the analogies. Then we went on to analyze the Old Testament with genuine *Yeshivabuchas* who knew it in Hebrew. It was a great class and a great time to be a teacher, full of what today we call 'teaching moments.' The campus was already very sharply polarized between pro- and anti-war and right and left – and the class was held in Hamilton Hall, by now occupied by SDSers , Black students from the Afro-American Society, and others. They were sort of besieging the Dean's office and would eventually sequester him there.

Jenny: Right. Here's the *Post* front page with a big headline 'COLUMBIA STUDENTS HOLD DEAN 24 HRS.' But back to your afternoon class....

Richard: So first I milled about with the students, and then it was time for me to go upstairs to my Humanities class, to which everyone had unexpectedly shown up! I greeted them and said something like: 'I know there's a lot going on downstairs and like me, you all have opinions about it, but today we're finishing Spinoza, which is a very hard subject and I've worked very hard to prepare for the class so if you've also prepared and you want to keep reading Spinoza, the subject is Freedom. So we took a vote and it was unanimous for holding class! We did, and it was a very lively discussion. After 50 minutes, I went back downstairs and now the entire lobby was jammed with students. Some, mostly Blacks, were ostensibly guarding the door to the Dean's office. It was clear that they would remain there and hold the building until they got an answer form this Dean, who was a sweet jock named Harry Coleman. I hung out with the kids and made a little speech about what the student movement was doing in Europe, and around 7 pm I got hungry and realized they would stay there all night and sleep on the floor in the classrooms. I had no interest in that so I went home to Julie for dinner. I had already had a big day.

Jenny: The next day must have been even bigger, right?

Richard: Looking back I would say it was one of the biggest and *happiest* days of my life! I don't know where all that energy came from. It was like education in action.

Instructor Richard Greenman teaches outdoors.

Jenny: That's what's written on your sign in this picture in the *Post:* The sign stuck to a tree over your head reads: 'Dick Greeman's class, Education in Action, meets here. 2:00.' And below a *Post* editor wrote a caption reading 'Instructor Richard L; Greenman teaches outdoors.' Like they can't read? They've always got to put an extra '*n*' in our name.

Richard: That picture was taken a few days later, after the Big Bust, during the actual strike. You can see the bald patch on my head where the doctor shaved it after I got clobbered by a cop, but we're getting ahead of our story. ... The next morning I made sure to get up early and put on my 'professor's disguise' (tweed jacket, rep tie, khakis, button-down collar and pipe) and return to the campus refreshed and ready. I put on an *espresso* and opened the *N.Y. Times,* which had been delivered around 6 am. Lo and behold, he headlines announced that during the night the Columbia students had occupied two more buildings! The Black students of SAS were holding out in Hamilton, and by mutual agreement, the Whites and SDS had seized two more. The hard core of SDS were ensconced in President Kirk's luxurious office with a Rembrandt on the wall (which an art history student claimed was probably *school* of Rembrandt). The others were in Fayerweather, where I had lots of friends because it was occupied mainly by grad students, students from professional schools and intellectual type undergrads from Barnard and Columbia. You can imagine I was totally elated when I read the headlines, and so I ran to the subway and down to 116th Street to see what was happening. At that hour, the campus was deserted. I walked up to Low Library and the first thing I saw was my favorite SDSer Mark Rudd sitting the window sill of President Kirk's with one foot in and one foot out and I couldn't tell if he was coming or going.

Jenny: The headline of the *N.Y. Post* reads 'Columbia Rebels Seize More Buildings' and there's a front page photo of students boosting themselves up to the window into President Kirk's office in Lowe Library.

Richard: Yes, that was taken during the excitement the night before while I was home in bed. Now it was the cold light of dawn. I had missed out on the long, lonely night the drastically reduced group of occupiers had spent in the *sacro sanct* of Columbia University waiting for a police bust in at any minute. It must have been scary in there cut off from the world. So there was Mark and I showed him the newspaper headlines and said, 'Mark don't be a schmuck, we've won. Get back in that building!' We've laughed about that together many times over the last years.

Then I went over to Hamilton Hall where my office was and where the Black students had now set up a serious barricade and let it be known that they were in solidarity with SDS on the demands over the gym, Vietnam, and over the punishment of students who had demonstrated. Soon some of the other professors who taught at Hamilton started showing up, as well as an old friend of mine, Sydney Von Luther from 1199 a Black union organizer whom I had worked with for years through Columbia CORE trying to organize Columbia's cafeteria workers (mostly Black and Puerto Rican) into a union. In fact, back in the 30's, James Wechsler, the student editor of the Columbia daily *Spectator* who was later the editor of the *N.Y. Post* for many years) got in trouble for supporting the cafeteria workers under autocratic Columbia President Nicholas Murray Butler, whose sister had the concession of the cafeteria and was as violently anti-labor as her brother, a former Republican vice-presidential candidate. When Columbia's football cheerleaders chant 'Who owns New York? We own New York!' they ain't just whistling Dixie.

My friends in CORE and I had previously tried to get help from the restaurant workers union, but that union finked out on us. Local 1199, however, did not. And thanks to our effort, all Columbia cafeteria, buildings/grounds, and later, secretarial workers are unionized and have benefits today. This – like the preservation of Morningside Park – is one of the great long-lasting victories of Columbia '68 I'm still proud of.

Jen: That's great, Dad. So let's get back to when it all started. We're at Hamilton Hall the first morning of the occupations.

Richard: So Sydney, the other teachers and I, almost spontaneously, became a nonviolent faculty cordon in front of Hamilton to avoid violence and because we sympathized with the students inside and didn't want them attacked. Sydney had lots of Civil Rights experience, and so did some of the other sympathetic faculty members whom I knew and who were also locked out of their offices. We were thus able to fend off a crowd of aggressive, jock-like White students who wanted to charge in and mix it up with the Black students inside. Who organized this phalanx, which later took form as the anti-strike 'Majority Coalition?' I was told at the time that Dean Truman or people from Truman's office had gone around to the fraternities the previous night and whipped up opposition among the conservative students. It was from this spontaneous group experience that the famous Ad Hoc Faculty Committee I talk about in my article was formed. We then fanned out to do our non-violent picket in front of the other occupied buildings.

Jenny: Where did you end up, Dad?

Richard: I was sent over to occupied Fayerweather Hall, where students were starting to gather for early morning classes (it was either 8 or 9). Again, a phalanx of athletic-looking students appeared, all fresh-faced and scrubbed, carrying piles of books and demanding to attend their classes, in pursuit of which they were willing to break through the feeble barriers erected by the Weenie grad students and beat them all up. With a few other Professors I held onto the high ground at the top of the steps leading to the doors, from which I was able to look down at the gathering mob. I recognized a student in the crowd moving up, called out his name and said: 'Why Mr. So-and so, I've never known you to be up so bright and early and so eager to absorb knowledge.' Of course, that got them laughing and I persuaded them to sit down like gentlemen and scholars and discuss the matter, rather than having a brawl which would be unseemly on an Ivy League college campus. I told them 'if you're so eager to learn philosophy and political science, well there is something exciting happening here and now on this campus and we're part of it. So let's discuss it.' Isn't that what college is supposed to be about? Today, we would call it an ideal 'teaching moment;' It was in that context that I said something about education in action which got picked up by the next day's *N.Y. Times*.

Jenny: Right. Here's your quote: 'There can be no education and no thought that is divorced from action.'

Richard: So that's how I got them all to sit down on the lawn in front of Fayerweather, and we held a discussion – you could call it a teach-in. Next I gave the floor to a famous sociology professor, Amatai Etzioni, who was standing next to me on the steps.

Jenny: Oh yes, here's his picture talking in front of the crowd on page 5 of the *N.Y. Post* We can see your ear behind him while he's talking into the Radio 88 microphone. The caption reads: 'International expert on arms control placates students in front of Fayerweather Hall and things cool off a bit, for a while.'

Richard: Well things heated up the next day when William F. Buckley Jr., picked up that *Times* quote in his nationally syndicated column and hauled me over the coals.

Jenny: Yes, here it is in the *Post* from April 30. 'Professor Richard Gree*n*man of the French department announced, in the accents of Charlotte Corday, that 'there can be no education and no thought that is divorced from action.' The trouble with that statement is (a) it isn't true and (b) even if it were, it is no justification for what the authorities of Columbia have been tolerating.'

Richard: The next day I dashed off a note to the *Times*: 'Dear Bill, It's Greeman, not Gree*n*man and Marat, not Corday,' but he never answered. I bet one of his fact-checkers bit the dust that day.

Jenny: Of course, we're Gree*n*mans, but who are those other people, Marat and Corday?

Richard: Jean-Paul Marat, known as the 'friend of the people,' was the extreme left fiery Jacobin journalist and agitator of the French Revolution, hated and reviled as a monster by all conservatives. Obviously, Buckley had me in mind for the part. Charlotte Corday was a beautiful conservative young woman from the provinces who traveled to Paris, bought a kitchen knife and stabbed Marat in his bath (where he did his writing because he suffered from psoriasis). In my day, every student knew the famous painting by the revolutionary artist David, showing his corpse sprawling in bathtub.

Jenny: Now I remember. There was a famous theatrical production by Peter Brook of a play called 'Marat/Sade.'

Richard: Right, that was Peter Weiss' script: '*The Assassination and Persecution of Jean-Paul Marat as performed by the Inmates of the Asylum at Charonton under the Direction of the Marquis de Sade.'* I really savored the irony that Buckley was implying that I wasn't fit to teach while he didn't know the difference between Marat and Corday! It gave me a big kick that a pretentious prig of an intellectual snob like Buckley would've made such a really ignorant mistake.

Anyway, back to campus. After standing all morning in front of the occupied buildings, we faculty picketers and sympathizers ended up gathering in the graduate lounge at Philosophy Hall, where my Graduate Department, French and Romance Philology, had offices upstairs. The lounge was huge, comfortable and always had tea going. After some discussion, we formed an '*Ad-Hoc* Faculty Committee' to express our concerns in this crisis. I loved those Latin words, *ad-hoc* ('to this' purpose) which gave our spontaneous, unofficial gathering of liberal and radical faculty, mostly untenured, a bit of academic *cachet*.

'The Center Falls Out,' the analytical piece that I wrote for *Radical Teacher* at the time, criticizes the fact that the liberals caved in and that all that *ad hoc* good will and courage was co-opted by a few ambitious faculty members. So the article comes off negative. But what I remember best was how wonderful all of these people were. How our meetings, though a little bit chaotic, were full of passions, erudition, and fun. Here, for the first time ever, faculty members who had been infantilized by the Administration, found their voices. When we faced off against our former Dean, now University Vice-President, David Truman. It was a thrilling moment which made me think of the beginning of the French Revolution when the Estate General first met at

161

Versailles and for the first time the Third Estate, the middle class, was allowed to stand up and speak for itself. I have such clear memories of my colleagues, like Jeoffrey Kaplow, a young Marxist History Professor and specialist of the French Revolution, with a clear high voice and a brilliant sarcastic wit. He's an actor now in London, but still writes left-wing history. And of course there was Eric Bentley, the famous downtown theater critic, translator of Bertolt Brecht and founder of a local cabaret called The DMZ (after the so-called Demilitarized Zone in Vietnam). Columbia had given him a professorship, and he now loudly threatened to resign. Also, Terry Hopkins and Emmanuel Wallerstein, two brilliant semi-Marxist global analysts from the Sociology Department who went on to found the Braudel Institute to study global long term economics. I shouldn't forget Alexander Erlich, an old Polish Socialist, the son of Polish Socialists murdered by Stalin, whom I later met on the Broadway Subway with a red cocarde in his lapel, on his way to a Socialist May Day meeting. These were wonderful colleagues and people who are still – those who are alive – committed to the same ideals.

After Dean Truman told us *ad hoc* faculty that it didn't matter what we thought and that he was going ahead with his police plan, he left the hall under cries of 'shame!' Then we made a plan to get together and to provide a *cordon sanitaire* protection for the students by non-violently blocking the buildings that had been occupied. Including Avery Hall, the Architecture School, whose students had erected a symbolic blockade of beautiful cardboard with ribbons. We were expecting a blood bath, which is exactly what happened two weeks later. So we all fanned out to different places. I really wanted to go to Hamilton Hall, partly out of my sympathy for the Black students and partly because that's where my office was.

But I was sent to a tricky spot, the entrance of Low Library in whose basement the police had their headquarters. A bunch of faculty members were standing on the porch, on the concrete steps that lead into the big door, maybe 20 of us there, including Eric Bentley and several others I knew very well. We were allowing police and other officials to go through our line as a matter of course. Suddenly, a whole phalanx of burly guys in trench coats came barreling up, and I put up my hand and said something like 'we're faculty, officers of the university, what's your business here/identify yourself,' and they didn't even slow down. The first guy walked right up to me, raised his arm and out of his sleeve came a blackjack with which he wrapped me on the top of the head (as my colleagues told me later). I didn't see anything but I sure felt it. I started to go down, but I was so f-ing mad that I punched him in the balls. I don't know if he felt it. I hope so. Anyway, the troop of plainclothes goons marched through us and into Low.

Now I tried to sit up, and my colleagues look horrified since I was bleeding so beautifully (as the most trivial scalp wounds will). They helped me to my feet, and when I touched my head where it hurt and looked at my hand, I could see it was all covered with blood. And, of course cameras were all flashing because this entrance was where the press had gathered. WKCR the college radio was broadcasting remote, the Post was there and people from TV. Never at a loss for words, I stood tall and held up my hand on which the blood was quite visible, and announced to the assembled press what had happened. And that's when the picture was taken that you see on the front page of the next day's Post.

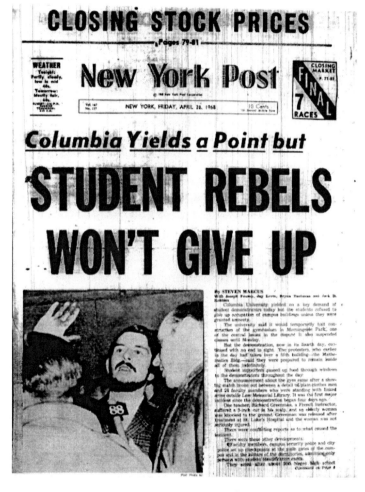

Jenny: This was about 1 am on Thursday, April 26th right? The headline of the Post says, 'STUDENT REBELS WON'T GIVE UP.' The caption reads 'Richard Greenman shows what he claims was blood.'

Richard: Didn't Mark Twain once say: 'I don't care what they write about me as long as they spell me name rights?' So this was my Andy Warhol '15-minutes of fame.' My only regret is I was more famous for getting hit over the head than for what was in my head. But I was feeling elated.

Jenny: Elated? How?

Richard: Yes, elated that I was able to seize the time (as the Panthers were saying) when the press was focused and focus it on the inevitable consequences of bringing carloads of heavily armed police to campus to enforce the trespassing laws in the middle of the night. This was a storm-trooper operation. I was able to express this in a way that might make a difference. Just then the big door opened and a faculty colleague who was working with the administration came to ask how I was (he had heard the story) and to extend David Truman (the Dean's) offer of help/concern. He held out his hand and, of course, with my flair for the dramatic, I shook hands with him and covered his hand with blood. I said to him, 'Take this back to David Truman and tell him the blood of faculty will be on his hands if he continues with this police business!' He was a colleague from the Russian Institute who came form an old Menshevik family and took guitar lessons in Jersey with your Grandmother Mira. I think I felt comfortable enough with him to pull a stunt like that. The next thing that happened was comical. I thought of your mother.

Jenny: Oh, geeze, she must have been worried out of her mind.

Richard: You don't even know

Jenny: Um, I think I might!

Richard: So as soon as I thought of Julie I realized I needed to telephone her and reassure her because she must be going crazy. But here I was on an occupied campus and the only place I could use a phone was down in the administration office, which was filled with police! Of course, how could I go down there?

Jenny: No cell phones, eh?

Richard: No! So after having cavalierly dismissed Truman's offer of assistance I find myself needing to use the phone, and probably the toilet too! Here I am, thoughtlessly fearless when confronting a phalanx of goons, suddenly going to pieces thinking of my wife at home! Anyway, I knocked on the door, and most humbly (now) asked if I could use the phone. They took me downstairs and I could see the whole police command. I called Julie.

164

Now Julie was staying nearby at the apartment of Peter Haydu, another faculty member of the French department (whom I heard from just a few months ago, a propos of the Columbia Reunion).

So I had his number and I called. I spoke to Marie-Helen, Peter's wife, and I told her what was happening and she's telling me that Julie's hysterical. They were listening to the radio (WKCR), which was reporting just then that they'd hit a French professor and he's going down, right then. Right now in Julie's point of view! In any case, it was being simulcast (but 10 minutes late) so my wife is hearing on the radio that I'm dead and I'm on the phone trying to convince her I'm not! I mean, a head wound bleeds a lot, but if you don't have a concussion or crack your skull, it's OK. What hurt was the stitches! After the phone call I dragged myself through now-deserted streets – the cops were rounding everyone up – and walked into St. Luke's hospital. As luck would have it, the guy on duty in the emergency room was a Columbia man with little sympathy for the rebels. Let's just say he didn't take too much care to make the stitches gentle! Well, I met Julie and we went home.

Jenny: That's kind of a big day! So, what do you think was the result of all this?

Richard: The result was that David Truman and President Kirk finally understood what was happening and what *would* happen – that it wouldn't only be my blood. That it would be a blood bath and they called it off. I can just imagine what the police felt, and what contempt they must have had for these 'liberals' on campus who couldn't make up their minds; and it well may be that the reluctance of the police to return may have allowed us to continue our occupation of buildings much longer. Anyway, that was the upshot. The police were called off, the students were jubilant, and the whole situation was transformed. There was no way that Kirk and Truman could 'cry wolf' again or that Mayor Lindsey and the police department could come back. We won more time! And in that time, more buildings were occupied, and more attention was focused on the Six Demands. High school students and outside agitators begin showing up on campus. More important, the majority of Columbia Students had time to argue the issues and eventually come over to the position of SDS, SAS and the sit-ins. That picture of my bloody hand was published the next day, Friday, and that was a new day at Columbia. The occupation had a new lease on life.

Sadly, it was during that period that the *ad-hoc* faculty committee – from having heroically defended the students – ended up getting boxed up in a neutral, and somewhat ambiguous, position between the student strikers on the one hand and the administration on the other, and eventually co-opted, demoralized and dispersed by ambitions faculty opportunists.

Jenny: Yes, that's the story you cover in the article 'The Center Falls Out.' That's a great title and it sounds familiar, like I should know the reference, but I don't. Where did you get it from?

Richard: I'm not surprised you asked. The title is a quote from Leon Trotsky' *History of the Russian Revolution* where he say that 'in a crisis the center falls out' meaning that liberals become irrelevant and you end up with polarization between Reds and Whites. But my left academic colleagues for whom it was written didn't get it either. They thought I was (mis)quoting William Butler Yeats, a moderate, who, in a famous poem, *The Second Coming,* wrote:

> *Things fall apart; the centre cannot hold;*
> *Mere anarchy is loosed upon the world*
> *The best lack all conviction, while the worst*
> *Are full of passionate intensity.*

Great poetry, but not quite what I meant. As for the rest of the story of the strike, I tell it in detail in the article 'The Columbia Rebellion' where you can read about me and Julie both crying while watching the students being hauled off campus during the 'big bust' a week later. So Mayor Lindsay's cops finally agreed to come back to Columbia, and this time they out-did themselves in brutality – perhaps out of peak at being thwarted the first time by a quick-witted French Instructor.

Richard: Oh, Jenny, before we end this interview, there's one more story about Columba 1968 which will interest you as an actress.

Jenny: Let's hear it!

Richard: Well, back in the 60's your mother and I were close friends with the Broadway and TV actor Hershel Bernardi, whom we met through Grandma Mira. Well Heshie was an old Wallace Progressive and sympathized with the 1968 Columbia Student Strikers. At the time, he had just finishing playing Tevye in *Fiddler on the Roof* on Broadway and was touring with his own program of Yiddish theater in English. So after the Big Bust, he volunteered to

 sneak his players through the police cordon around Columbia and present a Left-wing play (I think by Peretz) called *Gymnasium.* It's about a Jewish student in Tzarist Russia facing anti-Semitism, and Heshie asked me to introduce the play to the packed hall of students and make sure they understood that *every word* in this play was written before 1910. You'll see why in a minute.

The plot goes like this: a boy and his parents are burning for him to study, but the quota for Jews at the gymnasium is infinitesimal and bribes, *etc.* are

required to get in. (Raya Dunayevskaya told me of a similar humiliating experience in her own Russian girlhood.) Finally the boy is accepted at some distant gymnasium and moves to that town with his parents. But on the first day at school, he comes home at noon with his new school uniform all messy and announces that he and his classmates are on strike (against discrimination). This is the climax of the play. It's the big scene when the father (played by Heshie), shocked out of his mind at the idea of all that he has sacrificed for nothing, tries to talk the boy out of striking. He launches into a set-piece monologue, a long litany of all the world's problems, each punctuated with an ironic cry of 'strike!' (*'So you don't like discrimination? Strike! So food prices are too high? Strike!*). Finally the old man runs out of steam. He starts getting convinced by his own ironic arguments. And in the end, instead of raising his palms with irony and rolling his eyes in incredulity every time he gets to the word 'strike,' the poor father looks at his son and says, humbly and quietly, 'So, strike.' My eyes are swelling with tears just in the telling.

Well you can imagine the incredible reaction this audience of striking Columbia students. Many of them, like me, were wearing bandages as badges of honor after the Bust and many were having the same problems with their own Jewish parents. They couldn't believe what they were hearing, and every time Heshie pronounced the word 'strike' the audience went wild shouting: 'Strike! Strike! Strike!' for a full minute. And then Heshie said the next part of his monologue, ending in 'strike' and it all started again! I think it took poor Heshie twenty minutes to get through that five-minute monologue, but he was overjoyed. What an audience! What jubilation! And what a powerful thing theater can be, right Jenny?

Jenny: Right, Dad!

From Paris to Prague: the Spirit of '68 Lives! [1969]

Introductory Note [2008]

In March of 1969, I had the opportunity to travel to Europe in the wake of the thrilling May 1968 Student Uprising and General Strike in France. Still smoldering were embers of the (to me) equally significant Prague Spring of radical reform within Communist Czechoslovakia – not to mention the growing student movements in Italy, Germany and Britain. My goal was to catch up with old international comrades, to learn first hand what had transpired in Europe during that revolutionary season, and to observe for myself what remained as a result of the exciting mass struggles that had come close to overthrowing the powerful conservative regimes of two industrialized countries.

Particularly exciting to me at the time was the coincidence of parallel near-revolutions taking place in Gaullist France and Stalinist Czechoslovakia: the one a conservative pillar of the self-proclaimed 'Free' World, the other of the nominally 'Socialist.' This coincidence confirmed my long-held belief that the two allegedly 'ideological' adversaries of the Cold War were in practice rival imperialisms bent on world domination. Both types of exploitative regimes manipulated ideological conflict in order to regiment their disaffected populations against their respective 'Communist' or 'imperialist' enemies and repress legitimate internal dissent as treasonous disloyalty. For me, this agreed-upon Cold War myth had too long inhibited any possibility of international class unity among the oppressed within the Eastern and Western blocks - the indispensable ingredient in any future socialist world. Now, suddenly, simultaneous revolts from Paris to Prague had changed all that.

Moreover, the demands of the both Eastern and Western rebels movements (self-management, participatory democracy) were strikingly similar. So were their methods (spontaneous self-organization, student-worker alliances) and their spirit (lively, radical, optimistic, humorous). So was the response of the authorities (panic and over-reaction which mainly provoked more sympathy for the rebels). Further, these different international movements inspired each other and recognized themselves in each other. The living symbol of this convergence between rebels East and West was 'Red' Rudy Deutschke, a young Marxist rebel against East Germany's Communist regime who, once expelled, became a leader in West German SDS (socialist student society) and was tragically assassinated by a reactionary egged on by the right-wing

Springer press. This East-West internationalism extended to the U.S. For example in August 1968, when the Russian tanks rolled in to crush the Czech rebellion and the protesters at the Democratic Convention – also victims of police violence — put up signs reading 'Welcome to Czechago!' We in SDS and the U.S. left also attempted to reach out internationally, although in that pre-Internet and pre-cell-phone era this was not always easy. The International Student Conference we hosted at Columbia in the Summer of 68), my 1969 trip to Europe, and the dispatches I sent home were among such attempts.

If these 40-year-old 'dispatches from the European front' have any interest today, it is to remind us that for quite a while after and in many lands, the revolts of 1968 remained, as the slogan went, 'Just a Beginning.' Who could be sure such beginnings might not still lead to new, higher struggles. And indeed, some of the fires lit in that era are still glowing embers today, despite decades of government and media campaigns to demonize or trivialize the truly radical and internationalist spirit of the '60s.

The defect of these somewhat breathless eyewitness chronicles is the other side of the same coin: their excessive revolutionary optimism, which predominates despite the evidence I give indicating that the movement was in decline and the establishment tightening its grip on power. 'Pessimism of the intellect; optimism of the will' (the motto of the Italian Marxist Antonio Gramsci, who spent many years in Mussolini's prisons) was my mood.

Paris One Year Later: 'Gauchistes' Everywhere

(Paris, March 18, 1969) [87] As soon as you return to France you begin to notice it: 'gauchistes' seem to be everywhere. From the windows of the bus leaving the airport the highway walls proclaim: 'Power to the Workers' Councils,' 'The Struggle Continues,' 'May Will Bloom Again,' 'C(ommunist) P(arty) = Betrayal,' *CGT* [Communist Union]= *CRS* [Police Riot Squad].

What do the French mean by 'gauchistes'? Literally 'leftists,' but it really means *ultra-leftists* since last Spring the official Left (the Communist Party its affiliated unions along with the social-democrats and theirs') did its utmost to contain the worker-student uprising and then joined with de Gaulle in negotiations to call it off. As for the derivation of 'ultra-leftism,' back in 1919 Lenin wrote a pamphlet called 'Ultra-Leftism: An Infantile Disorder in Communism,' paternally comparing the radical ideas of his his opponents in the Party to a childhood disease like the measles. In 1968, Dany 'the Red' Cohn Bendit turned the tables on Lenin with a radical bombshell entitled 'Ultra-Leftism: The Cure for the Senile Disease of Communism.'

Ten months after the 'Events,' the 'spirit of May 1968', from dying out, seems to have become a permanent feature in France. Wildcat (unofficial, non-union-sanctioned) strikes, generally rare in France, have spread everywhere, and workers no longer give notice to the boss before striking or limit their strikes to a day or week as in the past. The traditional Left organizations – the unions, the Communist and Socialist Parties, even the traditional Far Left sects – are dragging their heels behind the struggle. At the present moment, the most active elements are the high school students and the workers in sectors that were passive last May.

These *gauchistes* (workers, students, employees) are mostly new, previously apolitical elements who first entered the struggle last May. They are so numerous that they are no longer easily recognizable. Almost any type of person may be seen reading Marx, Mao, Bakunin or a copy of *Action* in the Metro, and often the most militant individuals are outside of any organized Anarchist, Trotskyist or Maoist sect. The three factors that seem to unite this new French ultraleft are youth, combativeness, and total scorn for both capitalism and the traditional (especially C.P.) Left. These *gauchistes* are often politically confused, usually disorganized, but nonetheless capable of concerted action. They are a real specter haunting both de Gaulle and the CP-CGT: the right and left poles of the French establishment.

---

[87] Anniversary of the Proclamation of the Paris Commune, March 18, 1871.

It's not the boss what pays, it's the struggle!'

The CP-CGT is caught in the middle of a cross-fire between *gauchistes* and de Gaulle's government, with it two-faced policy of considering the Communists 'respectable' when it needs to negotiate and Red-baiting them when it doesn't. Today the CP's tactic is trying to co-opt the struggle. Worker militancy has been both high and successful. Three weeks ago, for example, the auto workers at Le Mans (Renault) and Sochaux (Peugeot) pulled off big wildcat strikes over working conditions and despite the opposition of the CGT, won big victories. Far from demanding money, moreover, these workers demanded an equalization of pay, breaking down all the hierarchies and categories that divide workers. The CGT, on the other hand, had arranged to meet with the bosses representatives 'at the summit' in early March and wanted everyone to keep quiet so as not to rock the boat. At the meeting, however, the bosses refused to talk. Since the CGT bosses could no longer control the workers, they had lost their usefulness for the bosses and there was no point in continuing to deal with them.

Scorned on both sides, the CGT decided to call a one day 'nation-wide work stoppage' on March 11 in order to prove its militancy. (The unions here traditionally prefer limited work-stoppages, announced in advance and thus totally harmless, to actual open-ended *strikes*, which are not respectable or controllable.) The CGT was very careful to avoid the word *grève* (strike) as well as to make sure that the wildcat strikes were settled first: nothing scares them more than the idea of a strike taking off and spreading. The plan was for the traditional Mayday-type parade from the Place de la République to the Bastille, and the Communists brought in goon-squads from every part of France to keep out the *gauchistes* and maintain 'law and order.' At three o'clock in the afternoon, the CGT began the parade with prepared slogans like 'We Want a Six Percent Raise!' and 'Reopen the negotiations!' The students and *gauchistes* were shunted into a side-street so that they could only join the parade at the very end. After waiting a couple of hours, it became obvious that the same CGT marchers kept marching in circles past the same spot in order to keep the *gauchistes* bottled up. Finally, some Maoists broke in and a fist-fight started then some Anarchists pushed through and the Postal workers made a place for them. Many CGT workers were visibly confused and embarrassed at their leaders calling for 'Law and Order' against young *gauchistes* shouting 'Down with Capitalism!'

At five o'clock, the *gauchiste* end of the parade finally got into the street. By this time, many young workers and members of other unions had come over to the ultra-leftists. The *gauchiste* contingent stretched all the way from the République to the Bastille – easily 25,000 to 30,000 demonstrators – shouting: 'National Interest = Capitalist Interest,' 'It's not the boss who pays off, it's the struggle,' 'Sochaux-Le-Mans. Yes! Negotiations, No!' and singing the

171

Internationale. At the Bastille, the Communist officials immediately dispersed the demonstrators and sent them home while the cops moved in from the side-streets to beat up the now-isolated *gauchistes*. (This sort of « division of labor » between the CGT and the CRS riot cops explains why you often see 'CGT=CRS' on the walls). The street-fighting lasted until nine o'clock and spread all over Paris.

'Contestation' on the Job

These dramatic clashed are only an outward manifestation of a constant struggle taking place all over France and at every level: offices, factories, high schools, universities, unions, action committees. Nobody seems to do any work here any more; a permanent political discussion has been established in the most unlikely places. A friend of mine works in the offices of a big construction company which was not actively on strike last May. All the employees are technicians or white-collar. There have been so many political discussions there since May, the office has been renamed 'the Soviet'. One day the boss came in and said: 'Listen, you can't work and talk at the same time. Things have got to change.' Someone answered, 'Right, things have got to change,' and they all went back to their discussion. Elsewhere, on a production-line, the men were holding a discussion at work. Again the boss came in and said: 'You can't work and talk at the same time.' 'Fine,' came the answer. 'We'll stop working,' and they did.

It's the same in the schools. One day, I was invited out to the University of Paris at Nanterre, a spin-off of the Sorbonne in a suburban slum and the home of the 22 March Movement (the student group, now disbanded, whose actions set off the May Events). There I sat in at a philosophy seminar taught by an old friend [Jean-François Lyotard from *Socialisme ou Barbarie* days]. After a while, someone said: 'There's a comrade here from American S.D.S.' and immediately the seminar was transformed into a political discussion group about the U.S. — SDS, the Panthers, wildcat strikes, and rank-and-file caucuses. No one seemed to worry about the school work. Most striking: the students and the professor (a *gauchiste*) in that class were on a first-name basis and spoke to each other with the familiar '*tu.*' In France, that's a real revolution.

At Nanterre, more than anywhere, the walls speak. Every night the school is occupied by the cops who tear down all the posters, and the walls have been repainted grey three times. Over the door is written: 'Grey: boredom, emptiness, monks – France!' Elsewhere, one reads: 'Never work! ' 'Participation is like a lollypop: after you suck the sugar, you're left with the stick (i.e. nightstick),' 'Long live Anarchy,' etc. At Nanterre, as elsewhere, there is no student organization of the general-purpose SDS variety. But there are meetings and actions every day. All you need to do is grab a bullhorn or put up a poster, and you get from 50 to 1,000 people ready for a discussion or an action. Organization seems perhaps unnecessary when everyone is political. Still, there is a great deal of confusion and many problems.

Action Committees and Micro-Parties

The Action Committees (in factories, schools, neighborhoods, etc.,) were the original organizational creation of the May-June revolt, but they never quite got to the level of federating in nation-wide strike committees or workers' councils (mostly on account of the obstructionism of the unions and CP). Nonetheless, the Action Committees (ACs) were an effective organizational expression for the May struggle, and they broke down all relations of leaders/ranks, theoreticians/doers, old politicos/newcomers, giving everyone a chance to speak, work, and struggle. But AC's are only good when there are actions to organize, and in the months since May-June they have mostly run out of steam. At the same time, the ideological sects or *groupuscules* (micro-parties) have attempted to raid or co-opt the ACs, using them as recruiting grounds for new members, and the sectarian infighting has discouraged many from participating.

The *groupuscules* themselves have had a tremendous influx, but at the same time there have been dozens of splits and such a sectarian spirit that no one will talk to anyone else until the very moment when they have to unite against the pigs or the *Stals* (Stalinists). I count four varieties of Anarchists, five each of Trotskyists and Maoists, various Left-Communists, and of course the *Situationnistes*, who are constantly expelling each other like their predecessors, the *surréalistes*. Every combination is possible. There are Maoists who consider that Lenin was counter-revolutionary because he allowed the Soviets to die but imagine that Mao's state-sponsored Cultural Revolution in China represents the power of the workers' councils! Every group, of course, claims to represent the 'true content' of the May revolt. For some, it proves that all you need is workers' spontaneity; for others, the cause of its failure was the lack of a vanguard party with the correct Marxist-Leninist line. Few, unfortunately, have attempted a real analysis of what was new in May or attempted to revive a genuinely Marxist methodology.

Nonetheless, even this sectarianism and confusion has been fruitful. A whole forgotten libertarian and ultra-left tradition which had simply been erased from history by the Stalinists, has now been revived. People are reading Rosa Luxembourg, Georg Lukacs, Anton Pannekoek, Alexandra Kollantay, Trotsky of course and studying movements like the German Left of 1919, the workers' councils, Ukrainian Makhnovism, Spanish anarchism, etc. People who had never heard of Marcuse and for whom Marx himself was only a name last May are now discussing forgotten prewar Italian Communists like Gramsci and Bordiga (Lenin's target in 'Ultra-leftism: a childhood Disease.')

Limits of Spontaneity?

173

Nonetheless, with the decline of the Action Committees and the disappearance of the multi-tendency of 22 March Movement, there is an organizational void on the extreme Left that the competing sects are organically incapable of filling, since each considers itself to be the unique vanguard party. Even semi-anarchist « open » groups like *Passer-Outre* (Move On) have been obliged to define themselves politically and thus, implicitly, to exclude other tendencies. All attempts to create a united front of the *groupuscules* have run aground on the rock of sectarianism. Ideally, the members of the *microparties* would unite in a pluralistic action movement, each maintaining its identity, bringing its organizational skills, and proposing its solution, but remaining submerged in the mass of activists. However the tendency, inherited from Bakunin, Lenin, Trotsky, Mao, of sectarian factionalists is to enter mass arenas in order to co-opt, rule or ruin. Our own SDS is already experiencing such tensions.

The problem in France, however, is that the best and most militant of the newly radicalized elements belong to no organization whatsoever. Often, the most militant actions are organized on the spot, without the need for any any outside organizers. This, of course, is the greatest sign of strength of the new consciousness here. Since everyone now has his or her own polities and is ready to act, each individual is in a sense 'organized.' But there is a corresponding weakness: faced with the highly organized, bureaucratic Communist Party, with its professional staff of organizers, its mass press, its front organizations, etc. the unorganized extreme Left inevitably loses out. Spontaneity works fine as long as there is no rival organization willing and able to co-opt the movement.

A Bureaucratic *Putsch*

I saw this up close this weekend at the special Convention of the radical National University Teachers' Union (SNE-Sup), where the French Communist Party's *apparachiks* pulled off a successful bureaucratic *putsch*. SNE-Sup played a key role in the student-worker revolt last spring when, under the leadership of the Leftist, Alain Geismar, it backed up the student strike with a teachers' union strike, giving the students a respectable « cover » and a first link with organized labor. Moreover, it has been a valuable center for new ideas and struggle against the university as a capitalist institution. With the CP takeover, it will no longer play that role. The CP faction stands for limited university reform in cooperation with the government and for pure trade-union demands for the teachers. Any criticism of the content of the university is considered 'adventurism' by them, and the average conservative professor considers the CP more respectable than the ultra-left. The CP takeover was a triumph of bureaucratic maneuvering so disgusting that, in the long run, one hopes will rebound to help the *groupuscules* in the union. The first act of the new CP leadership was to adjourn the Convention before the question of a projected eight-day strike could be discussed. From now on, all decisions must

174

first be studied by the National Office before the members can even hold a discussion. The ranks are not supposed to take any initiative.

The ultra-leftist defeat in SNE-Sup is not a tragedy, provided the militant and pro-student elements are able to reorganize at the rank-and-file level. In fact, having a revolutionary leadership at the head of a traditional union was a kind of paradox anyway and hampered the *gauchistes* in developing their politics, since they were always bogged down in day-to-day trade-union issues and constantly obliged to mute their radicalism in the name of unity. Nonetheless, it still turned your stomach to watch a Stalinist pig (ironically named Professor Innocent and wearing a dark suit and starched collar) take over from Geismar and his radical gang and then cut off all political discussion by immediately gaveling the Convention to a halt. To contend with this kind of adversary to contend with, it is clear that ultra-left sentiments alone are insufficient. . . .

Marseille, March 31, 1969

The prolonged wildcat strike of the railroad workers on the Western lines of the French National Railway (SNCF) obliged me to stay an extra few days in Paris: hence the lateness of this article. Wildcats are a totally new phenomenon in France, and the seemingly endless wave of rank-and-file walkouts has the government the unions, and management climbing the walls. This new capacity for self-mobilization among French workers is one of the most promising and one of the few real 'gains' of the May-June 1968 general strike. If a generalized movement of *contestation* [conflict] starts up again here in the near future, it is certain that the workers, rather than the students, will be the 'detonators' this time around. Although the government and the official Left try to ignore it, the economic crisis of which last Spring's movement was a symptom is still wide open and the workers are reacting. Under the headline 'Lawlessness,' a conservative columnist writing on the front page of the super-serious daily, *Le Monde*, complains that the workers won't listen to their leaders any more. 'Has France gone crazy?' he asks. 'Where are the unions?' A good question…

The Western railway strike is a good example of this new type of movement. The rank-and-file launched it with two specific objectives: job security and better working conditions. The French railroad, nationalized under the Communist-Gaullist coalition after the Second World War, is state property, but the worker's problems with management are the same as back in the good old free-enterprise USA. The government/boss is cutting back on 'unprofitable' passenger service and laying off men while continuing to offer cheap freight hauling for big business. At the same time, it has 'rationalized' work schedules to the point where the workers can no longer lead a human existence. They must be ready to pick up a train on an hour's notice (Sundays

175

and holidays included), and after a run they must spend hours of their 'free' time hanging around some dirty provincial station miles from home waiting for another run. As a result, an engineer may be made to run an express after two or three days without decent sleep and still be responsible for the lives of hundreds of passengers. He spends the better part of his life dozing in railway cafés or in coaches between hauls.

Naturally, the rolling personell were the backbone of the strike and the first to take off work. The unions, with the Communist CGT in the lead, immediately tried to maneuver the workers back onto the job. Their argument was that management wouldn't even begin to negotiate as long as an 'illegal' work stoppage was going on and that the workers were thus 'hurting their own position' by striking. (Evidently it is better to negotiate from weakness than from strength.) This time, however, the men were not duped. They held general assemblies in every depot twice a day to discuss their affairs and sent the union leaders back to talk with management. Meanwhile, *Humanité*, the Communist daily paper, ran a front-page banner headline declaring 'THE NATIONAL INTEREST IS THE WORKERS INTEREST' and told the striking workers, 'At a time when the government is preoccupied with its problems with the National Railway, aren't you afraid your strike will add to these problems?'

Class collaborationism seems to have no limits here. Even George Meany[88] wouldn't dare go that far in public. But of course he doesn't have the prestige of revolutionary 'Communist' party to back him up. By March 22, nonetheless, the strikebreaking union leaders managed to get some of the men back to work with vague promises, and *Humanité* joyfully proclaimed: 'One by one, the depots are decided to stop the strike in order to deny management and the government any pretext to act against the rolling personnel.' Obviously, for them, a strike is merely a pretext. In fact, the strike is not really over. The depots at Orleans, Toulouse, Poitiers and elsewhere voted only for temporary returns to work.

Behind the maneuvers of the unions and the official Left lies a political problem: the upcoming national referendum proposed by President de Gaulle in order to reaffirm his power, seriously shaken by the near-revolution nine months ago. As usual, de Gaulle has managed to get his opponents up against the proverbial wall by making them fight on his chosen ground. The

---

[88] *2008 Note* In 1969, Meany was the ultra-conservative President of the AFL-CIO who backed Nixon and hated anti-war demonstrators. Alas, his successors have gone even farther in give-backs and concessions to U.S. corporations.

referendum has been the favorite weapon for manufacturing popularity under right-wing 'strong men' from Napoleon II to Franco to Stalin. This particular one is a beauty. The electors will be asked to vote 'yes' or 'no' to a package of contradictory proposals. One part will help France's impoverished provincial regions to develop their economy, something everybody wants. The second part allows de Gaulle to abolish both the Senate and the Constitution (which he himself imposed ten years ago in another weighted referendum). What is astonishing - at least to the naïve - is that the whole official Left is going along with this electoral farce and seriously campaigning for people to vote 'no'. Moreover, the big rush to end this nasty railroad strike was due more than a little to the desire to calm the bourgeois public and prevent another pro-Gaullist stampede. All is grist for *Humanité's* mill. The class struggle must cease as soon as something 'really important' and 'political' like a Gaullist referendum comes around.

International Politics Among the *'Groupuscules'*

Now that a shooting war between Russia and China is a real possibility, every vanguard party, no matter how tiny, has taken its position for one side or the other and discovered some form of justification in 'Marxist' theory. 'Theory' seems mainly to be a device for determining which side to back in the various ongoing inter-imperialist conflicts. This taking sides then permits each revolutionary group to forget about actual class conflict between rich and poor *within* each nation or block (e.g., Nigeria/Biafra, Israel/the Arab states, Russia/China). The trouble with the present Sino-Russian conflict is that there are too many variables among the possible alliances. Thus *Lutte ouvrière* (Workers Struggle), a Trotskyist group, backs Russia over China because the former is a 'workers state, however bureaucratically degenerate,' while the latter is merely a 'petty bourgeois state.' So far, so good... But since *Lutte ouvrière* is obliged to consider the theoretical possibility of the combination U.S.-U.S.S.R. uniting against. China-(France?) their editorial adds that in that case they would back China. On the other hand *Rouge* ('Red,' formerly JCR *Jeunesses communistes révolutionnaires*)[89] a relatively new group which has grown tremendously since May, seems to lean towards China. *Rouge* considers both Russia and China to be 'workers states, bureaucratically deformed,' and the criterium of selection is apparently that of their *degree* of bureaucratic deformation . . . I had been unaware that Marxism supplied a barometer for measuring degrees of bureaucratic deformation in workers states, but I am always willing to learn.

Action Committees

---

[89] *2009 Note. Rouge* is still published weekly. The Trotskyist LCR (*Ligue communiste révolutionnaire*), a "100% Left" Party with a popular presidential candidate (the handsome, charismatic young postman Olivier Besancenot) has recently transformed itself into the *NPA,* the New Anti-Capitalist Party.

At the suburban Nanterre campus of the University of Paris last week it was the anniversary of the March 22 movement, and the student newspaper celebrated it by inviting a group of celebrated establishment journalists to answer the students' questions about distorted press coverage of the movement. We were all packed into a huge amphitheater when most of the journalists showed up. Just as one of them started into a pompous and self-justifying speech, the lights went out and when they came on again the man's face was covered with black paint. We all had a good laugh, but I have to brag that the pie thrown at [head of the military draft] General Hershey's assistant at Columbia last year was more daring and funnier. I was supposed to lead a discussion about American SDS after the journalists were disposed of, but there was such total chaos (both the lights and microphone were eventually cut off) that we had to adjourn to a small group upstairs. Nanterre has become so chaotic that it is now impossible to hold any kind of general assembly. At the same time, the Action Committees have died out and the March 22 movement has been dissolved. As a result, although almost everyone at Nanterre is a *gauchiste*, there is absolutely no possibility of organized discussion or action. Nanterre is what the French call a '*bordel*' (disorderly house).

In general, the Action Committees, created out of last Spring's nationwide struggles, are on the wane. Since there are no longer large masses in motion seeking a form of self-organization and self-expression, the Committees have been reduced to the role of information exchanges where they have not been entirely gobbled up by one or another of the *groupuscules* and transformed into front groups. As a result, the thousands of ultra-Leftists who were 'born' in the May struggles have mostly abandoned the Committees to their fate and now come together only for big actions.

The Provinces

This tendency is less marked in the provinces, if I can judge from my experience in Toulouse and Marseille where Action Committees are still functioning more or less. But in France, the provinces tend to lag behind Paris in most things, and it may just be a matter of time. At Toulouse, they were discussing the creating of a Coordinating Committee to Link the Action Committees, and there were two proposals: one for a centralized CC made exclusively of delegates from the ACs with decision-making powers and the other for a CC that would merely exchange information and leave the initiative in the ranks. The Trotskyists were for the first proposal, since they would be likely to have the majority on the Committee. But the others saw that such a CC would merely become one more political leadership without a base calling for actions which no one would follow. On the other hand, the ACs alone, with no political philosophy and few actions develop are already empty shells and are withering rapidly.

It is hard to conclude on the state of the movement in France. Despite the pervasive sectarianism and the bureaucratic behavior of the *groupuscules*, May has left many positive factors: 1) the new freedom and initiative among the workers, as evidenced by the wildcats 2) the thousands of new ultraleftists whose presence is felt everywhere, 3) the mass diffusion and discussion of revolutionary ideas, not only of Marx and Lenin, but of a whole critical, anti-Stalinist Leftist tradition that had long been buried, from Trotsky and Rosa Luxembourg to Lukacs, Pannekok, the German Left, the Council Communists and the Anarchists.

Resistance in Russian-Occupied Czechoslovakia [1969]

(Prague, March 30) Ever since Russian tanks 'fraternally' invaded Czechoslovakia last August to prevent the spread of the reform movement known as Prague Spring, finding your way through the labyrinth of Czech politics is about as difficult or as easy – as finding your way through the labyrinth of streets of medieval Prague. The local street signs and house numbers – removed last August by the population in order confuse the invading Russians - have not yet been replaced. At first you are totally disoriented: how to find your way to a home or public building, even with a map, when you don't even know the name of the street where you are standing? The answer is easy: ask anybody. Within two minutes you will be surrounded by a crowd of three to a dozen Praguers, of whom half will speak a little English or German, all arguing about where such-and-such a building used to be and offering to take you there. You realize that such amenities as addresses are superfluous in a country where people have real confidence in each other.

It is the same with politics. Here again, the 'street signs' are down. The official press prints only what the government, under Russian pressure, wants people to know (i.e. damn little) and few pay attention. But not an event takes place in Czechoslovakia that isn't known by 80% of the population within two days. The grapevine is better than any newspaper. The cleaning lady in the Ministry of Interior tells her son, a university student, who meets a worker from the Jawa factory whose brother is in the Fifth Regiment, etc., etc. By nightfall, the latest shift in government policy or the latest resolution of a certain factory or group of journalists is table-talk in every café and restaurant. And do people talk! Finding a Czech who isn't interested in talking politics is like finding for a Frenchman who isn't interested in talking about food or women. In cafés, on street corners, in homes, everyone is talking. I can state without reservation that I have never experienced a freer atmosphere in my life than in poor, suppressed, censored, occupied Prague. If you want to know what's happening here, ask anybody.

Appearance and Reality

Once you make contact with people, it is relatively easy to get behind appearances and discover the reality. For example, when I arrived I was shocked to find the streets literally full of soldiers carrying sub-machine-guns. 'So this is what 'occupied' means', I thought grimly. Not exactly. To begin with, the soldiers were Czech. I never saw a single Russian uniform in Prague, although I was told that the Russians were poised in camps and barracks just outside the city. This new form of repression using Czech troops was only days old. It was imposed after the Czech ice hockey team beat the Russians on March 28, and the people went wild in the streets. After the Russians angrily protested the alleged sacking of the Aeroflot offices by demonstrator, the

Dubcek government promised them to keep law and order on the streets. Two young Czech soldiers with automatic rifles were assigned to accompany every middle-aged Czech policeman on his rounds. As a result, between soldiers actually patrolling and those on their way to and from their duty assignments, the streets were full of soldiers. And what soldiers! Every one a Schweik.[90] All young, 17-20. Beatle-cut hair hanging over the backs of collars. Ties askew or pulled down at the throat. Boots unpolished. Automatic rifles slung casually behind their backs or even leaning against trees (!) The uniforms looked more like the pieced-together war-surplus you see at SDS meetings than anything you might see in a military parade. And everyone smiling, talking to passers-by and flirting with the girls as the black-uniformed, grey-haired policeman they were assigned to reinforce stood scowling.

I witnessed a comical scene when a policeman tried to do an ID check on a kid caught playing the guitar in an underpass. The soldiers allowed a crowd, apparently sympathetic to the kid, to gather around the crime scene, and while the cop was distracted arguing with the crowd, they let the kid slink away. I spent an hour in a café drinking with one of these soldiers. He was a student. He lived with his folks. He was simply part of the population. The last thing he would dream of would be to shoot at his fellow citizens and comrades. Later, a journalist explained to me that the only result of this 'martial law' in Prague was to demoralize and neutralize the police. How can a cop act like a cop when he is being followed wherever he goes by two of these smiling SDS-types carrying machineguns? Again, you see how the unity of the population, however passive, is their strength.

More realities: When Premier Dubcek cracked down on the journalists at *Rude Pravo* (the Party organ) the papers were full of resolutions of support for the government from factories and trade unions. Again, I was shocked. I had thought the unions supported the new press freedoms. Later, I spoke to an ex-Party-member in the know. He told me that the fired journalists had all been rehired by the metal-workers union paper at their old salaries and that the 'resolutions' were meaningless. Apparently, the resolutions all began with pro forma statements of support for the Party and government, which the papers printed. But they also went on to criticize, albeit in Aesopian language, the crackdown and to support the journalists. The real sense of the resolutions was censored out. Again, the political unity is there, albeit hidden.

---

[90] The simple-minded Czech soldier who ingeniously avoids combat in Jaroslav Hasek's 1923 satirical anti-war novel, *The Adventures of the Good Soldier Schweik in the Great War.*

Student-Worker Allies

The 'student-worker alliance,' which we all *talk* so much about not only in American SDS, but in the French Left and in German SDS, is not an idea but a reality in Czechoslovakia. It is a reality based on actual political forces and has genuine roots in Czech society. It exists both on the top and in the ranks. It is a matter of course for the student movement to send delegates to trade union meetings and for trade union officials to attend teach-ins and discussions in the university. This is because the trade union leadership and the universities are the objective 'base' of the reformers in the government and turn to each other for support whenever the pressure is turned on. But there is more. Groups of workers and individuals also come 'unofficially' from the factories to the universities to discuss political ideas, and it is in these informal discussions, as well as in the factories themselves, that the ideas of workers' councils and workers' control of production are beginning to be popularized.

How is this so? The first conversation I had in Prague was with a university professor with whom I had made an appointment ostensibly to discuss academic matters. As soon as his office door was closed, we began to talk politics. Like everyone else I later spoke to, he was pessimistic about the perspective of continuing and deepening the 'Spring' movement under the combined pressure of the Russians and the party-state, whose 'socialism with a human face' was looking more and more like old-fashioned Stalinism. But he was still hopeful, and his hope was based, not on any government 'reformers,' but on the workers. 'The workers have not yet had their say. They are the backbone of the movement.' This I heard from him and many others during my stay in Prague. He also talked of the hope of a European revolution coming from France or Italy and breaking up the domination of Europe by the two superpowers. This was also a common idea.

Like many intellectuals he too had 'done time' in the factories during one or another of the purges, and he felt no separation from them as an intellectual. Let me insist that he was no extraordinary individual and that I met him by chance. I soon learned that many Czech workers are former students or intellectuals and that many more are the sons and daughters of pre-war professionals and intellectuals who have been in the factories for at least a decade are thoroughly proletarianized. This factor, combined with the high level of Czechoslovak culture, its long proletarian tradition, and the fact that it was the only Eastern country which was thoroughly industrialized even before the war, makes for a highly intelligent and politicized working class. Moreover, the government, since it calls itself a 'workers' government,' has always maintained a fiction of political life in the factories, pressuring workers to attend endless meetings. Now that fiction threatens to come to life, and with it the threat of real workers' power. Nothing scares the bureaucrats, and even more so, the Russians, more than this as yet untapped potential among the workers. The two short, symbolic general strikes they have pulled off since August are merely a hint of the kind of concerted action they are capable of.

Ambiguities

If this national unity in the face of the foreign occupiers and their local henchmen is a fact of life in Czechoslovakia, it is an ambiguous fact. First, let me get one thing out of the way: there seems to be no chauvinism, no specifically anti-Russian (much less anti-socialist) remarks here. The same people who are adamant about getting the Russians out will insist on telling you that they are still grateful for the liberation by the Russians in 1945. The opposition is political and highly sophisticated, and it is directed as much against the local Stalinists as the foreign ones. All the talk about 'anti-socialist forces' having organized the March 28 demonstrations (after the Czech victory in the hockey game) is pure propaganda. The mass outburst was totally spontaneous and totally unplanned. Moreover, the crowd was extremely good humored. Several participants I spoke to were convinced that the sacking of the Aeroflot (Russian airline) office was a provocation carried out by Stalinist agents and designed to pave the way for a new crackdown. Subsequent events (the Russians' ouster of Dubcek) seem to confirm this view.

The ambiguity lies rather in the basis of this unity in relation to the Dubcek reformers in the government. Dubcek was never more than a Communist bureaucrat 'with a human face,' hand picked by the Russians when they finally realized that Novotny (his conservative predecessor) was a loser. But people had the same kinds of illusions about him that many Americans did about Clean Gene McCarthy last year. They focused all their revolutionary aspirations on his person, although he never said or did anything to justify such hopes. Naturally, everyone was happy about the new freedom of discussion that reigned after last January, but many – particularly among the workers – were more than dubious about proposed economic reforms which might lead to speedup and increased pressure on the workers in the shops. It was only the Russian invasion that really united the people behind the Dubcek team, and this support was wearing thinner and thinner as Dubcek proved himself a more and more pliant tool of the invaders in subsequent months. Whether or not this growing rank-and-file opposition to Dubcek from the Left would have burst out into the open is now a moot question. His replacement is clearly an old-line Stalinist, and no one is likely to have illusions about *him*.

The replacement of Dubcek by the conservative Stalinist Husak is, from one point of view, clearly a blow to the 'Spring movement,' clearly a sign of increasing Russian pressure and old-line Stalinist strength. Yet, in another sense, it may prove a two-edged sword. The situation is now totally clear, and workers and students are hardly likely to respond to the same demagogic appeals for 'calm' and 'unity' from the lips of a Husak. In fact, Husak's appeals have been based entirely on the threat of dire punishment. If the new clarity of the situation provides the workers with the freedom of action they seem to have been moving toward, the Kremlin may yet regret removing Dubcek. In any case, one thing is clear: the masses now know they have only their own strength to rely upon. The Czechoslovak drama is far from being over.

Twenty years after: 1968 in Historical Perspective [1988] [91]

An Elegiac Evocation

A42 · The Chronicle of Higher Education · May 4, 1988 · **Students**

Participants in 1968 Student Takeover at Columbia U. Return to Campus to Celebrate 20th Anniversary

Roger Grossman, professor of French at U. of Hartford, at the 20th anniversary of the student takeover at Columbia U.

Nineteen sixty-eight (sigh!)... What a wonderful year that was! Rebellions breaking out all over the f–king place. From Paris to Prague, from Berkeley to Berlin, from Mexico City to Chicago - in the ghetto, on the campus, in the jungles of Vietnam, even within the councils of the Vatican - revolution is the happening thing.

People in motion – all kinds of people. People thinking, acting, daring, participating in an unprecedented historical crisis on an unprecedented international scale. Sending sparks of inspiration and solidarity across frontiers of nationality, age, ideology, and class. Sparks illuminating a moment of world-historical significance, challenging the old order and illuminating possibilities of a different way of being, a new human order.

The place where the spark was kindled was Vietnam. There, poor peasants, city workers, Buddhist monks, and nationalist intellectuals led by the Communists under Ho Chi Minh successfully defended themselves against brutal attacks, first by the French Army and then by the Americans – the 'anti-colonialist' Americans, whose 1776 Declaration of Independence was included *verbatim* in the Basic Program of the Vietnamese National Liberation Front. The Vietnamese were ingenious in their audacity, fighting with bicycles and bamboo sticks against B-52s and flame-throwers. Their popular rising during Têt (the Vietnamese New Year) inspired solidarity and sympathy around the world and inaugurated the year of the rebels. Images of beautiful Vietnamese faces and bodies agonized in torture and defiant in dignity girdled the globe through the technological wizardry of television. In the flickering light of the tube My-Lai became the global village.

---

[91] Published in *New Politics* on the occasion of the 20th Anniversary of the May 1968 uprisings.

From deep down in another colonial jungle – the Magnolia Jungle of U.S. racism – came another spark. Struck by Rosa Parks, kindled by Martin Luther King and the brave young people of SNCC and CORE, it burst into flame and burned its way through the cities of the oldest and most complacent of capitalist 'democracies,' incinerating the vestiges of McCarthyite conformity and awakening a new generation of white youth to the joys of sex, drugs, rock and revolution.

France: May-June 1968

In response to police repression of anti-Vietnam war protests, the Latin Quarter is occupied by student rebels – eventually by rebel youth of all classes and all ages demanding nothing short of a new society. Their slogan: 'All power to the imagination!' As in 1789, 1830, 1848, 1871, Paris is in revolt. Eros is in the ascendant. Handwriting on the walls: 'The more I make revolution, the more I want to make love – the more I make love, the more I want to make revolution.'

186

The spark spreads to the aircraft and auto factories, then to the railroads, the buses, the labs, the big stores, the administrations. In every school, factory, office  people are organizing 'Action Committees' to coordinate their struggle and reorganize their workplace. Power is in the streets. President de Gaulle, *le grand Charles*, is mysteriously absent.

Ten million French and immigrant workers are on a general strike. They have their own agenda. Not higher wages, but workers' power, self-management, an end to hierarchy. Corporate managers and Communist union officials are equally nonplussed at the popular slogan, 'Humanity will finally be happy when the last capitalist is hanged by the guts of the last bureaucrat.' The detonator was the student uprising; the powder charge, the working classes. The target, the whole established order... In short, a pre-revolutionary situation.

Czechoslovakia: August 1968.

Half a million Russian troops invade Czechoslovakia to crush attempts to democratize and humanize the Communist regime. The massive resistance of students, workers, intellectuals and reform-minded Communists sparks worldwide sympathy. Behind the Iron Curtain solidarity demonstrations are held in Poland, Hungary, East Berlin, even Leningrad. In the U.S., protestors brutalized by the Chicago police at the Democratic Convention brandish signs reading 'Welcome to Czechago.' 'Welcome to Prague' is spray- painted on the streets of Berkeley during the battle for People's Park.

187

Although the Czech experiment in 'socialism with a human face' is forced to capitulate before the armed might of what is euphemistically known as 'Actually Existing Socialism,' workers and students, imitating their French counterparts, continue to form Action Committees demanding civil liberties and workplace democracy.

Internationalism

In all these movements, internationalism prevails over national chauvinism and racism. When the French government deports 'Dany-the-Red' Cohn-Bendit (a Jewish German national prominent among the Paris student rebels), thousands of French workers and students parade through the streets chanting 'We are all German Jews.' The General Assembly of Student-Worker Action Committees call for 'The Abolition of the Status of Foreigner in France!' – this despite the French Communist Party's patriotic appeal to 'national feeling.'

The unity of the New Left, East and West, is incarnated in the person of 'Red'

Rudi Dutschke, the dissident East German Communist student who became the outstanding leader of the SDS in West Berlin. His shooting by a right-wing fanatic echoes the shots that killed Martin Luther King the previous week. In Mexico City the sham internationalism of the Olympic Games is unmasked by victorious U.S. athletes raising their clenched fists in the Black Power salute and by the protest of the Mexican students - brutally slaughtered in the Plaza of the Three Cultures by the police of the ruling Institutional Revolutionary Party.

Nineteen sixty-eight: a year of triumph and tragedy. A moment when the news was dominated, not by the pronouncements of boring bureaucrats, but by the daring deeds of people in protest and masses in motion. At a time when we ourselves were the spectacle we watched through the magnifying and distorting lens of the media. When bold, surrealistic slogans like 'Do it!', 'Burn, baby, burn!', 'All power to the imagination!' 'Freedom NOW!', and 'Everything is possible!' seemed perfectly reasonable. A time when everyone was young, when rebellion was in the air, when life meant struggle and it was exciting to be alive.

Do I wax nostalgic? Looking backward over two decades, one is tempted to paraphrase François Villon, the student-rebel-poet-thief of 15th Century Paris, and inquire: 'Where are the riots of yesteryear?' However, the purpose of the proceeding exercise in elegiac evocation is not to poeticize the remembrance of things past. It is rather to recall to the reader's mind true-life images of an actual world-historical moment: memory-pictures which, from today's viewpoint, would seem fantastic, were they not factual. With these images in mind, then, let us attempt more soberly to evaluate the movements of the 1960's in historical perspective: the positive, the negative and the prospects for the future.

Backlash, or the Sixties Suppressed

If nothing else, the worldwide mass revolts that culminated in the revolutionary year 1968 disproved for our generation the pervasive myth of the invincibility of the system. Since 1968 we have undergone two decades during which the establishment has devoted the full force of its apparatus of repression and propaganda to the task of erasing the memory of what happened in the '60s. The rebellions, near revolutions, and mass protests have disappeared down the memory hole as far as official history is concerned. In a frantic effort to avoid an inconvenient repetition, the media and the ruling elite have pulled out all the stops in their campaign to discredit and destroy even the memory of that glorious decade.[92]

---

[92].*Update, June 2007.* New proof of 1968's still-potent charge. – after not twenty, but now forty years: Nicolas Sarkozy, the successful Right-wing candidate in last month's French Presidential election, devoted his final speech of the campaign to…. 1968-bashing! According to Sarko, we 68'ers are responsible for today's 'intellectual and moral relativism,' 'brought cynicism to society and lowered the political and moral level.' Further more, we 'encourage criminals.' 'We must turn the page of May-68' Sarkozy concluded (*Le Monde,* May 2, 2007).

For example, the media create and perpetuated the ugly myth of anti-war protesters spitting on returning soldiers, when in fact the movement set up G.I. coffee houses near Army bases where soldiers could relax, be themselves and escape for a moment the brutality and brainwashing of Basic Training. It is remarkable that despite this orchestrated slander campaign, so many people in  the United States continue to be wary of foreign adventures in places like Nicaragua and El Salvador, to the point where the Reagan Administration, which came to power eight years ago with the destruction of Nicaragua as the number one item on its agenda, has had to face total failure. Indeed the derogatory phrase 'Vietnam Syndrome' (labeling a cure as if it were a disease!) is designed to conceal is one of the most remarkable phenomena of world history: for the first time in human memory the native population of a powerful imperialist nation (including many in the military) forced the abandonment of an oppressive war of conquest against a rebellious semi-colony. Neither the Athenian *demos* nor the Roman *plebs* had the courage and wisdom to effectively oppose their own imperialist leaders. The result was the destruction of democracy in Greece and Rome. The people of the United States have every right to be proud of our record of resistance and our continued opposition.

The Balance Sheet

Among the other great achievements of the '60s was the end of two centuries of legal segregation and oppression of America's Black former slave population. Add to this the official recognition of the rights (and the historical oppression) of women, gays, Hispanics, and the handicapped. Moreover, the dawning awareness of the danger to humanity's survival posed by pollution and nuclear war represents a new and universal consciousness capable of uniting the mass of humanity in a common struggle. Finally, the establishment has not forgotten that our movements, however feeble and disorganized, succeeded in unseating and forcing the retirement of three of the most powerful and popular rulers of dominant nation states: Lyndon B. Johnson, Richard Nixon, and France's Charles de Gaulle.

It is hardly surprising that the battle of 1968 did not end in a decisive knock-out against world capital in its 'private' and bureaucratic forms. What needs remembering 20 years after is the fact that we won a couple of rounds on points and struck a nasty left jab which sent the Establishment reeling to its corner. Nor is it surprising that the forces of repression and reaction returned to the fray stronger and more determined to crush the revolutionary elements; indeed it is in

190

the nature of things. As Rosa Luxembourg so elegantly put it, 'Every revolution is doomed to failure except the last one.'

A Failure to Build on Victories

The real shortcoming of the movements of the '60s was not that we failed to annihilate a vastly superior antagonist, but that we failed to acknowledge, consolidate, and build on some of our very real and remarkable victories. For example, in the United States in 1970, the youth movement achieved a very high stage with the first nationwide general strike of students – spontaneously organized in response to Nixon's invasion of Cambodia, the repression of the Black Panther Party and the murder of Black protestors at Jackson State (Miss.) and White students at Kent State (Ohio). For the first time a majority of students, not just in elite schools like Berkeley, Columbia, and Ann Arbor, but in the hinterlands, was prepared to defy the authority of schools, parents, and the live ammunition of the police and the National Guard in full awareness of the potentially deadly consequences of their commitment. Moreover, the 1970 protests were not confined to the 'single-issue' of winding down a losing and unpopular war. They also struck to the root of the most critical domestic issue of the decade: Black liberation. If personal self-interest – the threat of the draft – may originally have awakened the student youth to politics, in the end they called the whole system into question by their actions.

The tragedy of 1970 was that far from building on what can be seen historically as a remarkable victory for spontaneous direct action – thwarting the plans of the Nixon-Kissinger Administration to expand the war in Southeast Asia and eradicate the militant Black leadership – the movement retreated into quietism and despair. Instead of planting the flag of victory on the high ground that had been conquered in an open struggle and congratulating themselves on their new power, the students

191

succumbed to pessimism. Unaccustomed to measuring tactical victories in terms of a long range revolutionary strategy the students, and to some extent the Black militants, mistook a partial gain for a defeat. This failure to consolidate and capitalize on a new, higher stage of struggle had both subjective and objective causes.

The Scuttling of SDS

On the subjective side, the break-up of SDS in 1969 deprived the student movement of a national organization in which to gather and channel the new energies or prepare them for the next stage of struggle. This organizational quasi-suicide cut the new forces of radicalized youth off from each other and from a core of experienced, seasoned leadership capable of orienting the expanding movement. The Progressive Labor Party, the Weatherpeople, and the other self-appointed elites and vanguards in SDS bear a heavy responsibility for disarming and disorganizing the radical student protest movement at the very moment it was about to achieve majority status and provoke what a Presidential Commission on Campus Unrest described as an 'unparalleled crisis' in American history. Through their 'rule or ruin' tactics, the Maoists and Weatherpeople more-or-less deliberately scuttled a fast-growing, radical, mass-based youth organization with a distinguished history. By turning their backs on the SDS tradition of participatory democracy and multi-tendency radicalism, they reneged on the promise of further mass organizing and political growth among the majority of youth. By opting for obsolete, elitist forms of struggle – vanguardism and terrorism – they effectively alienated the sympathies the movement had slowly gathered over years of escalating struggle. Worse still, they destroyed the vehicle through which it could develop further. [93]

The self-proclaimed super-revolutionary vanguardists in SDS were in effect *retrogressionists* with respect to the new forms of organization – radical, spontaneous, community-based, self-developing – which were the historically specific creations of the 1960s. Moreover, by refusing to recognize the role of youth and students as a new revolutionary subject with its own inner dynamic, they cut off the possibility of alliances with other actors on the revolutionary scene: Blacks, women, national liberation struggles, and the working class.

To form effective alliances, a social group must be organized and capable of united action, of throwing its weight into the struggle alongside of other radical social forces. In the modern world, youth and students represent such a force. In

---

[93] *2008 Note.* On the occasion of the refounding of SDS this Winter, remorseful Weatherman Mark Rudd ruefully recounted dumping the SDS membership files into Lake Michigan. Imagine how much more powerful the spontaneous campus risings of 1970 would have been if connected and coordinated through this national network.

May 1970 half of the U.S.'s 8 million students and 350,000 faculty members were on strike against racism, imperialism and university complicity with the war machine. This was a considerable social force in itself, one capable of opening and prolonging a political crisis and of lending important weight to other social forces – the Blacks, the minorities, the women – who were already in motion. If something like the French student-worker revolt of May 1968 with its general strike of 10 million was probably not on the agenda for the U.S. in 1970 (for reasons we will discuss later) there is no doubt that a golden opportunity was lost.

The Role of Youth

Let us note the historical lesson for future reference: like the Black liberation struggle and the women's movement, the students and youth need and are entitled to their own organizational vehicle for self-development and struggle. The course of history *may*, in some objective sense, 'subordinate' the youth within the broader struggle of the workers, but for elitist super-revs to choose to subordinate it to their chosen idea of 'true vanguard' is dangerous nonsense.

Granted, the U.S. is different from France, but if the French worker-student uprising of May-June 1968 proved anything, it proved that a student movement could serve as a 'detonator' for a social revolt that would unleash the fundamental economic antagonists in the social struggle – the workers *versus* the capitalist state – and involve the near-totality of the population in revolutionary activity. It proved that social revolution – despite the hoary prognostications of decades of liberal theorists and neo-Marxists – was still on the agenda in advanced capitalist countries. Most of all it proved (in the root sense of 'tested') the fragility and vulnerability of the seemingly invincible hegemonic bureaucratic-capitalist superstructure – the progressive modern state. The spectacle of the police in disarray, the government paralyzed, and the army confined to barracks (for fear of fraternization) is a specter that continues to haunt the corridors of power - even if the radicals have momentarily forgotten it. Like the failed pan-European revolutions of 1848, like the doomed Paris Commune of 1871, like the abortive Russian Revolution of 1905, the revolutionary year 1968 heralded the appearance of new revolutionary subjects, revealed new forms of struggle, and foreshadowed future possibilities.

The significance of 1968 twenty years later is less in its more-or-less predictable failure, than in its promise for the future. Call it, if you like, a 'flash in the pan.' It was nonetheless a flash sufficiently bright to illuminate, however briefly, the possible shape of things to come. This being the case, we have no choice but to

193

return to the history of the rebellions of 1968 as to a living lesson, a roadmap which *may* point to possible pathways – perhaps the only roads – toward human survival and a new society.

What Was Missing?

Let us look, first of all, at the negatives: the reasons why the rebellions of 1968 did NOT result in world revolution. I do not share the analysis of the celebrated Marxist philosopher Herbert Marcuse, whom the media presented as the inspirer of the worldwide student revolts, but who in 1968 publicly opposed them.[94] Marcuse's earlier revival of Hegalian Marxism (*Reason and Revolution,* 1941) and his synthesis of Marx and Freud (*Eros and Civilization)* were certainly seminal for many in the New Left. But by the 1960s Marcuse was seeing only negativity ('The Great Refusal') in our epoch of world-wide rebellion and theorizing workers in terms of *One-Dimensional Man* (his 1964 book).[95]

---

[94] Marcuse was appalled by the student tactics of strikes and occupations. Having been hounded out of Nazi Germany as a Jew and a Marxist, Marcuse defended the 'liberal' U.S. university system, where he had been welcomed, as a sanctuary for free inquiry. The sight of students taking over campuses must have reminded him of the Hitler Youth. We rebels exposed U.S. universities – supposedly 'value-free' – as complicit with the Vietnam war, carrying out secret military research and processing students into future officers and docile corporate employees.

[95] Please see my essay, 'A Critical Examination of Herbert Marcuse's Thought,' *New Politics* Vol. VI, No. 4.

On the other hand, Marcuse's analysis did have the virtue of focusing attention on a salient feature of the 1960's: revolt in the 'periphery.' Whether we consider the national liberation movements on the geographical periphery of the industrially developed world, or the 'peripheral' elements within it – the racial and ethnic minorities, the women liberationists, the youth, the unemployed, the disaffected intellectuals – we are looking at elements on the fringes. The fact that this rag-tag assortment of illiterate peasants and alienated intellectuals, dark-skinned ghetto-dwellers and middle-class students, outsiders, freaks and so-called 'lumpen' proletarians succeeded in uniting to knock the establishment off balance, is a remarkable testimony both to the fragility of the system and the maturity of oppressed humanity in our epoch of capitalist decadence.

The received wisdom of traditional 'Marxism' (Communists, social-democrats, even Trotskyists) considered these diverse 'elements' as essentially passive at best, and at worst as potential reactionary shock-troops in moments of crisis. Only under the 'firm leadership' of the advanced proletariat and its 'revolutionary vanguard' (the Party), it was believed, might they 'go over' to the revolution. Yet 1968 presents the spectacle of these very peripheral elements joining forces, generating their own leadership, mounting new and ingenious forces of struggle, and provoking a social and political crisis – a *breach* in the continuity of authority. This radical rupture was all the more remarkable in the absence of two elements considered essential for the overthrow of capitalism: a world economic crisis and of a generalized intervention on the part of the working class.

Limits of the Struggle

The Sixties' revolts erupted during a period of relative prosperity – the post-WWII boom of capitalist expansion. Unionized workers in the West, relatively well-paid, were considered integrated and consumerized. Futurists worried over the problem of 'leisure time.' Students, more or less assured of lifetime employment at places like IBM, were free to reject capitalist society on moral grounds. The mass strikes of the working class in France and Czechoslovakia were the exception, rather than the rule. It is not surprising, given their isolation, that they did not develop in an insurrectional direction and confront the armed forces of the state.

Whereas Marcuse and others dismissed French workers' general strike as a sort of historical conditioned reflex, a throwback to the traditions of 1848 and 1871, one might argue the contrary case. The decision to stop short of the ultimate confrontation (and thus avoid a bloodbath) was perhaps a sign of the collective maturity and tactical wisdom not only of the French (with their bitter memories of the massacres of July 1848 and the 1871 Commune), but also of the Czechs (who could hardly have forgotten the fate of the insurrectionary Hungarian Workers' Councils of 1956). It is hardly astonishing that the workers of France and Czechoslovakia chose not to become martyrs in the cause of an unlikely world revolution. What is astonishing is the fact that the overwhelming majority of the French workers refused to accept the Grenelle Agreements (including wage raises of up to 72%!) negotiated for them by the Communist and Socialist trade unions. It wasn't *more* money they wanted, but something else: new human relations in production. (A mass meeting of 25,000 actually booed the CGT leaders off the platform at the huge Renault factory at Boulogne-Billancourt near Paris.)

Astonishing but True

What is astonishing is the fact that during the French general strike, many enterprises actually resumed production under worker self-management and began exchanging their products with those of neighboring farmers, thus stripping the commodity-fetish off their labor and creating an embryonic socialism in the course of struggle! What is astonishing is the fact that many workers (backed by the students) continued to face the police in full-scale battles to defend their occupied factories long AFTER the official Communist- and Socialist-led unions had 'settled' the strike and attempted to stampede the workers back to work with false reports that 'all the other' factories had returned. What is astonishing is the fact that the Czech workers, often led by rank-and-file Communists, actually intensified the organization of democratically elected factory committees AFTER the Russian invasion put an end to Dubcek's reforms.

Clearly, if these workers had no taste for traditional revolutionary martyrdom, they had no taste for traditional reformism either. If the Czechoslovakian mass strike had spread, say, to Poland in 1968 (instead of 1981), the Czech resistance might have taken a less passive, less 'Schweikian' form, and the outcome might have been different... Similarly, if the French general strike had spread into Britain and Germany – as it did in a drawn-out form in Italy during 1969...

But, not so astonishingly, it didn't. It didn't for perfectly clear, objective reasons. The world economy was still enjoying the autumn of the long post-World War II boom. France, for example, had undergone a remarkable period of modernization and expansion during the Gaullist decade of 1958-1968, and in the U.S., L.B. Johnson was still able to deliver guns *and* butter, to pacify part of the labor movement and to co-opt an important sector of the Civil Rights movement by recruiting its leaders with paid jobs in his bogus 'War on Poverty' – all the while escalating his much more real and more costly war on Southeast Asia.

Only a Flash in the Pan?

Let us return, now, to our point of departure – Marcuse's critique of the movements of the 60's as essentially 'marginal' and their negative depiction as a mere 'flash in the pan' of no historical significance. History buffs and gun-freaks may recall that the expression 'a flash in the pan' refers to the misfiring of an old-fashioned flint-lock musket. The flint strikes a spark, the spark ignites the powder in the pan, but the main powder-charge in the breech fails to ignite. There is a blinding flash, but no bullet. This is an apt description of what happened in 1968.

On the other hand, the 60's revolts – be they of youth, oppressed minorities or peasants in the periphery – did display the potential to act as *detonators* (our 'flash in the pan' image again) for flare-ups of serious class conflict involving the essential polar antagonists of modern industrial society: the wage earners who produce goods and services *versus* the stockholders whose corporations own, manage or control the means of production and the state. Moreover, in both France and Czchoslovakia, the rebels and strikers had the active sympathy of the general population, further isolating the power structure to the point where the Army and even some of the police could no longer be counted on. As we have seen, these pre-revolutionary situations flared up for a few weeks only and then, unable to go forward, died out, like a flash in the pan. But does this render them meaningless 'throwbacks' (Marcuse) to a bygone age of class struggle? Not necessarily. The fact that a musket may misfire on one or another occasion does not render it any less a deadly weapon. Perhaps the powder was wet. The wet powder in this case standing for the absence of an economic crisis. Better timing next time. And speaking of next time, there is a

197

striking time-lag – a *décalage* or out-of-phase character – between the period of widespread social and political crises of the 1960's and the period of generalized economic crisis we are entering today, East and West. Given this *décalage*, it is not altogether surprising that the revolts of the 60's remained largely confined to 'the periphery' and retained a quality better characterized as 'revolts' or 'rebellions' than as 'revolutions.' (Hence the essentially symbolic, even theatrical quality of many of their tactics, from non-violent sit-ins to Days of Rage, or from showering the stock exchange with dollar bills to planting bombs under it.)

Meanwhile, the brief flash of 1968 stands like a beacon of hope, illuminating the capitalist landscape, pointing to the vulnerability of the powers that be and to the potential of new revolutionary subjects like youth and peasant farmers to ignite a general conflagration.

Some Hairy Theories

Nothing fails like failure. On the negative side, the objective isolation of these 'peripheral' movements from the central, essential class struggle of labor and capital led to some hairy theories with unfortunate practical consequences. Among the more innocuous of these deviations was Charles Riech's theory of The

Greening of America (1970) which predicted the peaceful transformations of the oppressive, exploitative and brutal institutions of U.S. capitalism through a revolution in consciousness ('Conn III') which would take over as soon as the long-haired students of 1968 were old enough to become Chairmen of the Board. In practice, the 'Long March through the Institutions' (as it was known in German SDS) changed little besides style.

Author's self-portrait as Natchayev

Equally idealistic but far more pernicious were the various vanguardist theories based on the elitist dogmas of the 'backward-ness' of the masses and its corollary, the need for a 'Party' of heroic self-proclaimed revolutionaries to lead them or set them an 'example.' Although couched in the language of Marxism-Leninism-Maoism, this ideology was a reversion to the ideology of the 19th Century Russian Populists – the 'Narodniks' against whom Lenin had had to struggle to lay the basis for Russian Marxism. Yet in the lull that followed the explosions of 1968, many European and American radicals, impatient with slow, dialectical development of mass movements and hungry for shortcuts to revolution, unwittingly reinvented the idealistic 'serve the people' ideology of the Russian students of 1870 and unconsciously aped the anarchist and populist bomb throwers of 1880-1914.[96]

Whose Violence?

On the level of the movement as a whole, incalculable damage was done by confusing the necessity for revolutionary violence (for example, self-defense as practiced by the original Black Panthers and Deacons for Defense; the militant occupation of private property and public space) with the counter-productive practice of individual terror. Rather than representing a step forward, the cultivation of individual violence was an index of the movement's isolation and decline.

Finally, the very weakness of the 60s rebellions (the absence of an economic crisis and generalized class warfare) paradoxically revealed the secret vulnerability of the power structure. Despite its monopoly of guns, police, prisons, political processes and information media, the Establishment's hegemony was severely (if momentarily) shattered by our rag-tag army of outsiders and freaks. The vaunted stability of de Gaulle's monarchy-by-referendum proved to be a house of cards, and it was not for nothing that Nixon whined about a 'pitiful, helpless giant.' The Emperor, albeit armed to the teeth, for a moment stood naked for all to see.

History, like geology, does not move forward at a uniform pace, but rather in fits and starts. Long periods of apparent uniformity are followed by volcanic moments of rapid transformation, summing up all that has come before and illuminating much of what is to come. I very much agree with George Katsiaficas[97] who characterizes the 1960's as such a 'world-historical' moment. Thus the rebellions of 1968 (like the unsuccessful revolutions of 1848 and 1905) may be seen as heralding the appearance on the historical stage of new revolutionary subjects and new forms of struggle that may develop at a later date.

If this be the case, the forces of social revolution that were forced into retreat two decades ago, may very well, following a historical pattern of 20-year cycles, return to the fray with the coming of a new generation. How have conditions changed since 1968? Will the balance of forces – subjective and objective – be more or less favorable for the Return of the Social Revolution?

---

[96] This repetition of history as farce would be laughable were it not for its tragic consequences – for the radicals themselves, for innocent by-standers, and for the movement. From my own N.Y. circle, Ted Kapchuck is dead and Dave Gilbert and Kathy Boudin are in jail for life. We have already seen how SDS was dismantled in the name of this 'revolution.'

[97] For the best overall view of the Sixties, I recommend George Katsiaficas, *The Imagination of the □New Left: A Global Analysis of 1968,* South End Press, 1987.

Favorable Signs (in 1988)

To this inveterately optimistic observer, the objective signs look favorable. To begin with, the strategic capability of the U.S. as policeman of the capitalist world has sharply declined since 1968. Twenty years ago U.S. imperialism was able to mount a prolonged full-scale invasion 6,000 miles from home against a seasoned Vietnamese guerrilla movement with a protected rear and lines of communication to allies in Russia and China. Today, tiny Nicaragua, surrounded by Contra bases, more or less abandoned by the U.S.S.R., stands defiant, only 600 miles from the U.S., after 8 years of concerted attack. Meanwhile, Washington's credibility lies shattered by the Iran-Contra-cocaine scandal. In comparison with the non-entity of [G.H.W.] Bush, Singlaub and North, Nixon and Kissinger loom like giants (and even Nixon's bumbling White House Plumbers look professional).

If the Monroe Doctrine is showing signs of wear, the Brezhnev Doctrine seems altogether in shambles. The rumble of tanks moving, NOT out into Czechoslovakia but home from Afghanistan (with their tails between their treads) can only be sending one message to East Europe's Communist dictators Husak, Geirik, Jarelzowsky and Company: 'Sink or swim. It's every man for himself, boys!' Not only did Gorbachev knock the military props out from under the ruling bureaucrats of the Warsaw Pact, he also removed the ideological props. Whatever *glasnost* and *perestroika* may mean in Russian, translated into East German, Hungarian, Czech, and Polish they have got to revive the hopes (and fears, for the bureaucracy!) of 1953, 1956, 1968, and 1981 respectively. Be that as it may, the rigid, bi-polar Cold War system with enforced social immobility based on the mutually agreed upon threat of the 'Enemy Without' is a thing of the past. The genii is out of the box. The superpowers suddenly don't seem so super any more, and humanity has less reason to fear and more reason to dream and to dare.

Economic Crisis?

On the economic front, it is clear that the world's dominant economic systems are on the brink of crisis.[98] On the one hand, it is difficult to imagine the U.S. economy escaping the logical consequences of a rapidly declining balance of trade, a huge internal debt (both governmental and private), and billions of uncollectible loans to impoverished Third World countries. With savings

---

[98] *2008 Note.* Ruefully re-reading my 20 year-old doomsday prediction I am reminded of the humorous brag: « We Marxists have predicted five out of the last three recessions. » On the other hand, the objective conditions I noted in 1988 – debt, speculation, balance of trade, plant-closings, globalization – continued and intensified, while many of the regulations put in place in the 1930's to prevent another 1929-type Crash were removed. I don't want to be an I-told-you-so, but I told you so.

institutions in deep trouble and the stock market, unchastened by Black Monday, battening on unhealthy speculation, laundered drug-money, and unproductive takeovers, it is likely that things may get a whole lot worse before they get better.

Whereas in 1968 the labor bureaucracy would drag a relatively well-paid layer of the working class 'part of the way with LBJ,' today plant closings, cut-backs, and take-backs have eroded the influence of the social-patriotic class-collaborationists of the AFL-CIO. How long can the Johnny-One-Notes of the UAW go on trumpeting 'Buy American' when it is obvious to every worker that 'American' companies are in fact transnational and that the job security of U.S. workers has been sacrificed on the altar of cheap labor in foreign lands? And if management can get away with paying garment workers 16 cents an hour in El Salvador, what chance does any worker – White, Black, or Latino – have asking for $16 an hour or even $6 an hour in L.A.? The answer is, 'Let's put the INTERNATIONAL back in UNION!' (Are you listening, International Ladies Garment Workers' Union?)

The beginnings of an anti-imperialist Central America solidarity lobby within the AFL-CIO is evidence that many U.S. workers understand that they are being forced to compete with the victims of anti-union rightwing dictatorships propped up by U.S. workers' tax dollars. Meanwhile, the situation of the Black and Hispanic labor force in the U.S., bad enough in 1968, has if anything worsened. To this reservoir of anger and revolt, Reaganomics has added millions of women forced into the labor market for survival, and thousands of skilled white workers who have been thrown out of work or forced into low-pay service jobs.

Capitalist Internationalization

The internationalization of capital has been the cutting edge of a generalized attack on U.S. labor's historical living standard – an attack designed to reduce us all – White, Black, male, female, young or old, to the level of subsistence.

Cutbacks in health care, housing, education and job safety combine with 'deindustrialization' to increase our insecurity and fear. All this takes place with the tacit complicity of the AFL-CIO leadership who blame everything on the Japanese and provide an easy out for the politicians and the corporations. As a result, union membership has declined to the level of the 1920's. Only a new, militant and internationalist labor movement (allied with other community forces) can possibly turn this situation around.

On the other side of the 'deindustrialization' equation stand the new proletarians of Korea, Taiwan, and the other 'Little Tigers.' A generation ago, they were peasants. Today they are industrial workers in the most advanced and most profitable sector of the world economy, increasingly impatient with low wages, long hours, harsh conditions, and the U.S.-backed authoritarian regimes that enforce them. Unlike the peasant guerrillas of the 1960's, these workers have the power to attack the system where it hurts.[99]

Some Big 'Ifs'

If the internationalism that characterized the movements of the 60's comes back to life and creates active links of solidarity among the workers in the various branches of the new multi-national capitalist system, then 'everything is possible' will cease to be a mere slogan. If the new subjects of revolution that revealed themselves in the mass movements of the 60s – the youth, the women, the oppressed minorities, the poor peasants, the new working class of educated technological and office personnel – join forces with these industrial workers in a situation of economic crisis, then humanity may yet find a way to its humanness and in the process save itself – and this beautiful world – from destruction.

These are all big 'ifs' – hypotheses based on selected evidence using an historical method that by definition lacks the verifiability (repeatability) of physical science. They are the best – indeed the only hopeful – hypotheses we have. Possibilities... Perhaps slim possibilities, but possibilities nonetheless, and thus a pathway opened toward a solution to the crisis of a society so decadent, so hell-bent on self-destruction, that the alternatives of 'socialism or barbarism' might better be restated as 'socialism or planetary extinction.'

There are so many time-clocks ticking their way toward an all-but-inevitable Armageddon that, without the hypothesis of worldwide social revolution, it is

---

[99] *2007 Note.* Twenty years later the Asian Tigers have been joined by China, a 2000 pound industrial Gorilla – with a new, militant proletariat of billions. Let us note that in China in 2006, there were 87,000 violent strikes and uprisings necessitating armed intervention according to *official* reports which likely underestimated the situation. The global proletariat, contrary to Western postmodernist, 'End-of-Work' dogma, has not 'disappeared.' It has merely changed its address.

202

only a matter of which form of annihilation we will succumb to first. An 'accidental' thermonuclear war *à la* 'Strangelove' or one unleashed by maniacal theocrats in Pakistan or Israel? The destruction of the ozone layer or the greenhouse effect? Overpopulation or universal starvation provoked by drought due to the destruction of the world's rainforests?

Species Questions

'People do make their own history, but not in circumstances of their own choosing.' Marx's remark is particularly poignant today when we may soon run out of circumstances (not to mention people). What were once class questions, social questions, political questions, have been qualitatively transformed into species-questions: questions of global survival. The global order, dominated by multinational conglomerates more concerned with short-term profits than future economic development (and increasingly propped up by repressive military-bureaucratic regimes), no longer even pretends to offer long-tern solutions. Reformism, once the hope of liberal and social democrats, is (paradoxically) a viable possibility only in the Eastern Block. (In the U.S., liberalism – our chief antagonist in 1968 – has become taboo: the 'L' word).

Thus if we eliminate Divine or extraterrestrial intervention, we are forced to the conclusion that only human activity on a world scale – the mass activity of the powerless and oppressed, be they landless peasants and sweated laborers in the Third World, rebels fighting the 'socialist bourgeoisie' in the Second, or the relatively privileged technological new working classes in the post-industrial First World – can prevent extinction and open the way toward the reconstruction of a rational, humane society.

To be sure, such a radical perspective sounds hopelessly Utopian today with Thatcherite neo-capitalism triumphant. Like everyone, I have my moments of despair. But then I think back to the rebellious world of the Sixties, to a time when 'Bliss was it in that dawn to be alive/ But to be young was very Heaven!'[100] I also remember that what happened once can happen, in perhaps more favorable circumstances, again. The 'flash in the pan' that sparked up in the Sixties was like a flare illuminating a dark battlefield. Its momentary brilliance revealed a capitalist adversary much weaker than we had imagined and a host of global allies we didn't know we had. Not enough to win, but future times may be more favorable. Today, we see the circle of the rich and powerful growing smaller and smaller, the numbers of excluded and exploited growing larger and larger, and with it their resentments, their hopes

---

[100] William Wordsworth's recollection of his experiences in the French Revolution (the *Prelude* of 1850.)

and their world-wide demand for justice. *'Ce n'est qu'un début! Continuons le combat!'* ('It's only a beginning! Keep the struggle going!')

Part IV:

Back in the U.S.S.R

The Death of Communism and the New World Order [1992]

Since the fall of the Berlin Wall in 1989, the ideologues of the Right have been congratulating themselves on the death of so-called Communism and proclaiming the everlasting triumph of neo-liberal free-market capitalism as the happy End of History. However, the collapse of the Evil Empire came as a total surprise to these very Cold Warriors, who insisted on seeing Gorbachev's radical and irreversible moves as mere feints designed to throw the West off guard. For example, George Will was still writing 'Liberalization is a ploy' on the very day the Berlin Wall came down! As a result, the U.S. security establishment blew the chance to ally with Gorbachev when he still controlled the Soviet Union and could have prevented the proliferation of unstable new nuclear states (certainly one of the greatest diplomatic blunders in modern history). Today, the same ideologues and 'intelligence' experts are trumpeting the death of Marxism and the millennial triumph of a new capitalist World Order. However, the nature of what died in the East and what is struggling to be born is far from clear, and their new prognostications may prove just as illusory.

Western experts and Sovietologists had long been unanimous that Russia's closed totalitarian system was impervious to change from within, and could only be contained from without by military means. On the other hand, serious independent Marxists like Leon Trotsky and Victor Serge, who understood the inner weakness of the Stalinist bureaucratic regime and the deep resistance of the workers, prefigured today's transformations a half century ago. As early as 1936, they foresaw the trend toward privatization, and Serge spoke specifically about the dangers of revived nationalism and Islamic fundamentalism.[101] So much for the idea that the collapse of Stalinism has 'disproved' the validity of Marxism! As Serge wrote just before his death in 1947: 'A poor excuse for logic, pointing an accusing finger at the dark spectacle of Stalinist Russia, asserts the failure of bolshevism, and therefore of Marxism and even socialism... A facile attempt to conjure away the many problems gripping the world and which won't go away in the foreseeable future. Aren't you forgetting other failures? What was Christianity doing during the [recent] social catastrophes? What happened to liberalism? What was the end result of conservatism, whether reactionary or enlightened? Did it not give us

---

[101] See Trotsky's *Revolution Betrayed,* and Serge's *Russia Twenty Years After,* especially his new 1947 Preface, 'Russia Thirty Years After.'

Mussolini, Hitler, Salazar and Franco? If it were a question of honestly weighing the many failures of different ideologies, we would have our work cut out for us for a long time. And nothing is over yet.' Serge died believing that it was reasonable to hope that the Russian people would eventually overthrow totalitarian Communism and move in the direction of democracy and a humanistic form of socialism.

However the Revolutions of 1989, while they did revive the democratic and socialist hopes of the East European anti-Communist revolts of 1953, 1956, 1968 and 1981, did not fulfill them. These early, ill-fated freedom struggles all bore the same revolutionary stamp of mass self-activity – from the 1953 Berlin workers' uprising following the death of Stalin, through the 1956 Hungarian Revolution with its Workers' Councils, to the 'socialism with a human face' of the Prague Spring of 1968, and the original Polish Solidarity movement of 1981. Their more or less explicit aim was democratic workers' control of society, that is to say socialism. Yet when the incubus of totalitarian Communism was finally lifted, what happened? Far from fulfilling the early expectations of freedom, democracy, revival and reform, the Revolutions of 1989 ushered in a dismal period of passivity, demoralization, political stagnation, economic chaos, hardships, shortages, and unemployment; of narrow nationalism, internecine warfare, and authoritarian rule. Indeed, as East Europe and the ex-Soviet lands slide deeper into this morass, the only 'light' at the end of the tunnel is apparently the dim possibility of the restoration of capitalism! And what kind of capitalism? Not the growth of small business, but an IMF-dictated bitter pill of austerity that can only lead to Latin-American-style dictatorship, debt and dependency! In fact, the fresh-minted 'democrats' around Yeltsin openly declare that a 'Pinochet-type solution' might be desirable if the masses, whose sufferings get worse daily fail to support what are euphemistically called 'reforms.'

How do we account for this horrible retrogression on the day after a victorious movement for liberation? Is it possible to found any rational hope for a socialist-humanist reorganization of society in the wake of the collapse of 'Communism?' To answer these questions we must begin by stating that the 'Communism' which collapsed in Russia and East Europe bore as much relationship to the liberating ideas of Karl Marx's Communist Manifesto as the Spanish Inquisition did to the ideals of Jesus' Sermon on the Mount. It was not communism, the theory and practice of human self-liberation, that collapsed in 1989 but Stalinism, a totalitarian system of bureaucratic class rule based on anti-working class terror and forced labor in the interest of the Party-State apparatus: the dominant *privilgensia* or *nomenklatura*.

It is history's bitterest irony that this bureaucratic totalitarian system first took root on the ruins of a genuine popular revolution, the Soviet Revolution of October 1917. The Russian Revolution turned sour when the expected world revolution failed to rescue the Soviets from poverty, isolation, backwardness, and continuous capitalist attacks. Eventually it degenerated into Stalin's bureaucratic tyranny. Yet the fact that its new rulers, while constructing a system resembling fascism, derived their privileges and power from state, not private property and continued to pay lip-service to a bastardized form of Marxism, has led to endless ideological confusion. However, the proof that the Stalinist bureaucracy's takeover was an anti-socialist counter-revolution has been obvious since the 1930's, when Stalin literally exterminated all the Marxists and revolutionaries in Russia including every member of Lenin's 1917 Central Committee but himself!

The Stalinist bureaucracy's cynicism and brutality were as ferocious as its legitimacy was flimsy. It murdered millions. Yet Stalinist economic planning, however crude and coercive, succeeded in turning a backward Soviet Union into the world's second industrial power with such speed that by 1945 Red Army tanks were able to overwhelm the industrial juggernaut of Nazi Germany, and Russia went on to compete head to head with the wealthy United States in a forty-year arms race. Today it is fashionable to dismiss Russia's state-capitalist command economy (and hence all forms of socialism and economic planning) as inherently inefficient. So let us recall that Communist Russia was able to industrialize during the Great Depression, when Western economies were stagnating, and that as late as the 1960s Khruschchev's threat to 'bury' the West economically was considered credible. On the other hand, as Victor Serge predicted, the absence in Russia of the essential socialist elements of democratic participation and intellectual freedom in the long run undermined the advantages of economic planning. Under Breshnev and his successors, efficiency declined to the point where Gorbachev's *glasnost* and *perestroika* reforms became necessities for the economic survival of the system.

What Marxists like Serge had anticipated – and what Western experts could not understand – was that Stalin's eventual heir (in the event Mikhail Gorbachev) would be obliged to initiate a profound revolution from above in order to solve two major sets of problems for the privileged bureaucracy he headed. The first was to end the economic and technological stagnation gripping the economy, raise productivity, and eliminate the system of police terror to the extent of making scientific progress and cultural life possible for the educated elites. The second was to somehow legitimize the scandalous illegal privileges of the bureaucracy whose rule was based on the fiction of administering socialized wealth in the interests of the 'true owners,' the working masses, who might one day wake up and demand an accounting. In retrospect, Gorbachev's reforms, although apparently slow and hesitant, were astoundingly radical, as was already clear to us in 1988.[102] Gorbachev realized that in order to revive the Russian economy, he would have to call off the ruinous arms race, which was eating up a huge percentage of the gross national product, and create the conditions for normal trade and exchange with the capitalist West. This entailed sacrificing the East European empire Stalin had established as a buffer-zone at the end of WWII while convincing his own military-industrial complex and his security apparatus to go along with him. To understand how radical Gorbachev was, try to imagine a U.S. President in 1985 convincing the Joint Chiefs, the FBI and the CIA to end the Cold War in a similar manner (and survive assassination)!

Moreover, Gorbachev understood that in the computer age, progress is dependant on the free flow of information, hence of ideas, and he began to take the clamps off of free expression through *glaznost*, much to the dismay of the Party ideologues and conservative KGB types. As a counterweight to the die-hard Stalinists and Cold Warriors on his right, Gorbachev opened up some space for democratic forces; but he understood that if democracy went too far he might very well need his old colleagues in the Party and the KGB, and he did not want to alienate them. This lead to his constant vacillation. This hesitancy was most evident where his last reform, the famous *perestroika* or economic restructuring, was concerned. Although Gorbachev's advisors had their 600-day plans (and Yeltsin's their 500-days) little was known about them and even less done. Why? For the simple reason that the bureaucracy was not then and is still not ready to take on the masses of working people in an open and decisive contest over who will ultimately own and profit from the economy, that is to say who will inherit the social wealth built up at great suffering by the Soviet people over generations during which these same bureaucrats (or their predecessors) told the workers to sacrifice in order to 'build socialism' for their children. Hence today's slow process of stagnation and decay, insecurity and price rises, all designed to demoralize the workers to the point that they will accept anything – even the IMF-Pinochet solution – in the name of reform, just to get things working again. Hence the encouragement of nationalism, even anti-Semitism, in order to divert attention from a potentially decisive class confrontation.

For what independent Marxists like Trotsky and Serge understood about the dynamics of the Stalinist system a half-century ago is still valid today. They believed that the ruling bureaucracy would be overthrown by the workers themselves within a generation or so, if there were no second (or third?) World War. In this they were overly optimistic. On the other hand these Marxists

---

[102] See above '20 Years After: 1968 in Historical Perspective' which appeared in *New Politics* in 1988 under the title, 'Reflections on 1968 and Beyond.'

foresaw that if the Stalinist system survived, the bureaucrats would inevitably attempt to integrate themselves into the world capitalist system and to turn their illegal privileges (ostensibly rewards for leading the workers to the promised land of socialism) into some kind of legal property. Trotsky saw this in terms of direct capitalist restoration; Serge through a process of joint-capital exploitation involving the West. Both were right. For the creation of this kind of Market Stalinism is, in essence, the program of the ex-Stalinist bureaucrats, freshly reborn as 'democrats,' 'nationalists,' and 'free-marketeers,' who have seized power in the ex-Soviet Union.

The process has been nicknamed '*nomenklatura* privatization' and it may be conceived as a kind of revolution-in-place. In this game, the ex-Communist bosses simply change hats, while remaining at their desks and in possession of the state-owned cars they drive, the state-owned mansions they live in, and the state-owned enterprises they manage. Only now the bureaucrats will be owners, not just 'servants' of the 'true owners,' the socialist workers. Thus commissars would become capitalists, 'Comrade Managers' would become 'Chief Executive Officers,' and the old Soviet *privilgensia* would become the principal stock-holders and directors of the social capital they formerly administered. And since the 'public sector' represents the whole national capital, even the U.S. multi-billion-dollar S&L and banking swindles pale in comparison with this massive theft of social wealth by a gang of inside traders. However, the would-be bourgeois have still problems. The first is the fear the workers won't let them get away with plundering the country. The bureaucrats have not forgotten the massive miners' strikes of 1989 and the amazing speed and boldness with which local, regional and national strike committees were formed these Marxists foresaw committees which moved immediately from pure economic demands to political demands. So while the self-proclaimed democrats in power pal around with Chicago-school economists and talk endlessly of 'reforms,' they haven't yet dared implement their full program of austerity and privatization out of fear of a massive reaction from below. Their low intensity attack on the rights and living standards of working people is demoralizing enough. Planned massive price rises have reduced everyone but the privileged to desperation. Salaries are next to worthless. Pensions are simply not paid on the grounds of a manufactured 'shortage' of money, while 'before our eyes, our systems of free medical care and free universal education are being dismantled without our permission, with no legal basis.'[103] IMF-imposed conditions for loans may give the bureaucracy a cover for attacks on the living standards of the people, but they also expose the fact that the bureaucrats want to sell the Soviet Union out to foreigners. (Thus there is an

---

[103] Nikolai Preobrazhensky of the Petersburg Party of Labor, quoted in *Bulletin*, U.S. Soviet Workers Information Committee, Vol. 1 No. 2, Nov. 1992, p. 36.

economic as well as a demagogic basis for the alliance of right-wing nationalists and Stalinist dinosaurs in opposition to 'reforms.')

Parenthetically, let no one imagine that what the Yeltsin gang calls 'free markets' has anything to do with the creation of small businesses and the development of capital through individual or cooperative labor. The principal successful examples of this type of capital formation are in the illegal private sector: an alarming growth of criminal mafias, swindlers and black marketeers. Bureaucratic restrictions, galloping inflation, and exorbitant new taxes continue to inhibit the actual creation of legitimate capitalist enterprises, so that even private farming, now technically legal, cannot take root – despite the ready market for produce. The 'market Stalinists' who now hold power are incapable of creating new private wealth and have only one plan: to expropriate the existing public wealth through '*nomenklatura* privatizations' and sell-offs of natural resources similar to those of the Reagan-Bush looting decade. For example the Mayor of Moscow recently transferred the assets of a large municipal enterprise to a new private company in which he is the principal stockholder.

So it is that the ex-Soviet Union is going to hell in a handcart and no one – East or West – is doing anything about it. Although the violent 'ethnic' quarrels in the Caucasus, the Crimea and the Baltics have not yet reached the stage of ex-Yugoslavia, all the elements are present plus an additional wild-card – nuclear weapons. Let us note that two significant factors in all this 'ethnic' violence have nothing to do with ethnicity. First, most of these conflicts are engineered by ex-Communist bureaucrats whipping up nationalist fervor in order to retain or expand their dictatorial power (and to make people forget their 'internationalist' Stalinist pasts). Second, the exacerbation of national quarrels serves as a diversion from the need to solve social problems, raise living standards, and establish practical democracy. As with the black on black 'tribal' violence in South Africa, much of the 'ethnic' violence in the ex-Soviet Union is provoked by the secret police in order to preserve minority rule – here that of the *nomenklatura* – and to prevent the working people from discovering and uniting around their common interests. Meanwhile, on the economic front, all over the ex-Soviet Union farms stagnate and factories cease production for lack of parts, yet Yeltsin's advisors, like Gorbachev's before him, have no practical plans for reviving the resource-rich Russian economy nor any intention of encouraging initiatives from below, be they collective or actual free enterprise. Of course the privileged and powerful are not hurting like the common people who have seen the buying power of their salaries and pensions decline at a vertiginous rate. The *nomenklatura* are quietly looting retail while waiting until the day when they can loot wholesale. Perhaps they feel that shortages and nationalist squabbles will create enough demoralizing diversions that the longsuffering Soviet peoples will eventually despair and willingly swallow the bitter pills of mass unemployment, homelessness, and the loss of healthcare and the social safety net in the name of 'austerity.'

212

On the other hand, the Soviet masses have suffered and labored, often heroically, for generations under totalitarian Communist bureaucrats who forced them to sacrifice in the name of 'socialism.' It is hardly reasonable to expect these same masses to sacrifice for another generation in order to enrich a few capitalists (in most cases the same bureaucrats) so that eventually the new wealth will 'trickle down' to them. Yet this is precisely the 'reform' Yeltsin's advisors are telling them they must accept! Hence, for the moment, we have *stasis* (which the Greeks understood as a violent and degenerative paralysis of a polity in the middle of an unfinished class war). This *stasis* is aggravated by unresolved antagonisms among sections of the *nomenklatura* itself, for the prospective bureaucratic bourgeois have already split into factions in anticipation of a division of the expected spoils.[104] The historic August 16, 1991 'attempted right-wing coup,' was little more than such a faction-fight played out in the streets, according to Boris Kagarlitsky, a leading spokesperson for the new Party of Labor and a socialist member of the Moscow City Council.[105] Kagarlitsky describes the 'coup' as an elaborate charade, staged with unarmed tanks and unloaded rifles, during which the Yeltsin people double-crossed the coup-makers and used the media to outfox the Gorbachev crowd in the generalized scramble for power. As a result of this spectacular political manoeuver, the Soviet Union, Gorby's stronghold, was dissolved to the advantage of Yeltsin's Russia. At the same time, the big provincial Party *apparatchiks* like Ukraine's Kravchuk, originally sent by all-powerful Moscow to be dictators over captive 'Republics,' suddenly converted to 'nationalism' in order to hold onto their local fiefdoms.

Within Russia, in the wake of the failed August coup, there was a great scramble to jump to the winning side. Every ex-Party boss from the Communist reformers around Gorbachev through Yeltsin's 'democrats' to various groups including neo-Stalinist and anti-Semitic nationalists (not excluding some of the coup-makers themselves) was born again as a free-marketeer. Yet within a year this unity of opportunists had fallen apart, as the representatives of the interests of the new entrepreneurs and those of the existing factory managers came to parliamentary blows over which privileged group should benefit most from privatization. In this struggle for spoils, the

---

[104] This split within the Stalinist ruling order was analyzed thirty years ago by two young Polish Marxists, Jacek Kuron and Karol Modzelewski, in an 'Open Letter' to the Polish Workers (Communist) Party that landed them in jail. Their brilliant analysis of the bureaucratic ruling class and the antagonism within it between the 'central political bureaucracy' and the managers in the field was prophetic, even if Kuron's subsequent political incarnation as an austerity Labor Minister provides an ironic commentary on the prophetic ideas of his heroic youth.

[105] See *New Politics* Vol. III, No. IV (New Series): 'Yeltsin's Successful Coup' by Boris Kagarlitsky.

factory managers have the advantage of being able mobilize 'their' workers against 'outside' exploiters by manipulating the existing unions and work collectives. Naturally, independent organizations of working people are anathema to both power-groups. Yet Kagarlitsky is certainly right that if there was a coup, it was Yeltsin who pulled it off. For 'Czar Boris' immediately used the victory of 'democracy' to vastly reinforce his own executive power to the detriment of actual democratic formations. Although Yeltsin called on the workers to strike and support him during the August charade and pledged that he would 'lie on the railroad tracks' if his reforms were accompanied by price increases, he has in fact attacked workers living standards while clamping down on the unions, both old and new. Among Yeltsin's first decrees was the banning of employee organization at the workplace (under the pretext of banning the Communist Party). The 'democrats' in power are also clamping down on grass-roots organizations and parties like Kagarlitsky's Party of Labor, but the popularity of these new groupings, although limited, seems to be growing. What are the perspectives for a socialist revival in the ex-Soviet lands?

Fifty years ago, Leon Trotsky died believing that despite Stalin's perversion of socialism, the basis of collective property and collective labor had been so firmly established in the Soviet Union that a 'political revolution,' merely by sweeping away Stalin and his cronies, would be sufficient to restore socialism. Whether his analysis was correct at the time is moot, for the political revolution has arrived, a half-century too late, and it is now obvious that it will take a acrimonious class struggle, perhaps a civil war, before the working people of the ex-Union can expropriate their bureaucratic-bourgeois oppressors. Moreover, such is the popular revulsion against the official Communism that justified so much suffering for so long, that, as Victor Serge predicted in 1947, it may be a long while before the mass of workers will be willing to listen to Marxist or socialist ideas. At the same time, the peoples of the ex-Soviet Union have so little experience with actually existing capitalism and have so many illusions about the consumer societies they imagine exist in the West, that they have no idea that their capitalist future will look more like Peru than like Switzerland. Although this would be tragic, some observers believe that the Soviet people will have to go through the actual experience of private capitalist exploitation before they are ready to overthrow it.

I, for one, am less pessimistic and I hope, for sound historical reasons. Let us return again to our original question: Why did the Revolutions of 1989, instead of marking a new beginning for humanity and fulfilling the libertarian socialist aspirations of earlier anti-Communist revolts, open the road to the most serious retrogression, including economic and political stagnation, a failure to develop the basis of democracy in a renewed civil society, a revival of bloody internecine religious and national struggles, and the apparent triumph of neo-liberal Reaganomics in the East? We have just explored the inner dynamics of the collapsing Stalinist empire, but for me, an essential part of the answer lies

214

in examining the unfavorable international environment and historical context. In order to understand the importance of this context of world-wide recession and rampant Reaganism, let us exercise our fancies and imagine it otherwise. Let us imagine, for example, that Russian 'Communism' had collapsed at the time of the world-wide revolutionary upsurges of 1968, rather than stagnating on for another twenty years. Imagine that in 1968 instead of the Russian tanks invading Prague, the spirit of Prague Spring (which did in fact spark sympathy movements in Poland and demonstrations in the Soviet Union) had invaded Russia. Imagine that the masses of students and workers in rebellion in France and Western Europe against both capitalism and 'Obsolete Communism' had poured across the Berlin Wall, not with the 1989 message of consumerism and contempt, but burning with the holy 1968 freedom-fire and bringing with them the kind of practical solidarity that people with mimeograph machines and experience in political parties and trade unions can effectively share with new movements just getting organized. Imagine a United States paralyzed by ghetto riots, anti-war demonstrations, and the collapse of adult authority. And while we're at it, why not imagine a self-organized workers' movement à la 1981 Polish Solidarity linking up with the wild-cat strike movements inflaming France, Italy, Britain and parts of the U.S., while the revolutions in Vietnam, Iran and Nicaragua keep the forces of imperialism off balance?

All of the above events did happen, albeit not simultaneously. However, there is nothing intrinsically impossible about our imaginary scenario, which certainly would logically have led to a genuine new world order based on spontaneous mass democracy and respect for human rights. What happened in fact, as we argued in our study of the Sixties, is that capitalism, after getting a good scare in 1968, counter-attacked and developed new techniques for suppressing rebellion and raising profits culminating in the recent decade of transnational high-finance looting, reactionary social policy, and militarism. The purpose of our imaginary exercise in the almost possible is not to argue that Communism collapsed 10 or 20 years too late for anyone's good, although that might turn out to be the case. It is rather to remind ourselves that the Revolutions of 1989 had the misfortune of taking place at the end of a decade of Reagan-Bush-Thatcherite neo-capitalist retrogression, during a period of high unemployment and economic stagnation, and that the political environment was not exactly supportive to socialism and democracy. For example, the unfortunate East German democrats, who toppled the vicious Honecker regime with demonstrations sparked by their little civic clubs, hardly had a chance to breathe before Helmut Kohl came barreling over the Wall with his Deutschmarks and his referenda and his plant-closings and privatizations. Nor did the sick, senile, cynical socialism of Mitterrand provide a shining example of solidarity for France's East European neighbors. Given this context of triumphant neo-liberalism, it was hardly reasonable to expect the poor Russians dragging themselves out of the radioactive mud of Chernobyl after 70 years of privation and brainwashing to come up with the clarity of mind to reject consumerism and espouse humanistic socialism without outside support.

However, there is nothing fated about this situation, and it could change quite rapidly. The 'boom' of the Eighties, which was not a boom in terms of working peoples' living standards, now appears to have paved the way for a bust. The false prosperity of U.S. military Keynesiansm seems to have reached its limit, and even Japanese capital has contracted dramatically. Despite the help of banking deregulation and massive bailouts, the capitalists can't play poker endlessly on borrowed money – sooner or later the hands will be called, and then it's pay up or fold. The political and social bankruptcy of neo-liberal capitalism is already evident in race riots, unemployment, homelessness, human rights abuses and growing economic inequality. Its financial insolvency can't be concealed indefinitely. Meanwhile, there have been encouraging signs of a revival of worker militancy in Britain and Italy.

To be sure, the death of so-called Communism left one and only one super-power, which, following its preordained victory in the Iraqi 'turkey-shoot' proclaimed itself the leader of a New World Order. However, the emptiness of that phrase was quickly revealed. Within a year it was obvious that under U.S. hegemony, not world order but worldwide violence and disorder still reign – and not only in the former Second and Third worlds, but increasingly in the First. As in the 1930's, the Western democracies are standing aside while genocide is practiced in the heart of Europe (Bosnia). Meanwhile, Kohl's Germany retrogressed to tacitly encouraging neo-Nazi-ism, Mitterrand's France refused to disavow the crimes of Vichy, and in the U.S., the Los Angeles revolt exposed both the racism of American society and the anger and despair of its underprivileged. New World Order notwithstanding, Bush's tin-horn victories over his former henchmen, General Noriega and Saddam Hussein, solved none of the problems that allegedly provoked those two ghastly U.S. invasions. As Panama sinks deeper into dictatorship, drugs and money-laundering, the intact Hussein dictatorship rearms, renews its armed attacks on the Kurds, Shiites and democrats, and remains a formidable regional power. If anything, Bush's paltry triumphs demonstrate the sickness and ineptitude of the Western policy of selling arms to all comers and of propping up corrupt tyrants with secret supplies of cash and weapons in order to 'tilt' against other perceived enemies.

Thus, Bush was afraid to campaign on his incomplete Gulf 'victory' for fear of watching his fabricated pro-war consensus unravel in a new Iraq-Gate of illegal deals with Saddy-the-Baddy. Indeed, even during the jingoistic media blitz against the mind of the U.S. public that was arguably Bush's greatest Desert Storm victory, his support was so thin that both of the two anti-Gulfwar demonstrations in Washington attracted more actual participants than Bush's ballyhooed multi-million-dollar Victory Celebration in the Spring. The subsequent electoral defeat of the architect of the 'New World Order' revealed both the superficiality of 'manufactured consent' and the depth of the economic crisis. Meanwhile, right in the U.S.'s back yard, the revolutionary and popular movements in the tiny countries of Nicaragua and El Salvador

216

remain undefeated and have forced the U.S.-backed right-wing governments into uneasy stand-offs. One recalls that the destruction of the revolutionary movements in Nicaragua and El Salvador was at the top of the foreign policy agenda of the Reagan-Bush New Right when it took office in 1980. The survival of these two minuscule nationalist-revolutionary movements after twelve years of massive U.S.-orchestrated repression (and especially after their abandonment by their Russian allies) represents a clear defeat for the New World Order.

In El Salvador, the guerillas of the FMLN succeeded in fighting the right-wing army to a standoff, despite billions of dollars in U.S. military aid. The U.N. - supervised truce can help open some political space for the teachers, trade-unionists, peasants, Catholic human rights workers and left politicians to organize against the Salvadoran death-squad oligarchy.[106] At the same time, tiny Nicaragua continues to stand defiant against U.S. imperialism even after the electoral victory of the conservative Violetta Chamorro over the revolutionary Sandinistas. In spite of the painful setbacks in health and education following Violetta's election, her bourgeois government refuses to concede to U.S. pressures on questions of sovereignty, and she maintains the Sandinista Army and Police intact in order to keep the C.I.A.-backed *Contras* at bay and to defend the national interest.[107] These are small and ambiguous victories, to be sure. But they are signs that U.S. hegemony is vulnerable to an international revival of social struggles around issues of sovereignty, human rights, land reform, the environment, and decent conditions of life and labor. And the U.S. solidarity movement as well as the generalized public revulsion against Vietnam-type adventures deserve part of the credit for the success of this resistance.

Back in Russia, moreover, despite the apparent domination of IMF-Yeltsin 'free market Stalinism', the ultimate battle between the bureaucrats and the workers for control of the economy has yet to be decided. The 'backward' Soviet people still reject the profit system as immoral if not illegal, and the true spirit of communism may yet take its revenge on the fat-cat ex-Communist

---

[106] *March 2009 Note.* The FMLN has just been elected by a majority of Salvadorans, ending decades of ARENA party death-squad government.

[107] Precisely because Nicaragua has refused to become another Honduras or Guatamala, the Chamorro government is not receiving the promised U.S. aid that may have won her votes. Moreover, by submitting to the (momentary) will of the majority, the Sandinistas have set a unique precedent among vanguard parties and avoided creating yet another bureaucratic tyranny to besmirch the name of socialism. If the Sandinistas are able to deepen their links with the masses and hold onto their arms during this period of retreat into legal opposition, they may yet teach the world a new lesson if and when conditions become more favorable for revolutionary resurgence.

bosses who hypocritically preached it only yesterday. Moreover, there are promising developments like new movements among the Russian trade unions, regional and national strike committees, the potential radicalization of workers' self-management collectives in the old state enterprises, and the recent foundation of the Party of Labor, based on these movements, which may take root if political freedom is maintained.

If ever there was a time to think and act globally, it is now. The Cold War bogeyman is no longer there to frighten people into numbed paralysis. No longer can 'anti-Communism' be used to suppress U.S. popular movements, as it was against generations of labor organizations and civil rights groups, from the Wobblies to Martin Luther King. Conversely, Communist agents and parties can no longer be used to divert popular mass movements into pro-Russian channels or to betray them as the Stalinists did in Spain in 1936 and in France in 1968. Nor can ex-Party bosses like Yeltsin any longer use the excuse of 'aiding the capitalists' to suppress the champions of labor and human rights in Russia. However bleak the post-1989 scene may be in appearance, the historical reality is that an incubus has been lifted that was sapping the life-blood of the revolutionary movement.

Indeed, whatever may have kept the East European revolts of 1953, 1956, and 1968 isolated from each other, today nothing keeps Western movements from uniting with their Eastern comrades except mutual misconceptions. These are many, and representatives of the U.S. labor bureaucracy, the CIA and State Department are busy directing disinformation campaigns at Russian workers to spread illusions. For example, anarcho-syndicalist militants I spoke with in Moscow report that the U.S. economy is being presented as some kind of worker-controlled peoples' capitalism since workers' pension-plans had stock in their companies! However, groups like 'The U.S.-Soviet Workers Information Committee' have taken the initiative to solicit and publish materials on workers' and socialist struggles in Russia, to make materials about conditions and forms of struggle in the U.S. available there, and to organize discussions and exchanges. These efforts must be expanded.[108]

It is time to extend the kind of solidarity work that has proven both effective and mutually enriching in Latin America to the struggling peoples of Eurasia. Internationalism must be the order of the day, beginning with information exchange, direct contact and material aid to social movements struggling in the ex-Communist lands. Nor should North American wage earners allow phony patriotism, like the Japan-bashing of Lee Iacocca and his labor lieutenants of

---

[108] For example in 2009 by the Praxis Research and Education Center in Moscow www.praxiscenter.ru

the United Auto Workers International (sic!), to blind us to the fact that the transnational corporations are playing on national fears to create competition among workers, depress everyone's living standards, and degrade the environment world-wide. An injury to one is quite immediately an injury to all, for the cheapening of labor, whether in Salvador or in Siberia means lower wages in North America as surely as the radioactive fallout from Chernobyl affects the milk we drink.

With the end of the Cold War, a global solidarity movement to create a new, truly human world order becomes a practical possibility, and only such a global movement can effectively oppose the destruction of the world by globally-organized capital in its private or state form. One hundred-fifty years ago, when the industrial revolution was new, the rallying cry of the First International was 'Working people of all countries unite, we have a world to win.' Today, the capitalist system has exhausted all its progressive features and has nothing left to offer the world but the consumerist rat-race for the 'lucky' few and the barbarism of endless wars and famines for the vast majority of humankind. As we enter the 21st Century, we not only still have 'a world to win,' we also have a planet to lose.

Lenin Horizontal and Vertical

Lenin's Contradictory Heritage

For almost a century, generations of revolutionaries have looked to V.I. Lenin as a model to learn from and emulate. Some are attracted by what we could call the 'horizontal' Lenin (and I'm not talking about the mummy Stalin put on display in Red Square). For us, Lenin was a principled revolutionary, one of the handful of socialist internationalists who denounced the imperialist nature of the First World War at its outbreak in 1914 and refused to follow the mainstream German and French Socialists, Anarchists, and labor leaders who had turned patriot over night, voted for war budgets and exhorted their workers to murder each other in the trenches. Three years later, Lenin wrote *The State and Revolution,* reviving Marx's radically horizontal vision of the Paris Commune in the context of the 1917 Russian Revolution. Lenin's vision is one of self-organized workers overthrowing the reactionary state (Power Against in John Holloway's terms), reorganizing society on a democratic basis (Power To) and replacing the centralized bureaucratic and repressive apparatus (Power Over) with cooperative self-activity until the state 'withers away.' Lenin penned that 'anarcho-syndicalist' tract while hiding in Finland, and the writing breaks off when he returns to Russia to carry out its anarcho-syndicalist program: 'All Power to the Councils *(Soviets)* of Workers, Soldiers and Peasants!'

This is the Lenin Victor Serge observed at Comintern Congresses, simple in his worn *émigré* clothing, carefully listening to delegates, workers and anarcho-syndicalists from Spain, Italy around the world, always asking probing questions. The Party leader Serge depicts patiently arguing and explaining his points, often placed in the minority by his comrades; the Lenin whose greatest threat to his opponents was to resign Central Committee and go directly to the revolutionary sailors. This 'horizontal' (or 'libertarian') Lenin comes to the fore again in 1923-24, significantly after a series of strokes removed him from the exercise of state power. Now we see him criticizing Communist bureaucracy, attacking 'Commu-Lies' in the official press, ultimately calling for the 'removal' of Stalin.[114] I think it is important to remember this horizontal Lenin today, when Right-wing revisionist historians try to present the horrors of Stalinism as the straight continuation of Leninism (and Leninism as the

---

[114] See *Lenin's Last Struggle* by Moishe Lewin

220

continuation of Jacobinism) in order to discredit *any* revolutionary change as leading *necessarily* to totalitarian ends. As Serge pointed out in *From Lenin to Stalin* the fact that Stalin took power by liquidating all of Lenin's surviving revolutionary comrades and replacing them with sycophantic bureaucrats is in itself proof of the discontinuity of their regimes. As for Bolshevism 'containing the germ of Stalinism,' Serge famously replied that it makes little sense to judge a healthy person, whose living body contains many different germs, on the basis of those found in his corpse.

This is not to deny the 'vertical' side of Lenin, whose 1903 *What Is To Be Done?* presented socialism as a scientific theory defined by intellectuals and proposed the creation of a top-down, militarily organized revolutionary party to bring it to the masses. At the time, Trotsky presciently remarked that Lenin's formula was an excellent formula for taking power, but would reveal itself as tyrannical once in power. Ironically, after 1917, Trotsky adopted the same vertical, vanguardist 'Bolshevik-Leninist' model and transmitted it to his anti-Stalinist followers in exile, thus perpetuating a profoundly anti-democratic tradition shared by Maoists and neo-Stalinists alike. Lenin and Trotsky must be held responsible for what Serge believed to be the Party-state's most tragic error – the creation of the *Cheka* secret police, an extra-judicial inquisition with power to arrest, try and execute counter-revolutionary suspects on the basis of dossiers and without the right of self-defense. Serge also blamed the Party for the bloody repression, without attempt at negotiation, of the 1921 revolt of the Kronstadt sailors, who were demanding 'free Soviets' and economic reforms, most of which the government soon adopted as the liberal New Economic Policy at the end of the Civil War.

Revolutionary or State's Man?

I believe we can still learn a lot from Lenin – as long as we are also learning from Lenin's mistakes and not repeating them. Raya Dunayevskaya, in *Marxism and Freedom* and elsewhere speaks of Lenin's 'ambivalence,' but that little word hides as much as it reveals when you get to specifics, which Raya never did. Kronstadt was off limits with her, as it was with Max Schactman. So was the decline of the Soviets and the factory committees under Lenin, which Maurice Brinton irrefutably documented in his 1970 *Solidarity* pamphlet *The Bolsheviks and Workers Control, 1917-1921* (subtitle: *The State and Counter-Revolution*). Rather than ambivalence, I think it is better to speak of Lenin's 'contradictions.' The primary contradiction in Lenin is between the statesman and the revolutionary, a contradiction that is reflected in the contradiction between the nationalist and the internationalist.

Lenin may have taken power in Russia as a revolutionary internationalist – boldly gambling that the 'coming' European Revolution would soon relieve Russia's isolation and backwardness. But once Lenin held state power over the territory of the former Russian Empire, he necessarily incarnated both Russia's national/imperial interests *and* the self-preservation imperatives of a party holding national state power. Those interests and imperatives were not necessarily identical with those of the international proletariat, and when Lenin, the statesman in power, had to choose between these competing interests, he acted more as a nationalist than as an internationalist, more as a statesman – a man of the state – than as a revolutionary. Once isolated within the borders of the Old Russian Empire, a vast underdeveloped land with a huge peasantry and a small, if highly concentrated and highly conscious proletariat, Lenin's government faced an impasse, and the state swallowed the revolution.

 Although I have walked through Red Square in Moscow on many occasions, I have always refused to visit that horrible granite mausoleum within which Stalin placed Lenin's mummified body, depriving it of its final rest, against the wishes of both Lenin and his widow Krupskaya. What humiliation, what horror for a modest man like Lenin to lie forever exposed to strangers' eyes! Lenin's mummy lies 'in state.' Ironically, the revolutionary has been totally subsumed by the State's Man, placed on view to legitimise Stalin's all-powerful counter-revolutionary State. As Engels wrote in *Peasant Wars in Germany* (1850):

> The worst thing that can befall a leader of an extreme party is to be compelled to take over a government in an epoch when the movement is not yet ripe for the domination of the class which he represents and for the realization of the measures which that domination would imply. What he *can* do depends not upon his will but upon the sharpness of the clash of interests between the various classes, and upon the degree of development of the material means of existence, the relations of production and means of communication upon which the clash of interests of the classes is based every time. What he *ought* to do, what his party demands of him, again depends not upon him, but upon the degree of development of the class struggle and its conditions... [115]

In 1885, in a letter to the Russian Populist revolutionary Vera Zasulich, Engel's argued that a leap forward into a peasant Utopia based in the *mir* (village commune) was out of the question, as capitalist economic forces would necessarily dominate Russia: 'All governments, even autocratic ones, are in the last analysis nothing more than the executive organs of the economic necessities of the national situation.'

---

[115] http://www.marxists.org/archive/marx/works/1850/peasant-war-germany/index.htm

222

Lenin and the Bolsheviks faced this dilemma very early. In 1918, they made a Devil's pact with the Kaiser in return for peace. What was Lenin protecting if not his capital (Petrograd/Petersburg) – symbol of state power? There were other options. Soviet Russia could have tried to trade space for time by retreating to the vastness of Russia and waiting for the Allies to defeat Germany. Such a defensive strategy had defeated Napoleon's invasion in 1812 and later it would beat Hitler. Both Mao in China, and later the Sandinistas in Managua, preserved their revolutionary strength by such strategic retreats. What might have happened if the new Russian Republic had refused to sign the humiliating peace treaty with Germany? We can't rewrite history, but we can at least *imagine* some latent possibilities: German lines stretched into the depths of Russia in the cold. Peasants revolting against German exactions of their grain and livestock. Gguerrilla warfare. Intensive anti-war agitation propaganda among German soldiers – themselves peasants and workers, many of them social democrats. German soldiers fraternizing with the Russians, deserting to the other side. The war ending. The German Army in Russia collapsing, forming its own Soldiers' Councils, marching *back* to Berlin to support the ongoing German revolution, full of socialist ideas. A new internationalist army of revolutionary soldiers of all nationalities. Garibaldi's dream. This scenario is more or less what Bukharin and the *majority* of the Bolshevik Party proposed, and Lenin got his way only by threatening to resign and split the Party.

Apparently, Lenin in power acted as a national statesman, not an internationalist revolutionary. The moment he put the interests of his Party, his government, and Russia ahead of the chance to advance the world revolution by a bold gamble, he put Russia on the road to what Stalin would call 'socialism in a single country.' True, the Reds in Russia might have succumbed to the German-backed Whites like the French Communards, but they would have left a glorious example for future generations instead of blocking the horizon of the international working class with a monstrously 'successful' revolution. In addition, once Lenin became a State's Man he ruled as a virtual dictator and allowed the Soviets to wither away. The Communist Party, rather than acting as the most revolutionary of the parties contending *within* the Soviets, transformed itself into a party-state apparatus which took over the trade unions and choked off the power of the soviets. This was in total contradiction with what Lenin wrote in 1917 in *State and Revolution* where he restated Marx's notion that the need for the state would wither away as the masses took charge of running society through the Soviets. There were, of course, a million reasons for Lenin's back peddling, as Trotsky and his followers have been reminding us for 70 years. We could list the depletion of mass energies during the years of Civil War, famine, and White terror, as well as the need to reorganize defence and production. These are the traditional justifications for the improvised statist system known as 'War Communism.' But such excuses are only valid if one equates 'the health of the revolution' with the maintenance of Communist state power over the territory of the former Russian Empire; that is if one equates the disease with the cure. Lenin and the Bolsheviks' imperative to hold on to state power not only strangled the self-development of the revolution *within* Russia, it also thwarted the development of the world revolution, whose eventual victory was – let us remember – the *sole* justification for a Marxist workers' party to take power in an overwhelmingly peasant country just on the verge of capitalist development.

What Lessons to Draw?

As for lessons, 1917 proved that world capitalism was so ripe for revolution that a proletarian socialist party, backed by the peasantry, could take power in a semi-feudal country. It also proved that Engels was 100 times right in his dire warning that 'the *worst possible thing*' that could happen to a revolutionary party would be to take power where conditions were not ' ripe' for the class on which it was based. Engels predicted that this party would inevitably be turned into the instrument of other, powerful forces which it could not resist. And indeed, the Leninist Party-State did become the historical instrument by means of which Russian capital developed at breakneck speed using police methods rather than the market to drive the peasants off the land and into the factories. Lenin's Party-State was such an ideal instrument for this historic task that despite Stalin's bloody mismanagement, it was able to build a Russian war machine powerful enough to defeat the most advanced and powerful capitalist nation in Europe – Nazi Germany. On the negative side, this actually existing Russian state-capitalism called itself 'Communism' and thus distorted and degraded the word and the ideal for a whole epoch. The obvious conclusion that the majority of workers of the 20th Century drew from the Russian Revolution was this: ' Socialism equals shortages and a totalitarian police state. Never mind the excuses. We've seen the broken eggs. Now show us your omelette.' Thus, by taking and holding power in backward Russia in the name of socialism, the Bolsheviks unwittingly closed off the revolutionary socialist alternative for a whole generation, paving the way for fascism's rise.

The tragedy of the Russian Revolution seems to indicate that the anarchists were absolutely right to condemn the state as *necessarily* oppressive and to fear ' workers' dictators.' It is high time for socialists to stop using Marx's misleading (because ironic) phrase 'dictatorship of the proletariat' as our goal. As if any 21st century worker hearing the word 'dictatorship' would stay around long enough to listen to the explanation of what this phrase *really* meant in the original context.[116] Its continued use is literal proof of the Left's

---

[116] Marx considered big money domination of parliamentary democracy as a *de facto* 'dictatorship' in the interests of the wealthy classes. He concluded, that real democracy would rule in the interests of the poor majority, hence a workers' 'dictatorship.' Marx soon abandoned this feeble and confusing joke, but unfortunately Engels revived it after his death.

'religious' attitudes and fetishistic ancestor-worship. (Even the Catholics finally gave up on Latin and translated the Bible into comprehensible modern English!) Indeed, one suspects that socialists who still talk about ' proletarian dictatorship' (instead of workers' councils, for example) secretly fantasize themselves as little Bolshevik dictators in black leather trench coats. John Holloway makes a very useful distinction between 'power *over*' (the bosses, cops and bureaucrats), 'power *against*' (the revolt of the billions) and 'power *to*' (the potential of humans to create, to build, to organize themselves, what Engels called 'the invading socialist society). What socialists *should* be doing is reaffirming the lessons that Marx *and* the anarchists drew from the Paris Commune. Don't 'take over' the state (Power Over).'Smash' the state (Power Against) and replace it (Power To) with expansive, democratic, self-created organs of workers' power like the Commune, the soviets, the workers' councils under popular control with elected delegates paid workers' wages and subject to recall.

During the Red Years 1917-1919, the Russian Revolution was considered both a national and an international event – the first link in a chain of popular and socialist revolutions provoked by the insane slaughter of WWI. That is why the bourgeois governments of Britain, France, the U.S. and Japan did everything they could to destroy it. Thanks to Lenin the statesman, a *national* incarnation of the 1917 revolution survived in the absence of, and even at the expense of, the *international* revolution. From the beginning, the Bolsheviks intervened bureaucratically in the affairs of the German, Hungarian, French and other workers' parties, reinforcing bureaucratic tendencies at the expense of self-development and extra-parliamentary action. Worse, from the beginning, the Russian state dealt with other states with truly Bismarkian *realpolitik,* making deals with reactionary governments and sacrificing non-Russian workers in the interests of its own survival: for example, with Germany over Finland in 1918, in China in 1927 (alliance with Chiang), in Spain in 1936, the Stalin-Hitler Pact in 1939, the Yalta agreement over Greece (and elsewhere) in 1945. That contradiction is the tragedy of the 20th Century, and Lenin, like Oedipus, was the hero who unwittingly brought down the plague on the city while using all his brilliance and courage to save it. The name of the plague was revolutionary nationalism, and it swept over Russia and infected the world socialist movement for nearly a century. Lenin died of these and the other contradictions of government's impossible situation. His brain split apart and a cerebral hemorrhage destroyed it. Dying, he tried to reign in Stalin, his evil genius, and put that wily Georgian Genie back in the bottle. But the brutal Stalin was merely the incarnation of those ' terrible forces' he had unleashed and about which Engels spoke so prophetically.

Lenin was a great-souled individual, who tragically overreached himself. Stalin was a power-mad brute and a bloody villain. But if the question of the extermination of the Old Bolsheviks were posed historically, dialectically, one would have to say that developing capitalism in Russia needed to purge its management of the potential moral or political obstruction incarnated by those old revolutionaries. State-capitalism – like the market – has no conscience. Like Lenin, the Old Bolsheviks were *subjectively* internationalists and thus guilty of the crime of 'Trotskyism' – that is to say of Marxism and of humanism in general. In any case, their scruples were obstacles to the totally ruthless exploitation of the Russian masses in the name of rapid, forced industrialization that Russian capital required in order to survive and compete in the world state-system... Which was the name of the game, once the Soviet state began signing Devil's pacts with reactionary bourgeois governments. To be sure, Lenin remained *subjectively* an internationalist. I believe he was sincere. But he *acted* like a Russian statesman, a state-builder like Tsar Peter I, and he re-founded the Russian state along the modern, scientific lines necessary to catch up with the capitalist West.

What other lessons can we draw from the Russian tragedy? Already in 1871 the Commune proved that working people could govern themselves and create a new society out of their own creative self activity. It proved in practice that socialism is indeed the *practical* goal at which the workers' movement aims. Those were its positive lessons. The Commune's negative lesson was that unless the revolution spread out from besieged Paris to the rest of France and beyond, it was doomed. As we have seen, this lesson applied as well to the Russian Revolution a half-century later, but with a twist. Instead of being doomed to annihilation by capitalist forces from *without*, it succumbed to capitalist forces from *within*. The positive lesson of 1917 was the discovery that workers' councils were the self-created *form* of workers' power, the horizontal means by which the revolutionary masses could direct their own destiny. Just as the 1871 Commune finally answered, *in practice*, the question of the state in Marx's time, so the new edition of the Commune, the federation of Soviets – self-organized workers', peasants' and soldiers' councils – answered it in Lenin's. The Russian workers themselves created this new *Soviet* form of mass self-activity and self-organization during the 1905 Revolution, but it was not 'discovered' by Marxist theoreticians like Lenin, Luxembourg or even Trotsky, who was President of the Petersburg Soviet in 1905, until it resurfaced in 1917. This *form* of self-organization was rediscovered during the 1956 by the Hungarian Workers' Councils during their revolution against Stalinist state-capitalism. Lenin's greatest theoretical contribution was to recognize the potential of the soviets on the eve of revolution when he rewrote Marx's study of the Paris Commune in *State and Revolution* at the moment when the horizontal power workers', peasants' and soldiers' soviets was rivaling that of Kerensky's vertical Provisional Government (dual power). Indeed, in my opinion the greatest deed in Lenin's life was to carry out the program of *State and Revolution* by placing ' All Power to the Soviets' on the banner of a reluctant Russian Social-Democratic Party *(Bolshevik)*.

Unfortunately the discovery of workers' councils was *not* the lesson that the historical Left – from Lenin on down through Stalin, Trotsky, and their present-day epigones – drew from the victory of the Soviets in 1917. Quite the contrary... For decades the Left has buried the importance of this precious example of worker self-organization: actual proof that socialism, defined as worker self-management, is possible; and that the socialist project flows from the *actual movement* of the developing working class and is not just a Utopia spun from the heads of idealistic intellectuals. Instead, what we have heard repeated a thousand times as the lesson of 1917 is 'The Party, The Party, The Party.' It is humbling to recall that as early as the 1920s there were lucid Marxists like the Dutch Communists Anton Pannekoek and Herman Gorter who clearly saw these contradictions, developed the concept of what they called ' Council Communism,' and predicted that Lenin's government could only lead to state-capitalism. I have never understood why later Marxists like Tony Cliff and Raya Dunayevskaya – once they had broken with the Trotskyist position of defending Russia as some form of ' workers' state' and analyzed the full-blown Stalinist system as ' state-capitalist' – did not return to or even pay much tribute to those veterans of the early Communist movement who saw state-capitalism coming and resisted it 20 years earlier. Or why they clung to the Leninist party in practice if not in theory.

The Twenty-first Century presents our generation of toilers and rebels with a situation of stark simplicity. As we have seen, the Twentieth Century witnessed many popular revolutions, and self-designated 'Marxist' parties and 'national liberation' movements came to power in a dozen countries. Yet not one such regime actually improved the material and moral condition of the workers. Now, practically all these 'revolutionary' regimes have converted to the capitalist free market.[117] But not necessarily to the 'free society' which according to liberal ideology supposedly flows from it. Indeed, the post-Communist elites have for the most part clung to power and retained their privileges. In the ex-Soviet lands, Commissars of state industries have morphed into CEOs, siphoning the wealth accumulated by years of workers' sacrifice into private, offshore bank accounts. In the Peoples' Republics of China and Vietnam, the leaders of the Communist Party and the Army continue to use their monopoly of power and police-state apparatus to discipline an increasingly rebellious working class. Yet these were the very regimes that were held up as 'revolutionary' examples during the rebellious 60's and 70's when my generation of activists was struggling to change the world.[118] Similarly, the inspiring mass-based anti-colonial

---

[117] With the exception of North Korea. Alas, Castro's Cuba, abandoned by Russia and desperate for hard currency, has permitted a limited revival of Batista-era gambling and sex tourism – this time Euro- rather than Dollar-denominated – a tragic expedient for a once-promising revolution.

[118] Yet the evidence was plain that the Russian, Chinese and the North Vietnamese leaderships were playing global power politics and using the lives of the Vietnamese

revolutions that erupted in Africa since the 'Fifties degenerated into corrupt bureaucratic or military dictatorships.

As a result of this tragic paradox, 'communism,' 'socialism' and 'revolution' became dirty words to many embittered working people and disillusioned intellectuals, especially in countries that have actually experienced such regimes. After so much idealism and tragic self-sacrifice, who can blame them? Meanwhile, since the 1980s, neo-liberal politicians and pundits have endlessly repeated as a self-evident 'lesson of history' that *any* form of organized resistance leads inevitably to a new *gulag*. Yet despite the Thatcherite dogma that 'There Is No Alternative' to capitalism, since the '90s, new resistance movements have arisen around the planet proclaiming 'another world is possible.'

Paradoxical as it may seem, I believe that the collapse of Stalinist 'Communism' in 1989 and its subsequent transformation into *nomenklatura* capitalism, have simplified many questions that have divided the Left for years. Although it *appears* that the fall of ' Communism' has discredited both Marxism and the very idea of revolution – the media take this as dogma – it is only the *appearance* of fact. As I argued above in 'Communism's Collapse,' the Stalinist model was the very opposite of Marxism – an exploitative, oppressive, anti-worker bureaucratic tyranny. Indeed, the collapse of this totalitarian system actually *vindicates* the ideas of critical Marxists like Victor Serge (as well as the anarchists and other revolutionaries) who resisted the Stalinist 'alternative' from the beginning. The fact that the Stalinist systems in Russia, China and elsewhere were able to make smooth transitions to market capitalism *without* a bloody, restorationist counter-revolution is proof that these systems were already based on the exploitation of labor by a privileged minority.

In any case, the necessary pre-condition for the emergence of a genuine socialist alternative is openly to reject Communism's state-capitalist model euphemistically called 'actually existing socialism' by its Left apologists. Socialists and revolutionaries must also rethink our organizational models, in particular the role of the vanguard party. The discrediting of Stalinism opens a space for revolutionaries to revisit the dissident revolutionary tendencies which opposed vanguardism in the past, beginning with the anarchists, the council communists, the Dutch Left, and the Luxemburgists who were already critical in Lenin's time. It also invites us to study contemporary alternative models like the mass movements developing in Latin America today. Examples range from

---

resistance as pawns – plain to those of us whose horizons went beyond Mao's *Little Red Book.* Indeed, much of the U.S. anti-war movement considered itself 'Maoist' even after Mao allied himself with Nixon and Kissinger against the Russians and to undermine the anti-U.S. resistance in Vietnam, Russia's ally (the result of the famous 'ping pong diplomacy' of 1971).

the *Zapatista* communities in Chiapas, Mexico to Brazilian peasants invading private lands, to Bolivian indigenous movements to the Argentine *piqueteros,* the neighborhood assemblies presented in the collection *Horizontalism: Voices of Popular Power in Latin America*[119] not to mention workers occupying and running abandoned factories as shown in Naomi Klein's film *The Taking.* These movements inspired John Holloway's 2002 book, *Change the World Without Taking Power* – a brief for the horizontal cause I agree that we must get rid of oppression ('power over') both now and in any future society. Unfortunately, the Billionaires who have that power now will not give it up voluntarily – even as their system collapses –and they have the monopoly of legalized violence through the governments, the laws, the police and the military. In other words, as Marx observed writing about the Paris Commune, the people must first 'smash the state' before they can build their new society, their democratic, expansive, self-organized and self-limiting 'non-state.' Holloway fails to explain how the Billions' power *against* might succeed in taking the war toys away from these dangerous children so that peoples' power can at last emerge.

There is no consensus yet on how to create a genuine socialist alternative, although there certainly is a consensus among reasonable people about what paths to *avoid.* Every Twenty-first century worker knows what genuine socialism *isn't.* None desire to live under a top-down military-bureaucratic dictatorship with no right to speak out, organize and strike. So if another world really is possible and if that much-abused word 'socialism' still has any positive meaning, it would refer to some kind of cooperative commonwealth, a federation of democratic, open societies where people are economically as well as politically self-governing. Moreover, in today's globalized economy such a commonwealth must be planetary – and ecologically sustainable.

Sound good? The problem is 'how to get *there* from *here*? We can start by asking: 'What form(s) of organization(s) will best enable the working people of the planet to unite, overthrow the existing order, take charge of the economy, reclaim the political sphere and create such a world?' Note that we are not asking the question ' what form of organization is likely to be most effective in enabling a revolutionary group to seize and hold power?' That is another question, which Robespierre, Lenin and Mao (as well as Mussolini, Hitler and the Ayatollah) answered concretely at different times and places. Our question includes the problematic of what happens *after* the revolution: ' How to change the world without ending up under yet another new form of exploitative tyranny?' The issue is one of ends and means, but not in the moralistic sense of whether not positive ends 'justify' the use of negative

---

[119] Edited by Marina Sitrin, AKPress, 2006.

229

means, but practical consequences of certain means as observed in history.[120] In politics means and ends are inseparable because the ends you get have inevitably been shaped and affected if not determined by the means employed to get there. With this relationship in mind, let us proceed with the unraveling of what Marxists used to call ' the organizational question.'

Spontaneity *vs.* Organization: a False Opposition

The debate is usually framed in terms of 'spontaneity *versus* organization' which actually confuses the question, since no socialist ever suggested that we can unite to change society without getting organized! Without organization of some kind you end up with localized riots, such as those that took place in many US cities during the 1960's (and more recently in France) where people destroy their own neighborhoods (instead of at least wreaking so havoc on the banks downtown). Anarchists, syndicalists and socialists all agree on that point: Organization is our strongest weapon. 'Don't mourn for me, organize!' famously said Wobbly organizer and song-writer Joe Hill the day the copper bosses had him shot on a frame-up charge in Utah. And today, the name of the game is 'billions *versus* billionaires,' and the only way for us to win is to organize *globally*.

Once past the false dichotomy 'spontaneity/organization' we are free to compare and contrast different *forms* of organization as they have appeared in history. On the one hand we find the traditional vertical political party with a permanent apparatus and a definite program. On the other, we have the ephemeral *self*-organization of the masses into horizontal workers' councils, soviets, mass assemblies, federated strike-committees and the like. These two *forms* have very different characteristics as they develop historically.

Let's begin with political parties. Parties – whether parliamentary or revolutionary – tend to be organized vertically, like pyramids, with information and power flowing downward from leaders. Thus even revolutionary parties tend to reproduce the *bourgeois* division of labor, exalting the intelligence and will of the leaders (CEOs or Commissars) and encouraging passivity and unthinking acceptance ('company loyalty' or 'party discipline') among the members. Party leaders may be more or less democratically selected, but they tend to perpetuate themselves in office, where they are apt to accumulate privileges and special interests. Furthermore, all parties develop through their relation to the *state*, which Marx and Engels defined as the government's repressive apparatus ('special bodies of armed men, police, prisons etc.') whose essential purpose is to defend the power of the few over the many.

---

[120] For example, If your end is building a democratic society in a country like Iraq, bombing, invading and occupying the place is not an appropriate means. On the other hand, if you want the oil . . . "We had to destroy the place in order to save it," famously said an American officer whose men had just napalmed a village in Vietnam.

Parties generally either aim at sharing state power through their influence in parliamentary and governmental institutions (electoralism, reformism, social-democracy) or at taking over state power through insurrection (as practiced by Blanquists, Bakuniinists, Maoists, Castro/Guevarists on the Left, and nationalists, fascists, and religious fundamentalists on the Right). The ever-flexible Lenin used both tactics successfully, with Bolshevik representatives in the *Duma*[121] and an underground cadre of professional revolutionaries.

In any case, all political parties aim at mobilizing the masses to put their leaders in power – whether by means of 'the bullet or the ballot' as Malcolm X succinctly put it. Theoretically, the benefits of power should flow back or trickle down to the masses as reforms or as revolutionary decrees overthrowing capitalism and instituting socialism. To be sure, reformist or revolutionary governments can and do accomplish many positive social objectives – depending of course on the degree of internal democracy, the honesty of the leadership and its commitment to principle as well as on the level of pressure from below, as is being demonstrated today in Bolivia and Venezuela. But over the long haul, the general tendency when leaders of pyramidal parties have taken power is that they perpetuate themselves in office, develop interests other than the general interest they officially 'represent,' evolve into bureaucratic castes, accumulate privileges, and eventually become corrupt – unless they are under constant pressure from organized mass movements. And when a radical, reformist or revolutionary party is in power, its rank and file militants are caught in a double-bind where out of party loyalty they hesitate to support, much less organize, oppositional movements considered disruptive.[122]

Horizontal Structures

Now let us look at the organizational pyramid from the base up. Here we find various horizontal forms of self-organization like strike committees, councils, networks, committees of correspondence and mass assemblies. Their basic mode of operation is that information and power flow upward from the base and information circulates both horizontally and vertically. Such assemblies, for example the revolutionary Paris *sections* in the French Revolution in 1791-93, the Paris Commune of 1871, the self-organized Russian *Soviets* of 1905 and 1917, the sit-in strikers of 1936 and 1968, and most recently the Argentine *piqueteros* and assemblies – often remain in permanent session. Their participants are able to pool their information, analyze it, come to decisions and respond to changing circumstances rapidly and flexibly. They unite thinking and doing, combining ' legislative' and ' executive' functions (as

---

[121] Russia's first parliament, granted by the Tsar in response to the revolution of 1905. It was as powerless as is today's *Duma* under Putin.
[122] For example in Brazil, after President Lula's *Workers' Party* compromised with neo-liberalism and turned its back on the landless peasants' and workers' movements, the left wing reluctantly had to break away and form a new party.

Marx said of the Paris Commune). They are in direct connection with the mass movement. They sense its moods and can respond rapidly to changes, take advantage of favorable moods, or fall back when militancy declines.

Such forms of self-organization encourage, develop and depend on the initiative and clear thinking of their participants; they thus overcome the 'let-George-do-it' passivity of many union and party members who are tempted to look to the leadership for direction instead of thinking for themselves. During the great strike waves of 1905-06 in the Russian Empire, Rosa Luxembourg observed the apparent paradox that ' spontaneous' strikes were more likely to succeed than those planned by the Bolsheviks, Mensheviks and trade-unionists. Today, we are able to recognize in the social phenomenon which Luxemburg analyzed a century ago in her *Mass Strike* pamphlet is a form of what scientists call 'emergent' behavior: self-organization from below. Over the past half-century the Newtonian/Cartesian Positivist model of cause/effect, conductor/orchestra has been superceded in fields as far-ranging as subatomic physics, cosmology, biochemistry, brain physiology and cybernetics, and replaced by the more dialectical paradigm of order emerging – under certain conditions – out of the chaos of myriad interactions. Like the Internet, for which today's global movements have an affinity, bottom-up forms of social self-organization are expansive.

On this historical model, when social movements grow beyond the factory or local level, they learn to network and federate on the industry, regional, national and now (with Internet and airplanes) global levels – without any need for a pre-existing bureaucratic structure likely to become a locus of power. To be sure, in order to federate, councils and assemblies must delegate authority. But delegation does not necessarily mean creating a new ruling elite; not when delegates are chosen from the ranks for specific purposes with limited mandates to express their comrades' views at regional assemblies and to bring back reports of what is happening elsewhere. In principle, delegates are paid at normal workers' wages, and their mission accomplished, they rejoin the mass, while others replace them, thus developing leadership skills of confidence, communication, and strategizing. Such responsible activities are truly 'schools of communism' – not for an elite leadership but for the participants as individuals and as a group, be they workers, farmers, neighbors, student activists, etc. These practical 'schools' develop the confidence and self-reliance which alone can turn multitudinous individuals into a revolutionary force. Today, scientists study such 'feedback-loops' by means of which amalgamations of individual cells 'learn to learn.' They are observed for example in development of the human brain, the growth of cities in history, and the algorithms of 'smart' computer programs designed to model such emergent behavior.

Organizations, we have seen, are not only means to an end, they shape ends. Which of these two organizational forms, the vertical or the horizontal, the

232

party or the workers' councils, is most likely to lead to the goals of liberty, equality, and economic democracy? Which is most congenial to socialism defined as the self-management of society by the producers brought about by the efforts of the producers themselves? Given this definition, shared by Marxists and Anarchists alike, it is clear that true socialism can only come from below. It can occur only when hundreds of millions of working people have developed the consciousness to unite *en masse*, the initiative to defeat the forces of capitalism and the state, and the confidence to undertake the reconstruction of society *on their own*. In my opinion, the only way billions of humans can develop these capacities is through the *experience* of making their own decisions through their own organizations and suffering the consequences. Obviously, this historical process of self-empowerment is bound to be lengthy and difficult, and certainly working people will build many organizations, including parties, along the road, but only through such a process can socialism so defined emerge.

Weaknesses of the Horizontal Model

The history of Lenin and Leninist-type parties shows, in the starkest terms, the fatal flaws in the vertical model of organization. But we must also look at look at the weaknesses of the horizontal workers' council and mass assembly models. The most obvious weakness is that such phenomena tend to be ephemeral. They mainly spring up in periods of intense militancy, in pre-revolutionary and revolutionary situations, and they tend to dissolve when this militancy declines or is defeated. They may remain as informal networks of workers and in the memory of the participants, as they did in Russia between 1906 and 1917 somewhat to the surprise of both the Mensheviks and the Bolsheviks. But otherwise, they leave no trace, except in the theories of the 'Council Communists'. Workers' councils, mass assemblies and strike committees are creatures of revolution, like the legendary salamander that lives only in fire. They must either triumph as they did in 1917 – in which case they become the nerves and lineaments of the new society to which they have given birth – or disappear into history, perhaps to rise again from their ashes like that other creature of fire, the phoenix. They are the incandescent incarnation of the socialist project, illuminating future possibilities; but short of a victorious revolution (which in a globalized economy must be planetary), they remain ephemeral.

The obvious great advantage of the party-form of organization is its enduring existence through time, its ability to absorb the lessons of past defeats and prepare itself for future struggles during periods when the mass movement has subsided. This advantage is particularly important in countries where dictatorship and repression make it necessary to maintain an underground network. Thus it is not surprising that over history, revolutionary workers have attempted to incarnate their will and intelligence in the more permanent and structured parties, associations and organizations that have sprung up to represent them in various countries at various times, with greater and lesser success. The problem is that often the masses have not been able to control these organizations, which become alienated as bureaucracies and turn against them. The classic historic example dates back to 1914, when the leaders of the Socialist parties in France and Germany each voted to support their imperialist government and led the French and German workers into a fratricidal slaughter. In 1918 the German Socialists crushed the revolution that had put them in power. In France in 1936 the Socialist and Communist Parties and trade unions acted to contain the spontaneous general strike,. Likewise in 1945 they channeled the revolutionary energies of the Resistance into rebuilding bourgeois France and in 1968 they sold out the worker-student rebellion. In 1995 and again in 2002 the unions and Left parties diverted a nationwide mass revolt against pension 'reform' and allowed a right-wing boss' victory. The problem is not that such bureaucratic organizations 'fail.' It is that they succeed far too well – as agents of the class enemy among the workers.

Of course the word 'party' didn't always mean a bureaucratic organization like the French Socialists and Communists or the U.S. Democrats and the Republicans. In the 19th Century, people often spoke of the 'party' of labor, the anti-slavery 'party, the 'party' of capital, even the 'party' of caution using a small 'p' to indicate general opposing forces in society. This is how Marx and Engels used the word in their correspondence. For us moderns, the word refers exclusively to the specific, local, ephemeral political Parties (large 'P') whether 'revolutionary' or merely electoral. This difference in usage has led to ideological distortions. Thus the Stalinist Communists read Marx retrospectively through the lens of their vertical vanguard party fetish, when the context makes it clear that he was talking about the general movement of the workers' self-organized struggle. In this sense, the 'actual movement,' the historical 'party' (small 'p') of worker socialism persists through time. It throws up its own thinkers (or co-opts professional intellectuals from other classes), develops its own world-view, theorizes its own struggles, and learns from its defeats and partial victories while attempting to unite to struggle for immediate objectives. Such critical thinkers are the 'organic' intellectuals of the oppressed class, their writings the record of its experience. They are, collectively, 'of the party' – the party of revolution – whatever their historical relation to the existing political parties of their place and time. Is it possible to imagine the emergence of such an international party of the world's working classes in the Twenty-First Century? That is the challenge we attempt to take up in Part I (Is Another World *Really* Possible?)

---

[126] Jim Hoberman, 'Who was Victor Serge and Why Do We have to Ask?' *Village Voice* Nov. 30, 1984.

Who was Victor Serge and Why Do We Have to Ask?

James Hoberman first asked this ironic question twenty-four years ago in the *Village Voice,* and alas it is still, alas, relevant today.[126] Jim was just launching the *Village Voice Literary Supplement* and he chose to kick off the first issue with round-up review of a number of Serge's books (mostly translated by me) on the cover . He even took me to lunch. Serge has always had secret admirers like that. Unfortunately, he always had all the right enemies, too. On the one hand, Serge has been revered for generations by 'a kind of secret international of admirers who read, reread and recognize themselves in his books' reports the French writer and former Serge publisher François Maspero. This international includes writers and intellectuals as diverse as I.F. Stone, Irving Howe, Dwight Macdonald, Eric Fromm, Octavio Paz, John Berger, Yevgeni Yevtushenko, Edgar Morin, Régis Debray, Adam Hoschild, Christopher Hitchens and Susan Sontag. The reader will find, at the end of this essay, quotations from their letters praising Serge and encouraging me as Serge's biographer-translator.

On the other hand Serge still remains outside the canon of Western literature and political thought. Indeed, how to fit him in? A quintessential internationalist in an era of exacerbated nationalism, Serge spent his 57 years wandering this planet as a stateless exile. His novels, written in French by a Russian, fell between the cracks of two national literatures. Serge remains a stranger not only in world of letters but also on the political Left. Indeed, the very richness of his complex identity as literary artist and revolutionary militant has apparently worked against him in both camps: Trotsky, in the throes of political polemic, dismissed him as a mere 'poet.' As for academic literary criticism, who ever heard of a Marxist militant writing serious literature? On the political front, Serge was derided by orthodox Marxists as an 'anarchist,' scorned by anarchists as a 'Leninist' and by Communists as a 'Trotskyist.' However, although Serge's successive political affiliations - libertarian anarchist, Bolshevik Communist, Trotskyist, socialist humanist - may appear eclectic, if not contradictory - his political evolution was in fact consistent. The central concept which guided Serge's conduct throughout his revolutionary career was what he conceived as the militant's 'double duty' to defend the revolutionary movement from *both* its external enemies (right-wing counter-revolutionaries) and its inner enemies (left authoritarianism, intolerance and bureaucracy). Serge first discussed 'double duty' in print in *Literature and Revolution* (1932), and it may be his most original contribution

235

to revolutionary morality. The problem, of course, was how to balance these two duties of criticism and support from inside a movement? Although one could argue with the politics of any one of Serge's judgements (discussed below), I find his attitude of double duty as a whole exemplary – in the sense of setting an example to be followed.

Moreover, as distinct from many Western writers and intellectuals who flirted at one time or another with Communism – names like Hemmingway, Dos Passos, Howard Fast, Malraux, Koestler, and Silone come to mind – Serge was a revolutionary and an internationalist more or less from birth, and he remained such to his death. Thus in the 1930s and '40s Serge's books were attacked or ignored by the Communist Party and its liberal anti-fascist sympathisers (for whom criticising Stalinism was considered treasonable in face of the threat of Hitler). Yet, during the 50s, Serge the die-hard socialist was of little interest to Cold War institutions like the (CIA-sponsored) Congress for Cultural Freedom which did so much to establish the reputation of other anti-Communist intellectuals. Marginalized during his life, Serge was nonetheless a mainstream figure whose uniquely intense involvement recapitulated the experience of millions of Europeans whose social struggles energized the first half of the Twentieth Century. Participant-witness to revolutionary events in several countries, survivor of ten years in various prisons, author of some twenty books, Serge's life history reads like a novel. Indeed, he himself retraced his radical's trajectory from Brussels to Paris to Barcelona to Saint Petersburg to Berlin to final exile in Mexico City in his *Memoirs of a Revolutionary* and a series of what he called 'witness-novels'. His itinerary may be briefly summarized as follows:

Victor Serge (1890-1947)

Stateless son of exiled anti-Czarist Russian parents wandering Europe 'in search of good libraries and cheap lodgings' Victor is born 'by chance' in Brussels, Belgium 'along the roads of the world.' On the walls of his parents' humble lodgings, he later recalled, 'were the portraits of the hanged': 19th Century Russian revolutionary martyrs for freedom. (See illustration.) These included the legendary N.I. Kibalchich, a distant relative who helped carry out the *Peoples' Will* death sentence on Czar Alexander II in 1881. Home-schooled by these penniless exiled intellectuals, Victor grows up reading Shakespeare and Chekov in cheap editions with his mother and learning science from his father, a passionate, impecunious positivist who scorned public schooling as 'stupid bourgeois education for the poor.' The young Kibalchich thus imbibes the heady traditions of the Russian revolutionary *intelligentsia* while growing up desperately poor on the streets of Brussels. So poor that at age eleven he watches horrified as his younger brother dies of malnutrition, while he himself survived on pilfered sugar soaked in coffee that little Raoul refused to eat. 'Throughout the rest of my life,' he recalled, 'it has been my fate always to find, in the undernourished urchins of the squares of Paris, Berlin and Moscow, the same condemned faces of my tribe.'

At age fourteen Victor is living alone, his mother having returned to Russia ill with tuberculosis and his father struggling to support a second family. He is active in the Young Socialist Guard and falls in with a group of young rebels who are far too militant for the staid Belgian social-democracy. Soon they turn to anarchism, which 'demanded everything of us and offered everything to us.' By 1906, fifteen-year-old Victor and his gang of Brussels apprentices are writing, typesetting, printing and distributing their own radical anarchist sheet, *The Rebel*. Victor writes under the pseudonym *Le Rétif* and shows a precocious maturity of style. The comradeship of other teenage rebels replaces Victor's disintegrated nuclear family, even as the French individualist doctrine of ego-anarchism eclipses the broader social revolutionary tradition of his Russian forebears.

Police photos of Victor (in Russian blouse) and the Tragic Bandits of Anaarchy:' Raymond 'la Science' Callemin (guillotined), Edouard Carouy (suicide in prison), Jean de Boë, survived Devil's Island and returned to the Brussels labor movement.

At eighteen Kibalchich-*Le Rétif* heeds the call of Paris, where he barely survives tutoring Russians in French and translating Russian novels while devouring the contents of the Sainte-Geneviève library, lecturing on anarchist individualism, editing the individualist journal *l'anarchie,* debating (and occasionally brawling) with right-wing French nationalists.

Meanwhile, his working-class Brussels buddies, angry, desperate, impatient of waiting for Utopia, unwilling to become 'masters' or 'slaves,' have turned to 'illegalism' - the anarchist practice of 'individual repossession' of property 'legally stolen' by the bourgeois exploiters. In 1911 they join up with a desperado named Bonnot and begin terrorizing Paris as the 'tragic gang' of anarchist bank-robbers - the first to use automobiles for the fast getaway (the police had bicycles). The bandits' fate is indeed tragic: death in gun battles, Devil's Island, the guillontine. Victor is appalled at the bloodshed, but out of solidarity he defends the comrades with his pen: 'I am with the Wolves.' Victor and his lover, Rirette Maitrejean, are arrested at the office of *l'anarchie* where they also live. Victor is sentenced to five years as an 'accomplice' - essentially for refusing to rat on his comrades. Conditions in the French penitentiary at Melun are harsh. The inmates are forbidden any news from the outside, even as WWI grinds on with German shells exploding nearby. Serge's first novel, *Men in Prison* (1930) is an effort to 'liberate himself from the experience' of those 1,820 days of silence, solitude, starvation, filth, brutality and mindless discipline.

Released from prison in 1917, Victor is expelled from France and comes back to life in Barcelona, where he works as a printer, participates in a revolutionary uprising and publishes his first article signed 'Victor Serge.' The title: 'The Fall of a Czar.' Soon Serge is attempting to reach revolutionary Russia via wartime Paris, where he is arrested a 'Bolshevik suspect' and held for over a year as in typhus-infested camps where – ironically – he meets his first actual Bolshevik. Exchanged for a French officer held by the Soviets, he arrives in January 1919 in Civil War Petrograd (later Leningrad, now St. Petersburg). On the ship to Russia he falls in love with Liuba, the daughter of another  repatriated revolutionary, the Jewish anarchist Alexander Russakov, who shares Victor's Utopian dreams and hopes for the fledgling Soviet Republic. They are shocked to discover the besieged revolutionary capital, no longer the scene of the lively debates and mass assemblies of 1917, lying silent, frozen, grim, surrounded by White armies armed by the victorious Allies. Serge's second novel, *Birth of our Power* (1931), chronicles his transition from Barcelona ('this city we could not take') to Petrograd the city the revolutionaries had taken. The ironic title of Serge's third novel, *Conquered City* (1932) [127] plays on the ambiguities of political power exercised by revolutionaries under civil war conditions.

After taking his bearings in Russia among the anarchists, moderate socialists and more or less disenchanted intellectuals, Serge decides to commit himself to the revolution and eventually joins the Communists, whom he sees – despite his anarchist's misgivings – as its essential backbone. The Party immediately puts Serge's talents to work on the staff of the new Third (Communist) International, writing, translating, and organizing the Latin Languages publications section. He lives and works at the Hotel Astoria, commandeered by the Soviets, and eats at the table of the Executive with Zinoviev and other top Soviet leaders. He helps organize the first Comintern conferences in

---

[127] Both translated by Richard Greeman, Doubleday, Garden City, 1967 and subsequent editions. New York Review Books Classics will republish *Conquered City* in 2010.

Moscow, where he acts as an unofficial guide to the anarcho-syndicalist delegates from France, Spain and Italy – among them, old comrades. To them, he confesses his fears about the increasing lack of freedom in Russia and his efforts – sometimes successful – to use his influence to save or succor Russian dissident anarchists fallen into the hands of the *Cheka* political police. His published pamphlets like *The Revolution in Danger,*[128] aimed at winning the sympathies of French anarchists to the Soviets, are much less critical of the revolution.

In 1921 Serge's loyalties are severely torn by the revolt of the Cronstadt sailors' Soviet (composed of anarchists and dissident Communists) and its subsequent repression by the Communists. The sailors had seized the strategic island fortress to press their demands for more freedom, and the government was refusing to negotiate. Serge participates in the unsuccessful attempt to mediate the conflict by the U.S. anarchists Emma Goldman, Alexander Berkman and Serge's anarchist father-in-law, Russakov. He looks on in anguish as volunteer Communists and rebellious Soviet sailors battle on the ice

Vienna, 1924: left to right Serge, with moustache, Gramsci, and Vlady held by Lucien Laurat

floes, locked in deadly fratricidal combat. After withdrawing briefly from politics to an unsuccessful French anarchist agricultural commune on Lake Ladoga, Serge accepts a Comintern assignment in Germany. There, the prospect of renewed revolution poses a last hope for saving the isolated Soviets from smothering under a bureaucratic dictatorship in Russia. In Berlin, where Victor, Liuba and their from smothering under a bureaucratic dictatorship in Russia. In Berlin, where Victor, Liuba and their young son Vlady live under an *alias*, Serge serves the Comintern as a publicist and journalist. Serge's articles on Germany reporting on galloping inflation, mass unemployment, mutilated

---

[128] Translated by Ian Birchall (London, Redwords, 1997)

veterans begging, strikes and abortive *putsches* were written under the pseudonym 'R. Albert' which I recognized in 1964. They are now available as *Witness to the German Revolution.*[129] He also doubles under various identities as a militant or 'agent' (in those days there was little distinction). When the German Communists are outlawed after the *fiasco* of the March 1923 Hamburg uprising, Serge flees with his family to Vienna, where he works for the Comintern press service and associates with Georg Lukacs and Antonio Gramsci.

In 1925, despairing of renewed revolution in the West, Serge makes the suicidally idealistic decision to return to Russia and join the last-ditch anti-bureaucratic fight against Stalin and his allies as a member of the Left Opposition led by Trotsky. Expelled from the Party in 1928, arrested, interrogated for weeks in the notorious Lubyanka prison, search is released after his arrest provoked a scandal in Paris. Soon after his release, Serge suffers a near fatal intestinal occlusion and vows that if he recovers, he will devote the time left at liberty to preserving the truth about the revolutionary upheavals he had experienced in the form of an epic series of 'witness-novels' – more lasting and superior, he thought, for the 'formation of consciousness' of new revolutionary generations than formal history. Given the political impasse of Stalinism usurping the banner of socialism and his own precarious situation as a semi-prisoner in a police state, it was a reasonable political choice to devote his energy to the long-term hope for socialism.[130] Between 1928 and 1933, Serge is able to complete and publish in Paris three novels – *Men in Prison, Birth of Our Power* and *Conquered City* (about the siege of Petrograd). He also publishes two books of non-fiction: *Year One of the Russian Revolution,* the first comprehensive, documented history of the great events of 1917-1918 to appear in the West (preceding Trotsky's *History* by two years) and *Literature and Revolution,* a critique of both 'socialist realism' and vapid bourgeois literature. Meanwhile, in Leningrad Serge is living in 'semi-captivity,' under constant surveillance, scrambling to make a living in a society where every door is closed to him, watching his beloved wife Liuba being driven insane by the persecution and his colleagues of the Soviet Writers' Union being driven to suicide or silence. Serge ekes out a precarious living for his family translating into French novels by Gladkov, Chaguinian and Sholokov as well as (anonymously) volumes of Lenin's *Works.*

---

[129] Translated by Ian Birchall, (London 2000).
[130] Cf. Serge's letter to Marcel Martinet Dec. 25, 1936 which dispels the Philistine myth that Serge, the consummate literary artist, became a writer as it were accidentally as a 'substitute political action.'

**Victor, Vlady and Liuba in 1928, one day after
Serge's release from prison.**

In 1933 Serge is again arrested and interrogated for three months in Moscow. In a letter prepared for publication in case of his arrest and smuggled out of Russia at the last minute, Serge defends individual freedom as essential to socialism and describes Stalinist Communism as 'totalitarian.' Refusing to confess to anything other than his personal opposition to Stalin's 'general line,' Serge is administratively exiled to Orenburg on the Ural, where he is joined by Liuba and teenage Vlady, already a budding artist.

Soon Liuba, now incurably insane and secretly pregnant, returns to Leningrad for psychiatric treatment. Deprived of work, Serge continues to write and survives in part on the postal insurance when his manuscripts sent abroad are mysteriously 'lost' by the Russian mail. Despite the cold, constant hunger and periodic harassment by the GPU political police, these years of deportation are – ironically – luminous years thanks to the solidarity and intellectual stimulation within the group of exiled Communist Oppositionists. Like Serge,

Liuba by Vlady 1935 these seasoned fighters have refused to capitulate to Stalin's betrayal of the revolution's original principles. Condemned and deported, they are paradoxically free to think and speak their minds. Serge depicts the hardships but also the beauty of these exile years in his 1939 novel *Midnight in the Century.*[131]

---

[131] Translated with a Preface by Richard Greeman, Writers & Readers, London, 1982. *Verso* is planning to re-issue in 2010.

241

Meanwhile in France, the 'Victor Serge Affair' has become a *cause célèbre* – embarrassing to the USSR at a moment when Stalin is desperately seeking an alliance with France against Hitler. After protests by intellectuals, militants and trade-unionists – along with the personal intervention of (then) pro-Soviet writers André Gide and Romain Rolland - Stalin eventually agrees to allow Serge and his family to leave Russia. But Serge remains in deportation since no Western democracy is willing to grant a visa to this dangerous anarchist (the French still have the 1917 expulsion order against him). Finally, Belgium agrees to open its doors. In April 1936, Serge and Vlady are reunited in Moscow with Liuba and baby Jeannine and board the train for Warsaw, but at the Polish border the GPU seizes Serge's manuscripts completed in captivity: among them a poetry collection and two novels ('the only ones I had time to polish'). Although Serge was able to reconstruct his poems from memory (published as *Resistance*[132]), the novels remain lost, despite persistent searches in the Moscow archives. [133] We only know their titles and subjects: *Lost Men* (about the 'tragic bandits' of French anarchism) and *Men in the Blizzard* (about the Russian Civil War).

Serge's arrival in the West, unlike Solzhintisin's a generation later, is greeted by silence – except for the Communist press, which slanders him as an 'anarchist bandit,' and the Soviet Embassy, which strips him of his Soviet nationality (the only one he ever had). From precarious exile in Brussels and, later, Paris), Serge struggles to support his insane wife and their two children – mostly by working in print shops – meanwhile writing furiously to unmask the 'big lie' of the Moscow show trials and Stalin's murderous intrigues in Republican Spain. Although he continues to support Trotsky and translate his books into French, Serge's support of the POUM (an independent Marxist party in Spain) [134] earns him the sectarian scorn of the orthodox French Trotskyists, further isolating him. Serge watches helpless when Andreu Nin, the POUM's leader in Barcelona is kidnapped and tortured to death by Stalinist agents, but by organizing and international campaign from Paris and thanks to the intervention of British Independent Socialists, he is able to save Nin's colleagues from death at the hands of a Communist kangaroo court set up in Republican Spain. In France, Serge's scrupulously documented, eyewitness books and articles exploding the myth of Russian Communism are greeted with silence by complacent intellectuals hypnotized by the 'anti-fascism' of Communist-manipulated popular fronts. His *From Lenin to Stalin* and *Russia*

---

[132] Translated by James Brook with an Introduction by Richard Greeman, City Lights 1972.
[133] For details, please see my 'Victor Serge Affair and the French Literary Left', *Revolutionary History* Vol. 5, No. 3.
[134] The anti-Stalinist Unified Marxist Workers' Party, often and erroneously described as 'Trotskyist.' George Orwell fought in its militia (*Hommage to Catalonia*).

Twenty Years After[135] remain classic accounts of Stalinist Russia. Meanwhile, Serge and his comrades are living in a 'labyrinth of pure madness' as Stalin's agents kidnap and murder Trotsky's supporters in the middle of opulent, indifferent Paris. The French capital paralyzed before the looming war is the background of two Serge novels, *The Long Dusk* (1946) and *Years Without Forgiveness* (unpublished until 1972).[136]

When Paris falls to the Nazis, Serge – accompanied by his companion Laurette Séjourné and his son Vlady – joins the exodus on foot and survives a Luftwaffe attack on the Loire. By now Liuba has moved to an asylum near Aix-en-Provence where she is well cared-for (she lived into the 1980s) while Jeanine is being looked after in by peasants the country.

Villa Air Bel; Foreground, Varian Fry. Background standing: Jacqueline and Aube Breton and Victor Serge

The three refugees eventually find sanctuary in a Marseille villa rented by American heiress Maryjane Gold and Varian Fry of the American Refugee Committee and shared with André Breton and his family. Marseille is the last possible exit-point for refugees trapped in Vichy France, and Serge immediately re-baptizes the villa *Air-Bel, 'Espère-Visa'* (Hope-for-Visa). During anxious months of waiting, Serge works daily on the manuscript of his masterpiece *The Case of Comrade Tulayev*[137] and participates in the now-legendary Surrealist games and the Sunday gatherings with artists like Max

---

[135] Translated by Max Schactman. See new edition edited by Susan Weissman, which also includes '30 Years After the Russian Revolution' (1947) considered Serge's political testament, Humanities Press, New Jersey, 1996.
[136] Serge, *The Long Dusk* (French title *Les derniers temps* or *'End Times'*) translated by Ralph Mannheim, The Dial, N.Y. *.Unforgiving Years,* translated with an Introduction by Richard Greeman, New York Review Books, N.Y. 2008.

Ernst, Victor Branner, Alfredo Lam organized by Breton. Underneath the gaity Serge and his fellow refugees aware they are caught in a deadly trap. Vichy France has closed its borders and agreed to 'surrender on demand' to the Gestapo all anti-fascists refugees in its territory. Serge is on the Gestapo's list and those of the GPU and the FBI as well. Despite persistent efforts by Dwight and Nancy MacDonald in New York, Serge is refused a U.S. visa. [138]

 Finally, Serge and his son are able to secure Mexican visas, thanks to the solidarity of comrades of the POUM (now settled in Mexico) whose lives he had earlier saved in Spain. They board one of the last refugee ships out of Vichy France only to be arrested in Martinique and held for four months in Ciudad Trujillo (where he writes *Hitler Contra Stalin* for a Mexican publisher). After being again detained in Cuba, Serge gains what will be his final exile in Mexico City in 1941. Here Serge finds himself isolated – unable to publish, boycotted, slandered and physically attacked by Stalinist agents, cut off from Europe by the war. Nonetheless, it is in Mexico that Serge completes his most enduring work – *Memoirs of a Revolutionary, The Case of Comrade Tulayev* and *Unforgiving Years* – all written 'for the desk drawer.' He investigates Trotsky's assassination and collaborates with his widow, Natalia Sedova, on a biography *The Life and Death of Leon Trotsky.* He also studies psychoanalysis, writes a short book on pre-Columbian archaeology and meditates on consciousness and death. He explores the meaning of the war not only in theoretical and political 'theses' but also in terms of dreams, earthquakes, volcanoes and luxuriant vegetation. All these elements come together in *Unforgiving Years,* which he finishes in 1946. In 1947 his heart gives out, stressed by the altitude and exhausted by years of prison and privation. Penniless and stateless as usual, Serge is buried in a pauper's grave registered as a 'Spanish Republican.' His posthumously published *Memoirs of a Revolutionary* conclude:

> . . . Of this hard childhood, this troubled adolescence, all those terrible years, I regret nothing as far as I am myself concerned [. . .] Any regret I have is for energies wasted in struggles which were bound to be fruitless. These struggles have taught me that in any man the best and the worst live side by side and sometimes mingle - and that what is worst comes through the corruption of what is best.

---

[137] Translated by Willard Trask. New York Review Books in 2005. Preface by Susan Sontag.
[138] For a wonderful read, see *Villa Air-Bel: World War II, Escape, and a House in Marseille* by Rosemary Sullivan, Harper-Collins, 2006.

Well, now that we have seen what a remarkable individual Serge was, now it is time to address Jim Hoberman's other question, 'Why do we have to ask?' Apparently, Serge's books have had almost as hard a life as their author. Politically, their author had made 'all the right enemies' on both the left and the right. 'Difficult to write for the desk drawer alone when you're past fifty,' wrote Serge isolated in Mexico at the end of WWII. 'Yet in every publishing house there are two conservatives and at least one Stalinist. I'm beginning to think my very name is an obstacle to publication.' Two of the manuscripts languishing in Serge's desk drawer were masterpieces: *Memoirs of a Revolutionary* and *The Case of Comrade Tulayev*. But there was little hope in post-war Paris, what with paper shortages and the influence of the Communists in publishing. No luck either in New York and London, even with the help of Dwight MacDonald and George Orwell. And although the posthumously published *Tulayev* and *Memoirs* eventually did achieve the status of 'classics' (albeit 'neglected classics') for a variety of reasons Serge has remained marginalized.

Even today, Serge's socialist politics continue to disturb the consensus. Unlike the conservative Alexander Solzhninitzyn, who in the 1970's and 80's became the poster-boy of a whole generation of right-wing Johnny-come-lately anti-Communist 'New' Philosophers, Serge criticised Communism *from the left* and remained unfashionable during the 'greed-is-good' era. Peter Sedgwick, the British translator of Serge's *Memoirs* and *Year One of the Russian Revolution,* showed in a truly seminal 1963 essay how Serge was a red *before* it became fashionable in the Thirties and remained one *after* they had abandoned a cause which 'they had only embraced in its addled flesh.' [139]

Meanwhile Serge's prestige as a revolutionary participant-witness, oft-quoted by historians and political scientists, has tended to obscure his status as a literary artist. For example, political scientist Susan Weissman's recent book on Serge takes the position that 'writing, for Serge, was something to do only when one was unable to fight.'[140] At the same time, the sorry example of the wooden, propagandistic literature produced by Communist under the ideological banner of 'Socialist Realism' (which Serge polemicized against) has given revolutionary writing a bad name. This prejudice tends to combine with the traditional prejudices of 'art for art's sake' to reinforce a false

---

[139] Peter Sedgwick, *Victor Serge and Socialism*, International Socialism (1st series), No.14, Autumn 1963, pp.17-23.
http://www.marxists.org/archive/sedgwick/1963/xx/serge.htm
[140] Susan Weissman, *The Course Is Set on Hope* (Verso 2002) p. 67. The book's main argument (previously advanced in Weissman's Glasgow PhD. and in several articles) is that 'Serge's critique of Stalinism was the core of his life and work' (p.6), and she gives short shift to his anarchist years, his poetry and fiction, and, curiously enough, to manuscript material in the Serge Archive at Yale (which her bibliography doesn't cite). Since Weissman doesn't speak French, perhaps she was unable to consult these untranslated documents.

dichotomy between art and politics in which Marxist-inspired literature is *ipso facto* dismissed as propaganda. Meanwhile, the very 'Marxist' literary critics that apparently used to avoid Serge because of his embarrassingly anti-Stalinist themes now agree with the postmodernists that 'authors' no longer exist

Serge with Laurette Séjourné and the painter Dr. Atl, in front of newly erupted volcano of Paracutin, Mexico 1944

(only '*textes*'), that 'authenticity' is an illusion, and that the idea of a 'message' in literature should be consigned to the dustbin of 'grand narratives.' However, what's wonderful about Serge is that his politics appear in his novels not as propaganda, but as organic ground and underlying vision, as intuition of the world's myriad inter-relations. His uniqueness and perhaps his greatness as a novelist was to have brought to bear his authentic insider's experience and Marxist consciousness on one of the central themes of modern literature: the tragedy of   revolutions gone awry. Yet despite the 'organic' nature of the politics in Serge's fiction, his reputation as a novelist may have suffered from an unthinking critical assumption that there is a necessary contradiction between a committed Marxist revolutionary *and* an imaginative creator − a contradiction about which Serge had this to say:

> Poets and novelists are not political beings because they are not essentially rational. Political intelligence, based though it is in the revolutionary's case upon a deep idealism, demands a scientific and pragmatic armor, and subordinates itself to the pursuit of strictly defined social ends. The artist, on the contrary, is always delving for his material in the subconscious, in the pre-conscious, in intuition, in a lyrical inner life which is rather hard to define; he does not know with any certainty either where he is going or what he is creating. If

the novelist's characters are truly alive, they function by themselves, to a point at which they eventually take their author by surprise; and sometimes he is quite perplexed if he is called upon to classify them in terms of morality or social utility. Doestoevsky, Gorky, and Balzac brought to life, all lovingly, criminals whom the Political Man would shoot most unlovingly.

As far as academia is concerned, Serge seems to have been abandoned to the 'no-man's-land between politics and literature departments, where he as yet remains an un-person. Another reason for academic neglect of Serge as a novelist may be his nationality – or rather his lack thereof. As a (stateless) Soviet Russian who wrote in French and died in Mexico, Serge also falls through the cracks between departments traditionally organized along the lines of 'national' literatures. As a result, there are as yet no PhDs on Serge in any French university,[141] nor will you find 'Serge, Victor' listed in French biographical dictionaries and literary manuals. Yet Serge is arguably as important a novelist in the political *genre* as Malraux, Orwell, Silone, and Koestler who have been largely studied to death. More bad luck for the writer whom Régis Debray sees as a 'magnificent loser.'[142]

Of course, to be properly understood, Serge is best situated in the Russian *intelligentsia* tradition of his expatriate parents. He inherited his father's scientific culture (physics, geology, sociology) while his literary culture (he was raised on Shakespeare, Hugo, Doestoyevsky, and Korolenko) came from his mother, whose family was apparently connected with Maxim Gorky.[143] By his concept of the writer's mission, Serge saw himself 'in the line of the Russian writers' [*dans la ligne des écrivains russes*]. And although he borrowed freely from cosmopolitan influences like Joyce, Dos Passos, and the French Unanimists, Serge developed as a writer within the Soviet literary 'renaissance' of the relatively liberal NEP (New Economy Policy) period. Indeed, during the 1920s, Serge was the principle transmission belt between the literary worlds of Soviet Russia and France. Via his translations and regular articles on Soviet culture in Henri Barbusse's *Clarté* he introduced French readers to the post-revolutionary poetry of Alexander Blok, Andrei Biely, Sergei Yesenin, Ossip Mandelstam, Boris Pasternak and Vladimir Mayakovsky as well as to fiction writers like Alexis Tolstoy, Babel, Zamiatine,

---

[141] Serge the novelist is better known in US and British French departments, with two PhD. theses: my own (Columbia 1968) and Bill Marshall's (Oxford) later published as *Victor Serge: The Uses of Dissent* (Berg, NY/Oxford, 1992)

[142] « L'échec, c'est ce qu'il y a de plus difficile à réussir. » *Préface* aux « *Carnets* » de Serge (Actes Sud, Arles, 1985).

[143] Serge went to see Gorky as soon as he arrived in Russia in 1919, but declined an offer to join the staff of Gorky's newspaper. During the Civil War, Serge depended on Gorky's relationship with Lenin to intercede to save anarchist comrades from being shot by the *Cheka*.

247

Lebidinsky, Gladkov, Ivanov, Fedin, and Boris Pilniak – his colleagues in the Soviet Writers Union. (I have often wondered why few if any of the Western academics involved in the once-fashionable 'Marxist literary criticism' project have paid attention to Serge's theories and practical Marxist criticism. Today, 367 pages of Serge's *Collected Writings on Literature and Revolution* are available in English translation thanks to that curmudgeonly British Marxist, the late Al Richardson.[144]

By the mid-1930s, all of Serge's colleagues (with the exception of Pasternak) had been reduced to silence (suicide, censorship, the camps). 'No Pen-club' wrote Serge in exile, 'even those that held banquets for them, asked the least question about their cases. No literary review, to my knowledge, commented on their mysterious end.' Only Serge – because he wrote in French and was saved from the Gulag by his reputation in France — managed to survive. Only Serge had the freedom to further develop the revolutionary innovations of Soviet literature and to submit the world of Stalinism to the critical lens of fiction in novels like *Midnight in the Century, The Case of Comrade Tulayev* and *Unforgiving Years.* As one Russian scholar put it in 1983: 'Although written in French, Serge's novels are perhaps the nearest we have to what Soviet literature of the '30s might have been...'[145]

Victor Serge and Me

Although I was a French major at Yale College (and later a grad student in French at Columbia and the Sorbonne), I first heard about Serge in the U.S. socialist movement. *The Case of Comrade Tulayev* was on a recommended reading list I got from the Young Peoples' Socialist League.[146] I read down the

---

[144] Francis Boutle, London 2004.
[145] Neil Cornwell, *Irish Slavonik Studies 4*, 1983.
[146] The list was probably prepared by Irving Howe of *Dissent*, who had written a

list as far as Orwell's *Hommage to Catalonia,* Malraux's *Man's Fate,* and Hemmingway's *For Whom the Bell Tolls,* but lost it before I got to *Tulayev.* Curiously, no one ever mentioned Serge to me as a lit student in France, where his books were out of print in the Fifties, although certainly everyone in the *Socialisme ou Barbarie* crowd had read them. So it was back in the States in 1962 that I 'discovered' Serge in the shipping room of a used book store in New York, where I was waiting to be paid for copies of Raya Dunayevskaya pamphlets I had left on consignment. My eyes fell upon a pile of French paperbacks about to be shipped to I.F. Stone, whose *Weekly* I had read since boyhood and who had become almost a family connection through my future wife, Julie Gilbert. Curious, I browsed the pile. They were all by the same author: Victor Serge. When I sensed the bookseller returning from his inner sanctum, I impulsively pocketed the first book in the pile – rationalising 'Izzy won't have time to read all these.'[147] At home that night I opened the book, and I've been hooked on Serge ever since.

In 1963 I got a French government grant to Paris to do research on Stendhal (still my favorite novelist) a project I soon abandoned for Serge after another wonderful bit of luck. During a weekend in Paris, my older brother, a highly successful Madison Avenue advertising executive, picked up a Serge novel for 5 francs (a buck) at a bookstand on *quais* and handed it to me in a *café.* 'Where did you find this?' Peter waved vaguely towards the Seine, but the next day I scoured the bookstalls and discovered the *bouquiniste* Teulé, who had a great stock of pre-WWII Serge paperbacks in mint condition. Teulé recalled hearing Serge speak before the War at the *Musée du Soir,* a center for proletarian culture created by Serge's friend Henry Poulaille. During the Occupation, when Serge's books were banned, Teulé had hidden a stock in his cellar. I told Teulé of my enthusiasm for Serge, and he asked me if I would like to meet his artist son, who was also spending the year in Paris on a grant. Vlady and I hit it off like brothers from the very first moment. We communicated instantaneously thanks to a shared socialist culture and a Russian-Jewish heritage of self-ironic idealism. Vlady Kibalchich was a man of vast reading and culture, having been 'home-schooled' through various exiles by his father, a polymatch who had benefited from a similar non-academic education. Only later, when I saw Vlady's murals in Mexico, did I realize what a stupendous painter he was. Please give yourself a treat and visit his monumental Mexican murals (and erotic engravings) at www.vlady.org. Vlady loved to talk about Victor, who had been a patient and supportive single parent through the most difficult trials and whose work and ethos he admired. Vlady was delighted when I told him I wanted to translate Serge's novels into English. I was also encouraged by Peter Sedgwick, the British socialist and contributor to

---

marvellously insightful chapter about *Tulayev* in his *Politics and the Novel.*

[147] It was no loss to Izzy. The 'book' I swiped was *Le Tournant obscur* a section of Serge's *Memoirs* which was published separately by mistake.

International Socialism, who was translating Serge's *Memoirs of a Revolutionary* for Oxford Press.[148] Back in the States, I got in touch with Eugene Eoyeng, a young editor at Doubleday, whose list already included *The Case of Comrade Tulayev*. In our enthusiasm, we concocted a plan to get Doubleday to publish not one, but a trilogy of Serge novels. To tempt the higher-ups into investing their good money in an obscure out-of-fashion foreign author of indeterminate nationality and non-conformist politics, I hit on the idea of asking the serious Serge fans I knew to write endorsements (which could later be used as blurbs) promoting my translation project.

Dwight Macdonald, who with his wife Nancy[149] had worked tirelessly to rescue Serge from Vichy France, replied: 'I can't think of anyone else who has written about the revolutionary movement in this century with Serge's combination of moral insight and intellectual richness.' Irving Howe, whose YPSL reading list first pointed me to Serge replied: 'To me he has seemed a model of the independent intellectual in Europe between the wars: leftist but not dogmatic, political yet deeply involved with issues of cultural life, and a novelist of very considerable powers.' The urbane Henri Peyre, my old French professor from Yale, replied offhandedly: 'Victor Serge is as worthy of a study by a scholar interested in ideas as is Proudhon, Georges Sorel or Charles Péguy. And he certainly counts also as a novelist - to me, far more than most of the 18th century novel which has been ridiculously overrated lately, and more than Robbe-Grillet and his vapid, skilled fiction and, may I confess, more than Beckett.'

Erich Fromm, who had known Serge in the Forties through psychoanalytical circles in Mexico (and whom our student socialist club had to Yale in 1961) replied: 'I believe indeed that to rescue the humanist tradition of the last decades is of the utmost importance, and that Victor Serge is one of the outstanding personalities representing the socialist aspect of humanism.' The journalist I.F. Stone from whom I had 'borrowed' my first Serge book wrote: 'Victor Serge died in exile and obscurity, apparently no more than a splinter of a splinter in the Marxist movement. But with the passage of the years, he looms up as one of the great moral figures of our time, an artist of such integrity and a revolutionary of such purity as to overshadow those who achieved fame and power. His failure was his success. I know of no participant in Russia's revolution and Spain's agonies who more deserves the attention of our concerned youth.' Bertram D. Wolf, whose *Three Who Made a Revolution*

---

[148] Peter's splendid translation of Serge's *Memoirs*, was truncated by one fifth by Oxford University Press, busy cost-cutting as far back as 1963. The first complete English translation, with the cuts restored by George Paizis and notes by Jean Rière, will be published by NYRB in 2011.

[149] Nancy Macdonald was business manager of *Partisan Review* and founder of Spanish Refugee Aid Committee.

had inspired me as a teenager, wrote 'Serge's writing was simple, vivid, strong, written with an insider's knowledge, the insights of a passionate yet detached observer and participant, and the skill of a poet and novelist.' For Trotsky biographer Isaac Deutcher: '*The Case of Comrade Tulayev* is by far the best novel about the period of the purges – far richer artistically and more truthful historically than Koestler's famous book.'

These endorsements, which date from 1964, confirmed my judgment that Serge was indeed a major figure in both literature and socialist thought. The Doubleday project was successful, and my 1960s translations of *Men in Prison, Birth of Our Power*, and *Conquered City* were reprinted in Britain by Gollanz and then Penguin in Britain. In the 'Eighties the Writers & Readers Publishing Coop in London bought the rights to the trilogy and commissioned me to English a forth Serge novel, *Midnight in the Century*.[150] My latest Serge translation, the posthumous novel *Unforgiving Years,* came out in 2008.

My friendship with Vlady flourished for 40 years (he died in 2005) through long letters which Vlady scrawled on the margins of proofs of engravings he was pulling in his studio. We often talked about finding a home for the archive of Serge's manuscripts and letters, which disorderly Vlady had done his best to preserve in Mexico City for forty years. They were refused by both Harvard and Stanford, where we hoped they could reside next to Trotsky's. Finally in 1995 the Beinecke Rare Book Library at Yale University (my *alma mater* made a generous offer for the papers. This sale had the ironic result of making poor (dead) Victor rich, and Vlady and his sister Jeannine Kibalchich generously donated Victor's money to preserving and disseminate their father's works and ideas through an International Victor Serge Foundation. I was to be the Secretary, so I bought a *How To* book and registered the VSF as a US non-profit 501 (c) (3) Corporation, in order to

---

[150] Verso Books in London will be reprinting *Midnight* in 2010. Writers & Readers Coop, while it lasted, was the originator of the *Marx for Beginners* comics series and other wonderful books. It was founded by Glenn Thompson, a black American living in London, his wife Sian from Wales, Richard and Lise Appignanesi from Canada, and the English novelist art critic John Berger.

avoid paying taxes on the sale as well as on Victor's future royalties, and to attract *your* deductible contributions. [151]

The Foundation invested these funds in new Serge translations, research and in other 'Sergian' projects. In Moscow, our never-ending quest for Serge's lost novels – illegally seized by the GPU when he left Russia in 1936 despite the *Glavlit* exit permit[152] – attracted an enthusiastic group of scholars and activists, which led to the creation in of the Victor Serge Public Library and the Praxis Center in Moscow discussed below. As trustee of the international copyright to Serge's works, I have been active in getting Serge's major books (almost all out of print in 1997) republished in France and in promoting translations in various languages, including Russian, Greek, Spanish, Portuguese, Slovenian and English. Serge's modest royalties (and a few donations, mainly from me) enable new projects. For example, the Foundation spent the advance from the 2004 NYRB edition of *The Case of Comrade Tulayev* on an Arabic translation of *Memoirs of a Revolutionary* and on publishing Julia Guseva's Russian translation of *Unforgiving Years* published by Praxis in Moscow. The quest for Serge's lost novels also led us to the city of Orenburg on the Ural where Serge and Vlady had been held in exile in 1933-36 and where local officials, heady with Russia's new freedom to look at the past, were eager to learn more about their illustrious exile and make a place for him in the Municipal Museum next to Kravchenko, the Ukrainian national poet, who had been exiled to Orenburg by the Tzar during the 19th Century, and Pushkin. Alas, at this writing, Russia has again slid backwards into state terrorism, and the future of Praxis and the Victor Serge Library seem threatened.

---

[151] Checks made out to 'The Victor Serge Foundation' should be mailed to 16 rue de la Teinturerie, Montpellier France, 34000.
[152] For details, please see my "The Victor Serge Affair and the French Literary Left" (*Revolutionary History,* London, *V*ol. 5, No 3).

Victor Serge and Stalinist Political Terror: *The Case of Comrade Tulayev*[153]

When the dissident writer Alexandr Solzhenitzyn was expelled from Russia in 1974, the event was hailed as unique. His aura as an uncompromising resister to totalitarian oppression compelled instant respect, while his powerfully truthful novels and painfully detailed revelations about the inner workings of the 'Gulag Archipelago' exploded like bombshells. The Solzhenitzyn phenomenon shocked the conscience of the liberal West and provoked a major shift in the political-intellectual climate, particularly in France where former Leftists were overnight converted to a 'New' Philosophy of neo-liberal authoritarianism.

Yet four decades earlier, in 1936, when Victor Serge was expelled under strikingly similar circumstances, there was no such attendant hullabaloo, much any less shift in the political atmosphere as a result of Serge's unmasking of the mass persecutions, slave-labor camps, and sensational frame-up trials in Russia. Serge, too, had established a reputation both as an uncompromising literary artist and a dissident prepared to pay with his person for the right to criticize the Stalinist regime. Like Solzhenitizyn, his persecution had become a cause célèbre among intellectuals and literati.[154]

But no Swiss bank accounts were waiting for Serge and his family when, stripped of most of their belongings (including several manuscripts never recovered), they were escorted across the border to 'freedom.' No Nobel Committee awaited Serge, nor did publishers press him with lucrative offers or journalists flock to hang on his every word. On the contrary, ill and penniless, supported by a few friends on the independent Left who were scarcely better off than himself, Serge found himself boycotted by the liberal and socialist press and forced to fall back on his old trade as a proofreader to earn a precarious living in Brussels and Paris. Deprived of his Soviet citizenship, heaped with abuse by the pro-Communist press, Serge nonetheless managed to survive and to continue writing in exile. Although he labored mightily to reveal the explosive truths about the then-triumphant Stalinist system and to warn the world about the potential threat to humanity posed by Stalin's totalitarian power, his words fell on deaf ears.

Yet as we have seen, Serge's credentials as a witness were impeccable. An early supporter of the Russian Revolution, he knew its inner workings first

---

[153] Victor Serge, *The Case of Comrade Tulayev,* translated by Willard Trask, Introduction by Susan Sontag (New York Review Books, N.Y. 2004. $14.95).
[154] See Richard Greeman, 'The Victor Serge Affair in Paris and the French Literary Left,' *Revolutionary History,* Vol. 5, No. 3 (London, Autumn 1994).

hand, having worked closely with Lenin, Zinoviev and the other Bolsheviks during the Civil War. Moreover, Serge's pro-Soviet journalism, novels and *Year One of the Russian Revolution* (1930) had revealed it to the French-speaking world, much as John Reed's *Ten Days that Shook the World* revealed the Revolution to the English. His arrest in 1933 had thus provoked a sensation and led to a sustained campaign of protest by both intellectuals and revolutionary militants in France. The controversy eventually involved writers as famous as Gide, Rolland, Malraux, Barbusse, Ehrenburg, Pasternak and Gorky as well as several governments and ultimately Stalin himself, who as a concession to public opinion agreed to release Serge and allow him to emigrate in April 1936. This nearly unique event took place just before Stalin liquidated the Bolshevik 'general staff' in the infamous Moscow frame-up trial during which Lenin's closest comrades (Zinoviev, Kamenev, Smirnov *et al*) confessed to the most absurd anti-Soviet crimes. The timing of his release convinced Serge that Stalin had not planned the blood purge in advance. Otherwise, the dictator would never have allowed such a knowledgeable witness to escape.

Yet despite Serge's relative celebrity and outstanding credentials, his efforts to expose the bloody fraud of the Moscow Trials and the counter-revolutionary totalitarian system that spawned them went largely unheeded. This was as much a result of the indifference of Western intellectuals and of their popular front mentality, which rejected any criticism of their new Russian anti-fascist ally, as it was of Russian machinations. To be sure, Stalin's agents used every means short of assassination to neutralize Serge's dangerous testimony. On 1 July 1936, the Russian government stripped Serge of his passport and Soviet citizenship, thus placing him in the insecure position of a man without a country. Moreover, the Soviet consular official in Belgium withheld official confirmation of this change in status, which made it impossible for Serge to obtain travel documents and effectively sequestered him in Belgium at a time when he might have found an effective platform in Paris. He was also the victim of police harassment provoked by GPU inspired denunciations. He was accused of agitating among the striking miners and preparing to assassinate the King of Belgium. The police rented a flat on the first floor of the house where Serge lived and his apartment was searched on a regular basis. On one occasion, a policeman even searched the cradle of Serge's infant daughter while supposedly looking for arms intended for the Spanish republicans!

Unable to strike an effective blow against Serge personally, Stalin's government took revenge on his relatives in Russia. His older sister, mother-in-law, two brothers-in-law and two sisters-in-law – all apolitical – were arrested and disappeared into the gulag. Serge and his wife Liuba never heard from them again. The fate of his family must have weighed heavily on Serge and there is evidence that they held him responsible for their persecution. How could he fail to feel guilty, especially when faced daily with the spectacle of Liuba's severe mental illness, which can only have been exacerbated by the news from Russia? Collective guilt – the use of hostages to ensure the good

254

behavior of their relatives – was one of the most effective and barbarous methods employed by Stalin's Terror. Like the 'choices' imposed on the Jews in the Nazi camps, it imposed moral dilemmas of an exquisitely painful nature, designed to destroy the very souls of its victims. Only individuals with a powerful hold on life, a clear political vision and a coherent sense of selfhood could survive it and preserve their moral and psychological integrity. Serge was such an individual, as was his sister-in-law, Anita Russakova, who survived nine years in the gulag (Viatka, Vorkuta). Interviewed in Leningrad at the age of 83, she told me that she bore no resentment against Victor, although she was certain that she, her mother, sisters and brothers, had been arrested because of Serge.

Harassment and persecution were reinforced by attacks on Serge in the media. The Communist press demanded his expulsion from Belgium 'in the name of respect for the right of asylum', and a slander campaign was mounted in Paris by a former friend, Jacques Sadoul.[155] Parisian editors were pressured to refrain from publishing Serge's articles and magazines were closed to him – *La NRF*, *L'Europe*, *Vendredi*, *Le Populaire* – until the boycott was almost total. Only the Belgian daily, *La Walonie*, of Liege, the Catholic personalist review *Esprit*, and a few small circulation, far left journals like *La Revolution proletarienne*, *Les Cahiers Sparticus* and *Les Humbles* provided him with a regular platform. Unable to live by writing, Serge was obliged to fall back on one of the trades of his youth, proofreading, and to earn his bread correcting the pages of some of the very left wing papers that were boycotting him.

Along with Trotsky's son Leon Sedov, the Austrian Social Democrat Fritz Adler, the old Russian Marxist Boris Nikolayevski, the Yugoslav Communist Anton Ciliga, and a few others, Serge labored mightily to expose the wholesale slanders and falsifications spewing forth daily from Russia – fabrications which were swallowed by the bulk of liberal opinion and endlessly repeated in the press. It was a Sisyphean task. No sooner hand one enormous lie been exposed than two new ones were invented. But Serge was too deeply attached to Russia, its people, its revolution, and to the defendants, whom he had known in more heroic hours, to abdicate. Serge helped Organize a 'Committee for Inquiry into the Moscow Trials and the Defense of Free Opinion in the

---

[155] Sadoul was a captain in the French military mission in Russia who sympathized with the Bolsheviks in 1917. His *Letters from Russia* provided the French public with a sympathetic eyewitness account such as John Reed's *Ten Days That Shook the World*. Serge had known Sadoul during the heroic civil war days in Russia and worked with him in Berlin in 1923. In 1936 he published two widely circulated and translated articles urging a boycott of 'the bandit' Kibalchich. He characterized Serge as a common criminal, the 'brains' behind the Bonnot gang of 1911, an unscrupulous sneak who had attempted to hide his criminal appetites behind the anarchist flag at the 1913 trial and was once again using 'politics' to camouflage his complicity with the 'criminals' in the Moscow Trial. Trotsky published a forthright response attacking Sadoul's record and defending Serge's.

Revolution', which met in the backrooms of cafes in Paris. Its members included the Surrealist post Andre Breton, the pacifist Felicien Challaye, the poet Marcel Henry Poulaille and Jean Galtier-Boissiere, worker militants like Pierre Monatte and Alfred Rosmer, left journalists such as Georges Pioch, Maurice Wullens and Emery, and the historians Georges Michon and Dommanget. Serge had insisted on the awkward two part title, for he already foresaw the need to defend anti-Stalinist militants like Andres Nin in Spain from GPU inspired slander and assassination.

Meanwhile, Trotsky's own followers in France were apparently too preoccupied with their own sectarian squabbles to rise to the historic occasion. 'How vexatious, how disgusting,' Serge wrote to Trotsky, 'to see so much paper blackened over the personal chicaneries of Molinier [the leader of one of the rival factions] when they haven't found a way to publish a single pamphlet about our comrades in Stalin's jails!' [156] There was little Trotsky could do, since a week later he would find himself under house arrest in 'liberal' Norway, forbidden to write or even listen to the radio reports of his own trial taking place on Moscow!

Among the literati, Serge found sympathy from George Duhamel (who nonetheless felt powerless to act), Leon Werth and the Catholics around Emanuel Mounier. Serge had addressed a bold open letter to Andre Gide on the eve of the latter's celebrated voyage to Moscow and, far from taking offence, Gide met with him several times on his return. If Gide took the precaution of keeping his association with Serge a secret (so as to avoid the accusation of 'Trotskyist influence'), there is considerable evidence that he relied on Serge's information and advice in writing his 'Retouches' on the *Retour de l'URSS*.[157]

On the other hand, Romain Rolland, whose intervention on Serge's behalf had probably been instrumental in saving him, remained silent when Serge exhorted him to use his unique moral authority in the USSR by questioning the Moscow Trials. Serge ironized:

> *So many literary men have succeeded in keeping silence, gaily, with a supreme revolutionary elegance. They have found it possible to publish weeklies and monthlies and whole books without letting the truth glimmer through. That is a sign of great artistry. And it is a terrible danger.*

Even intellectuals who did express concern often confined their activity to

---

[156] Serge to Trotsky, 10 August 1936, in M. Dreyfus, the editor and prefacer of Victor Serge and Leon Trotsky, *La Lutte Contra le Stalinisme: texts 1936-39*, a collection of letters and published exchanges between the two men.

[157] V. Serge, *Carnets*, pp21-25; pp30-32; interviews with Vlady Kibalichich.

agonized hand wringing. Typical was Victor Basch, one of the heroes of the Dryfus affair and the chairman of the League for the Rights of Man. He gave Serge a long interview, promised that an investigation would be undertaken and did nothing. Serge did not give in to discouragement, for his struggle was not only to save the oppositionist comrades he had left behind in the gulag but also to keep their ideas alive. This task involved rescuing both Marxism and the truth about the Bolshevik revolution from the flood of Stalinist distortion. It also meant explaining how and why a liberating movement with the highest ideals became transformed into an oppressive totalitarian nightmare, that is to say, facing the biggest challenge to Marxist thought since the collapse of the Socialist International at the outbreak of the First World War.

In pamphlets like *The Sixteen Who Were Shot* and *Yagoda's End*, Serge used his insider's knowledge of Stalinist police methods and of the character of the old Bolshevik leaders to explain the enigma of the Moscow Trials, where outstanding revolutionaries like Zinoviev and Bukharin confessed to the most absurd crimes. However, it was in books like *From Lenin to Stalin* and *Russia Twenty Years After* [UK title: *Destiny of a Revolution*] (1937) and *Portrait of Stalin* (1940) that Serge explored the historical, economic, sociological and political roots of the new system which the Stalinist bureaucracy was erecting on the ashes of the Russian Revolution. Serge wrote these books in great haste, within months of his liberation. However, they have stood the test of time: Serge's accounts of the Soviet Union combine the insights of an eyewitness with the scrupulous documentation of a professional writer and the analytical acumen of a sophisticated Marxist. Ralph Manheim's English translation of *From Lenin to Stalin* has frequently been reprinted and is in constant demand for socialist education classes, while Serge's account of the Terror in *Russia Twenty Years After* has been complemented, but by no means contradicted, by more recent massive studies by Solzhenitsyn, Medvedev and Conquest.

Serge's analysis was no doubt strongly influenced by the ideas of Leon Trotsky, whose *The Revolution Betrayed* Serge was translating from Russian into French at the same time he was preparing his own books on Russia. However, Serge also draws on his knowledge of the various theories circulating in Russian prison and exile communities where surviving Left Oppositionists, often in sharp disagreement with each other, were attempting to describe Stalinism in Marxist terms. Like Trotsky's, Serge's writings were often prophetic. In *Russia Twenty Years After,* he foresaw that without genuine democracy and worker participation, the triumphant progress of Soviet industry would eventually bog down in a bureaucratic morass. He also predicted that if the bureaucracy were not overthrown by the workers, it would eventually make its peace with the Western bourgeoisie and invite capitalists into joint ventures to share in the exploitation of Soviet labor. Indeed, in an unpublished new preface entitled 'Russia 30 Years After' (1947), Serge foresaw the post-1989 wholesale rejection of Marxism along with the tarnished 'Marxism' of Stalinists as well as the rise of nationalist ideologies in its place, describing them as likely consequences of Stalinism collapsed in the absence of a proletarian revolution.

Although Serge's underlying methodology in these historical and sociological books was Marxist, his presentation was largely descriptive – letting facts, figures and accounts of the situation of the workers under their new Stalinist masters speak for themselves. I believe this was only partly because he was writing for the broadest possible popular audience and not just for Marxists. Serge was also convinced both that it was too early to classify the Stalinist system under a single theoretical formula and that such premature attempts would only lead to sectarian squabbles among dogmatists. Thus, although Serge was perfectly familiar with such formulae as 'degenerated works' state', 'state capitalism', and the distinction between a 'cast' and a 'class', he tended to reject labels in favor of more concrete descriptions of the actual relations between workers and their bureaucratic exploiters from which his readers could draw their own conclusions.

When Serge completed the manuscript of *Russia Twenty Years After* on Christmas Day of 1936, he heaved a sigh of relief. 'The militant's job is now completed,' he wrote to Marcel Martinet. 'I'm going to attack something completely different.' That 'something' was fiction, to which he was increasingly dedicated. Serge had experienced something of a rebirth in 1928, when he was expelled from the Russian Communist Party, arrested and questioned form months, and suffered a heart attack. He realized that he was 'politically dead' as far as Russia was concerned and resolved to devote what remained to him of life and freedom to literary creation designed to preserve the memory and inner meaning of the unforgettable people and events he had known and to which he was one of the few surviving witnesses. Although as a longtime professional revolutionary Serge retained a healthy suspicion of aestheticism, he began to see that artistic creation held the promise of leaving behind a significant and lasting testimony to the struggles and the mentality of a generation that the counter-revolutions he saw rising in Russia and in Germany now threatened with extinction. Serge's first three novels, written in semi-captivity in Russia, had chronicled the rise to power of the revolutionary movement and, through their subtle ironies, posed the paradoxical problem of defeat in victory – the anger within. The two novels he wrote in exile in central Asia were, as we have seen, confiscated by the secret police. Now at last Serge was free to write openly about Stalinism, and his first novel, *Midnight in the Century*, described the resistance of Oppositionists in prison and exile against the backdrop of collectivization. *Midnight* was mentioned for the Prix Goncourt in 1939, but suppressed, like its author, at the fall of France.

It was thus only later with his sprawling social and psychological novel, *The Case of Comrade Tulayev*, that Serge succeeded in capturing the essence of the whole society, from its summits to its depths, and to epitomize the world of Stalinism. And by the time the book was actually published, in 1948, Serge had died, isolated and impoverished, in Mexican exile. The life of Serge's books has been hard, yet tenacious, like that of their author. Boycotted by both conservatives and fellow travelers, they never achieved the success of works like Koestler's *Darkness at Noon*, Malraux's *Man's Fate*, or Rybakov's *Children of the Arbat* – arguably novels of lesser artistic merit and political penetration. Trotsky, who was an *afficianado* of the French novel, opted not to read them and his disciples have largely ignored them. On the other hand, Serge's novels, essays and particularly his *Memoirs of a Revolutionary* have enjoyed the loyalty of a steadily increasing readership over more than 50 years, with something of a boomlet in the 1960s in response to the rise of a new left. His books have also been translated into many languages. Indeed, Serge may be better known in English than in the original French thanks to the translations of the late Peter Sedgewick, an early contributor to *International Socialism*, and my own modest efforts.

Now that New York Review Books has consecrated *The Case of Comrade Tulayev* as a 'Classic' in a spiffy new paperback with an Introduction by the late Susan Sontag, it is at last possible to discuss Serge's masterpiece as a novel - that is to say as literature.[158] During the Cold War, Serge's qualities as a writer were mostly obscured by his stature as a revolutionary truth-teller. If Serge the witness was a beacon to the anti-Stalinist Left, he remained anathema to conservatives and fellow-travellers alike. And if academic historians and political scientists frequently quoted Serge's *Memoirs of a Revolutionary,*[159] the novels of this French-speaking Russian 'Trotskyite' evoked zero interest in university literature departments.[160] Today, Stalinism is mostly history, and Sontag is right on the mark when she writes: 'The presumptive case for exempting Serge from the oblivion that awaits most heroes of the truth lies, finally, in the excellence of his fiction, above all *The Case of Comrade Tulayev.*'

I will now proceed to make that case. Never has such a serene masterpiece been composed under such trying conditions. *The Case of Comrade Tulayev* was written during WWII by a penniless Russian revolutionary exile who was living literally 'on the run.' Expelled from the USSR by Stalin into a 'world without a visa' Serge was a stateless refugee whose name figured on the hitlists of both Stalin and Hitler. Serge began working on *Tulayev* in precarious exile

---

[158] Originally published in *International Socialism* No. 38, London Spring 1993.

[159] Victor Serge, *Memoirs of a Revolutionary*, translated by Peter Sedgwick with a Foreword by Adam Hochschild, (Sightline Books, University of Iowa Press, Iowa City, 2002).

[160] One honorable exception: Bill Marshall of the French Dept. University of Southampton, England whose splendid book on Serge, *The Uses of Dissent* (Berg, Oxford/NY 1993), escaped the attention of reviewers. On the other hand, political scientist Susan Weissman's widely acclaimed Serge study *The Course Is Set on Hope* (Verso, NY and London, 2001), true to form, dismisses Serge the novelist with an airy "Writing, for Serge, was something to do only when one was unable to fight." (p.110)

in Paris during 1939 in the wake of the moderate success of his novel of the Gulag, '*Midnight in the Century.*'[161] With war clouds on the horizon, Serge's position became shakier, and under government pressure Serge's publisher Grasset withdrew his critical biography of Stalin from circulation. When the *panzers* entered the northern suburbs of Paris, Serge and his family joined the southward exodus on foot and nearly penniless. Yet Serge's correspondence reveals him working hard on the novel in one temporary refuge after another. 'I'm constructing another novel,' he writes to the poet Marcel Martinet from Agen in the 'Free' Zone in February 1940, very different, very dramatic, describing the next period, the Trials...' All this despite of the cold and struggles for something to eat. The habit of working in instability on moving sands is useful to me.' He continued writing in Marseille, sharing digs with André Breton and Varian Fry while desperately searching for visas for himself and his family, and he took the manuscript with him when by miracle he boarded the last refugee ship to leave France. Arrested by the Vichy authorities in Martinique, he was sketched by his artist son Vlady in the prison-camp - characteristically at his typewriter. Stranded for months at Ciudad Trujillo, Dominican Republic, Serge again returned to his manuscript, which he completed in Mexico - his final exile - in 1942.

Serge wrote *Tulayev* with the calm determination of a stranded explorer setting down his observations before placing them in a bottle and consigning them to the waves. As he wrote to his American friend and supporter Dwight Macdonald in 1940: 'we have all been swept off by history toward unknown shores – with our poor compasses knocked off their axis.' Yet he adds 'I am working on another big novel on the darkest period. Like a painter working on his canvas on a Fifteenth Century galion searching for the passage to the Indies...' How did Serge find the inner tranquillity to write what may be his finest novel – conscious that he was writing 'for the desk drawer,' that is to say with little or no hope of publication? Work was always his refuge, and perhaps the creation of a literary world - even the grim world of *Tulayev* - served him as a kind of defence against the world that was crumbling around him and his own insecure position in it – symbolised by the earthquakes and volcanoes that haunted his imagination and dreams in Mexico. In any case, it was an act of courage and faith in an uncertain future.

Truth and Fiction

In a 'Note of the Author' Serge prepared in English for prospective publishers (none were found during his lifetime, despite help from Dwight Macdonald and George Orwell) he made the apparently contradictory claim that *Tulayev* was 'rigorously authentical (sic) in all its details, but also essentially fiction.' I think that Serge was suggesting two points here. The first is that *Tulayev*

---

[161] Serge, *Midnight in the Century,* *t*ranslated with an Introduction by Richard Greeman, Writers and Readers Publishing Cooperative (London 1982).

should not be read as a *roman à clef*. The second relates to the difference between history and literature. Serge underscores this first point in his disclaimer: 'This novel belongs entirely to the domain of literary fiction. The truth created by the novelist cannot be confounded, in any degree whatever, with the truth of the historian or the chronicler. Any attempt to establish a precise connection between characters or episodes in this book and known historical personages and events would therefore be without justification.'

To be sure, such disclaimers are often meant to be taken with a grain of salt, especially in cases of genuine *romans à clef*. Indeed, the fate of many of Serge's characters parallels that of known historical figures. Erchov, Serge's Security Chief, is engulfed in the purge he conducted and ends up shot like Stalin's henchman Yagoda. `Rublev' bears a certain resemblance to Bukharin. Stephen Stern is kidnapped by the GPU in Barcelona like the Trotskyist Kurt Landau. Kondratiev is compromised by what he witnesses in Barcelona, like the hero of the Winter Palace, Antonov-Ovesyenko, and, of course, Tulayev is assassinated like Stalin's rival, Serge Kirov. But the interest of the novel does not reside in fictionalized 'revelations' about real persons. Moreover, Bukharin, Landau, Antonov-Ovseyenko and other historical personages are mentioned by name in the novel in such a way as to frustrate the attempts of any reader searching for the 'precise connections' of Serge's disclaimer.

On a deeper level, lies the distinction between the truth of the historical chronicler and the truth of literary creation. Serge respected both. He chronicled the Stalinist Terror in his non-fiction works, but when he turned to the novel, he was aiming at a higher, more general truth: the truth of human experience lived, felt, and made meaningful through the structure of a work of art. He did so in the belief that fiction has the power to touch us on unconscious levels that arguments generally fail to reach. His friend the French writer Léon Werth understood Serge's intentions when he wrote: 'In *The Case of Comrade Tulayev*, nothing is historical - not in the sense that political philosophers and the authors of textbooks understand history.'

Serge understood that art alone can adequately convey the complex totality of human motives and circumstances that give an historical experience its human significance and communicate it to us in a way that makes it somehow ours. Solzhenitsyn made this same point in his 1972 Nobel Prize Speech:

> Art is capable of the following miracle: it can overcome man's characteristic weakness of learning only from his own experience, so that the experience of others is wasted on him. From man to man, augmenting his brief span on earth, art can convey the whole burden of another's long life experience, with its cares, colors and flavor, can recreate in the flesh the experiences of other men and enable us to assimilate them as our own.

It is through the interplay of character and circumstance that fiction accomplishes this 'miracle,' and that is why Serge insists on designating *Tulayev* first of all as a 'psychological (and social) novel.' If Serge's characters, like Solzhinitsyn's, are authentic in the sense that they are based on intimate observation, on real, rather than invented events and experience, it is through their inner life, the psychological complexity and freedom with which Serge's creative imagination invests them, that they strike us as authentic in the literary sense. As Serge wrote to Macdonald, '[my] novels are exclusively about atmosphere.' Again, Léon Werth is right on the mark when he writes:

> [Serge's] characters are not examples in demonstration, arguments in a proof...Their thoughts and feelings are not Victor Serge's. Victor Serge does not pass judgement on them based on political prejudices, on his social preferences or his personal morality. The novel is not for him a courtroom where a single judge, the author, passes final judgement on the innocent and the guilty. The characters are not judged according to a Koran or a Code. They live their lives, full of nuances and contradictions. Like the men and women they are. Creatures of flesh and bone whose behavior, secret thoughts, repressed emotions, even whose erotic lives are revealed by Serge. Serge doesn't prove. He describes.

Fifty years later, Susan Sontag grasped the same truth when she wrote of Serge: 'The truth of the novelist – unlike the truth of the historian – allows for the arbitrary, the mysterious, the under motivated. The truth of fiction replenishes, for there is much more than politics, and more than the vagaries of human feeling.' The point is not that Serge lacked or concealed his convictions - his socialist humanism certainly pervades the novel. However, for him there was no confusion between the militant and the artist. Serge's Marxist worldview resides in the novel on the level of imagination, as an underlying structuring element, like Dante's Christianity.

'Comets are born at night'

Tulayev is divided into ten chapters (or 'complementary panels' as Serge called them in a prospectus). Each is more or less self-contained. Each focuses on a different central figure, although several of the characters appear in more than one section. The plot evolves chronologically from the unplanned, almost accidental assassination of Tulayev, a high Party official, to the execution, a year later, of three men, all important Communists, who become entangled in the net of the investigation and are selected to take the responsibility for the unsolved crime. The reader follows the ramifications of the purge from a wide variety of perspectives: those of the investigators and those of the victims, including loyal Stalinists, oppositionists who capitulate, and diehard supporters of Trotsky's Left Opposition. According to Serge's prospectus, the plot 'ends

262

with neither optimism nor pessimism, in the expectation of war, with: life goes on.'

Rather than concentrating on the 'biography' of a single individual, Serge simultaneously develops a varied spectrum of characters in the manner of Dos Passos, Pilniak, and the Unanimists. The multiplicity of his characters, each of whom is 'central' for the time he occupies the stage, thus permits us to assimilate the experience of many lives and through them to recreate the life of an entire epoch. Serge was convinced that individual existences are only meaningful in relation to the existence of all, especially in the epochs of revolutionary transformation. By breaking the mold of the traditional novel, with its focus on the single hero, Serge's realism may be considered revolutionary. The structure of the novel could be termed 'polyphonic,' to borrow the expression coined by Solzhenitsyn to describe his own novels.

This loose, yet dramatic form permits Serge to illuminate many aspects of Soviet Russian society from the lives of Arctic fishermen and peasants on a *kolkhoze* (collective farm) to the inner sanctum of the General Secretariat in the Kremlin. He extends his canvas to Barcelona, where the Trotskyists are being hunted down as the embattled Spanish Republic is drowning in defeat and to Paris, where the massacres of old Bolshevik revolutionaries is greeted with pious platitudes and maddening indifference. Moreover, through flashbacks and biographical sketches of his characters, Serge opens an historical perspective and extends his story back in time to the heroic days of the Revolution and Civil War. The ten 'panels' of his fictional fresco thus open a vast panorama of Russian life and history and permit the reader to penetrate both the structure of the system and its origins.

The first panel is entitled 'Comets Are Born at Night,' and it stands as a kind of prologue to the various episodes that make up the body of the novel. Structurally, the chapter is framed by two unpremeditated, irrational actions. It opens as Kostia, a Young Communist employed at the Moscow Subway construction site, impulsively buys an expensive antique miniature portrait of a young girl with the money he has been saving for a desperately needed pair of boots. It ends when he impulsively shoots Tulayev, a high official whom he has never met, with a revolver supplied by his neighbor, a mousey old clerk named Romachkin. The two impulsive actions are symmetrical and opposite, as are the characters of the two men; yet on a psychological and thematic level, they are all, somehow, complementary.

Romachkin is a slightly ridiculous figure: a timid, aging, petty bureaucrat with colorless eyes and a grey complexion. A relic of the old regime, reminiscent both of the pathetic clerk in Gogol's *The Overcoat* and of Dostoyevsky's *Underground Man*, Romachkin's problem is that he thinks. His tiny room is lined with grey paperbacks and adorned by portraits of his intellectual heroes: Ibsen, Mechnikov, Darwin, and Knut Hamsun. Employed as a statistician in

263

the Office of Salaries of the State Cloth Trust, his job is to calculate the wages of the workers according to the directives that come down from the Planning Commission. Almost in spite of himself, he discovers that these figures add up to a lie: that each nominal raise in wages - based on new 'triumphs' of socialist production - is counteracted by depreciations of paper currency and by rises in rents, prices and taxes so as to actually reduce the workers' miserable standard of living. As he eats his sparse meal of cold gruel in the office cafeteria, he concludes, 'I am fleecing the poor.'

Romachkin becomes obsessed with the idea of injustice, of life's iniquity. For a while he considers the possibility that he is insane, reads up on schizophrenia, and consults a psychiatrist. The passage in which Serge describes his dialogue of the deaf with the bland, self-satisfied psychiatrist anticipates by thirty years the accounts of Soviet dissidents of the 70s who were confined to mental hospitals for insisting that Soviet reality should live up to its official ideology. 'You keep talking about the Constitution and the laws,' the doctors explained to the dissenter, Vladimir Bukovsky, 'but what normal man takes Soviet laws seriously? You are living in an unreal world of your own invention, and you react inadequately to the world around you.' 1 When injustice masquerades as justice and exploitation parades as socialism, the individual who lacks the cynicism to ignore the contradiction is ipso facto mad. Romachkin's psychiatrist ends up telling him 'not to worry' about injustice and recommends sexual intercourse twice a month. Romachkin departs reassured and amused 'The patient is yourself, Citizen Doctor,' he muses. 'You have never had the least notion of justice.'

The doctor's advice on sexual hygiene leads Romachkin to a Doestoyevskyan encounter with a young, half-starved prostitute in a dingy room in which a newborn baby is sleeping. It is in the course of this encounter that he experiences a revelation of his own iniquity and that of the world and sees the connections between his feelings and the nature of the regime. The girl is a peasant, a refugee from the forced collectivization drive that has ravaged her village. After they make love, she tells Romachkin the pathetic story of how her father tearfully slaughtered the family horse, who was starving to death because the government refused to furnish fodder. 'Where I come from, horses are more precious than children,' the girl states matter-of-factly:

> There are always too many children, they come when nobody wants them - do you think there was any need for me to come into the world? But there are never enough horses to do the farm work with. With a horse, your children can grow up; without a horse, a man is not a man any more, is he? No more home - nothing but hunger, nothing but death.

The girl's story is at once an indirect account of why this simple child of the country ended up as a Moscow prostitute, a political expose of the disastrous effects of Stalin's agrarian policy, and a commentary on the value of human life in Romachkin's society. It is typical of the way Serge compresses a wealth of meaning, social reality and experience into the rapid evocation of a minor character who never reappears.

The aging clerk is touched with pity and offers the girl an extra fifty kopeks. At the same time, his brain begins putting things together, making intellectual connections between his human experience and his mathematical calculations as a statistician. When the girl complains that business is slow, he thinks: 'Of course. Sexual needs are influenced by diet.' Out of his obsession with iniquity, he poses the question: Why? Who is responsible? Romachkin's confused feelings of anxiety and revolt are crystallized by his involuntary reactions to official propaganda. As he walks down a dark, deserted street, his consciousness is assaulted by a strident female voice:

> Insults spewed into the darkness from a forgotten loudspeaker in an empty office. It was frightful - that voice without a face, in the darkness of the office, in the solitude, under the unmoving orange light at the end of the street. Romachkin felt terribly cold. The woman's voice clamored: 'In the name of the four thousand women workers ...' Romackin's brain passively echoes: In the name of the four thousand women workers in this factory ... And four thousand women of all ages - seductive women, women prematurely old (why?), pretty women, women whom he would never know, women of whom he dared not dream - were present in him for an incalculable instant, and they all cried: 'We demand the death penalty for these vile dogs: No pity! (Can you mean it, women?)' Romachkin answered severely. 'No pity?' All of us need pity so much, you and I and all of us ...') 'To the firing squad with them!' Factory meetings continued during the trial of the engineers - or was it the economists, or the food control board, or the Old Bolsheviks, who were being tried this time?

The sudden, disembodied clamor and the fact that it is a female voice increase the shock value for Romachkin and the reader. Woman - mother, the Madonna - is traditionally associated with suffering and pity, and the encounter with the childlike prostitute, with which this passage is juxtaposed, has brought these tender feelings to the fore. The effect is heightened as Romachkin's imagination endows the factory women with bodies and brings them to life as potential lovers. Serge begins with documentary material - the radio broadcast - but goes beyond the technique of literary collage à la Dos Passos by drawing them into his character's stream of consciousness through rapid shifts between the outer and inner voice. It is also significant that the identity of the 'traitors' is left vague. What is important is that victims must be sacrificed to distract from the emptiness of the triumphs proclaimed by the regime and to shoulder the blame for the dismal reality behind the official lie. This is the truth which is slowly impinging on Roachkin's (and the reader's) consciousness.

Romachkin now returns to his apartment building to find the neighbors in a panic over a new purge of employees and new regulations concerning internal passports. 'They give you three days to get out, Comrade Romachkin, and you have to go somewhere at least 60 miles away - but will they give you a passport there?' Romachkin then retires to his room and picks up the newspaper. 'The face of the Chief filled a third of the front page, as it did two or three times a week, surrounded by a seven-column speech. Our economic successes...' Again, the documentary text merges with the subtext in Romachkin's mind. He knows that the 12% raise in nominal wages triumphantly proclaimed by the Chief is, in reality, a 30% reduction in spending power. As he reads the speech, he is terrified to catch himself thinking: 'How he lies!' The 'feeble, faraway, hesitant' idea that was born to Romachkin in the prostitute's room now possesses him totally. He knows why and who is responsible:

> The terrible thought which, until now, had matured in the dark regions of a consciousness that feared itself, that pretended to ignore itself, that struggled to disguise itself before the mirror within, now stripped of its mask. So, at night, lightning reveals a landscape of twisted revelation. He saw the criminal. It did not occur to him that his new knowledge might avail him nothing. Henceforth it would possess him, would direct his thoughts, his eyes, his steps, his hands. He fell asleep with his eyes wide open, suspended between ecstasy and fear.

For a moment, Romachkin forgets that he is nothing but a clerk, an office rat, a timid, colorless creature of routine and passive obedience. Nourished by the legends of pre-revolutionary terrorists, his mind instinctively turns to assassination. He manages to get hold of a revolver and spends his lunch hours in a garden near the Kremlin waiting for his opportunity. It arrives. The Chief walks within six feet of him, but Romachkin is paralyzed. He cannot act. 'We are all cowards,' he concludes, and he returns to his office - not a minute late. As an afterthought, he makes a present of the revolver - a thing of power and beauty, now useless - to his young neighbor, Kostia. Ironically, and unwittingly, he passes on his mission of justice along with the weapon.

Kostia is apparently everything Romachkin is not: young, healthy, self-confident, practical. Yet his first action, in the scene that opens the novel, is the purchase of the cameo, revealing at once his impulsive spontaneity and his unconscious yearning for an ideal of beauty and harmony absent form his harsh existence. In Serge's scheme, Kostia and his neighbor, Romachkin, complement each other, for each is only half a man. Symbolically, their two cubicles, separated by a thin partition, were once a single room - one of six in a collective apartment that now houses 22 people (reminiscent of the one Serge inhabited on Jeliabov Street in Leningrad).

The realistic detail is developed as a significant structure. The two men's desks are situated symmetrically, back to back, on either side of the partition, and at one point they sit facing each other, invisible, each contemplating the cherished object on which he has spent several months' salary: Kostia, with his portrait, lost in dreams of beauty, and Romachkin with his revolver, dreaming of doing justice. I think of that partition - it is hardly a wall - as a kind of semi permeable membrane which permits the passage of matter from one organism to another or between two parts of a single organism. In the scene just referred to the two men sense each others' presence and make contact out of a half-felt need to share their dreams. Romachkin hands Kostia the revolver to hold and notes that he looks like 'a proud young warrior.' Kostia, for his part, is merely amused. 'You will never use it,' he tells his timid neighbor.

Indeed, Kostia finds it difficult to take his fussy, eccentric companion seriously. If he is drawn to Romachkin's philosophical speculations, he views his character with indulgent and amused contempt. Their conversations are generally limited to the books which Kostia comes to borrow from his elderly neighbor. But even these exchanges are significant: Romachkin chooses a volume of Prison, published by the 'Society of Former Convicts' for Kostia to read and tells him that it contains 'the stories of brave men.' In fact, they are stories of assassins, of the daring pre-revolutionary terrorists who struck out at Czarist officialdom in the name of the people's will. It is as if Romachkin had passed the active and idealistic part of himself, symbolized by the book and later the revolver, through the membrane of the partition in order to give them new life in the body of a more vital organism. After he abandons his obsession with doing justice and passes the revolver on to Kostia, Romachkin begins to appear aged and shrivelled, as if the flame had gone out within him.

Kostia is led to revolt along his own inner, emotional paths, and here again it is through connection with a woman that his sense of iniquity and injustice is crystallized. The woman, really a girl, is Maria, a worker at the subway construction site where Kostia is employed as a timekeeper and Young Communist activist. Maria is a quiet, rather prim, inoffensive creature. One day Kostia remarks that she has been absent from work and learns that she has drowned herself in the Moskva after being humiliated by a Young Communist wall poster denouncing her as a 'demoralized, petty bourgeois element' in a manufactured campaign against venereal disease. The whole affair had been routine. The Central Committee had sent down a directive, and the local leadership had applied it, choosing their victim more or less by chance. Only Maria had taken it seriously. Her suicide note reads: 'As a proletarian, I cannot live with this filthy dishonor. Accuse no one of my death. Farewell.' Kostia is stunned:

Maria you little fool, why let yourself get so desperate? Everybody knows that men are bastards. Nobody pays any attention to the Wall Gazette, it's only fit to wipe your arse with! How could you be so dumb, you poor baby, oh for God's sake, oh hell!

Once again we are reminded of the psychiatrist's remark to the dissenter Bukovsky: 'What normal man takes Soviet law seriously?' Kostia, as a Young Communist, feels he is partly responsible. Faced with the pathetic little corpse in the morgue, his self-protective veil of cynicism drops away, and he connects with a powerful sense of grief and outrage. When the guardian of the morgue asks him under what heading to place the deceased, Kostia replies angrily: 'Is there a heading, `Collective Crimes'?' Henceforth, he too will be obsessed with injustice.

In contrast to Romachkin, who consciously planned but failed to carry through his act of justice, Kostia's act is totally impulsive. It is ten o'clock on a February night scintillating with stars. Kostia emerges, discouraged, from a dreary Young Communist meeting about work discipline at which he has said nothing, knowing that his ideas would be unacceptable: 'For more discipline, more food. Soup first! Good soup will put a stop to drinking.' But the magic of the frosty, starry night (a central, recurring image in the novel) revitalizes him as he strides along. Suddenly, a powerful black car pulls up and Tulayev gets out. 'Tulayev? Tulayev of the Central Committee? Tulayev of the mass deportation in the Vorogen district? Tulayev of the university purges?' wonders Kostia. Curious, he moves closer. Before he realizes what he is doing, his hand 'remembers the Colt' and an explosion shatters the night.

Only later does Kostia recognize the rightness of his unthinking act. It comes to him as a feeling of joy: 'Pure joy. Luminous, cold, inhuman, like a starry winter sky.' Kostia's healthy body and spontaneous emotion symbolically carry through the action of which the anguished, meditative, overly-intellectual Romachkin was incapable. As if by osmosis, the one half man completes the other to produce that rarity in totalitarian society - a whole man who is unafraid to act. Kostia's joyful sense of freedom contrasts with the frustration he felt at the Young Communist meeting where he despairingly censored his perfectly communist solution to the problem of work discipline. What Serge is suggesting is that if labor does not nourish the laborer and if the regime does not allow his just resentment to be expressed through the official Party of the Revolution, then this pent-up anger and revolt will inevitably take the form of primitive, isolated acts of terrorism - a reversion to the pre-Marxist methods of the Narodniks under the old Czarist autocracy.

The chapter ends as Kostia, overflowing with joy and excitement after his adventure, bursts in on Romachkin to find him lost in rapture reading an old French novel about innocence and romantic love, *Paul and Virginia*. After a brief exchange, Romachkin notices Kostia's exaltation and asks him what has happened. Naturally, Kostia cannot share his secret with anyone, least of all his eccentric old neighbor, about whose own assassination fantasies he is in any case ignorant.

Taking his cue from the old man's infatuation with *Paul and Virginia*, he replies: 'I'm in love, Romachkin, my friend - it's terrible.' This ironic role reversal completes the osmosis between the two half men. In the beginning it was Kostia who nursed the dream of innocent, romantic love, symbolized by the antique portrait of the young girl, while Romachkin dreamed of justice. Now, the old clerk is lost in romantic fantasies of bygone innocence, while the young avenger hides his exaltation under the ironic pretext of 'love.' At the end of the novel, in a kind of epilogue, Kostia, who has married and made a new life for himself on a *kolkhoze*, returns to visit Romachkin in his old room and makes him a present of the miniature, thus completing the exchange. This resolution is fitting both psychologically and thematically. Serge seems to be suggesting that the idealism of the old, pre-revolutionary liberal generation has run its course and that, henceforth, the impulse for justice will be incarnated by the rising generation of Soviet youth. As we will see below, this theme of generations, traditional in the Russian novel, is central to the structure and import of *The Case of Comrade Tulayev*.

The Social World of Stalinism

'Comets Are Born At Night' is a masterpiece of fiction writing that works on many levels. It could easily stand on its own as a short story. The action is complete and self contained. The characters are fully developed, and the underlying social, political and historical themes are totally integrated into the structure. Indeed, I am painfully aware that in interpreting Serge's text I have not done justice to the experience of it as a fiction. The story moves forward as a kaleidoscopic succession of scenes and interior monologues with a rapidity and density of texture the effect of which is inevitably blunted by summary and analysis. The action flows from the characters' psychology and circumstances in a way that makes us accept it as inevitable, and it is only on a second reading that one realizes how much significance Serge has packed into these twenty-odd pages. Although the focus is on the symbiosis of the two characters, the social world Serge reveals to us is already vast. Through the eyes of Kostia and Romachkin we explore an office, an apartment building, a construction site, a Young Communist cell, an illegal marketplace, the streets of several neighborhoods and (through the prostitute) a peasant village in the throes of forced collectivization.

Moreover, although Serge never preaches, we are made to understand the basic, underlying social conflicts of this world. The principle economic contradiction, the official 'triumphs' of the Five Year Plan and the actual misery of the workers, is expressed in the figures that haunt the fevered brain of the old statistician and in the long lines, empty shops, hunger, overcrowding, and squalor, physical and moral, which we experience through the protagonists' eye. It is symbolized by the dynamiting of the Cathedral of the Holy Savior to make room for a Palace of Peoples in which Romachkin, a believer in progress, wistfully assumes people will be happier. It takes its most poignant form in the poor peasant forced to slaughter the horse that 'makes him a man' and whose daughter has been 'collectivized' as a prostitute as a consequence of the state's intervention in the life of the village.

These social contradictions are the underlying cause of the omnipresent manifestations of the Terror - the never-ending trials, purges, and repressive directives proclaimed on loudspeakers, at mass meetings, in the newspapers and in the neighbors' gossip. A new purge, provoked, ironically, by Kostia's act of justice, will now spread its nightmare tentacles into every corner of society. It is the subject of the sprawling novel of which 'Comets are Born at Night' is the prologue.

What is striking here is that from the outset, and without preaching or polemicizing, Serge has succeeded in rooting this political phenomenon in the concrete conditions of life and labor of the masses, in the social contradictions engendered by these conditions. This depiction of the interconnections between material life, politics, and the fate of the individual soul could only be conceived by someone with Serge's profoundly proletarian and socialist outlook. Yet, as Léon Werth observed 40 years ago, unlike writers like Barrès, Serge does not confront the reader with theses. His Marxist outlook is operative rather on the deeper levels of imagination: politics as vision.

The Passage of Generations

Significantly, Kostia, whose spontaneous act of revolt unwittingly unleashes a new wave of terror, is only dimly aware of these connections. In the central panels of the novel, Serge develops characters who do possess a clearer systematic understanding of what is happening - old revolutionaries, Marxist theoreticians, veterans or sympathizers of the various inner-party oppositions. The lucidity of this older generation contrasts with the half-formed consciousness of Kostia's. The problem is that, like Romachkin, they are unable to act, albeit for different reasons. In the impasse of the Revolution for which they have lived and would willingly die, their theoretical knowledge is, for the moment, impotent. They come to recognize themselves as members of a doomed generation, prisoners of an irony of history that has transformed the victorious Party of revolution, incarnating the highest level of human self-consciousness united with will, into the blind instrument of a power-system that cannot permit that consciousness to survive. That is their tragedy.

However, here are alternative themes in the novel that run in contrary motion to the theme of the destruction of the old revolutionary generation in the purges, suggesting an olive branch of hope for revolutionary renewal after the deluge. The old theoretician Rublev gives voice to some of these hopes:

> ... We must cultivate consciousness. There is sure progress under this barbarism, progress under this retrogression. Look at our masses, our youth, all the new factories, the Dnieprostroi, Magnitogorsk, Kirovsk ... We are all dead men under a reprieve, but the face of the earth has been changed, the migrating birds must wonder where they are when they see what were deserts covered with factories. And what a new proletariat! Ten million men at work in 1927. What will that effort not accomplish for the world in half a century?

In the scheme of *Tualyev*, the theme of industrialization, of renewal through the machine, is intimately connected with the theme of the renewal of life through nature and the passage of generations. Construction and destruction are linked by a dialectical tension at the same time as the elements of hope in the novel are muted by the threat of war. I think that this is what Serge had in mind when he described his novel as ending in 'neither optimism nor pessimism, in the expectation of war, with: life goes on.' Serge prefigured this dialectical movement in his opening chapter in the apocalyptic image of the dynamited cathedral that will hopefully be replaced by a 'Peoples Palace' and in the symbolic osmosis that links the two generations exemplified by Romachkin and Kostia. As the novel moves towards its conclusion, Serge enriches this theme and elevates it to a cosmic level through a series of images relating to the stars. Thus humanity's regeneration, industrial progress and the cosmos itself are linked in a nexus of imagery that lends the novel its lyricism and sense of spirituality.

The theme of the fruitful connection between the old and new generations is implicit in Serge's treatment of all the positive characters: the Old Bolshevik Ryzhik with his Marxist theory of the ascension of a new proletariat, Rublev with his testament written for future generations. However, it is most fully developed in the story of Red Army leader Kondratiev. His mission to Republican Spain is a 'Journey Into Defeat.' He realizes that the magnificent courage of the Spanish masses has been betrayed and that he can do nothing to save the Republic from entering its final agony. His crisis of conscience is crystallized by his encounter with the young Trotskyist, Stephen Stern, who has been kidnapped by the Russian secret police in Barcelona and implicated in the Tulayev assassination 'plot.' Kondratiev tries vainly to save him and succeeds only in compromising himself. But Stern's courage and unflinching revolutionary lucidity infects Kondratiev. As the despairing old revolutionary meditates on the tragedy of a revolution turned savagely against its most conscious representatives, Stern's image comes unbidden into his mind: 'Forgive me ... There is nothing more I can do for you, comrade. I understand you very well, I was like you once, we were all like you ... And I am still like you, since I am certainly done for like you ...'

271

Back in Moscow, Kondratiev expects to be arrested at any moment, and his existence takes on an unreal, hallucinatory quality. After a sleepless night spent wrestling with suicide, he resolves to fight. Not for himself - he knows he is doomed - but for future generations. 'Somewhere on earth there are young people whom I do not know but whose dawning consciousness I must try to save.' His victory over despair is associated with the eternally recurring victory of dawn over the night:

> Morning brightened at the window, the street along the Moskva was still deserted, a sentry's bayonet moved between the crenulations of the outer Kremlin wall, a wash of pale gold touched the faded dome on the tower of Ivan the Terrible, it was barely perceptible light, but already it was victorious, it was almost pink, the sky was turning pink, there was no boundary line between the pink of dawn and the blue of the vanishing night, in which the last stars were about to be extinguished. 'They are the strongest stars, and they are going out because they are outshone ...'

The last stars of the night are emblematic of Kondratiev's doomed generation. A few - the strongest - will survive to mingle their light of consciousness with that of the dawning generation. Kondratiev now at last falls asleep. In his dream the image of the stars explodes into a vision of the birth of the universe. This vision then merges with other images of renewal – a sunflower, a young woman, salmon swimming upstream to spawn:

> Enormous stars of pure fire, some copper colored, others transparent blue, yet others reddish, peopled the night of his dream. They moved mysteriously, or rather they swayed; the diamond-studded spiral of a nebula appeared out of darkness, filled with an inexplicable light, it grew larger. Look, look, the eternal worlds! - to whom did he say that? There was a presence too; but who was it, who? The nebula filled the sky, overflowed onto the earth, now it was only a great, bright sunflower, in a little courtyard under a closed window, Tamara Leontiyevna's hands made a signal, there were stone stairs, very wide, which they climbed at a run, and an amber torrent glided in the opposite direction, and in the eddies of the torrent big fish jumped, as salmon jump when they go up rivers ...

Serge's next paragraph slyly invites us to interpret the dream: 'When he shaved, about noon, Kondratiev found fragments of his dream floating in his mind; they did him good. Old crones would say ... But what would a psychoanalyst say? To hell with psychoanalysts! The dream does him good because it symbolizes his reconciliation with the life force. Tamara Leontiyevna represents the new generation to whom Kondratiev wishes to reach out his hand. She is also the sexual mate with whom Serge hints he will be united at the end of the novel. Thus historic consciousness, human reproduction, the life cycles of animals and plants (the fish, the sunflower), and the ever-expanding Einsteinian universe are integrated into Serge's cosmic vision. The present is dark, he tells us, but life goes on.

Called upon to give a routine propaganda speech to the graduating class of the Red Army Tank School that evening, Kondratiev arrives in a state of dream-like serenity. He finds himself departing from the clichés of his prepared text in order to find 'words that are alive' to share with the young men who are soon to face death:

> '... Perhaps, young men, I shall never speak again ... I have not come here, in the name of the Central Committee of our great Party, that iron cohort ...' Iron cohort? Hadn't that phrase been coined by Bukharin, enemy of the people, agent of a foreign intelligence service?... to bring you the copybook phrases which Lenin called our Communist lies, 'Comm-lies!' I ask you to look at reality, be it baffling or base, with the courage of your youth, I tell you to think freely, to condemn us in your consciences - we the older generation, who could not do better; I tell you to go beyond us as you judge us ... I urge you to feel that you are fee men under your armor of discipline ... to judge, to think out everything for yourselves, Socialism is not an organization of machines, a mechanizing of human beings - it is an organization of clear-thinking and resolute men, who know how to wait, to give way and to recover their ground ... Then you shall see how great we are, one and all - we who are the last, you who are the first, of tomorrow ...'

Paradoxically, the Chief decides to pardon Kondratiev's defiant heresy - at least for the moment. Instead of being executed, he is ordered to Northern Siberia to administer the search for gold - gold that will be needed to finance the coming war. As he prepares to depart, he invites two representatives of the new generation to accompany him: Tamara Leontiyevna and a desperate young student whom he meets on a park bench. Kondratiev thus progresses from the consciousness of historical defeat, through despair to a precarious and almost paradoxical reintegration with the forces of renew

'Listen to the earth, listen to your nerves.'

Star imagery is associated with all of the positive characters - Kostia, Rublev, Ryzhik, Kondratiev - who experience moments of transcendent foresight. Serge's cosmic lyricism serves as a kind of counterweight to the horror of the historical catastrophe he has elected to chronicle. It reminds us that our short life span encompasses only a moment in a movement whose rhythms must be measured by generations, centuries and millennia. Within this sidereal time scheme - which begins with the explosion of nebula and includes the eons of biological evolution and the successive epochs of human civilization - our lives may be experienced as tragic, but perhaps not as meaningless. The tragedy arises from the reversal of our intentions and expectations, and even Marxism, the highest form of historical consciousness, is not exempt from such reversals (although it may also contain the only means of transcending them).

The tragic reversal of Serge's period (which is still ours) is that the great victory of the Russian Revolution, conceived as the first step toward the Socialist transformation of humanity, led to its opposite: the usurpation of the Marxist ideal by a bloody, anti-working-class dictatorship and the defeat of international Socialism for a whole epoch. In *The Case of Comrade Tulayev*, Serge depicts his collective hero at the moment of catastrophic self awareness.

To the insistent question 'What is to be done?' Serge can provide no easy answer. The situation, an historical impasse, is entirely new. Ryzhik's response is intellectual: 'Theoretical conclusions, the chief thing being not to lose our heads, not to let our Marxist objectivity be perverted by this nightmare.' Serge's response includes this but broadens it. Survive, live, think, build, look to the future - these are the messages implicit in the structure, imagery and emotional tone of *Tulayev*. We feel them in the sense of wonder that suffuses the scene where Ryhzik encounters another old Marxist during a prison transfer:

> 'Our meeting is absolutely extraordinary ... An inconceivable piece of negligence on the part of the services, a fantastic success compounded by the stars ... the stars which are no longer in their courses. We are living through an apocalypse of Socialism, Comrade Ryzhik... Why are you alive, why am I - I ask you! Why? Magnificent! Staggering! I wish I might live for a century so that I could understand ...'
> 'I understand,' said Ryzhik.
> 'The Left theses of course ... I am a Marxist too. But shut your eyes for a minute, listen to the earth, listen to your nerves ... Do you think I am talking nonsense?'
> 'No.'

The critic Irving Howe, commenting on this passage in his seminal book which poses the question of *Politics and the Novel*, remarks: 'This seems to me as good a prescription for the political novel ... as we are likely to get: amidst the clamor of ideology - the indispensable, inescapable clamor - listen to your nerves.' It is not that Serge poses this vision as a substitute for the Marxist interpretation of history: rather he completes it with a lyricism that encompasses the stars, the earth, the centuries, and the unique emotional response of the individual.

Just as the tragic poets of ancient Greece, Aeschylus and Sophocles, juxtaposed hymns and choruses celebrating man's triumphs and the harmony of the universe to the catastrophic fall of kings and heroes, so Serge's humanism and cosmic lyricism create the context for a tragic appreciation of the fate of the modern proletariat. Toward the end of the novel, Kostia, in a burst of enthusiasm, exclaims: 'The earth is revolving magnificently ... Can you see it revolving, our green globe inhabited by toiling monkeys?' The shift in perspective is bold and striking. We are suddenly transported from the dingy confines of a Moscow apartment to the point of view of a cosmonaut circling the globe, from clock time to evolutionary time. The human moment fuses with the eternal while both the Marxist and the Darwinian view of man are compressed into the phrase, 'toiling monkeys.'

Classical Greek tragedy achieves this double perspective through lyricism of its choruses and the presence of the gods that see beyond human pain because they are immortal. Choruses and gods create the distancing effect that permits the spectator to experience the tragic emotion intensely without being devastated. Where the ancients drew on mythology for their symbols of harmony and permanence, Serge draws on the sciences to round out his vision.

Nowhere is this clearer than in the final chapter of the novel, 'And Still The Floes Come Down,' which serves as an epilogue in which the tragic echoes of the shots that smash the skulls of Rublev and his co-defendants mingle with the reverberating strains of Serge's cosmic lyricism. As the threads of the plot are tied together and the characters are brought back for their final *exodus*, Serge introduces the curious figure of Filatov, an old Moscow proletarian, whose sole apparent function in the novel is to prolong the theme of the cosmos and relate it to the theme of justice, also central to the novel. Filatov is a rather simpleminded fellow, a son of the people who becomes Romachkin's first real friend and spiritual advisor. He lives, symbolically, in the shadow of a church, but his religion is modern science. Left a widower at the age of 55, Filatov has enrolled in the 'free night courses at the Higher Technical School to learn mechanics and astrophysics.' As he explains to Romachkin:

> Mechanics rules technology, technology is the basis of production, that is, of society. Celestial mechanics is the law of the universe. Everything is physical. If I could begin my life over again, I would be an engineer or an astronomer; I believe the real engineer must be an astronomer if he is to understand the world. But I was born the grandson of a serf, under the Tsarist oppression. I was illiterate until I reached 30, a drunkard until I reached 40. I lived without understanding the universe until my poor Natassia died.

There is something slightly comical in Filatov's naive mixture of science, Marxism and religion, but his very simplicity is also both touching and profound. Just as Shakespeare, in his dramatic irony, often puts wisdom in the

275

mouths of his commoners and fools, so Serge uses Filatov to explore the notion of a materialist spirituality implicit in his cosmological themes and imagery. Filatov continues:

> When she was buried at Vagankovskoye, I had a small red cross set up on her grave, because she was a Believer herself, being ignorant; and because we live in the Socialist age, I said: Let the cross of a proletarian be red! And I was left all alone in the cemetery, Comrade Romachkin, I paid the watchman 50 kopeks so that I could stay after closing time until the stars came out. And I thought: What is man on this earth? A wretched speck of dust which thinks, works, and suffers. What does he leave behind him? Work, the mechanisms of work. What is the earth? A speck of dust which revolves in the sky with the work and sufferings of man, and the silence of plants, and everything. And what makes it revolve? The iron law of stellar mechanics. `Natassia,' I said over her grave, `you can no longer hear me because you no longer exist, because we have no souls, but you will always be in the soil, the plants, the air, the energy of nature, and I ask you to forgive me for having hurt you by getting drunk, and I promise you I will stop drinking, and I promise you I will study so that I may understand the great mechanisms of creation.'

Serge's Filatov also connects with the Russian literary tradition in which the solidity and simple wisdom of an old man of the people serves as a foil for the anguished uncertainty of the educated. He recalls Platon Karatayev, the old peasant soldier whose proverbs for every occasion sustain the troubled Pierre Bezukov during the burning of Moscow in Tolstoy's *War and Peace*. He also anticipates the figure of Spiridon Yegorov, the old peasant prisoner whose moral values inspire Gleb Nerzhin, the hero of Solzhenitsyn's *The First Circle*. Both these figures are reflections of the Russian tradition of populist Christianity in which the peasant, the man of the soil, is seen as the 'real' Russia and the repository of its spiritual values. Serge's Filatov springs from the Russian soil too. He is the 'grandson of a serf.' But he also reflects the impact of 20th Century industrial, political and intellectual revolutions on the masses and he thus transcends traditional populist ideology.

Filatov sees the world in the image of the machine: 'I have not had time to think about the universe, Comrade Filatov,' says Romachkin, 'because I have been tortured by injustice.' 'The causes of injustice,' Filatov answers, 'lie in the social mechanism.' Romachkin has by now forgotten that he once dreamed of assassinating the Chief and has settled into life. He votes his approval of the execution of Tulayev's 'murderers,' but he is deeply troubled by his act. 'Did I betray pity? Should I have betrayed the Party if I had not raised my hand? What is your answer, Filatov, you who are upright, you who are a true proletarian?'

'The machine,' said Filatov, 'must operate irreproachably. That it crushes those who stand in its way is inhuman, but it is the universal law. The workmen must know the insides of the machine. Later there will be luminous and transparent machines which men's eyes can see through without hindrance. They will be machines in a state of innocence, comparable to the innocence of the heavens. Human law will be as innocent as astrophysical law. No one will be crushed. No one will any longer need pity. But today, Comrade Romachkin, pity is still needed. Machines are full of darkness, we never know what goes on inside them ....'

As long as society remains a 'dark machine,' pity will be needed. In their heroic attempt to create a 'transparent machine,' Serge's Old Bolsheviks experience what Engels called 'the tragic collision between the historically necessary postulate and the practical impossibility of its realization.' As the dark machine crushes them, they evoke the tragic responses of admiration, pity and fear. A new generation of 'toiling monkeys' will take up the struggle, preserving the continuity of Serge's collective hero, as the 'green globe' continues to revolve.

Praxis and the Victor Serge Public Library in Moscow

The opening of the Victor Serge Library in Moscow 1997 culminated a successful international project which began in 1995 with 'Books for Struggle,' a campaign I organized to 'send political dynamite to Russia' by shipping left-wing books and journals donated by U.S. activists and publishers to Moscow. To quote the 'Books for Struggle' Appeal: 'Russian activists and intellectuals have been cut off for seventy-five years from serious information about Western labor struggles and trends in socialist thought. Such knowledge is vital to the new Russian left that is struggling to find its way under the most difficult and confusing conditions.' During 1995-96 forty six cartons of donated radical material were collected and stored in the office of *News & Letters* in Chicago. The Victor Serge Foundation organized the shipment by truck, ship, and rail to Moscow via Hamburg. The Institute of Comparative Politology offered them a space – a near-miracle in high-rent Moscow. Renfrey Clarke, the Moscow-based Australian journalist, organized the actual miracle of getting them through customs, where Russian officials had impounded them. He enlisted the aid of an unemployed actor, who impersonated an irate *apparatchik* and cowed the officials. The next problem, was finding a place for the library in Moscow, where rents were skyrocketing.

In the Spring of 1997 Julia and Alexei Gusev announced the good news to comrades in the West. 'The Victor Serge Public Library in Moscow has been open since the 1st of May. It is the first and only Russian library to take up the task of acquainting the Russian public with scholarly and political literature of a left-wing (anti-capitalist and anti-bureaucratic) orientation. We are working in cooperation with the Self-Government Committee of a Moscow neighborhood,' the Gusev's continued. 'Books are lent out, there are classes and discussions, most recently on the 1936 Spanish Revolution. The Library Committee appeals to all organizations and individuals that would like to support the spread of left-wing ideas and the development of the workers' movement in Russia to help our work.' The Library welcomes donations of books and journals as well as financial contributions (see address below).'

With over 6,000 books and periodicals in Russian, English, French, German, Spanish and Italian, the Serge Library brings to the Russian public the radical, alternative traditions of democratic and libertarian socialism that were forbidden in Soviet times and are rarely discussed in Putin's Russia. It is the only center in Russia where readers can access a wealth of works written from critical perspectives on Marxism, anarchism, syndicalism, Trotskyism, feminism, trade unionism, literature, social science and the history of radical and workers' movements in various countries. The catalogue is computerized and available to other libraries in Russia. The Library is thus a treasure house for Russian students, academics, activists, scholars and youth who are trying to develop a critical view of the world and thinking about how to change it. Functioning as a neighbourhood public library, it also serves as a sort of clubhouse where discussions, lectures, seminars and gatherings of various left-wing organizations take place.

Another goal of the project was to create a center around the books where

members of the fragmented Russian 'new left' could come together for discussion and reflection around the donated books The Library was set up by he Praxis Research and Education Center, created 'on the initiative of representatives of various left-wing currents (from democratic socialists to anarcho-syndicalists), with support from the Victor Serge Foundation.' and named after Victor Serge (1890-1947) the Franco-Russian writer and revolutionary who incarnated the anti-totalitarian resistance to Stalinist Communism and whose ideas englobed Marxism and Anarchism. The Praxis Research and Education Center undertakes publications, research and international conferences. To date it has published Victor Serge's Memoirs of a Revolutionary, and novel *Conquered City* in Julia Guseva's Russian translations, as well as the papers of Praxis Conferences. Praxis is also known for its courageous public support of human rights in Chechnya (hence under government pressure). Today more than ever, Praxis needs international support.

Praxis Today

The good news is that Praxis Center and the Victor Serge Library in Moscow, of which I am one of the founders along with Julia and Alexei Gusev, has survived for well over a decade under the most trying conditions, both political and material. Indeed, we now have satellite libraries and active study groups in Ukraine and Bielarus. Our Moscow Public Library has twice been forced to move under political pressure. The officials simply closed the library (where we also served the neighborhood's needs with ordinary Russian general interest books) for unneeded 'repairs' which can only be done after we leave. Our struggle to maintain a space for study and discussion open to ordinary working people and scholars as has entailed exasperating skirmishes with Moscow City bureaucrats. Not easy to find a safe haven for what is now a huge collection of over 6,000 documents in five or six languages (all computer catalogued). In February 2009, the Library has once again been evicted from a community space which our comrades spent hundreds of hours rehabilitating. Renting commercial space in Moscow is simply out of the question. Fortunately, the Library has just found a new home: two rooms in a building owned by various free trade unions.

As for propagating anti-totalitarian socialist, humanist and anarchist ideas and publications in Russia's increasingly repressive political climate, this is the situation at present. Apparently we're still tolerated as long as we stick to translating and publishing serious books (well, mostly serious if you include the Russian version of my *Revolutionary KIT*). On the other hand the there have been serious problems finding printer willing to bring out *Radical Thought,* Praxis' feisty little magazine which satirizes the government and openly opposes the occupation of Chechnya. (Praxis has also been collecting material aid – books, clothes, etc – for Chechan refugees and works with the Chechan Human Rights movements – a very daring act under Yeltsin and Putin's murderous regime). As a result, *Radical Thought* now appears on line at www.praxiscenter.ru where it has many more hits per week than it ever had readers.

In terms of serious publications, as we have seen Praxis has already brought out a number of books by or about Victor Serge, translated by Ildar Rismukhamedov, Alexei Gusev and Julia Guseva, Praxis' librarian: *From Revolution to Totalitarianism: Memoirs of a Revolutionary* (2001), the novel *Conquered City* (2002) and an anthology entitled *Victor Serge: Socialist Humanism against Totalitarianism* (2003). Other anthologies include *Decadence of Capitalism* (2001) and *Left Communists in Russia*, 1918-1930s (2008). Other recent titles include Voline. *The Unknown Revolution*, 1917-1921 (an anarchist participant-witness' history of the Makhnovist movement), Maximilien Rubel's *Marx Critic of Marxism* (2006) and Stanislao Pugliese. Carlo Rosselli: *Liberal Socialism and Anti-Fascist Action* (2007). In the works are original Russian translations of Raya Dunayevskaya's *Marxism and Freedom,* Jurg Ulrich's biography of Lev Kamenev, Victor Serge's *Life and Death of Leon Trotsky* and *Libertarian Socialism,* an anthology of Daniel Guérin's anarcho-Marxist writings., Johathan Neale's *Stop Global Warming* and a collection of articles on 'The Anti-Authoritarian Left in XXth Century.'

How does Praxis do it? Praxis receives no grants from foundations or other big donors. Much of Praxis' success is due to the dogged idealism, dedication and hard unpaid work of Julia, Alexei and the comrades around them, many of them dissidents and activists from the 'Eighties. The Victor Serge Foundation recycles the meager royalties of Serge's books to pay for translations and printing costs, and Praxis has a few other international friends able to make donations in the low four figures. But we sure could use more help! Please end your checks to the address below.

Praxis' annual International Scientific and Practical Conferences have been more or less tolerated for a decade. The problem is finding a place to meet. The beautiful Andrei Sakharov Center (named for the great physicist and human rights hero), one of our former hosts, is now under government and church attack and may be forced to close. The pretext stemmed from a 'blasphemous' painting in an experimental art exhibition at the Center. The exhibition (and the Center) were trashed by Russian Orthodox vigilantes, who went un-punished. Indeed, the Center was prosecuted for 'provoking' this breach of public and is now tied up in court). Praxis works closely with the *Memorial* Society, whose volunteer staff of interviewers, archivists and historians has collected thousands of testimonies, not only of Stalinism's victims, but also of the anti-totalitarian socialist resistance during the Terror years. We held our last joint conference (July 2008) in the meeting on the top floor of the Plekhanov Foundation with a view of the Kremlin across the Moscow River. *Memorial's* offices in Moscow include a meeting hall in the basement. Alas, now *Memorial* is facing repairs and dearth of funds to pay the rent.

International Conferences attract both scholars and activists of various anarchist and anti-Stalinist socialist tendencies from throughout the ex-Soviet space (Ukraine, Belarus, Uzbekistan) as well as from France, Belgium, Switzerland, the U.K., Turkey, Iran, Denmark and India. The debates are sometimes riotous. But the scholarship is top-notch, based on serious research in the Soviet Archives. I am happy to report that at our 2007 and 2008 our network of anarchists, social-revolutionaries, critical Marxists, ecologists and radical democrats, achieved a remarkable consensus about what went wrong in the Russian Revolution, and we have begun orienting our discussions toward how to apply these lessons contemporary topics and the future. Which is my own preoccupation in this book, parts of which have appeared in Russian. For the past two years, Praxis, in alliance with various Green groups, has been holding 'scientific and programmatic' (Soviet Russian for 'scholarly and practical') conferences on the subject of Ecology and Socialism in an ecocological camp on the shores of the Black Sea in the Crimea. The air in the Ukraine since the Orange Revolution is much freer than in Russia. Internationalists are more than welcome. The interaction is intense (so is the partying, Russian-style). See our site for information about upcoming conferences. www.praxiscenter.ru

Tax-deductable financial contributions to Praxis should be made out to the 'Victor Serge Foundation' and mailed to 16 rue de la Teinturerie, 34000 Montpellier, France.

Political Terror in Russia Today

As this book goes to press, we have received the following Appeal was received from our comrades of the Praxis Center and Victor Serge Public Library in Mosow: 'On 19 January 2009 our comrade, human rights lawyer Stanislav Markelov, and young anti-fascist journalist Anastasia Baburova were assassinated in the center of Moscow. Stanislav Markelov, 34, defended the interests of victims of Russian government's policy in Chechnya, anti-fascists,

 activists of independent trade unions and social movements. As a convinced democrat and socialist he participated in various campaigns for justice and freedom in Russia and internationally. As some of you may remember, he was a co-chair of Praxis seminar on situation in North Caucasus at the Russian Social Forum in St-Petersburg, 2006. The murder of Markelov and Baburova is definitely an act of political terror. Most probably, responsibility for this crime belongs to ultra-right gangsters, whose activity is growing in Russia every day. Attacks on 'non-white' people on the streets of Moscow and other cities became something usual, and several prominent anti-fascists were killed recently. Other victims of political terrorism are oppositional journalists, principled critics of the existing Russian political regime – Anna Politkovskaya, Magomed Evloev, Mikhail Beketov...

The growth of pro-fascist forces in Russia is objectively encouraged by the whole political atmosphere in the country. While acts of political terrorism mostly go unpunished, the authorities and their mass media are engaged in hysterical propaganda of 'patriotism', authoritarianism, great-power sentiments, hostility towards external and internal 'enemies'. Under such conditions, criminals against humanity (both of present and past) are painted as 'heroes' and those struggling against them as 'traitors'. The last article by Markelov, 'Patriotism as diagnosis' (published on Praxis web-site) was devoted precisely to denouncing these awful ideas. And one hour before his assassination, Stanislav spoke at the press-conference protesting against pre-term release from prison of the war criminal Colonel Budanov, who raped and killed a Chechen woman. Stanislav was a legal representative of her relatives, he received many threats from supporters of 'heroic officer' Budanov – and was killed a few days after the latter's release...

The release of Budanov and the murder of Markelov are certainly linked, even if not directly: both characterize the real situation in Russia today. Though now the world civil society can't stop the political terrorism in Russia by its own forces, it could be able to exert pressure on Russian authorities by showing that their passive or even objectively encouraging attitude towards escalating fascist violence ruins the international 'image' of the Russian state, finally discredit in the eyes of the global public opinion. Therefore, we ask you to send letters to Russian Embassies in your countries, expressing indignation about political terrorism in Russia, demanding thorough investigation of murder of Stanislav Markelov and Anastasia Baburova and punishment of its organizers.'

So it is that eighty years after Stalin had Victor Serge arrested, forty years after Khruschev opened the *Gulag,* and twenty years Gorbachev finally ended the Stalinist Terror, the disciples of Serge are once again the victims of political terror in Moscow. We ask our readers to respond to this to this Appeal. I only met Stanislav Markelov once, but Yelena Milashina, Baburov's colleague at the independent news weekly *Novaya gazeta,* knew him well. She writes:

'Stanislav Markelov was an exceptional lawyer. He took on hopeless and dangerous cases. A Moscow attorney, he was constantly in Chechnya, representing the interests of the victims of extra-judicial punishment and torture. He also dealt with cases elsewhere of those who had been attacked by Russia's fascist groups. Stanislav defended those who were killed or humiliated by the State. He was a friend to our newspaper and its legal advisor. He was responsible for the civil cases of Anna Politkovskaya, defending those she wrote about. After the murder of Anna Politkovskaya, with whom Stanislav Markelov was closely linked through North Caucasian affairs, we realised that more of our people — the newspaper's journalists, lawyers and rights activists — could be next. After Anna was killed many people waited for the regime to speak clearly and take decisive action. What we actually heard would have better not been said. On Monday the list of our losses wascontinued by Markelov and Baburova. It's no surprise. We are not the only ones to pick up the message being sent out by the regime: all the country's fascist trash also understand it very clearly. The killers have no fear because they know they will not be punished. But neither are their victims afraid, because when you defend others you cease to fear. Those today who are fearful are the people who keep out of trouble, trying to survive these bad times, when the bad times (for some reason) never seem to end.

It was not by chance that Stanislav and Nastya had been friends for many years (she was only 25!) They were people who had an absolutely clear understanding of good and evil. Such abstractions acquire meaning when people act. Markelov and Baburova were both left-wing and anti-fascist activists. He had defended the anti-fascist group Anti-Fa, and she had been hired by the paper to write about neo-Nazis, and quoted Markelov in her articles. In April 2004 he was attacked in the Moscow Metro by five skinheads, who beat him up, shouting nationalist slogans and denouncing his work against Budanov. Anti-fascist activity too has become very dangerous. In October

2008 neo-fascist skinheads kicked16-year-old Olga Rukosyla to death in Irkutsk; and stabbed 27-year-old Fyodor Filatov to death in Moscow. In January 2009 the young leftist Anton Stradimov was beaten to death in Moscow. Racist violence is monitored by the excellent Sova Centre, which publishes regular updates on its web-site in Russian and English.

The daily *Izvestia* for 21 January 2009 offers another possible explanation. The killer carried out his assassination on a busy street in broad daylight. He did not drop his gun, but calmly walked into a nearby Metro station. And the 'Makarov' pistol is standard police issue. Was he a police officer? The police could have had a grudge against Markelov. In April 2008 there was a brawl in Sokolniki police station in Moscow. Five youths were beaten up, but were charged with assaulting police officers. One of the youths was represented by Markelov, who succeeded in having charges pressed against police. On the day of the murder, the case was at its peak

Part V:

Killing the Jews

Schindler's List or E.T. Goes to Auschwitz

Good intentions don't necessarily make good movies. Steven Spielberg's *Schindler's List* was inspired by the director's revulsion at ethnic cleansing in Bosnia and other forms of racism. His highly acclaimed film about the fate of Jews in Nazi-occupied Poland couldn't have come at a better time what with so-called "revisionist" historians denying the reality of the Holocaust and gaining credibility. Spielberg's moving story and vivid images will bring the reality of the systematic destruction of European Jewry home to millions of viewers, not only in the U.S. but also in Germany and East Europe, where the subject has been taboo for fifty years. Yet if *Schindler's List* has all the power of a major Hollywood production, Spielberg's deeply flawed film also embodies Hollywood's failings.

Schindler's List is based on the true story of Oskar Schindler, a Nazi businessman who saved 1100 Jews from the gas chambers. He did by employing them as slave laborers in an enterprise originally capitalized by squeezing money out of ghettoized Jews in Cracow, Poland. The exceptional story of the emergence of Schindler's underlying decency and of his remarkable success in beating the Nazi system deserves to be told. *Schindler's List* will certainly be seen by millions who will never be exposed to gritty documentaries like *Shoah* and *The Sorrow and the Pity*. With its happy ending and its focus on an identifiable Everyman character, Spielberg's film is able to confront mass audiences with a subject so horrifying as to be quite literally unbelievable.

But does *Schindler's List* truly succeed in awakening its mass audience to the reality of the Holocaust experience? Alas, in curious, but quite specific ways Spielberg's film actually invites its audience to deny that reality.

The Holocaust, a "Myth"?

To begin with, the film explicitly fails to contradict the revisionist thesis that Nazi's use of gas chambers at Auschwitz for mass extermination of Jews is a "myth." The first mention of the gas chambers in the film is a rumor, which Schindler's Jewish women refuse to believe: "Why kill us?" they reason. "We are valuable workers for the German war effort."

289

Then, as the film reaches its climax, these women, whose lives the audience had considered "saved" (Schindler had bought them from the Nazis), are shipped to Auschwitz by mistake. Our expectations are suddenly reversed. We witness the horror of the train entering the Death Camp... Night and fog, dogs and searchlights. The shaved heads of naked, terrified women herded into sealed chambers marked "Bath-Disinfectant." Hysterical farewell embraces: the terrible rumor was apparently true. As we watch and listen in horror, the shower-heads begin to hiss, and out comes – water! Fresh, cool, life-giving water to soothe and cleanse the parched throats and bruised bodies after the slave-labor camps and the cattle-cars.

This stunning anti-climax is never explained, and the audience is only too glad to have been spared the horror. Next morning, Schindler arrives like John Wayne and rescues "his" Jewish women for the second time. As the women re-embark on the train to safety, we get glimpses of dead bodies and smoking chimneys. Viewers who already believe in the gas chambers are free to imagine what they believe. So are Holocaust-deniers, who are free to imagine that the bodies represent workers who died of disease and the smoke from the chimneys comes from the factory.

Nothing has been shown but a shower-bath. At the heart of Spielberg's darkness there is – avoidance.

After this central anti-climax, his film has no place to go but down, and it wallows in bathos for the next un-dramatic hour or so. We are treated to endless scenes of tearful re-uniting, lip-quivering gratitude, and heroic modesty with "Schindler's Jews" (they are never referred to otherwise) standing around their Gentile savior in carefully choreographed groups with dumb grins on their faces, like the Munchkins after Dorothy has saved them from the Wicked Witch. The audience walks out numbed as if they had attended a B'nai Brith Awards Ceremony minus the boiled chicken.

The Jews of Silence

Even during the first half of the film, which is far more dramatic and historically grounded, "Schindler's Jews" are never developed as characters. Jews are depicted merely as objects of Schindler"s benevolence or as victim's of the Nazi's cruelty. There is no space in Spielberg's very long film for developed dialogues between Jewish husbands and wives or Jewish parents and children. Indeed, Spielberg's Jewish "characters" only get to speak when they are spoken to – by Nazi officials or by Schindler himself. The actors are reduced to speaking lines like "*Ja, Herr Direktor*" or later, tearfully and gratefully: "God bless you, *Herr Direktor*." Rarely do we hear Jews talk to each other.

290

The two exceptions to this rule are themselves remarkable for their curious ambiguity. One is the scene, cited above, where a Jewish woman passes on a rumor about the gas chambers to her companions and is disbelieved. In the other, a circle of idle Jewish men are shown schmoozing in a Krakow street, having just been herded into the ghetto and deprived of their occupations. They conclude that "Here, we are free." Again, at the heart of darkness – avoidance.

Visually, too, Spielberg focalizes his Jews almost exclusively through Schindler's Gentile eyes. For example, we look down with Schindler and his mistress (on horseback) from a cliff high above the Krakow ghetto as we watch the SS round up the Jews for the camps. Although the film is shot in black and white to give it a documentary flavor, during this scene the dress of one little Jewish girl is tinted red, which enables the audience, looking down with Schindler, to follow her individual fate during the roundup. Later, we see the red dress again through Schindler's eyes as the child's body is dragged by on a cart at Auschwitz while Schindler is loading "his" Jewish girls on the rescue train. Thus does Spielberg "individualize" Jews.

To be sure, during the scenes of the SS roundup of the ghetto Jews, we are shown a few examples of Jews taking action to save themselves. However, they are soon captured and brutally killed. In Spielberg's Krakow there is no salvation outside of Schindler's list (although in real life, some Jews did resist and even survive).

The visual and auditory messages are clear. There are two types of Jews: passive victims of the Nazis and passive benefactors of Schindler. The Jewish "characters" barely even rise to the level of stereotypes, their main function being to act as stand-ins for the actual names on the real-life Schindler's list. There is hardly a need for actors (as opposed to extras) in this production, although Ben Kingsley struggles manfully with the ungrateful role of the grateful Itzhak Stern, Schindler's Jewish accountant and reluctant confidant.

Indeed, Spielberg dispenses with actors and actually shows us the real-life survivors at the end of his film. A dozen of Schindler's Jews, most of them in their eighties today, file by the real-dead Schindler's grave, smiling and grateful and above all silent. As the survivors place stones on the tomb, the audience reads subtitles proclaiming their names – remembered from the famous List. I suppose one could argue with the authenticity of this dubious shift from fiction-film to documentary, but I would gladly have accepted it if only, at long last, Speilberg had allowed some real-life Jews to speak for themselves! No wonder Claude Lanzmann, whose documentary *Shoah* is made up entirely of first-person survivor narratives, protested *Schindler's List*.

Schindler Unmasked

Schindler alone is active in Spielberg's film. He is the omnipotent entrepreneur who pits his capitalist skills against the omnipotent SS and wins: first by piling up a fortune exploiting Jewish slave-labor, then by keeping his business going in the face of the "final solution," eventually by rescuing his Jewish workers.

In Spielberg's fable, the capitalist ethic is thus depicted ambiguously as saving humanity, or at least a remnant of Jewish humanity. To his great credit, Spielberg also shows us the larger reality, which is the fact that the camps were all slave-labor enterprises run at a profit for German businesses. What the film perhaps cannot be expected to show is the big picture – that Nazism was the final solution to the crisis of German capitalism.[162] To be sure, Spielberg's film makes tricking the Nazis look almost easy: a little bribe here, some psychology there and voilà! Of course, Schindler is as much a con artist as an entrepreneur, but he soon has the sinister SS buffaloed much as in the world of TV Hogan's Heroes pull the wool over the eyes of their cute dumb German captors.

This is the level on which Spielberg's film fails to convince both as document and as drama. Like Hogan's Heroes, Spielberg's Jews remain fat and relatively well-dressed throughout World War Two! They look nothing like the photographs of skeletal concentration camps survivors that horrified those of us who were alive in 1945 when the camps were liberated and which continue to shock today. In Spielberg's sanitized "ET Goes to Auschwitz" version of the Holocaust, Schindler's Jews are not even believable victims.

---

[162] The true story of the real Schindler shows how one decent businessman was able to save 1100 Jews without losing his life, indeed while amassing a sizable fortune. It is good that Schindler be remembered and his story told. But Spielberg's monocular and monopolist focalization on his fictional Schindler prevents the audience from asking the obvious question: why didn't more German businessmen save more Jews? I'm sure in real life it was much more difficult than in the movies, but the fact remains that German businesses like I.G. Farben profited from the slave labor camps and calculated down to the last gram of bread what was necessary to keep their workers dying slowly enough to maintain profits until the weak were gassed and sent to the ovens to be replaced by ever-new supplies of Jewish labor. Every mark and *pfennig* was accounted for. No one but Schindler – who in any case was apparently a Czech, not a German, and more of a con-man than a capitalist – seems to have though to keep them alive, even for the value of their skills. Schindler tried to convince his business colleagues to follow his example and fails. Spielberg's film thus depicts capitalism's ethic as both complicit in the Holocaust and resisting it. One cannot ask for more.

292

Thus, during the final self-congratulatory sequences set in Czechoslovakia, where Schindler has managed to install "his" Jews in a factory in his home town, the Jewish extras appear as chubby and grateful as the happy slaves on Scarlett O'Hara's plantation. In these crowd scenes Spielberg's well-fleshed extras are shown massed, Hollywood style, like Dorothy's Munchkins. Why didn't Spielberg, that stickler for visual authenticity, bother to hire out-of-work actors with AIDS as extras? After all, they used real midgets in The Wizard of Oz.

Even the extras' costumes fail to convince us they have endured five years in the camps. Their "slave" outfits look as fresh as if they had just been sewn by the mothers of the Hollywood Hills Jewish Center for their children's' Passover Pageant. No wonder there wasn't a wet eye in the house, when I saw *Schindler* at the East Hartford shopping mall Cinemas.

Even the character of Schindler, whom Spielberg does attempt to develop as an individual, gets spoiled and sentimentalized in these concluding scenes. Throughout the film Schindler had appeared as an opaque figure, a cynical bon-vivant who, having consciously chosen to make his fortune out of war and slave-labor, inexplicably stops short of implicating himself in the ultimate Nazi horror and chooses to invest part of his profits in bribes to save the workers who have made him rich. The poker-face he uses to deal with the SS is an ideal mask to conceal his motives from the audience and create a totally credible character whose singular aura is enhanced by mystery.

Then Spielberg throws it all away by having Schindler remove his mask before his final getaway. While his chorus of grateful Jews masses around his waiting Mercedes, Schindler breaks down blubbering about how many more Jews he might have saved if only he had drunk less Champagne! It is as if, at the end of Casablanca, Claude Rains, the Vichy Police Captain who saves Bogart, had begun beating his breast about how guilty he felt lining his pockets instead of exiting on the immortal line: "I am only a poor corrupt French official!" Alas, Schindler's tear-jerking exit scene is more of a homage to Dorothy's or to ET's farewells than to Claude Rains' and Bogie's tight-lipped, cynical/sentimental departure from Casablanca.

Schindler's weepy exit lines not only destroy him as a consistent character, they also undermine the logical premise of the plot by suddenly making it appear that this unscrupulous conman-cum-entrepreneur had secretly been nourishing some sort of benevolent plan all along! But only a cynical Schindler who had no scruples about spending his evenings wining and dining Nazi mass-murderers to win contracts could possibly have brought off this tour de force rescue under the very noses of the SS.

Spielberg's sentimentalized Hollywood ending not only breaks with dramatic consistency, it also violates historical reality. According to Thomas Keneally, the author of the nonfiction novel on which Spielberg based his film, the real Schindler actually fled with a small fortune in jewels he had stashed away.

The final horrendous inaccuracy occurs after Schindler's departure, when Schindler's Jews march off into the sunset over the green fields of Czechoslovakia (now in Technicolor like the Munchkins after Dorothy drops out of grim, black-and-white Kansas and saves them). As the camera pans back, the music comes up in a magnificent chorale of triumph and liberation, sung in Hebrew. One imagines some traditional Jewish song or one born of the Holocaust, like the authentic camp song "Peatbog Soldiers." But no! I immediately recognized the strains of "Jerusalem of Gold," the stirring anthem commissioned in 1967 to celebrate the victory of the Israeli Defense Forces over the Arabs – a hymn familiar to anyone who has been a tourist in Israel or attended an Israel fundraiser. Let's not even talk about the ideological twist this 1967 Zionist song gives to this story of the Holocaust – especially for the Jewish audience. Have Schindler's Jews been transmogrified by Spielberg into Rabin's Israelis?

One might also object to Spielberg's exclusive focus on Jews as Holocaust victims, to the exclusion of the millions of Communists, Socialists, Gypsies, Christians, homosexuals and resistance fighters who were sent to the camps. But again, my quarrel is with the film Spielberg DID make, not the one he didn't. To conclude: I had entered the theater with much trepidation, having grown up during the Holocaust, an American descendant of Krakow Jews and one who is easily upset by graphic movies. I left the theater dry-eyed, with a distinct taste of cold boiled chicken in my mouth.

Will the Real Holocaust Deniers Please Stand Up?

I have long believed that discussions of the Holocaust focused far too much attention on the murderous activities of the Germans and their pro-Nazi Axis accomplices, while neglecting the complicity of the Allied 'United Nations' and neutral governments. True, the Nazis, abetted by their French, Croat, Hungarian and other collaborators, performed the actual ethnic cleansing by rounding up the Jews, seizing their property, and shipping them off to the concentration-camps and the death-ovens – setting the example for today's Serb and Croat Red-Brown dictatorships to imitate. But Hitler's dream of a *Judenrein* ("cleansed of Jews") Europe could not have been achieved without the complicity of the U.S., Britain, Russia, Switzerland, the Vatican, *et al.* – any more than Milosevic's and Tudjman's dreams of ethnically cleansed Yugoslavia today.

I use the world "complicity" not in some vague, passive, moral sense, but in the strict judicial sense. For the neutral and Allied governments were witting accomplices before, during and after the fact of Nazi war crimes against the humanity – and what is more, accomplices who shared in the spoils of money and property stolen from the Jews! Consider the following: 1. The Allied governments were accomplices *before* the Holocaust in that they systematically shut their doors to the persecuted Jews of Germany and the Nazi-occupied territories who had legitimate grounds for seeking asylum under international law. 2. The Allies were accomplices *during* the Holocaust in that they systematically hid the knowledge of the death-camps, thus lulling the Jews into believing the Nazi cover-story of "labor camps" and enabling the Hitlerites to round up their ignorant victims "like sheep." 3. The Allies were accomplices *after* the Holocaust in that they systematically helped the Nazi war criminals to escape with part of the booty they looted from the Jews, while hiding their own part of the booty in secret vaults where the Jewish survivors could not claim it. Please allow me to develop these three deliberately provocative accusations in more detail:[163]

1) Jewish Exclusion By refusing the Jews (and left anti-fascists) asylum, the foreign offices of Britain, the U.S. and their dependencies in Latin America deliberately condemned millions to persecution and eventual death.[164] These

---

[163] Everyone interested in this question should start with Arthur D. Morse's pioneering exposé *While Six Million Died: A chonicle of American Apathy.*

[164] Imagine the effect of post-war economic development of the South American republics if their governments had taken in a couple of million Jewish engineers, businessmen, teachers, doctors, lawyers, scientists, skilled bakers, jewelers, tailors and mechanics. Within a generation or two, this leaven

governments uniformly refused to recognize Hitler's persecutions (including the murder of anti-fascists and other non-Jews) as an international emergency. Instead, they punctiliously enforced the most absurd provisions of their immigration codes and visa requirements. The notorious anti-Semitism of the classes from which Western diplomats were then recruited does not suffice to explain the systematic rejection of these useful and otherwise inoffensive refugees. Although the diplomats' vile upper-class caddishness was given free rein, the racist policy decisions were made at the top for reasons of state, racism being the health of the capitalist state.

This closed-door policy of the capitalist democracies faced with Hitler's campaign to create a "Jew-free" Reich during 1933-1945 was historically unique and a direct cause of the "Final Solution." After all, there was nothing new or original in Hitler's plan to scapegoat the Jews, persecute them, steal their property, and then get rid of them, leaving his Empire free of Jews. The *Fürher* was only following in the noble footsteps of European sovereigns over the centuries. In 1290, King Edward banished all Jews from England... In 1306, Philip IV expelled all Jews from France, seizing their property and money owed them... In 1492 Ferdinand and Isabella celebrated their marriage and the unity of the Spanish monarchy by expelling the Jews, and so on... However, previous to 1933-1945 other states had always been found willing to welcome the fleeing Jewish refugee populations, if only to use them, squeeze them, and expel them subsequently. The unique difference in 1933-1940 was the democracies' systematic refusal to follow tradition, leaving Hitler little choice but to introduce the "Final Solution."

2) Holocaust denial. By systematically ignoring, downplaying and keeping secret a multitude of reliable intelligence reports and survivors' tales establishing beyond reasonable doubt the existence of the death-camps, the Allied governments aided and abetted Hitler's maniacal crimes. Churchill, Roosevelt and Stalin were thus the original "negationists" whose denial of the Holocaust while it was happening enabled it to happen. There is no question that they "knew."

Although Roosevelt issued an order to his staff not to show him any documents concerning the Holocaust (Nixon didn't invent 'plausible denial') and turned a deaf ear to Eleanor's pleas for Jewish and anti-fascist refugees (among them Victor Serge), the other Allied governments officially acknowledged the fact Holocaust... And proceeded to do nothing to stop it. Nonetheless, on 24 August 1941, Radio Moscow transmitted the Appeal of the Soviet Jews: "The very existence of the Jewish people is today in doubt." On July 1, 1942 Jean Marin talked about "gas chambers" on the Free French radio broadcasting from

---

of European technical and entrepreneurial skill would have enabled Latin Americans to free themselves from dependency on the U.S., climb out of poverty and develop modern capitalist economies.

London. Finally, in December 1942, a declaration was signed by eleven Allied governments and the Free French Committee: 'The German authorities are carrying out Hitler's often repeated intention to exterminate the Jewish people in Europe.' [165] How widely was this epochal news circulated? In 1945, when the camps were finally liberated, the G.I.s and accompanying journalists saw the extent of the horror, they were totally incredulous. *Nothing* had prepared them for what they stumbled into on their advance through Germany and Poland.

All the justifiable furor over the *post-facto* scribblings of negationist 'historians' like Fourisson and his miserable defenders ironically serves to cloud the issue of the active complicity of the negationist governments and statesmen during the commission of the actual, and preventable, crimes against humanity. Instead of daring the raise the question of the guilt of Hitler's international accomplices, journalists and scholars touch at most on the question, "what could they have done?" The answer is: "a great deal." The conventional arguments over whether bombing the camps and the rails leading to them would have "diverted" planes from "important military targets" are hardly worth considering in the light of the useless bombing of Dresden. In any case, it was not by withholding the bombers but by withholding the truth that Roosevelt, Churchill, and Stalin ultimately condemned the European Jews to destruction.

It takes only a little historical imagination to picture what might have happened if the Allies had systematically used their radio, airdrop leaflet and underground propaganda apparatus to spread the word about the death camps among East European Jewry. By 1943, London was crawling with escaped Jews clamoring to tell their authentic stories in Yiddish and every language of Nazi-occupied Europe reached by Allied broadcasts and propaganda. Assuming the word reached only half the Jews and was believed by only half of them, the effort would still have resulted in a minimum of one million who could have hidden, run away, perhaps armed themselves and resisted. Now imagine the problems that a million refractory Jews would have created for Nazi administrators like Eichmann, whose vast and minutely-organized roundup operations depended on his victims' near-total passivity and cooperation. Apparently Eichmann had only a couple of hundred troops in his command. Imagine the diversionary effect on the Nazi war effort if troops had to be systematically diverted to hunt down, round up and guard these Jews.

But why not take this perfectly likely scenario one step further? Among the million-odd European Jews who might have heard and believed the truth about

---

[165] Denis Peschanski, "Extermination des juifs: que savait Vichy?" *Nouvel observateur* Sept. 18, 1997

the fate Hitler had in store for them if the Allies hadn't deliberately kept it from them, there would have been a certain percentage who would have attempted not just to escape, but to resist – as they finally did in the Warsaw Ghetto. For if many European Jews were a-political, pious and passive (like their non-Jewish counterparts), there were also plenty of hot-headed teenagers, Zionists, Bundists, Socialists, veterans of the First World War ready and able to fight. And if the Jewish resistance trapped in the Warsaw ghetto was able to inflict real harm on the Nazis with homemade weapons, what might a Jewish Resistance have accomplished if coordinated, supported and supplied by the Allies like the French, Italian, Yugoslav and other Resistance movements were?

There is nothing absurd about this notion. After all, the U.S. wartime OSS (Office of Strategic Services: predecessor of the CIA) went to great lengths to recruit its officers among such unlikely groups as labor agitators, Communists, Spanish Civil War veterans in order to drop them behind the Nazi lines and link up with their counterparts in the local *maquis*. So why didn't they send anti-fascist American Jews to help the Jews to resist? The sad fact is that the idea never occurred even, for example, to the Jews who were active in the French Resistance itself.

Forget, for a moment, the number of Jews who might have been saved by such a policy. Just think of the diversion it would have caused behind the Axis lines and of the number of Allied lives that might have been saved. And this at the minimal cost of extending to the Jews the same programs of propaganda and strategic support services the Allies aimed at stirring up the other peoples of occupied Europe; indeed at the "cost" of NOT suppressing the truth of the horrors of Nazism in the case of the Jews!

Excuse me for insisting at length on this point. The veil of "military expediency" has always concealed what seemed to me the blatant guilt of the Allies what is usually perceived as their "failure to help the Jews." But if military expediency dictated sparing Allied lives and materiel by encouraging the resistance of the Jews with the same cynicism with which the OSS encouraged the resistance of the Communists, the Gaullists, the Mafia, the Poles and *tutti quanti*, then the truth behind the veil is revealed. The truth is the predominance of Allied anti-Semitism and the complicity in Hitler's genocidal crimes of the original Holocaust deniers, Roosevelt, Churchill, Stalin and their aids.

3) After the fact: hiding the criminals and sharing the loot. It has now become general knowledge that the Vatican and the Allied Occupation forces and intelligence services (principally the OSS/CIA) conspired with neo-Nazi and anti-Communist networks throughout Europe and Latin American to organize the famous "rat-lines" which enabled thousands of notorious Nazi war-criminals to escape prosecution and reach safe havens. Indeed, the charge that the democratic governments were Nazi accomplices after the fact of the Shoah is barely controversial, since in recent years retired Allied intelligence officers have willingly told their tales, either out of guilt or in order to justify coddling Nazi war criminals as recruits in the anti-Communist crusade.

We now know how the "rat-lines" network systematically sought out Nazi war-criminals concealed under aliases in the teeming displaced persons camps, hid them in churches and monasteries, got them visas and false papers, organized their escape to Latin America, and employed them as advisors and agents. For example in training the torturers employed by the right-wing Argentinean *junta* and then loaned to the CIA to train the Nicaraguan *Contras.* So it is hardly a surprise that the world had to wait until most of the criminals had died natural deaths before learning how carefully and for how long they were protected.

The more shocking revelations of 1997 concerned the disposal of the booty the Nazi killers looted from the Jews they murdered. Not only did the Swiss banks knowingly welcome Nazi deposits that probably included gold from the teeth of death-camp victims, the banks also systematically concealed from the Jewish survivors and their relatives the records of their wartime holdings in order to embezzle the money for their own profit. Financial institutions in the U.S., Britain, and Sweden also profited by concealing confiscated Jewish wealth during the post-War period when Jewish Holocaust survivors continued to suffer and die on the road or in Allied displaced person camps for lack of money to pay for food and medicine. Hanna Arendt coined the phrase "the banality of evil" to describe the personality and activity of Nazi bureaucrats like Adolf Eichmann.

Looking soberly at the chaotic picture of half-destroyed Europe in the months after the victory of "democracy" over "Nazism," one almost has the impression that the Allies set out to finish the extermination job begun by Hitler. Indeed, in post-war Poland, thousands of returning Jewish survivors were murdered and despoiled with impunity. Jewish camp survivors wandered Europe for years as starving and homeless as DP's (Displaced Persons) with no support from the Allied governments and little charity from U.S. Jewish congregations, which had done little or nothing before and during the Holocaust for fear of bucking the government and attracting unfavorable attention to themselves, returning Jewish survivors.[166] On the one hand we see the Nazi victimizers rescued, coddled, and helped to flee; on the other the Jewish victims despoiled, neglected, persecuted, confined and forcibly prevented from fleeing to Palestine.

---

[166] I am not making this up. The official commemorative histories of local congregations which I have perused in West Hartford and Philadelphia while visiting relatives both explicitly express regret and embarrassment at their temple's inaction during the Holocaust years.

Why do I feel so particularly outraged, indignant and angry over all this particular hypocrisy? I had grown up believing that WWII was fought to defeat fascism and save the Jews from Hitler. At home, they worshiped Roosevelt. In my little bed I imagined the Allies were protecting me and other Jewish children against the ultimate Bad Guys. Then I learned the truth. We were betrayed. World War II was ending as when learning to read and learn about the world. Only once did I dare glimpsed a photo in a book of skeletal Jews in striped pajamas as a little kid. After that, I walked carefully *around* the place that book was kept. But my parents read papers and magazines like *The Nation* and the left-wing *National Guardian,* and our daily paper was the independent (no ads) *P.M.* whose star reporter was I. F. Stone, my hero and role model and a family friend. In 1946, he covered the refugee story and wrote a sensational book *Underground to Palestine* describing the plight of the homeless Jews in a heartless world. Also the Negroes: *P.M.* was the only paper that regularly covered the lynching of returning African-American G.I.s that was taking place all over the South. They got betrayed too. All this was discussed over endless cups of coffee (mine mostly milk) in our kitchen, and as they say, little pitchers have big ears.

At that time *N.Y. Post*, which most liberal Jewish NYers read, was violently anti-German, forgetting that Hitler had sent the all the German Socialists, Communists, trade-unionists and anarchists to the concentration camps before he hit on the Jews. This was the theory of "collective guilt" which Victor Serge satirizes in his novel *Unforgiving Years.* Then, a few years later, suddenly the 'Good' Germans were on our side against the nasty Russians and nobody talked about the thousands of Nazi administrators, profiteers, torturers, judges, police chiefs, professors who escaped the quickly-curtailed Nuremberg war crimes trials and were now back administering, judging, policing and professing, if not torturing.

I was eight, when the Jewish State was declared in Palestine. I learned that Jews could fight for themselves. Their cry was "Never again like sheep to the slaughter!" Sounded good. But how do you avoid going like a sheep when the whole world – including the democracies and the established European Jewish leadership – is telling you that the slaughter-house is a rest-home for sheep? Alas, many of these false leaders, these Judas goats, became prominent in Israel, as did the hardcore right wing Zionists who were ready to collaborate with Hitler to get more Jews into Palestine. So that even Israel, for political purposes, is involved in the denial of Allied complicity in the Holocaust.

If my voice sounds hoarse in this article, it's because I want to shout the truth from the housetops: put not your faith in princes!

Part VI:

Slaughtering Sacred Cows

Crimes Against Humanity

Mass Murderers
(Letter to the Editor *Hartford Advocate,* December 15, 1994)

Congratulations to President Clinton for having the courage to fire Surgeon General Elders for offending the nation with her disgusting talk of masturbation! Although decent Americans have long been justifiably outraged about abortion, the evils of masturbation have too long been kept under the covers. Yet, for each embryo that is murdered when a woman has an abortion, literally millions of potential human souls are destroyed every time a man commits the sin of Onan!

The time has come to speak out frankly: masturbators are nothing but mass murderers. They belong behind bars, where their actions can be kept under strict surveillance. Nor should so-called "juvenile offenders" be exempted. Boys adult enough to bring new lives into God's world are actually men. Let us hope that our radic-lib President, who has obviously learned the lesson of the 1994 election, will have the guts to join Newt Gingrich and the new Christian American Majority by sponsoring legislation to end this daily holocaust by making masturbation a federal offense.

Richard Greeman, West Hartford

Marching Against Onanism
(Reply to the *Hartford Advocate* December 22, 1994)

As an outward Christian soldier, I do agree with Richard Greeman's opinion ["Crimes Against Humanity," Dec. 15] that masturbation is a sin against our Lord, Jesus Christ. However, I do not agree that masturbators should be placed in prison! Onanists are not criminal; they are disturbed people who need our help, compassion and love.

For those who insist on believing that masturbation is harmless, I would offer the following facts: Every year in America, over 200,000 people are admitted to the hospital with masturbation-related afflictions, such as physical exhaustion and sore wrists; masturbation is the number one preventable cause of blindness in our country today.

I am a former masturbator who, with the help of God, overcame the semen habit. Now that I have kicked that satanic affliction I am assured a place in heaven. I also have a lot more money in my savings account now that I've stopped spending it on men's magazines, Kleenex, ostrich plumes, and laundry money for my sheets.

To those who wish to give up masturbation, I would offer the benefit of my experiences. When the urge to masturbate hits you, read the Bible (just not the "Song of Solomon). Try the new PeterPatch. Manufactured by Killpecker Pharmaceuticals of Cheyenne, Wyoming, the PeterPatch is stuck to the abdomen, just above the genitals, and periodically shoots (pardon the expression) saltpeter into your system, thus negating the sex urge. Contact MING (Masturbation Is Not Good), a nationwide support network for recovering Onanists. Just call 1-800-785-5783. Masturbation can be eradicated in our lifetime, but only if we work together!

Dean Fiora, Hartford

Master logic
(Reply to *Advocate* December 29, 1994)

Mr. Richard Greeman had very strong feelings against masturbation. (Letters, Dec. 15, "Crimes against humanity") So strong as to suggest making masturbation a federal offense. However, his argument against masturbation is ludicrous.

According to Mr. Greeman, masturbation is immoral because "literally millions of potential human souls are destroyed every time a man commits the crime of Onan." With that line of reasoning, there is nothing immoral about a woman masturbating. There is also nothing immoral about a sterile or infertile man masturbation. Yet, according to Mr. Greeman's argument, any type of birth control would be immoral as would total abstinence from sex.

I would suggest that Mr. Greeman think of a more rational argument, because this one will not get him very far.

Denise McNeil
Bristol

Get a Life

(**Advocate** January 5, 1995)

I am writing in response to Dean Fiora's letter to the editor ("Marching Against Onanism," Dec.22). Dean, it's attitudes like yours that create boundaries in a sexual society. Your strange fascination with anti-onanism is unhealthy and for the most part obnoxious. If someone wants to touch oneself in a most "impure" manner who needs your dung-slinging, fast-food Johnny-lately advice anyway.

Where is it written that self-exploration is as you have coined the term "a satanic affliction?" Which church official advised you of your "wrongdoing?" Remember Waco?
It sounds like you need one of two things: a)A lover, or b) A life.
Lee Olsen, Cheshire

Jerkin' for Joycelyn
(**Advocate** January 12, 1995)

I would have understood if Surgeon General Elders was fired after talk about legalizing drugs, or even when she claimed to support handing out contraceptives in elementary schools ["Crimes Against Humanity," Dec. 15]. But because she advocates teaching about masturbation in sex education classes. This incident just proves that the position of Surgeon General is entirely for show, a means for the White house to tell the public what the government wants them to hear.

Masturbation is a viable alternative to having intercourse. I challenge Mr. Greeman of West Hartford or an other "good" Christian to give me just one logical reason, not based on religious opinion, why masturbation should remain a stigma in our society. Mr. Greeman makes Hitler seem like a Boy Scout compared to the average Joe, equating the release of sperm through ejaculation to the slaughter of "millions of potential human souls." Little does he know that millions of spermatozoa are released every day, regardless, when a man urinates.

It is sad that so many people are ignorant in this country and very frightening that some are members of our government. If Mr. Greeman and his cronies in the Christian American Majority succeeded by incorporating their religious, moral beliefs into our laws and make, "...masturbation a federal offence," believe me, come the next election there will be some changes.

Mark Ramone, WECS Willimantic

It's Called Satire, Folks

305

(Richard Greeman replies, **Advocate** January 12, 1995)

Having been maligned in these pages as a member of the "Christian American Majority" who "makes Hitler seem like a Boy Scout" after humorously proposing that masturbation be made a "federal offense,"
(Letters, "Crimes Against Humanity," Dec. 15), I would like to defend my honor as an inveterate agnostic, occasional Onanist and firm supporter of ex-Surgeon General Joycelyn Elders.

It never occurred to me that anyone would take my absurd proposal literally. As a result, indignant masturbators and worried liberals have been ringing my phone off the wall all week. For the record, I was practicing *reductio ad absurdum* (not a form of coitus but a form of satire) when I compared a woman having an abortion (which supposedly makes her a "murderer") and a man masturbation (which by the same logic would make him a "mass murderer"). Indeed, the inspiration for this bit of adolescent silliness was Monty Python's Flying Circus, which I quote:

> Every sperm is sacred
> Every sperm is great
> If a sperm is wasted
> God gets quite irate

I did, however, hope to use irony to make some serious points. The first was to satirize the hypocrisy of the Clinton's post-election effort to climb aboard the conservative Christian bandwagon by firing Dr. Elders. (Slick Willy admits he did masturbate once, but claims he didn't come). I also wanted to satirize the hypocrisy of the so-called "Right to Life" movement, which is really about males using violence to control women's lives in the name of a perversion of "Christianity." (In contrast, the real Jesus defended the life of a whore and said to her hypocritical attackers: "Let him who is without sin cast the first stone.")

Alas, in America today the insanity of the violent Right has become prevalent to the point where nothing seems too outrageous to be taken seriously - even the absurd humor of a satirist playing the Devil's Advocate!

So let me apologize for any discomfort I may have unwittingly caused to readers who practice what may be the most fundamental form of love, self-love. Denise McNeill of Bristol ("Master Logic," Dec. 29) didn't realize how accurate she was in calling my argument against masturbation "ludicrous," a word the dictionary defines as "hilarious through obvious absurdity." Thanks, too, Denise, for being logical enough to recognize that my argument wouldn't apply to women masturbating. Not unsurprisingly, most of my indignant callers were female masturbators. Given the physiological advantage of the clitoris over the penis, they had a larger stake in keeping masturbation legal.

306

Thanks, too, to Dean Fiora ("Marching Against Onanism," Dec. 22), who took my absurdity one hilarious step further by inventing the masturbation-inhibiting "Peter Patch." Dean may be amused or appalled to learn that anti-masturbation devices employing electro-shock were actually marketed during the Victorian era. Parents attached them to their children's hands and genitals at bedtime to prevent them from touching themselves while sleeping. (One of Freud's most famous cases was a patient named Schwaber whose father was a leading German proponent of this invention and presumably used it on his son, who naturally developed paranoid persecution fantasies. Unfortunately, Freud refused to look at the evidence of actual parental abuse and instead used the case of Schwaber to spin out his theory that paranoia results from repressed homosexuality.)

Finally, it may be of interest to Mark Ramone ("Jerkin' for Joycelyn" Dec. 22) that the story of Onan in the Bible (Genesis 38) is not really about masturbation at all. Onan's sin was his failure to impregnate his brother's widow, as was the custom in patriarchal society (later codified in Mosaic Law, Deuteronomy 25). When Onan "let his seed spill upon the ground" he was practicing coitus interruptus, not masturbation.

Conclusion: not only is masturbation moral for girls, the Bible says it's cool for boys as well. And remember, folks, the great thing about self-sex is... it's safe and you don't have to look your best!

Yours Truly, Richard Greeman

Shoot 'em first and give 'em a fair trial later!

Woody Allen, in his good old days as a stand-up comic, used to run a hilarious routine that dramatized every schoolchild's worst fears. A police SWAT team surrounds Woody's parents' house and threatens through a bullhorn to use guns and teargas unless the kid comes out with his hands up – holding his overdue library book!

Woody's comic paranoid fantasy has turned into a tragic reality as U.S. law enforcement agencies increasingly resort to major military sieges and deadly force against citizens accused – but not convicted – of relatively minor offenses. This was the ultimate tragedy of Waco, Texas, in which dozens of innocent women and children were gassed and then burned to death in order to "protect" them against unproven charges of sexual abuse by a cult leader who was charged (but never tried) with minor violations of the firearms code.

David Coresh was indeed a maniac. But was he guilty of possession of illegal assault rifles? Since he was never brought to trial, we will never know. In any case, if convicted, he would only have served months, at most a year or so in jail. Well and good, but what about the agents he shot during the initial helicopter attack on his house?

On Friday July 9, 1993 an Idaho jury acquitted a man whose home was subjected to an 11-day Waco-like siege. Although Randy Weaver, a white supremacist and gun collector, in fact killed a Federal Marshal during the final shootout, the jury declared it was self-defense and rebuked the government for attacking Weaver's home. The jurors did, however, convict Weaver on the original charges that led to the bloody standoff last summer during which Federal sharpshooters hiding in the woods near Weaver's isolated cabin first shot his dog, who sniffed them out, then his fourteen-year old son (in the back), and finally his wife and 10-month baby, who were standing unarmed in the cabin door hundreds of yards from the stakeout – a sixteen-month operation which involved 400 agents and cost a million dollars.
Weaver may now serve several months in jail for a disputed sale of a gun to an undercover agent. But who will bring back the lives of his wife, his children, and the misguided Federal Marshal?

Apparently the U.S. law enforcement community – from publicity-hungry Alcohol and Firearms agents in Waco, Texas all the way up to the F.B.I., Attorney General Reno and President Clinton in Washington – are taking their inspiration from Rambo movies, old Westerns and SWAT reruns, rather than U.S. law, which provides that citizens are innocent until proven guilty in a

308

court of law by a jury of their peers. Instead of Perry Mason, we are seeing the government take the Late Show vigilante approach: "Come on, boys! Let's get up a posse, shoot 'em first, and give 'em a fair trial later!" This vigilante style has also infected the conduct of U.S. foreign policy. President Clinton, his ratings lagging, could not wait for the conclusion of the ongoing Kuwaiti trial of alleged Iraqi agents accused of a clumsy and unsuccessful plot against ex-President Bush. On the basis of a "conclusive" C.I.A. report which offered zero supporting evidence, the Arkansas gunslinger simply declared Saddam Hussein "guilty" and fired from the hip.[167]

Twenty cruise missiles and six civilian corpses later, the Kuwait trial is falling to pieces, grounded on the rock of faulty evidence, coerced "confessions" and a wacky story of bumbling drug smugglers and inexperienced "terrorists" so amateurish that not even the maddest of movie dictators would hire them to kill someone as important as ex-President Bush. Never mind, "justice" has already been done. But what ever happened to due process, diplomacy, sanctions, the World Court?

And while we're asking, what about Manuel Noriega, the Panamanian head of state and former Bush/C.I.A. operative whose spectacular arrest destroyed half a city and left hundreds of civilians dead and thousands homeless? Did the end – arresting an accused drug dealer – justify the means: reducing Panama to ruins by a massive military invasion? And if the U.S. routinely carries out unilateral armed attacks on foreign heads of state like Saddam and Noriega (not to mention Quadaffi and Castro), doesn't this practice legitimize what honest Americans fear most: terrorist attacks on our own leaders - or on innocent U.S. civilians? Will not foreign groups who cannot afford Marine battalions or Cruise missiles retaliate with car bombs? [168]

---

[167] Only governments that respect their own laws and follow due process can answer such questions and face such juries. But the U.S. was already putting Rambo tactics ahead of the law as early as 1963, when our soon-to-be martyred President John F. Kennedy authorized the assassination of President Diem of South Vietnam (an anti-Communist ally) and the attempted assassination of Fidel Castro (an opponent). Did JFK not symbolically sign his own death warrant by these lawless acts? Isn't that what Malcolm X meant by his controversial (and much misunderstood remark), "The chickens have come home to roost"?

[168] While we're on the subject of car bombs and asking embarrassing questions: Why didn't the F.B.I., who had been monitoring the blind Sheik of New Jersey and his followers for months, act to prevent the World Trade Center bombings? Was it only an "innocent blunder" that a CIA agent working under cover in a U.S. Embassy overlooked Shiek Rahman's name on the list of undesirables and admitted him to the U.S.? And why did the Immigration Department later commit another innocent blunder and grant a terrorist suspect like Sheik Rahman a special visa? Why must Clinton alienating Egypt, our only reliable ally in the Middle East, by dumping this hot

The moral of these tragic tales is clear. Lawlessness on the part of governments and law enforcement agencies is just as bad as lawlessness by professional criminals. Indeed it is worse. It destroys respect for the Constitution and the whole Anglo-American tradition of rule by law that begins with *habeas corpus*. It turns law enforcement into a military operation, inflicting arbitrary punishment before trial. Moreover, the innocent victims of official violence are just as dead, and less likely to get any compensation or retribution. Finally official U.S. lawlessness justifies others – i.e. foreign terrorists and domestic nuts – who take the law into their own hands. The Idaho jury that acquitted Randy Weaver yesterday understood these basic American principles. I wonder if Janet Reno and her boss Bill Clinton do.

Islamic potato in Cairo's lap? Finally, how come the U.S. is deporting Sheik Rahman for bigamy [!] instead of bringing him to trial for terrorism? (Trials can be embarrassing. First all those nasty rules of evidence and then those jurors... average Americans who have a nasty habit of thinking for themselves and taking every word of their oaths seriously!)

The *Dissertation française*: An Essay in 250 Words[169]

Years ago as a student in Paris, I was forced to learn to write a *dissertation française*. This is the formal five-part French composition obligatory for all subjects and occasions.

It consists of an Introduction, a Development in three parts (Thesis, Antithesis, Synthesis), and a Conclusion which must recapitulate the matter of the Introduction, mysteriously enriched by its passage through the triadic Development. Variations are inadmissible unless the writer is over sixty, dead, or both.

At the time, my rebellious spirit waxed indignant at this arbitrary imposition of form over content. It reminded me of that typically Gallic institution, the *Loy de chauffage* or Heat Rule, which obligates all *concierges* to send up billows of steam every November 15 and mandates the total cessation of same on April 15, regardless of the temperature.

Years later, however, I not only caught myself expounding these same Trinitarian or Pentagonal mysteries to my own students but discovered that the French *dissertation* had become the pattern of my own essays. Humbly, I acknowledged the genius of the French spirit and its gift to the world, the *dissertation*, which, by its formal rigidity, conveys a double blessing.

It provides that necessary obstacle which alone turns the potential of inspiration into the actuality of creation, much as the irritation of a grain of sand is necessary before the oyster can produce the pearl. Moreover, it has enabled generations of French authors who have nothing to say to do so logically, elegantly, and with every appearance of profundity.

---

[169] My response to a Yale Law School application question: 'Write an essay of 250 words on a subject of your choosing.' Originally published in *College English* (vol. 39, no. 5, January 1978)

311

The S-11 Anti-War Tax Revolt

Wake up America! Your pay-stubs are talking to you and telling an important truth you won't read in the papers or see on TV. Take a look at how much the IRS deducts from your weekly 'pay' – money you will never see.

Why do we wage-earners and salaried people put up with spending roughly 1/4 of our earnings supporting a government which uses our hard-earned dollars to send the U.S. army half way around the world, to endanger our lives through nuclear arms and pollution and to pay off the big corporations and their military stooges around the world who conspire to push down what's left of our declining standard of living?

Why? The answer is simple! The IRS takes the money out of our pay checks *before* we ever see it! "Tax Revolt" may have worked for rich Reaganite California businessmen and property owners who have "loopholes" to defend, but up till now, there has been no solution for average men and women who depend on a pay check to pay our bills.

How to Use your W-4 Form to Save Money
While Eliminating War and Pollution

But we do have the power to resist! The name of our "loophole" is the "Dependents" box on the IRS W-4 Form. When we list the number of our dependants, the employer is obliged to increase our exemptions by $1950 per dependant and reduce the amount deducted from our pay check accordingly. For example, an average salaried single person earning $23,400 and filing a W-4 Form as "S-11" (Single with Eleven Dependants) would have zero dollars to pay with the IRS out of earnings. The math is simple: just multiply the number of your "dependants" (including yourself) by the standard exemption of $1950.

Once you have filed your "S-11" on the W-4, you start collecting the FULL AMOUNT of your actual earnings, and it is up to the IRS to audit you and challenge your exemptions in order to get their greasy paws on your hard-earned cash after April 15. Now YOU are in the power position, and the burden of collection is on the government.

The fact of the matter is that the IRS doesn't have enough auditors to go after thousands of wage-earners who have filed "S-11." It would take them years and create total chaos if they tried. And every Anti-War Tax Resistor who stood up and demanded a trial would be spreading the idea of the S-11 Tax Revolt through the media and inspiring two more New Tax Resistors to join the Movement. One hundred Resistors would snowball into a thousand and a thousand into ten thousand if they even tried!

Some Anti-War Tax Resistors, acting in the tradition of Thoreau and Martin Luther King, may choose to go to jail, rather than submit to injustice. This would create even more public sympathy. Others might chose to submit to the auditor's decision, pay their taxes plus interest charges, and be no worse off than if they had borrowed the same money from a bank! If the government chooses to sue a group of us for "tax fraud," they will probably have to sue all of us under the doctrine of "no selective prosecution" established by the mass movement of young people who successfully undermined the Selective Service System in the 1970's by refusing to register for the Draft. The new Anti-War Tax Revolt promises to be just as effective as the Draft Resistance was.

S-11: The New American Family Way to End War

But where, you may ask, can you find eleven "dependants" to list on your W-4? Simple: start with the people you work and live with, the members of your union, women's group, Central American Solidarity group, religious organization, peace group, human rights group, anti-racist organization, ecology group or gay rights coalition. We all have our reasons – good reasons – to resist the government and its tax-extortion racket. Form a New American "Family," an affinity group of three, five, seven or eleven Anti-War Tax Resistors who agree to list each other as "dependants" and to be listed reciprocally by their friends. In the event that the IRS tries to audit one of us, the others can all show up at the audit as "proof" that they are dependants. More chaos results. More publicity. More sympathy. More "families" of Tax Resistors.

Steal this leaflet! Spread the word!

Let's create one, two, ten thousand "New American Family" affinity groups! Let's use the power of the alternate media and our existing network of organizations and newsletters to spread the "S-11 Revolution!" By the time the government catches up with the first Resistors – and the IRS often takes years to get an audit going – we will be a mass movement. (Indeed, the IRS has recently laid off hundreds of auditors, since the government does not want a staff capable of going after the "big fish" and it costs more in staff salaries to go after the "little fish" than what they can collect in unpaid taxes).

Forming "New American Family" affinity groups and linking them creates power and solidarity, brings people together in struggle rather than isolating them. The "S-11 Revolution" is a wonderful combination of idealism and good old American "tax-chiselling," of save-the-world altruism and plain self-interest, of mass organizing and do-it-yourself screw-the-government Americanism. It has the potential to create major problems for the war-

313

machine while bringing people together in struggle in a massive new movement which combines a basic economic (class) issue with the more overtly political issues of the nuclear threat, militarism and injustice.

Nobody Beats America!

(Note: Originally published as "Do patriotic symbols cover up fears, doubts?" in the *Hartford Courant (*Hartford, CT, February 9, 1992) This article was written short to fit the Op-Ed format, so it is interesting to see what the *Courant* editors chose to cut (sections underlined.) From a sharp, humorous blast in the style of Buchwald or Russell Baker (neither of whom run in the *Courant*) we end up with a bland, earnest article from which references to flag-burning, AIDS, unemployment, the Gulf War, and class antagonism have been deleted.)

As an American recently returned from a stay abroad, I am struck by the pervasive display of patriotic symbols and slogans in my native land. Everywhere American flags bristle forth from porches, lawns, auto antennas, even tee-shirts, while bumper-stickers and billboards boast: "NOBODY BEATS AMERICA! NOBODY!"

Driving home from Bradley International Airport down the flag-lined streets of my familiar West Hartford neighborhood I was puzzled: had Veteran's Day or perhaps Flag Day been moved back to September? Months later, I am still perplexed at the sight of frayed and faded Fourth of July flags drooping under a cold winter drizzle. Indeed, as a former Boy Scout I am often tempted to ring my neighbor's bells and remind them that respect for the flag demands that it be furled every sunset and burned (yes, burned, not thrown in the garbage!) when it is worn or damaged.

Yesterday, out for a walk, I was struck by "I'm Proud to Be An American" on a neighbor's bumper sticker. As I strolled on, I wondered how my friends in France, Canada and Mexico would react to it. Would they infer that as Frenchmen, Canadians and Mexicans they were considered somehow inferior to the owner of that particular Chevy? And if my foreign friends were not offended, might they not be intimidated by the aggressive displays of nationalistic slogans and symbols lining our suburban streets?

I began to wonder how comfortable I would feel as a tourist in France or Mexico (not to mention Germany or Japan) if my own eyes were assaulted by nationalistic emblems and appeals on the streets of every town and village. Suddenly my mind flashed back to old newsreels of flag decked streets in Japan and Nazi Germany during the early 'thirties when those two civilized industrial nations were overwhelmed by a massive inferiority complex wrapped up in paranoid patriotism.

Then I flashed on a muscular neighbour I observed this fall raking his lawn in an American flag tee-shirt that challenged: "TRY TO BURN THIS ONE, YOU A—HOLE!" I wanted to ask him if wrapping himself in the flag gave him the right to address other people as "A—holes," but I was intimidated. Nationalistic symbols and slogans do that.

Now I am wondering if my flag-waving neighbors are really all that proud of America or if, like the Japanese and Germans of the 'thirties, they may not be hiding their confusions, fears and doubts behind a defensive shell of patriotism.

Are they really proud of America's dying cities full of desperation, drugs, disease and homelessness? Of our foreclosed farms and rusting factories? Of our bankrupted public school systems? Our polluted waterways? Our race-torn communities? Our tax dollars bailing out the high-rollers and crooked directors of belly-up banks? Of our Desert Storm victory that left millions of Iraqi civilians dead or starving with "Hitler"-Saddam still in poser? Of Kuwait "liberated" for the benefit of a repulsive family of slave-holding oil potentates?

Are my mainly working-class neighbors not confused when they hear Mr. Bush and Mr. Iacocca blame U.S. unemployment on the Japanese and nobody asks why the Detroit executives who keep designing Edsels earn 17 times more than Japanese executives and get to keep their million-dollar jobs while 27,000 G.M. workers get fired in one day? Are my neighbors not just a little scared now that every American has at least one friend or relative who is out of work or one friend or relative who is dying of AIDS while nothing is being done about it in this great and glorious land?

Patriotic symbols and slogans are an effective way to stifle such worries, doubts and fears. The huge "NOBODY BEATS AMERICA! NOBODY!" billboard on I-95 hardly invites questions, but if we Americans do not ask questions, how will be find solutions to our very real domestic problems?

Anyway, who is this "NOBODY" we're all afraid will "BEAT" America? The Commies? Gimme a break! The answer, of course, is "NOBODY." And as long as we Americans are kept busy patriotically blaming this mysterious foreign "nobody" for America's problems, the "somebodies" who seem to be running this country – greedy speculators, fat-cat executives, sleazy bankers, venal officials, corrupt politicians, Mafiosi and media moguls – can go on looting America with the blessing of both political parties.

So now we are facing another election year so paralysed by stupefying patriotism that nobody dares advance a practical program to put Americans back to work revitalizing America's cities, cleaning up America's polluted lands, educating America's youth, housing America's homeless, and building an America thoughtful Americans can be proud of.

316

Last night I dreamed I was out walking in my neighborhood when a huge voice boomed: "Neighbors! It's time to come out from behind our flags and bumper stickers and talk to each other! There's nobody here but us Americans, and nobody can beat us!" - Then a very little voice added: "Unless paranoid patriotism turns us into our own worst enemies and we beat ourselves."

Silly Sectarian Songs

The Red Revolution

Tune: 'When the Red, Red Robin Comes Bob Bob Bob'in Along'
(new words 1960 by Richard Greeman and Bruce Berger [170]

When the Red Revolu-tion

Brings its solu-tion a-long, a-long,

There'll be no more lootin'

When we start shoot'in that Wall Street throng!

    Wake up, you proletarians!

    Don't sleep like seminarians!

    Expropriate barbarians!

    Form a workers' republic!

Exploitation and alienation will *dis*-appear.

Surplus value from *ca*-pital you will not find here.

    I'm just a red again

    Sayin' what I said again

    No boss 'ere long,

When that Red Revolu-tion brings its solu-tion along.

***

When the Red Revolution and its solu-tion

Take place, take place

All the workers then, they will rise again

As the *Hu*-man Race

    Black people lead the masses

---

[170] Bruce Berger, my Yale College '61 roomate when this was written, is a respected poet and author of prize-winning essays, notably *The Telling Distance: Conversations with the American Desert* (1990) and *There Was a River: Essays on the Southwest* (1994)

To kick the bosses on their asses.

And the new world will be without classes

With true, new, human dimensions.

So take no lies from those Commie guys

Or the *bour*-geoisie!

Don't depend upon Party dogma, depend, on *Thee*!

> Up the proletariat!

> Down with the bureaucrat!

> We'll win this race

When the Red Revol*u*tion and its so*lu*tion take place!

Cuba, *Si! Yanqui,* No!

Tune: Harry Belafonte's Banana Song. (New words by Richard Greeman and a busload of Fair Play For Cuba demonstrators picketing the CIA in Langley, VA in 1961)

Work all day in Havana fact'*ry*

> (Cuba, *Si!* Yanqui, *No!*)

Make exploding cigars for the bour-geoi-*sie*

> (Cuba, *Si!* Yanqui, *No!*)

Fi-del, *Fi*-del

> (Cuba, *Si!* Yanqui, *No!*)

> *

Well, the Yanqui come in the Bay of Pigs;

> (Cuba, *Si*! Yanqui, *No!*)

We shoot them down with our brand-new MIGs

> (Cuba, *Si!* Yanqui, *No!*)

Fi-del, *Fi*-del

> (Cuba, *Si!* Yanqui, *No!*)

America

Tune: America the Beautiful
(New words by Allie Gilbert and his daughter Julie Gilbert Greeman)

Oh beautiful, for specious skies,
for transgened waves of grain,
For topped-off mountains' majesty,
above thy plundered plains.
America, America,
God shed disgrace on thee,
And crowned thy hoods with stolen goods,
From sea to oily sea.

Brush Up Your Hegel
(or, Excedrin Headache number 8,675,538)

Tune:"Brush up your Shakespeare" from Cole Porter's Kiss Me Kate
(new words by Julie and Richard Greeman)

Brush up your Hegel
Start quoting him now
Brush up your Hegel
And the masses you will wow

If they say your philosophy's eclectic
Just go in to that ol' dialectic

If the masses you want to bring pleasure
Just explain Quality, Quantity and Measure

If you want to create a commotion
Don't forget Being, Essence and Notion

Brush up your Hegel
And they'll all kowtow

Brush up... (etc)

Poor Marx on one subject was not astute
He balked at the *I*-de-a Absolute

320

Then Lenin appealed to the *muzhik*
With Notebooks on Hegel's great "Logic"

Now History has moved one stage higher
With the new book by Dunayevskaya
Brush up… (etc)

I've digested Kant, Fichte and Schlegel
So why not some classes on Hegel?

I've been told that the abstruse old Prussian
Could have taught poor dear Trotsky some Russian

But now I could use a vacation
From continual double negation

Brush up… (etc)

With Raya I've tried to be patient
And wait for the second negation

To seek out the new revolution
In products of her convolutions

But today of abstractions I'm weary
Give me movement from Practice to Theory!

Brush up… (etc)

Kim il Sung

Tune: "Maria" from West Side Story by Leonard Bernstein
(New words by Ted Gold)[171]

Kim il Sung – I just met a man named Kim il Sung
Suddenly his line

---

[171] Ted Gold (1947-1970) of Columbia SDS and later *Weatherman* was killed in the townhouse explosion on W. 11th St. when a bomb he was tinkering with blew up. I recently rediscovered his forty-year-old song parodies in my own file of silly sectarian songs and publish them here for the first time in memory of the Ted I knew.

Seemed so correct and fine to me
Kim il Sung – say it soft and there's rice fields flowing
Say it loud and there's peoples' war growing
Camel Sung, I'll never stop knowing Kim il Sung

The most beautiful country in the world
KOREA (Korea, Korea, Korea)

White Riot

Tune: "White Christmas" by Irving Berlin (New words by Ted Gold)

I'm dreaming of a White riot
Just like the one Oct. 8
Where the pigs take a beating
And things start leading
To armed war against the state

I'm dreaming of a mass movement
With every slogan that I write
[line missing]
And the world will off you 'cause you're White

A Party

Tune: Bobby Darin's "Dream Lover" (New words by Ted Gold:

Every fight we lead astray
Without a party to lead the way
With a line that we can use
To organize the fighting youth

Because we need (we need)
A party (a party)
To lead the fight
We need a red party so we can learn to struggle right

Red party needs some bread
Another banker winds up dead
Red party likes to loot
But better still, we love to shoot

322

Because we need… (etc.)

Revolution

Tune: "On Wisconsin" by W. T. Purdy (New words by Ted Gold):

Revolution, revolution
Time to smash the state

Struggling hard to free the people
Every single day (off the pig!)
Boby Seale, Erika Huggins
From jail they must return
Or we're gonna take this fuckin' country
And BURN, burn, burn.

Weatherman

Tune of the Beatle's "Nowhere Man" (New words by Ted Gold)

He's a real weatherman
Ripping up the motherland
Making all his Weather plans
For everyone

Proposed Compulsory School Prayer

God of the world and its peoples,
Thou who see into the hearts of all creatures,
We, the innocent, beseech Thee to cast Thy stern Gaze
On the hypocrites,
On the charlatans,
On the sly deceivers
Who, speaking falsely in Thy glorious Name, manipulate religion the better to
prey upon Thy children.

If there be ministers of any faith
Christian, Hindu, Moslem or Jew,
Who trade on Thy Name for personal gain,
Who grasp at fame,
at power,
at wealth,
at sex,
Scourge their souls and smite them, O God of Truth!

If there be leaders of the people, statesmen and men of war,
Who call up hatred, violence, oppression, yea even murder and rape
Dividing thy Children clan against clan,
color against color,
creed against creed,
Scourge their hearts and smite them, O God of Peace!

If there be proud inquisitors and stiff-necked censors,
Who inflict the fetishes of any Sect on thy children,
Banning our books,
Reviling our customs,
Trashing our music,
Prying into our thoughts,
Our bedchambers,
Yea even to the secret places of our bodies,
Remind them of Thy Injunction "Judge Not!"
Burn their hearts with shame, stay their fell hands and smite them, O God of
Love!

If there be found in any Church, Mosque, Synagogue or Temple,
Moralizing malefactors of great wealth,
Who chastise Thy humble poor, slyly contriving to deny them public Charity
Grasping the milk from the infant lips of the teen Madonna

324

Yea and the school breakfast from the young scholar's aching belly
Smite them and bring them low, that they shall know the bitter crust of
humiliation, O God of Justice!

Teach us God of all humankind to love each other as ourselves,
To cherish all Thy children as sisters and brothers,
Knowing no alien
Among other clans,
Other colors,
Other creeds,

Teach us to find in our hearts forgiveness
for the self-serving,
for the power-hungry,
for the violent
for the greedy
for the impious hypocrites who take thy Glorious Name in Vain
The better to divide Thy children
one against another,
The better to oppress us,
The better to stifle all voices but their own!

Amen

Part VII:

Author's *Postface*

My Political Itinerary

I guess I was born a rebel. My parents were active Progressives (pro-Soviet until 1956) while my maternal grandfather, Sam Levin, an immigrant tailor from Russia, was a card-carrying member of Eugene V. Debs' American

Socialist Party.[172] During his Presidential campaigns, Debs barnstormed the U.S. on a train called 'The Red Special' making whistle-stop speeches in every town and city, including Hartford, Connecticut. That's how my grandfather got his autographed picture, a prized possession of his which I inherited along with his library of Socialist books. This makes me a 'red-diaper' grand-baby.

My Dad came from a middle-class progressive Roosevelt Republican background, but the First World War opened his eyes. Patriotic 'Teddy' Greeman served in four campaigns 1917-1918 as a U.S. Army ambulance driver under command of the French Army and won a Croix de Guerre for bravery while touring France's bordellos (marked with an X in his driver's book, which I also inherited and published, along with his war stories as *Grandpa's War*).[173] Teddy Greeman also saw a lot of gore and fell in with the Lost Generation until he met Grandpa 'Uncle' Sam (Levin), who helped him understand the underlying economic causes of all that senseless slaughter. Then he turned Left. When I was eight, he ran for N.Y. State Assembly on the American Labor Party ticket, the N.Y. branch of Henry Wallace's Progressive Party. Then the Cold War broke out.

In the 6th grade, at the beginning of the Witch Hunt, I was labeled a 'Communist' during Social Studies class by the son of a local 'liberal' Democrat politician, who must have heard his parents badmouthing mine. I had zero idea of what a 'Communist' was back then (we were 'pwogressives' at home), but I knew that label could get me in trouble. Never at a loss for words, I instantly retorted that I was not a 'Communist' but a *'commonist'* because I was 'for the common people.' This inspiration shut the pint-sized red-baiter's nasty little trap, won the approval of my 11-year-old classmates, and has defined my political outlook ever since.

The other reason I was destined at birth to rebel is the clubfoot I was born with – a fairly spectacular birth defect long considered incurable. Horrified, my

---

[1] Debs, a union organizer from Indiana, was the leader of the Socialist Party in its heyday as well as one of the founders of the IWW (Industrial Workers of the World). As an anti-war candidate, Debs took away a million votes from Woodrow Wilson in 1916. When Wilson declared war a year later, the 'great liberal' locked Debs up in Leavenworth Penitentiary for talking against the draft and kept him there for years after the War was over – which didn't stop Debs from running for President in 1920 and getting a million votes. 'I want to rise *with* the people, not *from* the people' said Debs. 'Do not expect any leader to lead you to the Promised Land, because if he could, he could lead you out again.'

[173] Edward Greeman, *Grandpa's War: The French Adventures of a WWI Ambulance Driver,* Writers & Readers, New York 1992. Dad was a great raconteur. When I collected his stories and showed them to Paul Fussell, the author of *The Great War and Modern Memory* replied he was 'filled with interested and admiration' Dad's 'pretty wit and laudable humanity' which was just the blurb I needed for the jacket.

parents must have imagined me hobbling around on crutches for life, like one of those beggars depicted in 17ᵗʰ Century *genre* paintings. Fortunately my parents found a German refugee doctor in NY who by 1939 had devised an effective treatment and I grew up completely normal – physically. I don't think my parents ever got over the shock and the shame of giving birth to a 'monster' (one of my 'cute' family nicknames) which may be the source of my various neuroses. In college, however, I learned that Lord Byron was also born with a clubfoot (incurable then) which didn't stop the dashing poet and romantic rebel from swimming the Hellespont, seducing the most fascinating women of his age and dying in the cause of Greek independence.[174] Clubfoot Byron became his own hero by picking up his pen and turning his shame into a blaze of arrogance, rebellion and splendid poetry – much of it subversive and satirical. The same Oedipal impulse, minus the poetic talent, probably motivates me to scale the battlements of capitalism and engage in mental strife with Vegetarian Sharks. Another thing that set me apart from the regimented herd as a boy is that I was no good at competitive sports. I spent most of my time alone reading, dreaming and constructing rubber-powered models out of sticks of balsa wood covered with tissue paper. Some of them even flew pretty well before crashing! I finally learned to enjoy sports in my 30s, when they went co-ed, but I still read lots of books and construct models – political models and RFOs (Revolutionary Flying Objects) like the eco-Socialist Utopias with which I conclude this collection.[175] On the other hand, I was good at making jokes and arguing. My finest hour as a teenage atheist was during a High School debate on school prayer. I proclaimed myself a worshiper of Zeus and demanded the right to sacrifice a goat in the Auditorium. My argument: 'Doesn't the First Amendment prohibit favoring one religion over another?' Only later in life, under the beneficent influence of some good grass, did I discover that I am, if not a personal devotee of Zeus, by nature more of a tree-hugging pantheist than a doctrinaire atheist (too negative for my temperament).

Although hostile to all monotheisms and nationalisms, I've always been comfortable with my religious/ethnic 'identity' as a secular Jew.[176] (I couldn't imagine being anything else.) I have a Jewish sense of humor and I'm attracted to Yiddish Culture. So much for 'identity' – that over-simplified and dangerous delusion! Most people 'are' many things all at once: not just 'Black' or 'Gay' or 'American' or 'Jewish' or Female' or 'Moslem.' Existentially, we

---

[174] Byron also translated Sophocles' *Oedipus Tyrannus* into English under the curious title *Swell-Foot the Tyrant*, transposing quite literally the two Greek words that make up the hero's name – but probably also alluding to his own swollen foot. (According to legend, baby Oedipus' feet,were transpierced and bound on the order of his royal parents before being exposed to die on a barren mountain.)

[175] My free *Revolutionary KIT* supplies materials and examples for building your own RFOs online at www.invisible-international.org and www.wikitopia.wikidot.com.

[176] Cf. *The Non-Jewish Jew,* a collection of essays by Trotsky biographer Isaac Deutscher.

all create ourselves out of our heredity, citizenship, education, gender, class, ethnicity, age, culture, occupation and a whole complex of unconscious attractions and elective affinities. Naturally, we must defend our own and everybody's right to fully develop all these identities without oppression or disrespect. But in my opinion, reducing politics to 'identity' blocks individuals from developing a true, rounded human identity and sows division where we need to have unity among the oppressed. In any case, I will remain Jewish until the death of the last anti-Semite.

Concerning Yiddish culture, I learned to appreciate it through my adorable mother-in-law Mira Gilbert (Jenny Greeman's grandma), who earned her living singing in Yiddish (among 18 other languages). Mira was born in Odessa in 1917 and was brought to Philadelphia in 1923 by her father, the Yiddish writer Berish Eppelbaum[177] and her mother Tzina, a progressive educator. Mira introduced me to the actor Hershel Bernardi,[178] formerly a child star on the N.Y. Yiddish stage, with whom she used to travel the Borscht Circuit of Jewish Catskill Mountain resorts. It was from them that I picked up the phrase 'Killing the Jews' - Borscht Belt slang for wowing the audience. In the hope of offending everyone, I have used that phrase as the heading for my chapter on Holocaust deniers (Part V). Far from being a 'self-hating Jew,' I joyfully embrace the self-irony and universalism of the Jewish Diaspora whose very exclusion enabled it to rise above narrow nationalism and produce the likes of Maimonodes, Marx, Freud, Einstein and Kafka. As for the Hebrew warriors and ignorant, intolerant, long-bearded theocrats who rule the State of Israel, how do they differ from the Ayatollahs and Holy Warriors of Iran?

In High School I grew a beard, learned to play bawdy folksongs on the guitar and refused to say the words 'under God' (which had just been added to the Pledge of Allegiance to the flag); all of this flamboyance upset my parents during the conservative, McCarthyite Fifties. During the Witch Hunt, it seemed better for Progressives to keep a low profile. By the Sixties Dad was marching down Fifth Avenue with his medals protesting against the Vietnam War. In college I became a Socialist, and I've been in and out of Socialist and Anarchist groups ever since. They taught me as much, if not more, than all my universities. I would like to recount this political education briefly here, since it helps explain how I came to the convictions that animate these essays. Many of the observations collected in this volume relate directly to my political involvements over forty years, and the reader has a right to know where I'm coming from.

My Political Education

---

[177] Novelist and weekly *feuilletonniste* in the Yiddish-language N.Y. Communist daily *Freiheit*.
[178] Heshie, and old Wallace Progressive, sympathized with the movements of 1968. See below my interview with Jenny about the Columbia strike.

1957+ As a freshman at Yale College I joined a vibrant student Socialist club called the George Orwell Forum. The Orwell Forum's faculty mentors were two committed independent Socialists: Bob Herbert, an instructor in Art History and Bob Bone, a WWII Conscientious Objector, who taught in the snooty Yale English Department. Bone was a great speaker, a popular lecturer, and had just published *The Negro Novel in America* - the first academic study of black literature. Naturally he was denied tenure – which scandalized me at the time. What wonderful mentors! Bone got us students involved with the Civil Rights and non-violent anti-war movements. He even took us down to New York City with him for Socialist meetings after which we all adjourned to the White Horse Tavern on Hudson Street to get drunk with the likes of Norman Mailer, Mike Harrington and Brendon Behan. Reading Orwell cured me of my parents' illusions about Russian Communism and the Orwell Forum put me in contact with Left anti-Stalinists who called themselves Socialists and meant it. Over the next four years the Forum held public meetings at Yale nearly every other month promoting socialism. Among the better known speakers we invited were (in no particular order) Norman Mailer (who was drunk and/or high and disappointing as a speaker but whom I beat at thumb-wrestling), Eric Fromm (who spoke on Socialist Humanism and filled Woolsey Hall, the biggest auditorium on campus), J. Farrell Dobbs (the historic Teamster organizer and Socialist Workers' Party presidential candidate), Raya Dunayevskaya (who had just written *Marxism and Freedom* and founded *News and Letters* Committees which I eventually joined), the literary critic Irving Howe, the sociologists Lou Coser and Seymour Lipsit along with various other *Dissent*niks as well as a speaker from the Fair Play for Cuba Committee. These are the names I recall, but there were others.

As a Yale Freshman I joined off-campus struggles including anti-war civil disobedience with the Committee for Non-Violent Action (CNVA),[179] protesting against the House Un-American Activities Committee (HUAC),[180] and taking part in Civil Rights sit-ins and marches as a member of the Congress On Racial Equality (CORE).[181] I can pinpoint the exact moment when I became a revolutionary rather than just a young rebel. It was my personal experience participating in the 1958 national Youth March on Washington for Integrated Schools – in the Spring of Freshman Year – that destroyed my faith in liberalism. Bayard Rustin, a black organizer from the War Resisters League (who had also spoken at the Orwell Forum) along with black labor leader A. Philip Randolph, had organized tens of thousands of kids,

---

[179] Committee for Non-Violent Action, the radical pacifist group based in Voluntown, CT.
[180] The House Un-American Activities Committee, whose decades of witch hunting did as much damage to civil liberties as red-baiter Joe McCarthy's brief reign of terror.
[181] Founded in 1942, CORE pioneered the use of Ghandian non-violent tactics in breaking down Jim Crow and spearheaded the Sit-Ins and Freedom Rides.

black and white and chartered buses from all over the East and Midwest to present our students' mild desegregation petition to President Eisenhower. Ike refused to receive it, but that was no surprise. The surprise was that our 1958 Youth March turned out to be the largest demonstration held in D.C. since the Thirties and the first time since Populism that so many 'Negroes' and whites had come together in common cause in our nation's still-segregated capitol city. Next morning, I eagerly opened the liberal *N.Y. Times* to read about our triumph. Ziltch. *Nada.* Not a line.[182] I can still feel my young man's anger in the pit of my stomach. And the conclusion in my mind: no way is this system ever going to reform itself or respond to sweet reason.

Today we have an African-American President, something none of us Civil Rights activists – who according to Mr. Obama made his election possible - ever even dared dream of! The fact that the U.S. electorate is prepared to elect an African-American represents an epochal advance in the struggle against racism. When I was in college, it was still 'Whites Only' and not just in the South. The heroic struggles of the Civil Rights generation have come to fruition, and a majority or near-majority of whites (more women than men) have overcome their prejudices and voted to put a 'Nigger' in a White House built by slave labor. Racism has always been the Achilles' heel of progressive mass struggles in the U.S. Historically, it divided and weakened the once-powerful Populist and labor movements. 'Black and White Unite and Fight! was the winning slogan of industrial mass unionism in the Thirties, but after the CIO got established, its leaders reneged on Operation Dixie and abandoned millions of black workers in the Jim Crow, Right to Work South. By the Sixties, lacking organization, frustrated, unemployed blacks (joined by some whites) were reduced to rioting in the cities of the North. Mr. Obama's election suggests the possibility, during the inevitable upcoming social and economic struggles, of class unity among U.S. poor and middle-class working people of all so-called races. Only such popular alliance - including male and female, gay and straight, immigrant and native-born, white, black, Hispanic and 'other' - can mobilize the necessary strength to defeat the well organized sharks of U.S. corporate capital.

As for the ineffable Mr. Obama, no man can serve two masters. So far he has served billions on a platter to his financial backers – the bankers and corporations who paid for his campaign (and broke the economy). As for all those folks who voted for 'Change,' danced in the streets on Election Night and traveled to D.C. to share in the Inauguration, the President has even-handedly thrown this electorate a few scraps of Chump Change. Mr. Obama's even-handedness reminds me of the Army cook who served 'rabbit stew' to the regimental mess. When a trooper complained that the meat tasted like horse, the cook confessed that his recipe called for 'equal' amounts of horsemeat: one

---

[182] At least the strait-line Republican *Herald Tribune* dutifully ran five paragraphs on page 46.

horse, one rabbit. Of course, as the crisis deepens, the President can be expected to make concessions to the masses who elected him (especially if they are militant and organized) and throw in a few more rabbits. The former community organizer may even *want* to do some good. Didn't FDR famously tell a delegation of progressives: 'I support what you propose: now make me do it.'? Does Mr. Obama's election contradict my 1958 conclusion about the system's inability to reform itself and listen to sweet reason? Not when the peace candidate's first act as Commander in Chief was to order the murder of 15 Pakistani civilians from the air and escalate the un-winnable Afghani War. Indeed, I have seen little evidence of change in the past 50 years. In 2002-03 the *Times* and other media willingly trumpeted Bush's false claims about Iraqi WMDs and Saddam's relationship with Osama, just as they had previously concealed the truth about the U.S. 'secret' invasion of Cuba in 1963 (the Bay of Pigs) and endorsed LBJ's lie about an alleged North Vietnamese attack on U.S. destroyers in 1964 (the Bay of Tonkin Resolution). And now Afghanistan has escalated into Obama's Vietnam without a whisper of opposition in Congress or the media. In 1964, Texas Populist Lyndon Johnson was elected by a popular landslide and used it to push through the War on Poverty and the historic Voting Rights Act. Four years later he abandoned politics in disgrace, having destroyed his immensely popular and progressive Presidency by escalating a war he inherited from his predecessor. Am I the only one alive who remembers? How come none of the pundits are making this analogy?

Returning to New Haven in 1957, by now I was a Beatnik (Hippies didn't appear until nearly a decade later) and met my first love (an art student who could have modeled for Jules Feiffer's 'Dance of Spring') at a Gregory Corso poetry reading. As a Freshman I also became a member of the Young Peoples' Socialist League (YPSL). The YPSL's leader was Michael Harrington, author of *The Other America,* the book that inspired the War on Poverty. The Orwell Forum invited YPSL's over-aged but still youthful spokesman to Yale, and Harrington gave such a wonderfully rousing Socialist speech that I asked to join on the spot. This remarkable youth organization exemplified what was truly new in the New Left: a rejection of both U.S. imperialism *and* totalitarian Communism. We YPSLs were all involved in struggle as anti-war and anti-racist activists, but we also knew our Marx and Lenin by heart and held full-scale political debates, defending our platforms with position papers (mysteriously known as 'documents') and oratory - always passionate and sometimes humorous. At YPSL summer camp I even dared contradict the adult leader of our movement, the formidable debater Max Schactman.[183] You had to be tough to be an independent Socialist back in the Cold War Fifties, attacked one side by the red-baiters and on the other by the Stalinist crypto-Communists who still held onto key positions in the Left movement. Both were formidable adversaries, and you had to stick to your guns. Last year, when the YPSL held its 50th reunion, a remarkable number of us 'youths' were still more or less Socialists and activists, and few if any had actually gone over to Right. Unfortunately, by the end of the Sixties many among the next generation of New Left students had reverted to Old Left Stalinism under the aegis of Stalin's Chinese disciple Mao Tse-Dung. Disillusioned, many later abandoned socialism altogether and some turned sharply Right.

By my Sophomore year the Twenty-Sixth of July Movement and its *Comandantes* Fidel and Raoul Castro, Che Guevarra and Camilo Cienfuegas had established a serious guerrilla presence in the Sierra Maestra mountains of Cuba and called upon Cubans to overthrow the U.S.-backed dictatorship of Batista. The rebels denounced the two props of its neo-colonial economy: sugar monoculture export agriculture and gangster-ridden Havana casino/sex tourism. I followed this struggle closely through friends in the N.Y. Socialist movement and a remarkable series of articles in the N.Y. *Herald Tribune* by Tim Hogan, a young reporter 'embedded' with the guerrillas, and I was thrilled when the people of Havana rose up in December 1959, overthrew Batista, and welcomed Castro and his guerrillas into the liberated capital. Here at last was a self-organized, self-proclaimed humanist revolution taking place in *my* lifetime after long years of apathy and reaction. With Jonathan Spence, Yale's exchange student from Cambridge University in England, I helped organize the first student trip to Cuba over the 1959 Spring break. Spence and the other students returned enraptured, and the stodgy *Yale Daily News* printed a favorable series on Cuba. We also promoted the Fair Play for Cuba Committee, which further enraged the scions of rich Latin American families who were an important contingent of the Yale student body.[184] One night a half-dozen of these *señoritos* put on nylon stockings to disguise their faces, heroically broke into my college room and attempted to abduct me in my pajamas - perhaps to shave off my beard, which presumably reminded them of

---

[183] Max Schactman, a brilliant polemicist, distinguished himself as a U.S. Communist Youth leader in the '20s, then as a follower of Leon Trotsky. He broke with Trotsky's defense of the Soviet 'workers state' after the Stalin-Hitler pact, proclaimed Russia a 'bureaucratic collectivist' society, formed Workers Party (later the International Socialist League, which merged with the old U.S. Socialist Party and became what is now the Democratic Socialists of America, or DSA. Got it?). When I encounterd Max in 1961, he was moving quickly to the Right, and sadly he ended up defending the Vietnam War and expelling us party youth *en masse*. At the same time, however, he still defended Trotsky's suppression of the 1921 revolt of the Kronstadt sailors, the point on which I dared to challenge him after one of his brilliant three-hour speeches.
[184] In those days, Yale recruited the sons of Latin American *latifundistas,* Harvard those of Middle Eastern oil potentates and Princeton the spawn of Southern gentry.

335

Castro's. After a brief scuffle in which my 5'4" roommate, the poet and pianist Bruce Berger, distinguished himself in my defense, the old Irish campus guard arrived and my aristocratic assailants fled the field of honor. None were disciplined, and I got off with an admonishment from the College Master, a biologist, to watch out or I would never get a job because of 'security clearance.'

The Fair Play for Cuba Committee, with its slogan 'Hands of Cuba!' was organized defend the Cuban revolution against attack from *Yanqui* imperialism. In 1961 we demonstrated at CIA headquarter at Langley Virginia to expose the 'secret' army the CIA was training in Guatemala to invade Cuba under U.S. air cover and establish a beachhead counter-revolutionary regime at the well-named Bay of Pigs. The *Times* and the rest blanked out our protest as well as the documented first-hand report from Guatemala published in the *Nation,* but I had a great time going down to D.C. singing with a busload of Hispanics (of course I brought my guitar) and improvising *¡Cuba si! ¡Yanqui no!* to the tune of Harry Belafonte's *Day-O.* [185] When the invasion finally took place, we were jubilant when the Cuban Popular Militias defended their revolutionary homeland so fiercely that the CIA-trained and equipped invaders were chopped up on the beach.[186] A half-century later I am still campaigning for 'Hands off Cuba!' or rather 'Hands Out to Cuba!' and to the Cuban Artists we want to bring to the U.S. as a first step to lifting the blockade and normalizing relations.

However as early as 1961, troubling reports were filtering out of Cuba. Camilo Cenfuegos, considered the most liberal of the Twenty-Sixth of July *Comandantes*, had disappeared in a mysterious air crash. Blas Roca, the head of the Stalinist Cuban CP (which before the revolution had attacked Castro's guerrilla war as 'adventuristic') was now put in charge of a new state party, superceding the Twenty-Sixth of July Movement which had actually made the revolution. The workers' trade unions were being dominated and curtailed by the state, with Che Guevarra in charge of the economy. Dissidents were being repressed, women demoted, Trotskyists arrested. None of these problems were acknowledge by the Fair Play for Cuba Committee, whose leadership was dominated by the Trotskyist Socialist Workers' Party. Apparently, the SWP had opportunistically replaced Trotsky with Castro as their poster-boy, and they had a positive explanation for everything, including the imprisoned Cuban Trotskyists, who belonged to a different Trotskyist sect and were 'probably counter-revolutionaries'. One night in New Haven in 1961, a man who had just returned from Cuba took the floor at a 'Hands off Cuba' meeting. He turned out to be Tim Hogan, the author of those thrilling 1959 *N.Y. Herald-Tribune* reports from the Sierra Maestra. After the meeting Hogan wandered the New

---

[185]Please see 'Silly Songs' in Part V.

[186] Kennedy reneged on U.S. air support (which probably got him assassinated).

Haven night with Jon Spence, Tom Doyle and me and told us his story. The *Trib* had fired him for being too radical, and the Cuban government, grateful for his contributions, had invited him to join the Ministry of Information. However, Hogan had seen too many things that disturbed him in Cuba to accept such a post. Now, he was back in the States and unemployed, his loyalties torn between the urge to testify to the truth about the Cuban Revolution and fear of giving ammunition to its Yankee imperialist enemy.

Thirty years earlier in Russia, the writer and revolutionary Victor Serge was caught in a similar dilemma when the Soviet Revolution started turning sour. Serge formulated his solution as the militant's 'double duty.' Defend the revolution against its external enemies: imperialism and reaction. But also against internal enemies : bureaucracy, conformity, dictatorship. Under Castro, Cuba went backward to sugar monoculture on state-run plantations, locking the island into dependency and leaving it undeveloped. Castro's famous Six Million Ton Harvest (during which U.S. volunteer cane-cutters consumed more than they produced) was sold at a loss when the price of sugar fell on the world market, as pre-revolutionary Castro had warned. Today Havana, the Cuban capitol, is once again famous in Europe as a retro (Batista era) center for Euro-denominated casino- and sex-tourism. Yet there are still fanatics on the U.S. Left who will malign you as a traitorous scoundrel if you dare suggest that Cuba is anything less than a 'Socialist' model. (Come to think of it, Castro used this same tactic in the campaign against 'Anti-Communism' by which he silenced opposition to Blas Roca's bureaucratic Communist take-over of the party and state. To these would-be censors I answer: How are revolutionaries supposed to learn from our past mistakes if we're not allowed to admit them? In any case, although all the new Latin American democracies correctly and proudly defend the Cuban revolution against the U.S. blockade, none seem eager to imitate the Castro regime.

1959-60 During my Junior Year, I was lucky enough to study at the Sorbonne in Paris. As opposed to the U.S. where we Socialists had been reduced to a marginal handful, France had several Socialist parties and a legal Communist Party with officials at the head of many unions and municipalities. There were even two parties to the left of the Left who were about to unite, and Mike Harrington of YPSL had given me the address of Jean-Jacques Marie, who was very much involved and who invited me to observe. At that time, France was quagmired in an endless racist colonial war in Algeria against the independence movement led by the FLN. By 1959, the Algerian war, escalated under a Socialist administration, had become even bloodier than the Indochinese (Vietnam) war the French had lost in 1954. This was because Algeria was considered part of France, making it both a race war and a civil war. White-settler Algeria was represented in the National Assembly like the Dixie states in the U.S. - with voteless Arabs and Berbers taking the place of our disenfranchised American Negroes. In 1958, a year before I arrived in France, the Algerian civil war had provoked the collapse of the Fourth French

337

Republic. General de Gaulle had taken power as a spokesman for the colonial Army and the militantly rightist Algerian white settler movement (both of which he subsequently double-crossed). In Paris, every Algerian on the street was considered a 'terrorist.' There were soldiers with sub-machineguns in front of every public building and great bus-loads of black-clad CRS riot-cops parked all over the student quarter. Censorship was strict. The drowning of hundreds of unarmed, peaceful Algerian demonstrators in the Seine remained an official secret for decades. Accounts of torture were also censored, although one book, *The Question* by Henri Alleg a French-Algerian Communist who had been tortured, did get through somehow and made a sensation. My observations in France lead me to the conclusion that internal democracy at home and imperialist war abroad are incompatible. This was the teaching of Thucydides, the 5th Century B.C. Greek historian who observed how the Athenian expedition to colonize Sicily provoked the fall of Athenian democracy. So in 1961 when Kennedy starting meddling in France's ex-colony Vietnam, I was well ahead of the learning curve. The Teach-ins we organized then were the beginning of what became a massive anti-war movement in the late Sixties. Thucydides' observation still holds: the first victim of Bush's Iraqi expedition was the U.S. Constitution.

As I arrived for my first day of class at the Sorbonne, a stunningly beautiful young woman handed me a leaflet inviting students to a public talk on the Algerian rebellion. Naturally I showed up breathless that evening at the *Mutualité* (Left Bank labor-Socialist conference center). Since Catherine was seated way across the room, I was able to concentrate  on the speaker: Jean-François Lyotard a Marxist philosophy teacher who had taught in Algeria. The sponsoring group was *Socialisme ou Barbarie* (Socialism or Barbarism) founded in 1949 by a group of highly creative revolutionary workers and intellectuals including Lyotard (later a post-modernist), Daniel Mothé (who worked in an auto plant), Alberto Meso ('Vega' of the Spanish POUM), Edgar Morin (the philosopher of Complexity/Emergence) and Cornelius Castoriadis, the brilliant Greek economist and philosopher whose powerful mind and personality more and more dominated the group.[187] I soon joined the group, whose anti-Stalinist socialism appealed to my own, and Castoradis' visionary account of a possible future democratically self-organized Socialist society free of hierarchy has stuck with me to this day. My final chapter here, 'The Archimedes Hypothesis'

---

[187] Cornelius Castoriadis, whom I knew under his various 'party-names' as *Barjot, Chaulieu,* and *Paul Cardan*, came out of the Greek revolutionary movement and settled in Paris after the Greek Civil War as a political exile. He was a leading light of the journal/movement *Socialisme ou Barbarie* of which I was a member during 1959-1960. Castoriadis broke with Marxism in the 60s (although he supported the May '68 student-worker uprising) and became a celebrated psychoanalyst and philosopher.

was inspired by reading Castoriadis' *The Content of Socialism* in 1959. My great contribution to this historical movement was to organize U.S.-style parties ('socializations') in order to attract some more young people to the group. But imagine my chagrin when I naïvely attempted to get a date with 19-year old Catherine and learned what everyone knew: that she was living with Castoriadis!. I think the experience of living in another political culture gave me a much broader perspective on U.S. culture and society than if I had remained in New Haven at WASPish, all-male Yale College for four years, and I'm appalled at the number of U.S. leaders today who speak no foreign languages and have never left the Great American Mall.

In 1960, back in New Haven for my Senior Year at Yale, I heard about Robert

Williams, an African-American Korean War vet and the author of the sensational book *Negroes With Guns.* Naturally I invited him to speak on campus at the Orwell Forum. Williams had become notorious in 1960 by organizing an NAACP[188]-sponsored NRA Rifle Club with other black vets in rural Pennsylvania and by defending his community against an armed attack by the KKK. Williams' perfectly legal NRA-NAACP Pennsylvania rifle club was the ancestor of the Black Panther Party for Self-Defense. I printed up posters headlining 'Negroes With Guns' and spread them all over Dixwell Avenue, the African-American section of New Haven. I also handed them out at black churches that Sunday. The posters came to the attention of the Dean of Yale College, who called me onto the carpet in his austerely imposing office. 'Mr. Greeman,' he said. 'Aren't you afraid of bringing violence on campus if you go through with this meeting?' 'Not in the least, Dean Devane,' I answered. 'I give you my word as a gentleman on that.' This left the Dean speechless. To make him feel better, I reminded him: 'Don't you remember appealing to us in your welcoming speech to the Freshman Class to overcome town-gown hostility and bring more members of the New Haven Community onto campus?' There was nothing left for the poor man to say. The night of the big meeting, the 500 seat auditorium was full, and half the audience was black. Williams never showed. By that time, he had been forced to flee to Cuba, but his lawyer, Conrad Lynn, an African-American Trotskyist, showed up in his place. However, instead of talking about Williams and the black liberation struggle, Lynn started a long lecture praising Castro's Cuba. Since I had the Chair, I was able to get the subject back to racism in the U.S. and particularly to discrimination in New Haven by drawing the crowd's attention to some flagrant examples. Immediately, a local African-American factory worker (who also a Korean War vet I later learned) stood up to speak. He identified himself as the new

---

[188] NAACP or National Association for the Advancement of Colored People, the major Civil Rights group at that time.

President of the NAACP and called for action against the liberal Democrats' Model City program which leaders of the black establishment were supporting in return for a piece of the real-estate action. A lively general discussion ensued and the result was the organization of a radical CORE chapter and two years of activism, fighting Kennedy's Urban Renewal program, spelled 'Negro Removal' as far as New Haven's Dixwell Avenue was concerned.

When the Williams meeting was over and the crowd had gone, I carefully cleaned up the auditorium before leaving for the benefit of Dean Devane. A few students, including a friend named Steve Adolphus, were still chatting on the sidewalk as I passed on my way to join the comrades at George and Harry's Pizzeria. Five minutes later, Steve showed up breathless: 'Did you see those two guys in trench coats on the sidewalk just now? Well, when you crossed the street one of them started to follow you, but the other grabbed his arm and said 'No, *schmuck,* you're supposed to give 'em a head start!'' I just laughed, and in all these years I have never been visited by the F.B.I. who mainly go after 'weak sisters' they can manipulate. A few years after LBJ pushed through the Freedom of Information Act in 1964, I applied to order a copy of my file. At that time it weighed in at 1200 pages, beyond my budget at ten cents a page. So I went for my CIA file (only 36 pages, mostly blacked out for 'security reasons') and discovered that every step of my 1969 European travels had been monitored. The lesson I learned as a young radical was this: don't go paranoid over idea that the cops and FBI are watching you. Assume they are doing a good job keeping track of your public activities, your phone, post and email. If you do something illegal, take the reasonable precautions but don't play games with them, it only gives them a wedge by letting them know you're worried and vulnerable. [189]

---

[189] I recommend Victor Serge's *What Every Radical Should Know About Repression: A Guide for Activists,* based on his study of the Tzarist Secret Police archives, captured by the revolutionaries in 1917, and still relevant.

In 1960 I encountered the Russian-born Marxist-Humanist philosopher Raya Dunayevskaya,[190] a former secretary to Leon Trotsky in Mexico who, had demonstrated that Communist Russia was, in Marxist terms, a state-capitalist society. Dunayevskaya had spoken at the Orwell Forum while I was away in France, and Jonathan Spence lent me her book, *Marxism and Freedom* which had a profound and lasting effect on me. Subtitled *From 1776 to Today*, her book traces the development of Marxism from its origins in French revolutionary thought, British political economy and Hegelian dialectics  through its full humanist flowering in *Capital* and the Paris Commune. She then analyses its degeneration at the hands of Social Democratic opportunists and Stalinist totalitarians and describes it persistence and restoration in the 1956 Hungarian Revolution of Workers Councils and the daily struggles of U.S. workers against capitalist automation. The morning after I read it, I hitch-hiked to meet her. Her Detroit-based organization was nearly unique in combining blacks and whites, workers and intellectuals, women and men on an equal footing. I soon became a member of her allegedly 'decentralized' Committees of workers and intellectuals publishing the monthly newspaper *News & Letters* out of Detroit, and I organized a local chapter in New Haven with an iron worker named Tom Doyle, who became a close friend and mentor. I spent that summer in Detroit, then the headquarters of the U.S. auto industry and of *News & Letters* Committees, where I learned a lot talking to workers. Despite my problems with *News & Letters* unacknowledged centralism and cultish sectarianism, I remained active for fifteen years and recruited a whole new generation of Marxist-Humanists before being pushed out of the organization on phony charges and for no other reason than my generally questioning critical-minded attitude. It saddens me that a group with such a humanistic philosophy and democratic principles should be so undemocratic and inhuman in its internal life. However, for objective reasons I continue to support the newspaper www.newsandletters.org as a unique source of U.S. workers' voices and Marxist analysis along with articles by youth, prisoners, black, gay and lesbian activists speaking for themselves. I also still consider Dunayevskaya's *Marxism and Freedom* the best introduction to the subject and have recently sponsored and prefaced Russian and Arabic translations of this fundamental work.

---

[190] Raya Dunayevskaya (Rae Spiegel 1910-1987) was an active Young Communist in the Twenties in Chicago. Expelled for 'Trotskyism,' she eventually made her way to Mexico and served as Trotsky's secretary. She broke with him over the Stalin-Hitler Pact and, along with C.L.R. James analysed the USSR as a state-capitalist society. In 1958, as leader of her own Marxist-Humanist group, *News & Letters* Committees, she published *Marxism and Freedom* establishing the underlying humanism of Marx's philosophy as the antithesis of Stalinist Communism.

The other big influence on me at that time was the work of Franco-Russian revolutionary Victor Serge (1890-1947), whose novels and books of history and journalism were written in French – my academic specialty. Several of my U.S. radical mentors were Serge fans and pointed me toward his books, at the time long out of print. (Curiously, I had never heard his name in France or in a French class.) Serge was a witness-participant in revolutionary events in Spain, France, Russia, and Germany during the first half of the 20th Century as well as a brilliant novelist in the French language. An early opponent of Stalinism with one ideological foot in Anarchism and the other in Marxism (and no foot in capitalism), Serge made all the right enemies, spent ten years of his life in various prisons, and died in poverty in Mexico. Back in 1961, when I first got my hands on one of Serge's books and read it in French, I instantly made up my mind

to translate his novels into English and make him the subject of my research. By chance, a Paris bookseller put me in touch with Serge's son and companion in exile, the artist Vlady, and we began a friendship that lasted until his death in 2006. Vlady was born during the Russian Civil War in 1920, grew up in Leningrad, and followed his father and his Left Oppositionist comrades into exile on the Ural, then to Belgium, France and Mexico. He was a marvelous conversationalist, knew everybody, and claimed to have 'pissed on Lenin' as a baby (his mother was one of Lenin's stenographers and took her baby to work, where Lenin picked him up and got wet). Vlady's magnificent painting and graphics are visible at www.vlady.org

1961+ As a graduate student, later Instructor and Assistant Professor at Columbia University in the Sixties, I participated in the anti-racist and anti-Vietnam war movements, and did some off-campus labor and tenant organizing with CORE. I also got around New York and hung out with Anarchists like Russell Blackwell, Sam and Esther Dolgoff[191] and radical journalists like I.F. Stone[192] and Daniel Singer.[193] After a summer working

---

[191] Co-founders, in 1954, of the Libertarian League. Russell Blackwell was an amazing man, a cartographer (like the anarchists Kropotkin and Reclus before him) who had fought in the ranks of the Communists during the Spanish Civil War and converted to anarchism after witnessing the Communist sabotage of the peoples' revolution. Under his influence, I got my first little red IWW (Industrial Workers of the World) card and Little Red Songbook. (I still work with the revived IWW.)

[192] 'Izzy' was a self-taught teenage investigative journalist from Philly who went on to write for the *N.Y. Post, The Nation,* and the short-lived Left daily *PM,* before being blacklisted during the Cold War. With his wife Esther, he began publishing *I.F. Stone's Weekly* out of his garage and made a decent living off his subscriptions (50 issues for $5.00 a year). I started reading the *Weekly* as a kid, and we became friends in the

with mainly black workers around *News & Letters* in Detroit, I arrived in New York as a Marxist revolutionary and began working to establish a new 'local' (what the Communists called a 'cell') in for my new organization - led by Trotsky's former secretary, the hereditary Bolshevik Raya Dunayevskaya and carry out my revolutionary duty. 'The revolutionary's duty is to make revolution,' famously said Che Guevara, who then proceeded to commit revolutionary suicide by wandering around in the Bolivian forest carrying a gun, ignored by everyone except the CIA who caught and shot him. Nonetheless, the revolutionaries of the Weather Underground and the French Maoists followed his suicidal formula in the Sixties, with disastrous results, alienating the public from growing radical mass movements and providing the cops with a legal pretext for repressing them. In contrast, what I would like to share here is my own small-scale experience of the day to day, nuts and bolts practice of a revolutionary movement with long-term goals.

What Do Revolutionaries Do?

What did I know at the age of 21 about being a revolutionary organizer and educator (propagandist)? Basically I improvised on what I had learned from experience working with seasoned revolutionaries of earlier generations in Europe and America and listening to their stories of yet earlier generations. I added what I gleaned from books, particularly revolutionary biographies and autobiographies, this oral tradition, now nearly extinct, which is what I am attempting to pass on here. So let's start with some basics. Revolutions happen when masses of people rise up. Conscious revolutionaries are like the yeast cells that leaven the dough. By 'revolutionaries' (as opposed to reformers and people of good will) I mean individuals who have become aware that the *system* (slavery, feudalism, capitalism) is the problem and who are prepared to struggle for fundamental change. To be effective, they must be part of the struggle, just as yeast or leaven must be mixed into the dough to let the bread rise. Through education and organization they help the masses to empower themselves in two fundamental ways: by connecting present struggles with the lessons of past struggles and the future perspective of a new society and by connecting local struggles to the global struggle to overturn capitalism. To maintain the continuity of such educational and organizational activities,

---

Sixties. Since he was quite deaf, he didn't mind me arguing with him at the top of my lungs. An early anti-Vietnam war advocate, Izzy exposed the fraud behind President Johnson's Bay of Tonkin Resolution. We student rebels adored him and invited him to address the Columbia University Counter-Commencement in 1968 when I was awarded my PhD in French with a thesis on Victor Serge. Ironically, the first Serge book I ever read, I swiped from Izzy!

[193] After writing for *The Economist*, Daniel Singer (1926-2000) became the European Correspondent for *The Nation*. A teenage refugee from Nazi-occupied Poland and later from occupied France, Singer was educated in England and epitomized the best of the European socialist tradition. Sane, soft-spoken and elegant, Daniel's international reporting set a high example.

revolutionaries must of course themselves be organized. The problem of revolutionary organization is a thorny one, which I grapple with in 'The Invisible International' and 'Lenin Horizontal and Vertical' (Parts I and IV).

To make revolution, the first thing you need is a publication, the revolutionary's major organizing, educational and outreach tool. A paper – even a flyer – which you can leave with people you want to organize so that they can continue to think about your conversation. A paper they might pass on to a friend. A paper with a contact address. A leaflet, a pamphlet, a newspaper or a book like this. Today that job has been made easy by computers, Kinko's and the Web. In the Fifties and Sixties we spent endless hours in print-shops or typing stencils and cranking mimeograph machines. Both *Pouvoir ouvrier*[194] in France and *News & Letters* practiced an original kind of revolutionary journalism, soliciting and printing the views of people in various struggles. This created what we would call today a favorable feed-back loop, giving a voice to people in factories, placing them in the context of a revolutionary perspective, building bonds between the paper and its readers. This process takes time, but it works.

My first move, after getting settled in N.Y. was to scout out an auto factory to whose workers I could distribute my monthly bundles of *News & Letters,* edited by Charles Denby (Simon Owens) a black auto worker at Chrysler's in Detroit and full of articles about the industry. There were no auto plants in the city, but Ford had built a modern, highly automated assembly plant (now closed) in Mahwah, N.J. out in redneck country, to which hundreds of black workers commuted daily from New York City, Newark and Jersey city. For a period of more than five years, every month our paper was published I did a distribution, putt-putting out to Mahwah at six am on my old 125cc motorcycle and handing out hundreds of copies to workers rushing in to punch a time clock. Workers distrust phonies, so I always dressed as what I was, a professional intellectual (in those days we wore ties and jackets). At the beginning, my future bride, Julie Gilbert courageously rode on the back of that $200 East German MZ bike and helped hand out the Marxist paper, and her charm may have softened its reception. Later other comrades, strapping lads like Mike Flug, Ray Ford, Bob French and Steve Handshu would reluctantly join me. Especially after I got kicked off the parking lot and then picked up by the local Sheriff and charged with Criminal Anarchy for distributing papers to carloads of workers leaving the highway near the plant gate. Distributing to cars can be hairy, as the workers are in a hurry and hostiles can take a swipe at you. But you want to give your paper to workers going *in* to the plant, where it might get discussed or left in the lockers for others to read. I used to get catcalls of 'Castro' from some older whites on account of my beard, but blacks were much more friendly once they had read the paper, and carloads would sometimes ask for extras.

---

[194] *Workers' Power,* the monthly factory bulletin published by *Socialisme ou Barbarie.*

Still it was very difficult to establish feedback under such conditions. What we were able to learn about conditions in the plant got into the paper and distributed: unbearable summer heat in the shop and discrimination in the union favoring older, white, skilled tradesmen against younger, black production workers. And then one day in the middle of the revolutionary month of May 1968, we Marxist-Humanists suddenly found ourselves in the middle of a major wildcat strike. A worker's caucus called The United Black Brothers of Mahwah Ford's had closed down the plant, taken over the union hall, and invited us in as honorary Black Brothers (only one of us, Ray, was black). Standing in the urinals, Steve Handshu, who was white (and blind to boot), heard a suspicious black voice down the row asking 'What's *he* doing here ?' Before Steve could think of a reply, a black voice from the other side answered 'He's here because he knows he'll never be free until the rest of us are,' which thrilled teenage artist Steve.[195] We soon discovered that the leaders of the movement had been reading our paper regularly, and two of them traveled with us over Labor Day for a *News & Letters* national convention in Detroit. While there, they also visited the United Auto Workers HQ (and ended up getting bought off by the union, as can happen when the ultimate goal seems too far off). Meanwhile, that very same month in France, a wildcat strike and sit-in at an aircraft plant in the North, co-inciding with the student occupation of the Latin Quarter in Paris, spread from factory to factory and turned into a General Strike which nearly brought down the government. I was not surprised to learn years later that the aircraft factory sit-in had been sparked by an old comrade from our *Pouvoir ouvrier* group (long since dissolved) who, as a rank-and-file militant, had earned the respect of his fellow workers and knew what to suggest – form a strike committee, occupy the plant, and send delegates to other factories - when the right moment presented itself.

Most self-styled 'revolutionary' sects are parasitic, rather than creative. Some think they can recruit by sending young members to swarm around demonstrations and meetings like flies hawking their papers. Other 'revolutionary' parasites join ongoing activist movements for peace and justice with the perspective of 'boring from within,' taking over the leadership, imposing from above what they consider the 'correct' political line. These 'rule or ruin' tactics lead to endless power-struggles and splits, inevitably weakening the cause and driving away sincere activists in despair. In the Sixties, 'revolutionary' sects like the Socialist Workers' Party (the largest of the Trotskyist parties), Youth Against War and Fascism (neo-Stalinist), Progressive Labor Maoists and Guevarists infested the anti-Vietnam War movement. It happened again in 2002, when there were two big national anti-Iraqi war demonstrations in Washington on two successive weekends because of disagreements between the leaders of two coalitions.

---

[195] See his current work at www.**handschusculpture**.com/

In contract, the example of that old French comrade, whose local intervention in 1968 may have sparked a General Strike, personal contact and participation in concrete struggles are the revolutionary's other important tools. You really have to invest yourself in a struggle and demonstrate your sincerity, loyalty and good sense to your comrades before you can expect to recruit them. In the Sixties, my work in the Congress of Racial Equality - organizing against racism in housing and organizing minority workers in low-wage industries - brought me into contact with black working-class militants like Don Petty and Blyden Jackson in New Haven, who also considered themselves revolutionaries. We all three then moved to N.Y., where Blyden became active in Harlem CORE. I joined CORE at Columbia and worked with Mike Flug helping the super-exploited Columbia cafeteria workers get union representation, a struggle which had failed in the Thirties and ultimately triumphed in 1968 with the support of the student strike. Over time, CORE student activists like Mike Flug, Will Stein, Anne Jaffee, Bob French, Judy Miller and Allan Wallach were won over to our Marxist-Humanist network, while Ray Ford came to us through the Maryland Freedom Union struggle, a CORE outreach project in Baltimore.

We were also active in SDS's predecessor at Columbia, the militant Independent Committee Against the War in Vietnam led by Dave Gilbert[196] organizing demonstrations, sit-ins and teach-ins (where my knowledge of the French Vietnam War came in handy). Our activity and our politics were gaining our local new members and influence among the most thoughtful activists. Indeed, we could have had a more powerful influence during the 1968 events and perhaps successfully defended SDS against Maoism and mindless 'revolutionary' violence, were it not for the intervention of the *News & Letters* leadership in Detroit, which broke up our great team and severed its members from the organic situation in which they had won respect. You see, *News & Letters* Committees were 'decentralized' in name only, and local committees were not really expected to improvise or act autonomously as our NY local did. This autonomy must have been perceived by Raya and the old guard as a threat to their power, because as fast as I could recruit new members, the leadership would move them to the 'Center' in Detroit. Thus on the eve of the 1968 upsurge, Mike Flug our local's most experienced and charismatic Civil Rights, labor and anti-war organizer was pulled out of the struggle and summoned to Detroit - presumably to further educate him and, I

---

[196] Gilbert was a wonderful organizer, simple, tolerant patient and well-informed. But after 1968 he lost his patience, joined the Weather Underground and ended up eleven years later taking part as a member of a half-assed 'Black Liberation Army' in the botched 1981 Brinks robbery in which two cops were killed. Dave, who is doing 75 years to life at Clinton prison in Danamora, N.Y., considers himself a political prisoner and is still resisting and thinking. You can read his writings at www.kersplebedeb.com/mystuff/profiles/gilbert.html and I'm sure he'll grin when he reads this.

now suspect, to remove them from my evil Anarchistic influence. The same thing happened seven years later, after I succeeded in organizing yet another new local in Connecticut, which the leadership simply dissolved, summoning my recruits to the Center and leaving me and Tom Doyle out in the cold. After years of denial, I finally let myself see the huge gap between 'Marxist-Humanist' theory (decentralization, self-development, anti-vanguardism) and practice.

Like I said, revolutionary organizations are problematic. The cult of Raya's personality in *News & Letters* was mild compared to other revolutionary cults like Gerry Healy's once influential *Workers' Revolutionary Party* in Great Britain, where discipline was zombie-like and female comrades were exploited as concubines by their leader. We will return later to the vexed 'party question.' Meanwhile, I hope that something useful and positive emerges from this experiential account of Socialist revolutionary practice as I inherited it and came to understand it. What I learned in that school is that practicing revolution does not mean substituting yourself for the mass movement like the *Che* or taking over its leadership or manipulating it like the Trotskyists. The model of the revolutionary I gleaned from the example of my Anarchist and Marxist mentors consists of participating authentically in the struggles of your time while openly sharing your revolutionary perspective in ways that invite others to think for themselves, organize, and empower themselves. In contrast to the military model of a 'vanguard of revolution' (watch out for that gun!) and the medical model of 'midwife to revolution' (easy on those forceps!) I like the biological metaphor - perhaps inspired by Antonio Gramsci's image of the 'organic' working-class intellectual - of us revolutionaries as yeast cells leavening the dough - or fermenting the beer if you prefer!

The highpoint of my activities at Columbia was the April-May 1968 student strike and occupation. Our Six Demands englobed university racism (Columbia's takeover of a Harlem public park), university complicity with the Vietnamwar (secret military research) and student rights (amnesty for the students disciplined for sneaking into the President's office to copy evidence of these secret contracts). The unity of black and white students and of students with community residents made for the power of that strike, which flourished even under Police occupation of the campus. I talk about my 1968 adventures and reflections on the Sixties in Part III ('Where Are the Riots of Yesteryear?')

1970+ In the wake of the Columbia Rebellion, I was invited to a forum on 'student power' at Wesleyan University in Middletown, Connecticut and ended up being offered a teaching job there, which I accepted against my better judgment on the assumption that after 1968 I was washed out at Columbia. True, Wesleyan was considered very liberal. 'Marxism' was fashionable in academia then, and I was an attractive candidate as both a serious scholar and a semi-famous radical. But having observed that there were three conservatives and one Stalinist in the Foreign Languages Department, I had a premonition they would unite to stab me in the back (which) they eventually did. So I tried to wiggle out of the deal by demanding more goodies (Julie was dying to leave N.Y. and I was afraid to disappoint her); but the Wesleyan administration took my arrogance for assurance, assumed I had another prospect, and ended up making us an offer I couldn't refuse: a white house with green shutters in the country for Julie and for me a sabbatical in France in the *first* year of my contract! My Wesleyan misadventure was thus a double case of mistaken identity. Wesleyan thought they were hiring an intellectual academic neo-Marxist, not a committed practicing Marxist. One winy evening, my Chairman wrote me a letter stating I was 'unfit to teach' at Wesleyan because of a televised anti-war speech I had made earlier that day at a mass rally in Hartford (see below). This censure was a blatant violation of my academic freedom, but the subsequent painful tenure battle taught me that however 'liberal' these elite institutions profess to be, the Old Boy system still trumps free speech.

The highpoint of my activities at Wesleyan was the May 1970 nation-wide student strike protesting Nixon's bombing of Cambodia, the shooting of student protestors at Kent State and all-black Jackson State, and the murder trial of Black Panther leader Bobby Seale in New Haven. The strike spread like wildfire to campuses across the country, marking a new nation-wide phase of the student anti-war movement and a new unity between black and white students. Unfortunately our national student organization, SDS, had been scuttled and dismantled by quarreling Mao-inspired factions, and it proved impossible to consolidate this new high stage of the struggle. Our strike movement at Wesleyan was a model of organization. The night the news of the bombing broke, I drove to the campus to find the student body completely zonked on the lawn waiting for a rock concert to begin. I asked to make a brief announcement over the PA and called an organizers' meeting for 3 am after the concert.

By 9 am there were flyers all campus over calling for a 'Town Meeting' at noon, and flying squads of students announcing it in every class. The plan was to have four five-minute speeches explaining the situation and then throw the mike open until everyone who wanted to had spoken. We had prepared three demands: U.S. out of Indochina, Free Bobby Seale and all political prisoners, End university complicity with the war machine. To present them, we chose a faculty member (me), the leader of the student anti-war group (Steve Talbot), one of the first female students (Dierdre English) and Isaac Barret, a black Air-Force vet on scholarship, whose call for unity won over the more or less separatist Afro-American students from Malcolm X House. After more than an hour of very open and passionate discussion, the students voted unanimously to strike and begin setting up committees to go out into the community and explain their demands. Subsequent Town Meetings reaffirmed the integrity of the Three Demands and the unity of black and white they represented. Nor did Summer vacation end the community outreach. (Indeed, some of those

348

Wesleyan Class of '70 rebels are still out there.)[197] I later adapted this organizing model – calling a Town Meeting (or general assembly), inviting representative speakers to present a coherent proposal, and then opening the microphone for full and free discussion – to other situations like the 1971 Middletown March and Rally which mobilized over 500 local trade-unionists, high school students and blacks, and I still recommend it as a way of empowering people.

As a newly-unemployed college French teacher stranded in Central Connecticut (Durham, then Hartford) during the Seventies, I went native. I grew my hair long, planted tomatoes and got involved in all kinds of grass roots activities and organizations from local strike support to anti-nuke, anti-war, anti-racist and Central America solidarity and environmental groups. The issues of U.S. intervention in Central America and later in Iran and Iraq were central to our preoccupations. We were a loose coalition of about a hundred Quaker pacifists, Unitarians, Liberation Theology Catholics, Puerto Rican nationalists and labor organizers (some still Communist Party members) but we had a much bigger audience. I had learned my organizational skills in the N.Y. Socialist movement, and I had a ball in Connecticut organizing rallies, demonstrations, sit-ins and crazy media events on a small, manageable scale. The most fun was being able to confront public officials on a local level, face to face. And to write nasty radical Op-Ed pieces for the local press and get them printed – often thanks to my sense of humor. I got to grapple with and embarrass the likes of Senator Thomas Dodd, Rep. Nancy Johnson and General Alexander Haig (Nixon's Chief of Staff and then CEO of Hartford's United Technologies).

In those recession years, thanks to Richard Nixon's instinctive New Deal atavism, unemployment insurance benefits were automatically renewed every six months as long as the unemployment rate didn't decline. It didn't, and I collected for 18 months. Since I considered myself more or less black-listed in academia during an acute job shortage, I turned to other ways of making a

---

[197] Like Mike Maselli who started a free health clinic on donated materials in 1971 and is now CEO of the Middletown Community Health Center still serving the poor and uninsured.

living. I applied to law school, got admitted, but couldn't borrow enough money to go. Meanwhile, the U.S. had moved into the New Age of personal growth, and without abandoning Marxism I dabbled in Zen, self-development, Gestalt, anti-psychiatry, encounter groups, Primal Therapy, sensitivity training and Non-Violent Communication. I was already in therapy for personal reasons. (I had fallen into a chronic depression after losing my job - like my Socialist Grandpa, Uncle Sam the tailor, during the Depression.) Psychology fascinated me, and for a while I even considered becoming a therapist. I studied books, went to workshops, sought supervision from the head of the local Community Mental Health Clinic and started a therapy group in my basement. But I soon figured out that until I had finished my *own* therapy and got rid of my own *meshugas,* I would lack the objectivity to see others clearly (the Freudian 'counter-transference'). So I closed my basement workshop but remained active in the humanistic psychology movement. This involvement scandalized my 'Marxist' peers, who rejected psycho-analysis as a petty-bourgeois, individualistic cop-out – while unconsciously acting out their own neurotic compulsions as authoritarian sectarians in the political field. Of course there is no basic contradiction between the discoveries of Marx and Freud, synthesized by Wilhelm Reich, Eric Fromm and Herbert Marcuse on whose theories I base my analysis of 'Religion and Repression in the U.S.' in Part II.

Reflections on Violence

I also began to reflect on the implicit violence of intolerant 'revolutionary' groups who label their opponents 'counter-revolutionaries' and repress internal critics. I shudder to think what these uptight true believers would do to folks like me once in power. Is pinning a political label on someone any different than pinning a bull's-eye to his chest for the convenience of future firing-squads? By the Eighties, Maoist and Trotskyist sects had begun systematically disrupting their rivals' meetings physically - in the name of revolutionary purity. Were they not acting out physically the psychological violence underlying sectarian organizations that claim to have a monopoly on political truth?

In contrast to the power-struggles and intolerance I encountered on the political Left, my experiences with the various non-violent movements I worked and acted with felt much more human and grounded. I engaged in civil disobedience for the first time as a Yale Freshman in 1957 in Hartford, refusing to take cover during an Atomic Attack Drill with a bunch of 'Christers' (as Bob Bone ironically called his Christian comrades) from the Committee for Non-Violent Action. I learned some non-violent tactics in the Civil Rights movement influenced by Ghandi, King and Bayard Rustin, and in the Eighties I worked with Quakers, Unitarians, *Catholic Worker* and Liberation Theology Catholics - both in Hartford and in Nicaragua, where Christian Base Communities among the poor were a mainstay of the Sandinista Revolution. These 'Christers' were usually more radical and more fun than the self-designated professional revolutionaries of the Left. Therapy had taught me how to get back to feelings, and I could see how the authenticity of non-violent actors who recognize the humanity of the adversary or oppressor could only produce positive results, both in practical terms and in preserving the integrity of the actor. In any case, it beats screaming 'Off the Pig' at a line of well-armed cops.

That was what was going down the morning of the Anti-Aircraft demonstration at United Technologies Board of Directors Meeting in Hartford in 1972. Before I went into action I was scared shitless, but I had the courage to face my shameful feeling and even share it with my comrades. After that I was overcome with the kind of calm where you feel simply *present.* Time seems to open up, and you do what you have to do right in the moment. So I walked over to the young student who was shouting 'Off the Pig' (or its equivalent) at the cops, and when he took a break I asked to use the bull horn. First I said hello to the cops, who were presumably almost as scared as me behind their uniforms, and I humorously suggested that for $8.50 an hour it was not worth the risk of injury in a fight with these wild-looking kids. '$9.25,' one cop yelled back, and I knew we had an understanding. Humor and honesty often have that effect, and I had acknowledged their humanity - the first step in non-violent communication. I then reminded the student protestors behind me that we had come here not to fight cops, who are only city employees, but the capitalist warmongers - the Board of Directors of United Tech meeting on the other side of the fence. I even added that, unlike the cops, many of their parents probably made money from UT stock via their retirement funds, as did the universities where I taught and they studied through their endowments, whereas the cops' kids were more likely to be drafted and sent to Vietnam. (Total authenticity is the necessary condition for non-violent communication.) So why were we picking a fight? Who is the real oppressor? Didn't we come here to protest Hartford's highly profitable capitalist arms industry? This non-violent political intervention worked so well that the student organizers asked me to repeat it that afternoon in front of 5,000 people at a mass Anti-Aircraft Rally and Rock Concert downtown in Bushnell Park. Apparently while I was flaked out on the lawn, media-hound Abby Hoffman had shown up (after the scary direct action) and provoked another confrontation with the cops by shouting 'Fuck' - thus transforming our serious anti-capitalist anti-war demo into a 'filthy speech' riot. My political rap went over even better this time, and everything got mellow again.[198]

Non-violence is powerful. On the historical scale, the massive non-violent struggle against institutional racism won us the 1965 Voting Rights Act which

---

[198] Ironically, a conservative Wesleyan alumnus' third-hand report to my Chairman of my scandalous televised 'performance' at the Rally led to my ultimate rustication from that distinguished liberal institution.

made Mr. Obama's election possible. During WWII the organized non-violent underground in German-occupied Denmark succeeded in saving the Jews; and through sabotage, strikes and boycotts it eventually forced the Nazis to pull out. In France, by contrast, armed attacks on Germans provoked massive reprisals against innocent French civilians and did little harm to the Nazi war effort – unlike the effective non-violent sabotage by 'careless' French railroad employees and workers in arms industries. Non-violence does not exclude militant force and takes advantage of the massive numeric superiority of the oppressed over the oppressor. The February (March) 1917 Russian Revolution that overthrew the Czar was non-violent to such a degree that citizens who didn't read the papers were unaware that the troops sent to shoot the strikers had fraternized. The Autocrat of All the Russias had abdicated when he learned that none of his government's orders were being transmitted, much less carried out. Mass non-violence is very powerful and I am convinced that the developing revolutionary Emergence will be largely non-violent (planetary strikes and boycotts, local land invasions, factory occupations). In any case, I agree with former Weather Underground leader Mark Rudd's conclusion that in the 21st Century, the revival of Maoist-type armed struggle would be suicidal, given the array of high-tech weapons of terror and forces of repression at the disposal of modern national-security states.

The only way to change the world today is by taking the war toys out of the hands of the powerful few, or rather out of the hands of the poorly-paid working-class troops and mercenaries they hire to repress us in every land. This necessary disarmament of capitalism's repressive apparatus will be the essential problem of the coming social struggles that capital's deepening economic and ecological crisis is engendering. I am morally certain that non-violence is the only practical solution when faced with high-tech superviolence, and that the global revolution will probably be carried out not by armed revolutionary *cadres* but by women of faith, people of color, the indigenous, young people and small farmers together with billions of us poor and middle-class *proletarians* who attempt to sell our labor-time for salaries or wages (hopefully with benefits). Our greatest weapon is talk: to remind our uniformed brothers and sisters that we're all in the same boat, talk them out of killing us and invite the to come over to our side. Perhaps we will succeed, like the Russian women and workers of February 1917 and the Portuguese who approached the troops with red flowers during the Carnation Revolution of April 1974, which overthrew Europe's oldest dictatorship. Let me close this parenthesis on Non-violence with an historical observation. Once soldiers fraternize and mutiny, their lives and safety depend on convincing the rest of their comrades in arms in other units to join them (rather than shoot them) and so such mutinies spread within hours. And one never knows when the first crack in the sea-wall of military discipline will open, allowing the flood of human sympathy, solidarity and desperation to pour through the breach. In the words of Leon Trotsky, on trial for conspiring to commit violence as the President of the Petersburg Soviet in the 1905 Russian Revolution, 'The strength of the masses is in their willingness to die, not in their willingness to kill.'

1975 After two years of unemployment, I found a job teaching French at the University of Hartford, just when our daughter Jenny was born. U.H. is a new private school, largely dependant on the local arms industry for financial support. Yet, like the cat who came back the very next day, I somehow managed to hang on for twenty years to retirement as an outspoken anti-war Socialist – despite being denied tenure twice (a record!). My career was saved in the end thanks to a campaign mounted by Charles Ross, our local AAUP president, the support of a fair-minded conservative Dean (former Navy carrier pilot) and to the sympathy of colleagues who had come to appreciate satirical jokes at Faculty meetings and hard work around faculty salaries and benefits. Needless to say, I continued my Central American Solidarity work, writing Op-Eds, organizing demos and a state-wide Teach-In at the University of Hartford in solidarity with the people El Salvador, oppressed by a U.S.-backed death-squad government.[199] I spent the summer of 1984 in Sandinista Nicaragua learning Spanish and observing the Presidential elections then in progress. I lived with a family in Managua, went to the Sandinista rallies (including one showcasing Jesse Jackson), and I hung out with Liberation Catholics, thanks to my connection with Father Tom Goekler from Hartford. Accompanied by a nun, I even got to visit the Open Prison where former *Somocista* National Guardsmen were being rehabilitated. I also stood on the Honduran border with Witness for Peace and visited our Hartford-Ocotàl Sister-City project. I saw no signs of political police or the kind of repression they have in Cuba. I read the conservative opposition press, which was far more violent in its anti-government attacks than any opposition U.S. paper (are there any?), and I talked freely with members of conservative opposition parties, whose election billboards were quite visible. I deliberately sought out the tiny Trotskyist, Communist and Maoist hard core splinter groups who were out of favor but also out of jail. (Quite a contrast with Cuba.) The Sandinistas won the 1984 election I had come to monitor, but the U.S. government and media, under Big Brother Reagan, simply 'disappeared' the unfavorable vote.

I wandered the country by bus, and saw signs of popular initiative and creativity, like cooperative workshops and a green energy project where they

---

[199] As I write these lines, the rebel has just been FSLN has just won the Salvadoran election, putting an end to 130 years of U.S.-imposed right-wing dictatorship after 40 years of resistance.

got gas and fertilizer out of pig-shit. Everywhere kids in school uniforms. No beggars on the street. Up in the war zones, friendly teenagers in mismatched camouflage carrying AK47s, polite to women and eager to ask a North American if he knew Michael Jackson. (Many Nicaraguans also knew about Jesse Jackson, then running for President, but they mistook him for Martin Luther King.) A young revolution. I was older (and taller) than almost all the Nicaraguans. Obviously a *Yanqui,* I experienced no anti-Americanism. This despite a U.S. blockade which left hospitals and clinics without basics like hypodermics, sterilization or X-ray equipments and farms without spare parts for tractors.[200] This despite U.S. backed right-wing Nicaraguan death-squads known as *Contras,* whose raids deliberately targeted teachers, nurses, and co-op organizers so as to prevent the popular revolution from succeeding. The night I arrived in Ocotàl they assassinated a local agronomist, and instead of attending a *fiesta* I was swept up in a crowd of mourner marching behind his body, held aloft by his comrades. While I was down there, a CIA training manual was found on a captured *Contra* recommending these targeted assassinations of civilians. Despite this U.S.-financed civil war against Nicaragua's 'aggressive Communist dictatorship,' the Sandinista revolutionaries managed to maintain an open society, dialogued within their own ranks and with other parties, and held free elections. Their worst mistake (aside from having mishandled the indigenous *Meskito* question on the East Coast) was reluctance to grant the peasants title to occupied lands of *émigré* counter-revolutionary landowners. These title-deeds would have made the agricultural revolution irreversible and assured the revolutionary regime of permanent peasant support against the U.S.-backed counter-revolution. I returned to Hartford inspired by the courage of this young democratic revolution, more determined than ever to struggle to make the U.S. government end its support of the *Contras.* I wrote, demonstrated, organized teach-ins and gave talks with my slide-show in public schools, churches, union halls, even a singles club (Hi, Sharon!). Reagan was asking for $100, 000, 000 in *Contra* aid, explaining away atrocities with the fable that the Sandinistas were massacring their own people and blaming it on the *Contras,* as illustrated below by a Hartford street-theater group.

---

[200] Our CT solidarity delegation brought down truckloads of farm tools and donated medical supplies.

Bedtime for Bonzo Players in front of CT Rep. Nancy Johnson's office 1985: Ranjon Batra plays a Sandinista pretending to be a *Contra*; John Bach is Bonzo and I'm Nixon.

1997-2008 By 1996 I was burned out teaching incurious undergraduates who were attending college only because their parents could afford the tuition (which I couldn't when Jenny was old enough for college) and who treated the professors like servants. After 22 years of teaching, the University of Hartford generously awarded me a Sabbatical, and I headed to Montpellier, the old university town on the Mediterranean where the rollicking Utopian satirist Rabelais had studied medicine during the Renaissance. After tasting Montpellier, I couldn't stand the idea of returning to Hartford, and the University Administration was more than happy to grant early retirement to its perennial gadfly. So here I sit writing this memoir in the sunny South of France awaiting the end of capitalism on the shores of the polluted, but still swimmable Mediterranean Sea. Here I devote my non-beach time to dreaming up Revolutionary Flying Objects, completing my biography of Victor Serge while publishing and translating his writings.[201] I also organize support for various internationalist causes among them: the Iraqi Freedom Congress (defending secular Iraqi Women and trade-unions)[202] and the EcoSocialist International Network, and I participate in the global justice and anti-Iraqi war

---

[201] My latest translation with *Introduction* of Serge's posthumous novel *Unforgiving Years* was published by New York Review Books Classics in 2008.
[202] Go to **http://www.ifcongress.com/English/index.htm** Also, http://www.uslaboragainstwar.org/

movements, traveling to Social Forums and Left-Wing conferences. I see myself less as an expatriate or a political exile (although a French passport might come in handy some day) than as a cultural refugee from malls and fast food (although they're now all over France which has a bourgeoning obesity problem). I began writing in French for the local left-wing daily *Herault du Jour* (from which some of the articles published here are translated). I called my column 'The World is my Country' – the motto of the radical pamphleteer Tom Paine, my hero, who agitated in Britain, America and revolutionary France and identify myself as an *'internationaliste new-yorkais.'*

Like so many Jewish radicals, I have emotional ties with Russia, and when Gorbachev took power, Jenny any I were among the first Americans to visit the USSR unhampered by official guides at the invitation of progressive, non-government labor and environmental groups *(informali)* including Socialist dissidents. Our experience as Western radicals re-connecting with the Russian anti-totalitarian Left after a 60-year gap was profoundly moving. I was able to make contact with Serge's sister-in-law Anita, who had survived 25 years in the *gulag,* and other anti-Stalinist resisters, as well as with scholars and activists interested in Serge. To fill their thirst for knowledge, I organized the 'Books for Struggle' drive, which shipped a container of 'political dynamite' to Moscow, where we created the Victor Serge Public Library and the Praxis Research and Education Center. Praxis, which unites Marxists, syndicalists, Anarchists, ecologists and radical humanists, opened its doors in 1997 and has translated and published in Russia a number works of Victor Serge and other anti-totalitarian Socialist writers. Today under the Putin regime, this project is under threat (see 'Stop Political Terror in Russia').

In December 1997 I was invited to newly liberated South Africa, to attend an International Conference in Cape Town called by the South African 'Workers' Organization for Socialist Action' (WOSA), some of whose leaders had recently emerged from years in Robbins Island, the Apartheid government's political prison where Nelson Mandela, now President, also served time. WOSA was loosely allied with anti-Stalinist revolutionary Socialist groups from other African lands as well as groups from Italy, Mauritius, Brazil, Australia etc. I went as a delegate from Praxis in Moscow. Our idea was to create a flexible, horizontal International Network for a Socialist Alternative, and turn the old world upside down by meeting in the Southern Hemisphere. This Network model was a healthy rejection of the usual top-down, hub and spokes, centralized model of yet another 'Fifth International' centered around a few intellectuals based in Paris or New York. Visiting Capetown and meeting these African and international revolutionaries was a thrilling experience. I thought something new might emerge, but sadly our

356

'international network' fell apart after a year due to inevitable sectarian power-struggles. Again the contradiction between libertarian theory and authoritarian practice.

This failure, and other experiences with the organized Left in which I had operated for so many years shocked me into rethinking a whole series of assumptions. It also inspired me to return to our 1968 slogan 'All Power to the Imagination' and seek a more visionary approach to revolution based on cybernetics, emergence theory and Quantum logic, rather than on non-dialectical Newtonian reasoning. Ideas I develop in my 'Archimedes Hypothesis' in Part I. I also imagined a kind of Utopian sci-fi novel, *The Revolutionary KIT,* in which a massive multi-player on-line computer game called 'Billions *versus* Billionaires takes over the world. I also began to think in terms of Utopias. Not Greeman's Utopia, singular, but Utopia*s,* plural – self-organized and federated through Internet. If you want to play at dreaming up *possible* Utopias (no Gods or extra-terrestrials) please join us in creating 'virtual worlds whose economy is based solely on human need, and not on profit' by visiting http://wikitopia.wikidot.com/ Let's pool our knowledge and ideas so we'll have some idea of where we want to go if we manage to survive capitalism's collapse.

Thank you for reading this far. I welcome your comments and criticisms at www.invisible-international.org

LaVergne, TN USA
18 May 2010
183141LV00006B/80/P